PRAISE FOR *VERMEER'S ANGEL*

Vermeer's Angel is Fr de Malleray's brilliant debut novel in an intriguing genre that could accurately be called 'Vatican Noir'. The author's detailed knowledge of the ecclesiastical backdrop and the artistic foreground make for a convincing 'high resolution' world in which ambition, morality, psychology, espionage and high drama intersect.

—PIERPAOLO FINALDI, Master of the Keys, The Catholic Writers Guild (UK)

Fr Armand de Malleray is a priest with acute spiritual insight. He also has a rare gift of knowing how to read and vividly communicate the grand designs, and the riches half-hidden, in the paintings of the old masters, as those fortunate enough to have attended his celebrated talks at London's National Gallery will attest. Now he has written a remarkable novel, a tale of Ostpolitik set in expertly orchestrated scenes alternating between the aftermath of Hiroshima and the collapse of Eastern European communism. Ingeniously interweaving the various strands of his fiction with real history, Japanese culture, Vatican diplomacy, Kim Philby's Soviet spy ring, and a penetrating analysis of art that makes painting come alive, this is not only a culturally sophisticated narrative, but a gripping read, full of human interest.

—ROBERT ASCH, *St Austin Review*. Writer, literary critic, and scholar, Robert Asch is co-editor of *StAR* and of the *St Austin Press*.

Armand de Malleray's stunning prose draws the reader into a world of intrigue and uncertainty where nothing is quite as it seems. This is more than just a novel, it is a haunting meditation on the significance of memory, identity, betrayal, guilt and the insatiable human yearning for the Truth.

—FIORELLA DE MARIA, author of *The Fr Gabriel Mysteries*. Award-winning novelist De Maria studied Literature in Cambridge and has published nine books with Ignatius Press.

Vermeer's Angel is a triumph of a novel. It is a startlingly broad canvas that crosses several continents, cultures and decades, unfolding for the reader subtle readings of both artistic masterpieces and men's souls. It is a novel about the loss of the self, caused by the atomic blast of modernity and the lingering radiation of older ills. It is a novel about memory and about self-betrayal, suffused with a gentle but persistent sense of the need to recover spiritual responsibility in a world of pragmatic compromise.

—DR BRIAN SUDLOW, author of *Catholic Literature and Secularisation in France and England* (Manchester University Press). He teaches at Aston University (Birmingham, UK) and has written extensively about Catholic literature and Catholic thought in France and England.

VERMEER'S ANGEL

Vermeer's Angel

A NOVEL
by
Armand de Malleray

AROUCA
PRESS

Permission for the publication of this novel
was granted to the author on 8 August 2022
by Very Rev Fr Andrzej Komorowski, Superior
General of the Priestly Fraternity of St Peter.

ISBN: 978-1-990685-65-1 (pbk)
ISBN: 978-1-990685-66-8 (hc)

Cover image:
Johannes Vermeer,
Woman with a Pearl Necklace, c. 1664

Arouca Press
PO Box 55003
Bridgeport PO
Waterloo, ON N2J 3G0
Canada
www.aroucapress.com
Send inquiries to info@aroucapress.com

DISCLAIMER:
The story, all names, characters, and incidents portrayed in this book are fictitious. No identification with actual persons (living or deceased), places, buildings, and products is intended or should be inferred. Where words and actions are referred to historical figures in the novel, they are consistent with the known behaviour and temperament of their authors.

CONTENTS

A Red Hat

"RED, YOUR EXCELLENCY? BUT LOOK how these traffic lights just turned from red to amber and now to green. Here in Japan, they call green *blue*. In Rome then, while you see red, some might see *white*."

As the luxurious Toyota Century sped up smoothly, leaving the traffic signals behind, Bishop Picerno Dorf smiled at his colleague's witticism. "Seeing white?" Yes, Monsignor Marco Altemps had to be joking. A *red* hat was more than Bishop Dorf had ever expected, or deserved. "And yet," he mused, "is not the red hat the last step before the white zucchetto? Why not wear *white* indeed, someday? Who could tell?" After all, he was only sixty-seven and, since his minor stroke last Christmas, he had taken steps to lower his blood pressure. "Red it is then, for now," the bishop conceded. "Destiny is an artist combining unexpected colours. How dull our lives would look in black and white!" When Picerno Dorf had been made a bishop ten years earlier, following Pope John Paul II's 1981 visit to Japan, he had replied to Altemps' congratulations, "I will share this purple with you, Marco." And soon enough, his assistant at the Asian Affairs had been promoted to Prelate of Honour of His Holiness, which entitled him to knot a purple sash around his thin waist. However, for the time being, both men were wearing impeccably cut and undoubtedly *black* Italian suits.

In pleasant mood, the two clerics had just left the American Centre in Tokyo where they had watched the premiere of *Supero*, a film about the strange life of Hiroshima survivor, Japanese artist and Communist spy Ken Kokura, after a best-selling novel based on genuine events. They had congratulated co-screenwriter Kazuo Ishiguro, the Japanese-born

British author whose own mother was a Bomb-survivor. The American cultural attaché had attended the projection, as well as the Japanese minister of Culture (or Monka-shō). Officially, Dorf and Altemps were representing the Papal Nunciature, where the chauffeur was now driving them back amidst heavy traffic. Through the window of the limousine, Bishop Dorf looked without particular interest at the wide façade of the Akasaka Palace, a government building. That boring imitation of Buckingham Palace evoked Europe to him: Europe, where he would finally return after nearly three decades spent in Asia.

Lowering his voice in the very unlikely event that the chauffeur understood their German dialect, the bishop confided, "Well, that film revealed practically nothing about me. You know what, Marco, I am almost disappointed. After all the fretting about possible scandal... The teaser for *Supero* was ominous for us churchmen, I grant you that: *He survived Hiroshima. He escaped East-Germany. Will he elude the Church?*"

"Much ado about nothing," Monsignor Altemps agreed, adding, "And yet, I'm glad we waited before leaking the news of your promotion. The novel made almost no mention of you, thankfully, whatever the author's sources had been. But who could tell what the film would disclose? If its scenario was to keep closer to the facts, you could have been portrayed as responsible for Kokura's death. After all, he collapsed when you denied him his request and died in hospital soon after. Of course, you couldn't know how he would react. In a way, I'm surprised it's taken ten full years for the media to exploit that incident. Thankfully, now the hindrance of scandal is removed. Starting with your intimate supporters, we can disclose your elevation to the cardinalate next month."

Bishop Picerno Dorf remained silent and turned his head towards the window, as if enjoying the sunset. He hoped that his friend wouldn't notice his frowning. It was about 6pm and the air was warm. He'd found it hard to focus on Easter the day before. Obstacles to his cardinalate had worried him, but a more personal sorrow weighed upon his heart, namely, the liver cancer of Monsignor Altemps. Only three days earlier, on Good Friday, Bishop Dorf had discovered his friend's well-kept secret. As he'd popped into the monsignor's office at the nunciature, one floor above his, Hana, the new maid, had interrupted her dusting and informed "His Excellency that His Reverence the First Counsellor would soon be back from chapel." (A very pious priest, Mgr Altemps offered Mass daily, even in Latin for the past two years. Not on Good Friday, however.) While waiting for his assistant, Picerno had browsed through recent correspondence on the desk tray. At the bottom of the pile, a medical letter from the Oncology department of the St Luke's International Hospital in Tokyo marked "Confidential" had attracted his attention. Simply put, Marco was given a year to live, or up to eighteen months if he reacted well to the forthcoming treatment. Picerno made sense, in retrospect, of his friend's two holiday breaks over the past five months. Mgr Altemps was a hard worker, whose vocabulary didn't include the word vacation. But of late, his sickness had manifestly compelled him to slow down.

Picerno had left the study before the First Counsellor stepped back in and had refrained from mentioning the dreadful topic so far. He'd struggled with the brutal fact of his friend's expected demise and couldn't decide whether he admired or resented his courageous discretion. He so wished Marco had dared to share the news with him. Truly, losing his long-time teammate made the red hat fade away somehow. The achievement he'd so much desired repelled him rather, when he considered that his faithful collaborator was preparing for death rather than for celebration. And so young—barely past sixty... The two men went back a very long way, having spent their early childhood in the same mountainous province of Alto Adige, or South Tyrol, in northeast Italy. In the absence of a third interlocutor their conversation often switched from Italian to Tyrolese spontaneously. And what of their plans, now? While the new cardinal would be based in Rome, Marco was meant to become the first nuncio in Japan. It was time, after seventy-two years with mere apostolic delegates and pro-nuncios in this Land of the Rising Sun. But with widespread cancer now, could he even take the position? He should, absolutely! The current pro-nuncio, Bishop William Carew, would learn on his return from the Easter holiday that he was promoted to Bonn, moving to Berlin in the summer. Hopefully, Marco hadn't informed Mgr Jacques Pommard, their director in Rome, of his cancer. Ah, what a setback... And when would a propitious occasion occur for him to tell Marco that he knew about his illness, and to express sympathy at last? On the other hand, action was needed, and if fate took Monsignor Altemps away, Picerno owed it to his friend to bring their work to completion.

The automatic gates of the nunciature closed behind the car. They had arrived. As he waited for Marco to walk round the limo, Bishop Dorf noticed the *Fushichō* or gold phoenix logo displayed on the radiator of the Toyota. He found the emblem gaudy. But it was time for some supper, and for planning their next move.

~~~~~~~~~~~~~~~~~~

Alone at last. Nestled in his antique Chinese armchair, a carved rosewood throne of the Qing dynasty (on permanent loan from the Chinese Patriotic Catholic Association, thanks to his friend Mingdao), Bishop Picerno Dorf swallowed another sip of whisky from the bottle just unwrapped. As connoisseurs might recall, Okayama Single Malt comes from the Miyashita distillery in the south of Japan, using half German barley. A delicate hint to their shared German-speaking youth in Tyrol, it was Marco's present that evening. It tasted bittersweet, though. After a first glass and some chitchat, Picerno had eventually addressed the cancer issue. Marco had become very upset on discovering his friend's indiscretion. He wouldn't admit that every document marked as confidential justified Bishop Dorf's interest.

"Neither did *you* share your heart problems with me, Picerno. I only found out when reading the label on your pill box at breakfast. But in my case it was *private* correspondence you read."

"Sorry Marco; it wasn't obvious to me just from reading the envelope, and once I had the letter in my hand, I realised that this threat to your health had a bearing on our plans. Why didn't you tell me about it?"

"Look, Picerno: I've always shared with you every piece of information that I thought relevant to our work. But my cancer is insignificant. For I will never, *never* allow it to hinder what we've been working for over the past years. You *must* get that red hat. Your vision for the Church in Asia is vital in the current context and, as we agreed upon, you must now come out of the wood. Your work behind the stage has achieved wonders and calls for consolidation, which only visibility will secure. Our friends and I do see red for you, no longer purple. As for me, doctors are mere alarmists seeking attention. In Salzburg, my aunt Gabriella lived a further thirteen years after having been diagnosed with cancer. If I don't outlive you, I might last long enough to see you turn white."

"I'm impressed by your dedication, Marco," Picerno commented while putting his hand on his friend's arm. "But what about *your* new position? You were to succeed me as the unofficial co-ordinator on the ground in Asia. Becoming the papal nuncio in Japan would have given you the clout necessary for our teamwork. If you remained in this nunciature as mere First Counsellor, you wouldn't be able to achieve much around here once I'm gone."

"I'm up and ready to become the nuncio in Tokyo. All will work according to plan, I'm sure, Your *Eminence*."

They had left the matter to that, and Marco had gone to bed. Lord, he *was* looking pale.

Later that evening, sitting in his Chinese armchair, Bishop Dorf whispered the enthralling words for the first time, "Picerno, Cardinal Dorf." Then, as if being introduced to himself, he added, "Delighted, Your Eminence! This red biretta suits you perfectly. A well-deserved reward for years of crucial service to the Church in Asia."

Now that the potential hurdle of the Kokura film had vanished, they would send the pre-invitations. April had just started. The formal announcement for the consistory was scheduled for 29 May and the creation of the new cardinals on 28 June. But it was essential to secure as early as possible the attendance of the most sought-after guests at his first Mass as cardinal on Sunday 30 June in his titular basilica—especially Mgr Jacques Pommard and Dr Pavel Shevchenko. He wanted some Oriental flavour. Marco had ordered floral displays of Chinese red peonies (that is *chi shao*), and the best duck and spring rolls in Rome would be served at the reception afterwards, in a grand *palazzo* (once owned by Marco's family) near Piazza Navona. Picerno could see in advance the entrance procession into his basilica of San Sisto Vecchio on the Via Appia, the famous church allocated to him as his cardinalatial title.

And Pommard would be there. He *had* to be. As the kingmaker at the Secretariat of State, Mgr Jacques Pommard would appreciate Dorf's accomplishment. He would smile at the new cardinal, as in Roman antiquity the most influential senators would welcome victorious generals on their triumph along the Via Sacra, hailing them by the name of the territory they had added to the Empire. It would not be Germanicus in his case, or Britannicus, or Africanus, but Asiaticus—or rather, Dorf modestly corrected, *Asiaticulus*, since his achievements in China and its periphery, however significant, were mere contributions to the long-term Asian strategy of Rome.

Bishop Dorf helped himself to another glass of whisky, trying to define the nature of his emotion. No, he was not ambitious. He was a realist. He wanted power for Rome, not for himself; and his contentment was to add his own limited successes to a series of similar steps walked by other churchmen before him, leaving behind them dusty, sweaty or bloody footsteps. Like the best choreographies, conquest couldn't be a one-man-show. He was not the only one playing on the Asian stage, and probably not the most important actor. Pommard had helped, and dear Marco had been indispensable. He had encountered fools, like Vaddak, and opponents like Ignatius Kung, the former Bishop of Shanghai, now settled in America after thirty years in prison. Dorf admitted that his understanding of politics, albeit deep, was not infallible. He had done his best to promote the Vatican's interests in this vast part of the world. Please God, others would continue his task. Not replacing him just yet, though! His red hat was not the end, far from it. Rather, it was a new mode of operation, in the limelight after decades spent behind the scenes.

Through the branches of the cherry trees in the nunciature garden, Picerno looked at the lit skyline. He had arrived in Tokyo less than a month ago. Officially, because his position as Vatican Delegate to the Observatory of Non-Proliferation of Nuclear Weapons in Asia (a microscopic department of the United Nations) was being relocated from Singapore to the Japanese capital. Unofficially, he was to prepare Marco to take over his role as field coordinator for the Church's Asian affairs, an activity he would still oversee with Mgr Pommard, but remotely, from Rome. The Pro-Nuncio in Tokyo had obligingly lent him two spare rooms at the Nunciature. But Dorf would very soon vacate them. An entire floor awaited him, in a Roman palazzo with high, intricate Renaissance ceilings.

The familiar screech of the fax machine by his desk interrupted the prelate. He rose from his Chinese throne with some apprehension. Concern about some last-minute obstacle to his promotion lingered at the back of his mind. The machine was slowly printing a confidential memo. Before the sheet could be extracted, its headline was enough to reassure the anxious diplomat. The Warsaw Pact had just dissolved, it announced. No big scoop there. He knew well that it had been coming. Nothing to worry about; although Moscow's loss of its Eastern European satellites would boost China as the main power in the Communist world. That would not help the Church's agenda in China, but it would prove that his path of measured concessions to Beijing was the safest. Another fax message was now printing. Small fry: just a British businessman to be released by the Iranians after being detained five years as hostage. "It's quite fitting," Dorf approved, "for one to be liberated on Easter Monday." He switched off his desk lamp, deciding that it was time to sleep.

As he walked by the bookcase, he tenderly brushed the cover of a thick volume. His old doctoral thesis by the title *The Anonymous Priest* had finally been translated into Chinese the year before. Summarising the two-volume original German version and making it available to Chinese readers had been a pet project of his for years. In 1971, Karl Rahner had deigned to take notice of Dorf's attempt to apply his concept of *anonymous Christian* to the priesthood in particular. Picerno had meant the Chinese version as a hint; one of those little signs which glitter through the often dull or dark mist of political negotiations. Thankfully Mingdao, his very discreet friend at the Chinese Patriotic Catholic Association, had confirmed the good impression made upon the Government. "At last, an approach of the Catholic priesthood compatible with sinicization."

As a result, Picerno had been invited to the Fifth National Congress of Catholic Representatives, scheduled to meet in Beijing the following year. Anyone who needed to know—like Pommard—would have acknowledged that Bishop Picerno Dorf was a key player on the Asian stage, more than ever. He took a spare copy of the leather-bound book and dedicated and signed the title page adding 'Cardinal-elect' before his name. Tomorrow, as soon as Pommard had confirmed the all-clear for his cardinalate, he would have the book posted to Mingdao in Beijing.

~~~~~~~~~~~~~~~~~~~~

First thing in the morning, still dishevelled and with his crimson slippers on, Bishop Dorf had walked into his office to check the news. Monsignor Marco Altemps, fully dressed and shaven, was already there.

"It's a mistake, Picerno. It has to be. Some misunderstanding."

Altemps tried to sound reassuring, which made his manifest bewilderment even more alarming. Losing his composure wasn't like him at all. And yet, as he stood by the desk of Bishop Dorf, his hands could barely hold the letter just found on the fax machine. Dorf gently led the sick monsignor to a chair and delicately took the sheet of paper from him.

"Let me read it myself in case I've missed something."

The note was short and handwritten.

Confidential:

For the attention of Bishop Picerno Dorf, Vatican Delegate to the U. N. Observatory of Non-Proliferation of Nuclear Weapons in Asia, Apostolic Nunciature in Tokyo.

Monday 1 April 1991

Dear Picerno,

The unofficial announcement you were about to make to selected acquaintances regarding the happy matter we discussed last week must be postponed. A difficulty has occurred. I would love to call it a glitch, but it sounds serious enough to require me to cancel our earlier arrangement. Feel free to call me for further details. Wishing you a blessed Easter Week,

J. Pommard.

Bishop Dorf slowly sat down on the end of his desk. His voice sounded surprisingly devoid of emotion when he uttered, "It's Kung's doing yet again. These Chinese Underground Catholics are relentless. They'll try anything to block me. They still distrust me and want the red hat on his head or on no one else's."

PART ONE
The Agent

CHAPTER I
Sunburnt Artist

Confidential: Authentic Confession of Ken Kokura, Japanese artist, art expert and former spy, handed to His Excellency Archbishop Mario Pio Gaspari, Pro-Nuncio in Japan, Tokyo, 21 January 1981. The confession is reliably based on the author's diaries dutifully kept over decades, and his personal archives.

AWAKENING TOOK ME MANY YEARS. It occurred by stages.

I first awoke on 10 August 1945 under a tent near Hiroshima, Japan. Sunlight filtered through the material above my head as I opened my eyes. It ached. A red disc with beams was spread against the tent above me. I realised later on that it was Japan's imperial Rising Sun flag, our *Kyokujitsu-ki*. Thirst, dire thirst was my first impression. They gave me milk, a little. I was lying on a stretcher in a field hospital, four days after the bombing of my city. My fellow-sufferers moaned and shrieked: a hellish lullaby. Around me, many had not awoken yet, and more never would. I was among corpses and unsure whether I was alive. I didn't know that my memory was dead. Later that day, when asked where I lived, what my name, age and profession were, I could find no answer. Evidently, I was a Japanese man, probably in my late twenties, although the picture they took of me has me looking like forty. My entire body ached. I was cut and bruised; skin was missing from part of my neck and shoulder, and I had lost the hearing in one ear. Thankfully my limbs still held together. But to what purpose, if my soul was amputated from every remembrance?

The doctors were overwhelmed. The main assessment of our condition was "alive" or "dead." Later they refined it, segregating the survivors into those sound of mind and those mentally unhinged. I fell into the latter category. I heard a nurse say, "They just bombed Tokyo!" I didn't know what "Tokyo" meant, nor "bombed." And who were "they"? In fact, what did I know, or remember? Oblivious to earlier times when order and peace prevailed, I could not even call "chaos" my first impression of the world. In children's tales, fairy godmothers lean towards the cradle and gift the newborn child with the talents fitting for the heroic mission that awaits him. I had at least four godmothers, called *Pain*, *Confusion*, *Dread*, and *Helplessness*. Like a child though, whose experience of life is only beginning, I assumed such a state of things was normal. It was all I had ever known, being one day old, as I felt. Hope, I couldn't lose, having never experienced it.

A few days later, blasting loudspeakers could be heard from our tents. But I didn't understand what was said. It was the Declaration of Surrender by Emperor Hirohito, although the word "surrender" was not mentioned apparently. Still, the music played in introduction sounded perfectly familiar to me. "Thousands of years of happy reign be thine; Rule on, my lord, until what are pebbles now, By ages united to mighty boulders shall grow, Whose venerable sides the moss doth line." Recognising the *Kimigayo*, the national anthem of the Empire of Japan, I immediately tried to get out of my stretcher and stand, saluting. But I collapsed miserably. Still, that 15 August 1945 was when my first memory surfaced. I then knew that I had existed before. It meant that I was not presently being born: I was merely awakening. That evening, under my bed sheets, I tried to explain to myself the well-known lyrics of the national anthem. Had there been a "Lord," once? What was he to me? Was he to reign forever? Such a prospect seemed to please those singing. They were probably his subjects. But they would not enjoy his rule unless he were kind. The "growing pebbles" puzzled me. Minerals don't grow like fruits do. How could small stones grow into boulders? What did it mean? It struck me, all of a sudden! Yes,

I had found the answer to the riddle. The stones remained the same all along. The one changing size was me. Or Japan. We were to become smaller than we thought ourselves. We first saw the stones as pebbles because ambition kept us floating far above reality, making things look smaller. Our sense of proportion was distorted, probably through hovering pride. If we became humbler, more attentive and respectful, smaller in our own eyes, we would see the pebbles grow before us, reaching the size of mighty rocks. They would seem to grow as we lost altitude, as through the porthole of an aeroplane landing. Coming closer, we might even discover that "the moss lining their venerable sides" was hair, for the pebbles turned rocks were our human brethren—people rather than minerals. Was that the reign of the Lord?

In a different part of the camp, I had seen sick children. One looked at me, an embodiment of bewildered innocence. I could hear others crying. I suspected that most victims from the bomb had been civilians. If only, I thought, their parents were still with them. But these poor little ones were prob-ably orphans by now. What future was theirs? Admittedly, I seemed to have lost my entire family, as they had. But I was a grown man. I decided that I could take care of myself, unlike them. That gave me courage, paradoxically. Only later did I learn the horrible irony: the bomber that had taken the mothers of so many innocents was named after its pilot's own mother, Mrs Enola Gay. It was as if, through that coincidence, that man was telling my orphan children, pointing at his bomber, "Behold your mother." And that mother, far from calling herself "Sorrowful" as she should have, bore instead the surname of Gay, that is, "joyful."

One week later, following my daily assessment, the staff ruled out mental alienation. I was separated from the lunatics and found myself merely among amnesiacs. By then we were housed in a concrete building, not under tents anymore. The authorities had gathered some hundreds of us from Hiro-shima, Nagasaki and probably from other bombed cities. Thin pouches hung around our necks, comprising whatever pieces of information had been found about us. I've kept mine all these years. It is here on my desk as I write, like a birth certificate. As if we were kindergarten children, we were shown elementary depictions of animals, fruits, trades, landscapes or musical instruments and asked to name them. The purpose was not to teach us our mother tongue anew, since most of us could still speak fluent Japanese. Rather, the slideshow was meant to unlock memories by association. My doctor had done his best to assemble the few clues I had tried to extract from my numbed memory. They were images and sensations rather than words or concepts. "Classroom"; "children"; "paintbrush"; "paint smell"; "kneeling"; "girdle"; "cup"; "silk"; "wave"…

Ah, yes, "wave" was my first victory, or blessing. I immediately recognised Hokusai's *Great Wave off the Coast of Kanagaw*, an iconic woodblock print from the early nineteenth century. The mental health nurse asked me to explain the picture. "It's a system," I answered her hesitantly. "It's a warning. An invitation." I was afraid of speaking further. After a silence, my speech was unleashed. As one diving into clear and fresh water, I was carried by a momentum from which it was impossible to refrain.

"Mount Fuji is Japan's highest mountain, and yet it appears very small in the background. In the foreground, the great wave seems about to crash down as if on the distant volcano. It's an illusion of perspective. In the foreground, to the left, another wave is forming. It has exactly the same triangular shape and colours as the smaller silhouette of Mount Fuji. The foam on the crest of the wave echoes the snow on the top of the dwarfed mountain behind. That wave looks like a larger replica of Mount Fuji. But since the great wave above is about to cover belittled Mount Fuji, as it seems, symmetry calls for a yet larger wave to threaten the bigger liquid replica of Mount Fuji." I looked interrogatively at the nurse. She was taking notes. I continued. "First we identified the relation between Mount Fuji and the Great Wave. Then we noticed the similitude between Mount Fuji and the Smaller Wave. So, looking at the Smaller Wave as a larger Mount Fuji demands yet another wave, that one enormously bigger than the Great Wave. It's an analogy of proportionality. Does it make sense?"

I stopped, as one feeling his way along a dark corridor. Some door stood slightly ajar before me. I was afraid of pushing it open. The nurse was listening to me invitingly. Feeling encouraged, I dared to unfold my hypothesis. "The question is: *Where* is that greater invisible wave? It does not show in the picture. Then it must be swelling *outside* of the picture. The audience is prompted to look behind them and check if that colossal wave, so much bigger than the already gigantic Great Wave depicted by the artist, is not right over their heads, just about to engulf them, exactly as the painted Great Wave is falling upon the three fishing boats." Standing on the opposite side of the table, the nurse playfully glanced over her right shoulder, as if fearing submersion. She had a very fine profile. As she turned her head back towards me, she smiled. Her smile was my first gift. Never until then had I experienced a gentle and gratuitous gesture. From my awakening, everyone's attention to me had felt hurried, concerned and professional. I realised that the nurse had meant her sideward glance as a friendly touch of humour. She was not *really* checking whether a colossal wave was swelling behind her. Rather, she had just been playing with me, like a sister might. It was a very small thing, but one that revived an essential part of my personality. Only then did I notice her stomach, and wondered how pregnant nurses were allowed on the front line. Or was war over for good?

The nurse had identified some mnemonic thread of mine and was trying to engage me further. I furtively returned her smile as she wondered, "Surely you haven't invented all this right now, just by glancing at the print laid before you. You must have found that explanation stored somewhere in your memory." I lowered my eyes, strangely ashamed, as if I had trespassed into significance—a foreign kingdom—without a passport. Meaninglessness was all I had ever experienced since awakening. Was I clandestinely coming home? After a silence, she went on, "Here on the table the caption reads, 'The courageous fishermen represent the indomitable Japanese people, rowing to victory against daunting odds.' You interpret the picture as a cautionary warning to a vulnerable audience. Is it a memory of yours, or did you just imagine this? Are you influenced by the country's defeat, or have you caught up with something familiar to you, emerging from your past? Could you have been an artist, perhaps, or an art teacher?"

Nurse Tanaka's smile had been my first present, reminding me of what a relationship is and unlocking my capacity for pictorial analysis. Unfortunately, this first success was soon undermined by a remark from my roommate at supper. "I told her nothing," Yamato boasted. "Why, the Americans destroyed our country and now, they send staff to extract intelligence from us survivors."

"But she's Japanese, not American," I objected.

"You moron, don't you know she's a *Nisei*! Hundreds of them have landed since the ignominious surrender. She may speak our language, but she was born and raised over there in the USA."

"Surely you're mistaken. I can tell American doctors and military, whereas she looks as Japanese as you and I."

"I don't care what she looks like or what year her parents left Japan. Now she's part of them, our sworn enemies. They trained her. Sharing any information with her lot is sheer betrayal."

That night upon my bed I turned my head towards the wall, hiding a few tears. What if my fellow amnesiac guessed that I mourned the smile of Nurse Tanaka—an American, an enemy? Had she deceived me? Had my trust in her been a mistake? And yet, she'd been right: I hadn't invented the interpretation of Hokusai's *Great Wave*, I had recalled it. It was a very promising improvement. It was a victory, and the nurse had given it to me. Could I call such a successful carer a fiend, a traitor? But if I suspected her, who could I ever trust?

The following day Yamato gave me my first *iaijutsu* lesson. For several mornings I had seen him sitting on his heels by his camp bed. He kept totally immobile for up to half an hour, breathing very slowly, his hands spread on his thighs. Then, suddenly, with awesome velocity he caught with both hands a bamboo cane hanging from his side and projected it forward as if it had been a sword. Drawing his mock *katana* from an imaginary scabbard was so natural to him that he must have been an army officer—or so he believed. I learned from him. Once as I was shaving, he pointed at my knees visible below my trunks. "What calloused knees you have! You must have been a camel in your previous life." After a fortnight, I felt surprisingly comfortable squatting for half an hour like him. I was much slower at drawing my bamboo cane, though. I had probably never been an army man.

Sometime later in August, all of us amnesic men were made to stand side by side along a low fence. Each of us bore a sign displaying his presumed name, age, profession and place of origin. Groups of civilians slowly walked by, looking with anxious hope at our faces. Some men were identified by a father, a wife, a daughter, by friends or colleagues. They would clasp and sob in disbelief. After an hour, no one had claimed me, though. Unlike my only friend Yamato, no wife had swooned on my shoulder. No son had leaped into my arms. No friend had uttered my name. I felt humiliated. Group after group had walked by, trying in vain to read my features. I stood discarded, like a lame slave, an unworthy item on this market of affection, of acquaintance, of history. How I wished for bonds with kith and kin. How I longed for human ties to assert my belonging to a family, to a village or a trade. But no thread—however tenuous—connected me with the warmth, love or sympathy of any fellow Japanese. If tenderness wasn't to be mine, would not hatred or jealousy at least help identify me? I would have worshipped any rival, any bully—if they had been able to tell me my name. Facing scorn, anger or vengeance would have been my delight, if they had revealed to me who I was.

I needed a name. Those of us still unidentified were shown a map of Japan and invited to pick the name of whichever town or village we fancied. That is how I became Ken Kokura, after a nearby city. Yamato was moving there, having been admitted into the new domestic police force. I had started drawing. It seemed the best thing I was able to do. The staff suggested I had been a calligrapher. It wasn't a promising trade in 1945 Japan. The country was on its knees and build-ers, doctors, bakers, electricians, mechanics or accountants were in demand. No one advertised for artists. However, I showed the head of the amnesia department at the hospital a few of my drawings, depicting fellow patients, trees of the nearby forest and wrecked military vehicles. Some of them were published in the local newspaper. Following Yamato's suggestion, I went to Kokura and managed to find a job as an illustrator for a magazine. I still suffered from nausea two or three times a day, and hearing was still muffled in my right ear. But I could breathe, walk and even sleep almost normally.

By then I had put together a little routine which involved my early morning sword-drawing meditation and exercise, and a lot of calligraphy. I had been lent three books full of coloured illustrations on European and Japanese paintings and drawings. I soon became very familiar with the depic-tions. The thinnest book was about Japanese folding screens. I recall one such six-part screen by seventeenth century art-ist Kanō Naganobu, *Merrymaking Under the Cherry Blossoms*, with four women carrying swords as they performed the "Okuni Kabuki" dance. A later, three-part, screen, repre-sented three elegant ladies indoors, the last one of whom was reading a letter. A magnificent bird came to speak with the middle lady. Its long colourful feathers, like Fra Angelico's archangels', filled the entire background. It was by Kitagawa Utamaro, an eighteenth-century artist whose work later inspired the French Impressionists. All images had become like friends to me. I wished I could have known more about their authors, but books and time were scarce. I seldom went out. I started wearing a green bow tie found in a charity shop. I am not sure why, but I felt safe and prepared once I had it around my neck.

A few months later, in March 1946, a foreigner asked for me through the newspaper I was working for. He was a youthful German representing a university near Berlin. He had seen a few of my published drawings. We met in the quiet archives of the newspaper. Through a Japanese interpreter, Heinrich affirmed that I had real talent. Would I like to study in Europe? His offer unsettled me. I had never left Japan—to my knowledge—and was afraid of travelling so far away. On the other hand, having no intimate acquaintances in my homeland, I felt a bit alien among my own people. I was most at home—or least estranged—when drawing and painting. We met several times over that week with Heinrich and with fellow-Japanese. He showed me various illustrations by Lucas Cranach and assured me that I could study in the hometown of the great German painter. Heinrich knew many anecdotes. He explained that a winged serpent was the signature used by the artist, after his coat of arms. I was fascinated by the intensity of several portraits by Cranach. One in particular seemed to awaken memories. It represented Martin Luther. I had no notion of who the German Reformer was and yet, his features looked very familiar to me. Could I have been a Christian before? I also recall vividly Cranach's depiction of Adam and Eve in the Garden of Eden. I knew the famous Christian myth, as many non-Christians did. It was part of the world culture and did not imply that one belonged to that religion. I asked Heinrich why Cranach had omitted the wings on the snake around the apple-tree. He answered with a smile that it was not a signature serpent, this time, although a pun might have been intended. Once again, I realised how patchy my remembrances were. Sometimes I was certain of having heard a sentence or seen a picture, while on other occasions things felt totally new to me. The doctor had warned me against *déjà vu*. I had become accustomed to feeling my way through memory mirages.

Later that week, our little group was sitting around the table in Yamato's tiny kitchen. His wife was out. We had had several Kirin beers. Yamato boasted of drinking Kirin beer always, as in Hiroshima, the Kirin reinforced concrete parlour building had miraculously resisted the blast and stood alone as a proud monument to our "happy life before the bomb." Yamato remembered the Kirin Beer Hall as a popular venue since its opening in 1938. He lifted a third bottle as a toast to "Kirin, the survivors' beer", and filled Heinrich's glass again. But the interpreter brought by Heinrich, still refused to drink beer. It irritated Yamato. The interpreter looked and sounded Japanese, although speaking fluent German and American. My friend Yamato had already warned me against him, assuring me that he was a *Nisei*, an American spy masquerading as a Japanese, like Nurse Tanaka. The interpreter praised Martin Luther and the vibrant Lutheran communities in America. He deplored the fact that in 1941 the Japanese Government had forced all Protestant churches to merge into the single *Nihon Kirisuto Kyoudan*. He hoped for religious freedom to be promoted under American rule.

Yamato slammed his bottle of Kirin beer against the table, shouting, "To hell with the Americans! Japan did not surrender to Washington, but to Moscow. We had signed a five-year neutrality pact with the Soviets in April 1941. Moscow only declared war on Japan three days after the Yanks had bombed Hiroshima. Nearly seventy of our cities had already fallen under American bombs and we hadn't surrendered."

"This is news to me," the other objected sarcastically. "I thought that Japan had capitulated to General McArthur, not to Comrade Stalin."

Yamato replied even louder, "We only made up our minds when across the sea the Soviet Army suddenly turned against

Hokkaido. That decided us, not Hiroshima, nor Nagasaki. Of course, the Yanks clamour that their atom bomb broke our morale. They want to be seen on the world stage as the victors, and will never admit that the sudden change in Moscow from neutrality to war was what caused our surrender."

Heinrich had to intervene to prevent a possible fight between Yamato and his interpreter (an American Lutheran, as Heinrich later told me). Back in my rented room near the newspaper building, I wrote down my impressions of the incident. Religion left me rather indifferent. I felt patriotic when listening to Yamato. My country had been so horribly wounded by American atomic weapons. But I also experienced a shameful inability to react. Never would I have been able to speak like Yamato (nor like the interpreter). Was I weak? Something in me was broken, as was to be expected after what we had been through. And yet, was not Yamato also a victim of the Hiroshima bombing? How did I differ? Unlike me, Yamato had a past, a wife, a history, a name. I only had pictures of old paintings. Would I be betraying Japan by accepting the invitation to study art in Germany? Yamato insisted that the two countries had been allies. Even though Soviet Russia now controlled territories east from Berlin, Germany felt close to my heart, culturally.

~~~~~~~~~~~~~~~~~~~~~~~~~~~

One week later, Heinrich and a dozen of us foreign students from Japan, Korea, China, Indonesia, Vietnam and Singapore landed in Dresden, having seen nothing of Vladivostok and Moscow where we had changed planes. My allocated seat during the flight to Moscow was next to a refined Indonesian man in his late thirties. Prince Azmy was a cousin of Sulaiman Shah, the ruling Sultan of Serdang. This is why he was always referred to later on as "Sultan." His relative, Tengku Rachmadu'llah, had been beheaded by the Japanese in 1943, which made me expect hostility on the part of my travelling companion. Instead, he shared with me precious memories of Europe, which he had visited on several occasions. By the time our plane reached the Ural Mountains, Sultan and I had become friends.

I imbibed every piece of cultural information he disclosed to me, in anticipation of the wealth of art history I expected to learn on arrival. Sultan missed France in particular, where he had accompanied his two Sultan cousins to the 1931 Colonial Exhibition. An aunt of theirs had married a Dutch painter and their young cousin Jacques had been their guide across Paris, then the cultural capital of the world. The Indonesian princes had soon become the stars of fashionable society, as Jacques introduced them to artists in vogue such as Mistinguett. Sultan made me feel dizzy and ignorant when mentioning his encounters with people about whom I then knew nothing or very little, such as Pablo Picasso and Salvador Dalí, or James Joyce (whom he met at his flat near "Rue de Grenelle") and Ernest Hemingway.

My new friend expressed friendly commiseration when I admitted that even the name of Fujita evoked no memory to me. The son of a general in the Imperial Army, Tsuguharu Fujita had left Japan for France in 1910. In Paris, he had soon become a leading painter of the *avant-guarde*. He had returned to Japan during WWII as an official War artist, but was now back in Europe, Sultan assured me. That I, a Japanese artist, should not even know my successful fellow-citizen settled in Europe sounded particularly dreadful to Sultan. He promised that he would introduce me to "Leonard Foujita," as the painter was known in France. I knew that we would soon land in Europe in an atmosphere very different from the one Sultan had enjoyed in the 1930s. In post-war Germany and Europe, there were food shortages and social tensions, while economic and political power had shifted to America.

Looking down through the portholes on approaching our destination, the three Japanese among us were horrified to discover what the Americans had done to Dresden, the once prosperous capital of Saxony. Thus, Hiroshima was not the only city that they had razed to the ground. It made me shamefully happy. Not for the victims, of course, but because of the feeling of fellowship experienced during our short visit. The woeful brotherhood of civilian sufferers at American hands extended far beyond Japan, I then realised. I had not chosen to be part of such a family, but it was better, much better than belonging nowhere. The physical pain was subsiding and the nausea no longer affected me daily. But my mind still bore the deep scars of what we had been through, my fellow victims and I. Because of structural repairs affecting part of the rail track, Heinrich had us travel down to Wittenberg by boat along the Elbe. He mentioned that the Arado Aircraft Factory on the outskirts of Wittenberg had been bombed by American and British planes, killing one thousand non-German prisoner workers. "But the rest of the city was spared, including the landmark 'Lutherhaus,' a former Augustinian Priory: see the top of its tower, to the right," he added, pointing at a reddish roof visible in the distance, behind the trees on the embankment. "Lutheran Yankee pilots respected the hometown of their religious Founder, even though he was German."

That April 1946 was my first spring in Europe. Our arrival coincided with the return of the Cranach paintings to the *Stadtkirche*, after several years in shelters for fear of the bombs. I took that coincidence as a good omen.

The spring and summer of 1946 glow in my memory as two of the most exhilarating seasons in my life. Albeit patchy, my numbed memory was giving signs of vitality, budding like the cherry trees on the banks of the Elbe. (Heinrich called them "Japanese cherry trees", explaining that they had been planted in the early 1930s as a token of happy collaboration between the Universities of Wittenberg and Hiroshima.) Like a child magically endowed with adult faculties, I was allowed to be an actor in the re-creation of my personality and of my destiny. Furthermore, the process of restoration taking place in my mind coincided with the reconstruction of the country, in full swing one year after the end of the war. Buildings and roads, factories and university departments rose around me in Wittenberg like collective equivalents of my neuronal effervescence, as fragments of memory seemed to assemble again in my mind, while my conscious habits and tastes grew in strength and specificity.

My early morning sword-drawing exercise had become an essential part of my day. How Heinrich had heard about it, I do not recall. Had I, or Yamato, mentioned it to him? Anyhow, on 10 August 1946, for my first "birthday", Heinrich presented me with a long rectangular parcel. Excited and confused, I slowly unwrapped what proved to be a genuine Japanese sword. Unsheathing it filled me with awe. Steel emerged from the scabbard, gradually, like a solid silver stream out of a hidden spring. It was so long that I felt it might never end. Once fully extracted, the naked blade glittered in the summer sunlight. "A very special paintbrush for a gifted artist," Heinrich enigmatically commented before walking out of my room. I knelt down with the weapon now tied against my hip. Japan, it seemed, had come back to me, or I to her. I tightened the silk scarf around my brow, spread both hands against my thighs and closed my eyes, breathing slowly.

Since my first awakening after Hiroshima, Yamato had explained to me elements of the sword handling spirituality. Master swordsmen did not carry swords, he had insisted. They *were* swords. Every morning in Japan, I had tried to become the sword—or my bamboo cane rather, for want of an actual weapon. I allowed no haste, knowing that the learning process would take years. Heinrich's present led me across an invisible threshold, it seemed. For half an hour daily, immobile, I would put to sleep any ideas, thoughts, memories and plans. I would forget even Wittenberg and would empty myself. I would overcome the illusion of separation between my limbs and the blade, between my own self and the world. Immobility allowed me to gather all my energies, or rather, to open myself to the universal movement until I became motion. Unsheathing the sword was to me what stretching its wings must be to a gliding eagle. I had to draw the weapon as fast as possible without endeavouring to be quick. I meant to complete the unique gesture of sword drawing in one continuous motion as a perfect loop, a seamless curve witnessed by none and yet, attested by the smoking candle set on the floor in front of me. If I were filmed, my blade would blow out the flame without being seen. Since modern films display twenty-four frames per second, just as many as human eyes can identify, so I was told, I hoped to reach beyond sensorial vision and to "insert" a twenty-fifth image and many more. My blade would swing faster than sound, I imagined—like Soviet jet fighters soon expected to break the sound barrier and venture into virginal silence.

I was still far from such an achievement, but I did not mind. I was learning a lot, both with my sword and in my books. Back at my desk by the window, or in the University library, I would examine the famous paintings of dead masters as stepping stones into reality invisible, like ornate stairs leading me towards the beauty beyond sight.

Food was still scarce in the shops, but Heinrich made sure that we Asian students were well provided for at the hall of residence. On the political level also, important things were taking place with the KPD and SPD merging into the Socialist Unity Party of Germany on 21st April 1946. Heinrich kept us informed, as very few of us Asians understood German on arrival. After five months of intensive language school though, most of us spoke it well enough. Heinrich managed to have all of us enrolled in the University courses just resumed after five years of war. What topic I would study had been decided as follows.

As much as an amnesiac can tell, I will always remember that conversation with Heinrich. He had become a friend and a mentor to me. His very frequent absences from Wittenberg on behalf of the University made me miss him increasingly. It was very hot that 29 August afternoon. Heinrich had just come back after a fortnight abroad seeking grants, staff and students. I never asked him questions about where he went because I am rather reserved; but I hoped that someday he might invite me to share in his work. So it happened as we strolled along Church Square after drinking at a beer garden. Suggesting we find shelter from the scorching sun, Heinrich pushed open the side door of the small *Fronleichnamskapelle*. We climbed up the narrow belltower and rested our elbows against its ancient banister, whose wood had been smoothed by the sleeves of generations of students from the Middle Ages onwards. A few of them had arrived in anticipation of the University opening a fortnight later, and were mingling with laughing policemen, down in the street.

Heinrich congratulated me on my admission into the Art History Department of the University. After submitting two papers on Cranach and Holbein, and undergoing three oral examinations, I had been enrolled directly into a postgraduate programme. Much to my surprise, I learnt that I would soon be asked to select a topic for a doctoral thesis. Heinrich and other acquaintances of his had high expectations for me, he confided. They were most happily perplexed at seeing how much I already knew about European paintings. There was no chance that I had learned all that by myself since my awakening after the Hiroshima bombing, a mere one year earlier. The only explanation, we agreed, was that I had thoroughly studied European art history before losing my memory. If I were about thirty, I could have completed a doctorate in Japan or even abroad. My heart sank at the thought of a printed doctoral thesis gathering dust on some university shelf, by a Japanese author everyone assumed was dead. The imaginary sight of the forlorn volume moved me as if it were orphaned, since I, its estranged father, was incapable of claiming it as my academic offspring.

Heinrich regretted that his enquiries in Japan on my behalf had been unsuccessful so far. My country was still in such a state of trauma that identifying any biographical data about a youngish-looking amnesic artistic survivor of Hiroshima would have been miraculous. He eagerly supported my interest in classical paintings. "We cannot expect to build a more just society if we don't know and understand our past history and culture," he insisted. "You, Ken, are already very familiar with the techniques of the late Renaissance and of classical depictions. It is all coming back to you at great speed. Professor Schulz liked your interpretation of Holbein's *Ambassadors* centred on the anamorphic skull. He told me yesterday, 'Ken has intuition. His Asian outlook on our masterpieces is refreshing and sometimes uncannily revealing. If he doesn't fall in love with the bourgeois lifestyle and superstitions depicted in these sixteenth and seventeenth century paintings, he could shortly join our team. Although I wonder,' Professor Schulz added, 'where in Japan did Ken learn so much about Christianity.'"

Heinrich was looking at me intensely. It made me very uncomfortable. I don't take praise well, especially when undeserved as in that instance. What was my merit in passively witnessing the consolidation of my wounded memory? On the other hand, was I under suspicion of remembering more than I admitted, or even of play-acting? To hide my unease, I tightened my green bow tie while pretending to look at a group of schoolchildren walked by teachers along the huge *Stadtkirche* opposite our little tower bell. They were so cute in their little uniforms. I wondered why I was feeling so close to them, nearly waving at them from above as if they had been looking for me. When I felt more composed, still staring at pedestrians, I murmured, "I don't know how to describe it. It is like blossom. Notions, technical vocabulary, images suddenly unfold in my memory. I wonder if cherry trees felt pain last spring when putting out so many soft petals. My petals are pictures, associations and connections unfolding along the arteries of my brain. Strangely, my reminiscences are all scholarly or technical. Nothing about my life, my parents, my family, my school years or my professional training ever surfaces. It is like walking along a road planted with cherry trees—one side in bloom and the opposite side barren. My personal memory is locked up or deleted, whereas academic notions sprout suddenly out of some unknown memory chest. I shiver mentally when I become aware of yet another remembrance, like this doctrine of 'salvation through faith alone' which burst in my mind out of nowhere last night, as I walked by the *Lutherhaus* on my way home. I could have recited entire arguments for and even against the Protestant thesis without recalling where on earth I could have read or heard them. It is frightening. Sometimes I wonder if I am not insane."

I remained silent, not daring to share my deeper concern, for fear Heinrich might frown upon it. The thought had occurred to me several times over the past weeks that Shinto was right about reincarnation. Had I not been someone else, in a previous life? Was not that other self trying to communicate with me now? Or was he taking control of me? Should I prevent it or welcome it? As if guessing my worry, Heinrich put his hand on my shoulder, commenting, "Why life mistreated us is a question that needs not hinder us. The only question is, 'How do we learn from it?' Or put differently, 'How do we clear the mess, bridge the gap, build up, excel and bear fruit?'"

Seeing that I didn't react, Heinrich then challenged me. "From this very tower, my friend, if we look back 429 years, we can see three young men chatting down there, along this very street. They are Dr Faustus, Martin Luther and Hamlet of Denmark. The three were in Wittenberg in 1517. Which one will inspire you, Ken? The daring scientist, the revolutionary friar, or the timid prince? You are shy by temperament. But you are also scientific and not superstitious. Ken, I invite you to become an innovative art expert. You are not tied to any particular culture or country. You are young and learned. You appreciate the great things taking place here. I told all this to my administrative superiors. Based on my recommendation and with the approval of Professor Schulz, they have selected you to join the international team of experts appointed by the Committee of Arts of the Council of People's Commissars.

As you know, major works of art which survived the war are currently being transported from Germany to Moscow for safekeeping. We must be very grateful to Soviet Russia for taking such pains in the name of world culture. Germany simply cannot guarantee the conditions needed for safe storage of so many masterpieces, let alone their restoration. You are to join the team led by Leonid Naumovich Rabinovich and Stepan Churakov. You will learn a lot from them, and it will provide you with irreplaceable experience and essential data for your doctorate."

Still leaning against the old wooden banister, I let the news of Heinrich's proposal unfold in my mind. It boded of a bright future and felt refreshing, like the breeze gently blowing through the wooden pillars of our narrow bell tower in the hot summer afternoon. I did not know the two art experts just mentioned by Heinrich.

He interpreted my silence as approval and, returning my smile, he explained, "German and Russian engineers have teamed up to improve the technology of radiography. Before the war, Japanese too came to learn radiography in Germany. One Dr Takashi Nagai was part of this joint study group. He used his knowledge for medical science. Like you, he survived the nuclear tragedy. The Committee of Arts of the Council of People's Commissars wants to retain Asian involvement in this scientific undertaking, Japanese in particular. The Commissars wish you to learn how to apply radiography in order to examine, authenticate and restore classical paintings. Our Indonesian friend Sultan, that is, 'Prince' Azmy of Serdang, and a Chinese trainee, will also take part."

I was about to object that I was not an engineer and felt little capable of mastering the technical knowledge required by the science of radiography.

Anticipating my concern, Heinrich reassured me, "Your mission will be to use the radiographical device provided, not to design it. Our leading engineer Professor Chimek Kravitz will explain to you how it works."

Of Moscow, I mainly recall Vnukovo Airport. I flew there a dozen times between November 1946 and 1947. On arrival, I was taken straight to the Fine Arts laboratory, above which accommodation was also provided. My rare and brief trips to downtown Moscow were to report to some officials. I was always accompanied. But I didn't mind my semi-claustration. At the laboratory, in addition to Sultan, my fellow inmates were called Dürer, Cranach, Velázquez, Raphael, Holbein, Vermeer, Monet, Rembrandt, Renoir and El Greco—that is, masterpieces painted by these geniuses.

I was introduced to the staff of the Committee of Arts of the Council of People's Commissars of the USSR (or "Sovnarkom"). Leonid Naumovich Rabinovich had been an artist before the war. As a junior Soviet army officer in Germany, he had led the search for the hidden paintings around Dresden on behalf of the USSR. Stepan Churakov was a prominent restorer who had overseen the safe transfer of the hundreds of works of art hidden in the Castle of Meissen, near Dresden, to Moscow and Leningrad.

When our team sat at table, I never tired of listening to Churakov's anecdotes. "In Weesenstein we had a shortage of labour for carrying, and we used the local population. Women, girls, and some boys worked for us. For a day's work, we gave them a loaf of bread and a bottle of Burgundy for two people."

I imagined the hundreds of masterpieces passing through the hands of German civilians, surely unaware of the immense value of the crates and parcels they carried onto the train for a mere loaf of bread. And what if they had damaged some paintings? What a narrow escape it had been, in so many cases.

Churakov had explained, "Guards were posted at the front, the middle, and the end of the train. Submachine gunners were on duty twenty-four hours a day. The train passed through Germany without problems, but in Poland troubles awaited us: in the flatcar, where the masterpieces of Raphael and Correggio had been loaded, the axle broke. We had to unhook the car. It was very hard to repair the axle. We stood there the whole day. Finally they let us go, but when we were not far from the station the train stumbled on the wheels of a handcar which seemed to have been deliberately put in our way. But all ended happily. On 10 August 1945, we arrived in Moscow. The first stage of the gigantic work was finished."

I realised that on that date I was still awakening under a military tent near Hiroshima, having survived the explosion four days earlier. Never would I have believed that, a mere fifteen months from then, I would be in Moscow as part of a task force to catalogue, assess and restore some of the world's greatest painted works.

As Heinrich had said, my mission was to learn from Professor Chimek Kravitz the science of radiography as applied to paintings. Professor Kravitz was quiet and conscientious. He was also passionate about his work. He first showed me a *pentimento* visible to the naked eye on El Greco's *John the Baptist*. At the foot of the Precursor of Christ, the tail of the lamb originally lay further to the left. The improved position gave the tail a shape similar to that of the scroll on the Baptist's staff. It provided a visual echo between the sacrificial lamb (a symbol for Christ) and the quote displayed on the scroll of the Baptist, *"Ecce Agnus Dei—Behold the Lamb of God."* I was moved when discovering such changes in the composition. It was like being taken into the artist's confidence as he refined symmetry or enhanced contrast. The three of us sat behind the protective partition. Ida, the Professor's wife (as I assumed) acted as his technical assistant. Looking for the first time at the X-ray screen was a revelation. Below the surface, the underdrawing revealed a wealth of information. Alterations to the composition were the most obvious ones. But data as tangible as paintbrush hairs stuck in the veneer or in sublayers, and even fingerprints, could be identified. Professor Kravitz's department benefitted from the latest radiological discoveries by Soviet engineers. No museum in the world could afford such state-of-the-art devices, the Professor assured me. In fact, our tools were secret prototypes, sometimes "imported" from outside the USSR.

On 10 October 1947, after several months of training, I was asked to pilot alone the descent into a painting. This is how it happened. We were testing a new micro infra-red camera which detected the nature of pigments without needing to take actual samples. Professor Kravitz had always been very reluctant to add or withdraw any substance from the original paintings. Instead, he advocated "non-invasive interventions," which our new device now made possible. This technical upgrade had been obtained by the Committee of Arts in response to a slander spread in some Western art reviews.

Jealous of the many treasures conserved in Moscow, so-called Vermeer "experts" in London and Paris were challenging the authenticity of several of our Vermeers. Our department had been ordered to refute the claim that our *Girl Reading a Letter by an Open Window* was a forgery by Han van Meegeren. Sultan was related to the Dutch painter and had been sent to The Netherlands to learn all that he could from Van Meegeren. The painting had been in Dresden for decades until its transfer to Moscow for safekeeping. But the "experts" pointed at another painting by the same title, which had recently surfaced in Austria where it had been hidden during the war. According to our adversaries, the Austrian *Girl*, not ours, was the original Vermeer. Stepan Churakov was determined to expose the defamatory attack from the West. He had tasked Professor Kravitz with authenticating our Vermeer "as a top priority for the Committee of Arts of the Council of People's Commissars of the USSR." As we looked at the painting in the laboratory, Comrade Churakov had insisted, pointing his right index at the frame (while his left hand lay on Ida's shoulder), "Professor Kravitz, the Western bourgeois experts are laughing at us. This *Girl* has become a threat to our Department and we shan't be fooled by her beauty. I want you to find out whatever she hides. If she betrayed us, then expose her. Make her confess whether she is genuine or not. I want to know everything about her. I want to know who sent the letter she is reading and whether it is written in Dutch, Russian or even in Japanese! I want to know if she picked these apples from the family orchard or if she bought them at the *Groote Markt*. I want to know what she did last night and whom she will meet this evening, and I want to know it even before she makes up her mind. So get to work, or else..." Comrade Churakov sometimes mixed hints of humour with his orders. It made them more intimidating because one was never quite sure to what extent the threat was to be taken seriously. I was even more anxious, then, when Professor Kravitz unexpectedly entrusted me with the delicate mission of piloting the descent into the *Girl*, while he would stand by.

The room was dark. Behind the protective partition, I sat at the control desk, a bit flushed when Professor and Ida Kravitz with their lab coats on came to stand at my sides. Tightening my green bow tie, I felt like a kamikaze pilot about to take his jet off the ground for the first time—hoping it would not be the last. It was essential to avoid any vibration which might blur the microfilming. To that end, the frame of the painting had been taken off and the canvas lay bare on foam stabilisers, pressed under rubber handles. It was as if the *Girl* had been put to sleep before an operation. In fact, the laboratory felt very much like a theatre. As a surgeon identifies a suspicious organ, I had selected the long green curtain hanging on the right of the painting. By contrast with attractive items such as the human figure or even the fruits on the carpet, mere folds in material are deemed secondary compositional features, so that a forger would be less likely to pay much attention to them. He would paint them well and elegantly from the beginning. But the true author of the work, and especially Vermeer, would probably improve this or that minor fold, according to that passion for detail which characterises his genius.

The camera was remote controlled, carried on rails above the canvas. Guided by the live pictures on my screen, I made my way towards the curtain area. It was like flying over an ocean, whose surface undulated with waves of blue azurite and lead-tin-yellow. As I slowly descended, the waters seem to open, turning into solid streaks of colours. Zooming further in, I found wide cracks, as we hoped would soon be observed on the Moon by our Soviet astronauts. I went further down. Now it was like hovering within a quadrangular mine pit. I realised that the squarish shape of the hole resulted from the fibres of the canvas fabric crossing at a right angle. At my sides, the Professor and Ida were leaning towards the screen, as anxious as I. Like speleologists exploring a quadrilateral rift, we could number the superimposed strata of pigment emitting different kinds of radiation according to their chemical composition. On our screen, we could separate the different chromatic masses and explore their angles as if looking at blue, yellow or brown clouds from below. It was soon clear that the long green curtain had been amended in several areas. Was that conclusive of Vermeer's authorship, though?

We took a break. Leaving the desk and screen, we walked to the painting and Ida opened the curtains to let the sunlight into the laboratory. I was mentally asking the *Girl* to confide in us. I wanted definitive proofs. Then occurred again one of these awkward intuitions I had become familiar with. As if talking to the *Girl*, I inquired, "Would you read a love letter standing in front of a bare wall? Perhaps in real life, but in a Vermeer, some symbol of love should hang above you—a framed Cupid for instance, as in that other *Lady Standing at a Virginal*." No sooner had I uttered that hypothesis that I became certain of its validity. I anxiously asked the Professor and Ida to obscure the room again as I ran back to the machine. I moved the camera towards the large empty wall above the young woman, zooming in and further in. This time, we did not need to dive very deep. A little below the varnished surface, our infra-red probe soon identified the straight dark lines of a rectangular frame within which soon appeared a yellow mane spread around the face of a chubby child holding a bow and a card. Cupid! For several centuries it had lain hidden there. A forger would never have concealed a Cupid there. We gasped with joy and disbelief. Now we had our proof! The *Girl* had spoken and was vindicated as a genuine Vermeer.

At the same time, I experienced a painful knot in my stomach, a terrible tension in my neck and a sudden headache. Such was the usual way my body reacted to these eerie moments of *déjà-vu*. Professor Kravitz switched on the light and stared at me with a mixture of admiration and suspicion. He asked me if Sultan had shared with me the information received from his relative in Amsterdam, the Vermeer forger Han van Meegeren. I denied it, adding that I had only learnt from Sultan a few general techniques used by Van Meegeren, such as purchasing genuine seventeenth-century canvases, applying Bakelite to harden the paint before baking his imitations in an oven and finally rolling them over a cylinder to increase the cracks. But Ida avoided my eyes. I felt deeply embarrassed, explaining yet again that memories came back to me unexpectedly. However hard I tried, I remained unable to access vast layers of my past, but on occasions, some connections occurred, and important memories emerged from oblivion like luminescent shells at low tide.

I could not help thinking about the *Girl*. The fake dust curtain drawn to the right of the painting had become a well-established compositional device in Vermeer's time. Such short curtains were actually spread across valuable paintings to protect them from dust and light. Vermeer had included it as a trompe-l'oeil. He was drawing the public's attention to the privilege of seeing what could have been concealed, namely, the young woman reading her letter. There was another curtain also drawn, to the left, casually left hanging on the open window. If that second curtain had been shut, the young woman could not have read the letter, for want of light. It struck me that a *third* curtain had been spread across the Cherub. It was the painted empty wall covering the original depiction of the little angel. A figure was hidden behind that painted veil—a child, believed to be the god of love. I had nearly missed it. But science and intuition had revealed his presence to me. What was written on the little card he mischievously held? If it was a message meant for me, what was I to do about it?

Later that afternoon, Comrade Stepan Churakov showed himself satisfied with our demonstration that the *Girl* was genuine. He asked us to put together the scientific evidence in an article illustrated with our microphotographs. It would "shut up these bourgeois experts" and would demonstrate "the scientific superiority of the methods of investigation of the Committee of Arts of the Council of People's Commissars of the USSR." On his return from The Netherlands three days later, Sultan confirmed that he had not leaked any information to me about the *Girl*. His testimony proved my discovery of the hidden Cupid genuine. Still, I had been deeply hurt by the momentary distrust of Professor Kravitz. The mere idea of usurping knowledge or faking deductive skills to gain prestige or promotion had never crossed my mind—until that day. I had simply been passionate about discovering the secrets of masterpieces. I now felt sullied by the brief doubt cast upon my enthusiasm by Professor Kravitz whom I admired so much. Similarly, Ida's esteem of me was restored, if not increased, and yet, something in my relationship to them both had been wounded. In retrospect, I realize that I was afraid of my discovery. What discovery? Not the hidden Cupid, but the fact that truth could become a means to some further end. Knowledge and achievements could be faked or instrumentalised, I had just learnt. Manipulation could bring me success. For the first time, I experienced temptation. On 12 November in Amsterdam, the Vermeer forger Han van Meegeren was found guilty. I longed to meet him, but he died six weeks later.

Professor and Ida Kravitz were ordered to fly to Wittenberg with Sultan and me. The Professor and his wife had been living in Moscow for years. But Comrade Stepan Churakov preferred our researches to be conducted from Germany rather than from the USSR capital. It would make our findings less political, he explained, thus broadening their influence across the Western world. Our equipment followed us. I became a frequent visitor to the little house of Ida and her husband, ten minutes' walk from the Art Department of the University. She encouraged me like an older sister would. Not *that* much older in fact: much younger than her husband, Ida could have been my wife, age wise, as well as his. She played the violin (so did he) and offered to teach me.

I knew I should have declined her offer.

CHAPTER 2
Showcasing Dissent

T THE TOKYO NUNCIATURE, BOTH clerics looked petrified. They would not even touch the glossy sheet with the fatal news, just extracted from the fax machine. How could their superior in Rome have been so pressured as to cancel Bishop Dorf's promotion to cardinal?

"I was thinking, Picerno... Any chance Mgr Pommard may be pulling your leg?" Marco Altemps ventured, looking unconvinced. "Look at the date. It was still April Fools' Day in Rome when he sent it yesterday."

Bishop Dorf silently gazed at the letter and suddenly burst out laughing. "Impossible! Of course, you're right Marco. I knew Jacques to be humorous, but I would never have suspected him of inventing such a deadly trick. Right, it's just past 11pm in Rome. He will still be at his desk. Let me call him right away, as he offered."

The line was engaged. On the second attempt, the suave voice of Mgr Jacques Pommard, Head of the Asian Section at the Secretariat of State in Rome, was heard.

"Hello Picerno. I'm glad you rang. Forgive me for going straight to the point as I must make another important call before midnight. Well, I was sent some further allegation against you. It's anonymous this time, and states that you are a 'Communist master spy,' no less."

Bishop Dorf held his breath. After a brief silence, Pommard encouragingly went on, "Congratulations, you must have done something good for various people to be so intent against you."

"What time is it in Rome, Jacques? Still long before midnight?"

"Yes, but I always go to bed late, don't you worry."

"Thanks for the April Fool joke, then. You nearly got me! It's already 2 April here, obviously, but Marco Altemps, sitting next to me, found you out. I'm putting you on loudspeaker by the way, so that he may join our chat."

Hearing no reply, Picerno insisted, "Seriously, do I have your all-clear for sending my pre-invitations?"

"I see... No, as per my note, this is called off. I wish it were a joke. I'm sorry for you, and for Marco."

"What! But you'd said my vetting process for cardinal was completed! Listen Jacques, anyone serving for several decades in my position is bound to face such accusations. It's part of the job. To my knowledge, it's already occurred three times. Is it again about my so-called luxury villa in the Shaanxi Province, paid for by the Chinese Communist Party? I was absolutely transparent with you when you first enquired, and you agreed that it would have been unpolitical to turn down the gift twelve years ago. So, yes, as I told you already, I still go to Xi'an about twice a year, essentially to keep up diplomatic contacts. The rest of the time, the house is used by clergy on vacation as a convenient base to visit Emperor Qinshihuang's Terracotta Army. You enjoyed it once, I remember. A pity you had to cancel your stay there last October, by the way."

"You bet I regret it! What a damned flu it was! Incidentally, there'd been a fourth allegation, but like the earlier ones, it was found inconclusive, or I would have told you. This fifth time, unfortunately, there seems to be evidence."

"Very well Jacques. Please fax me the compromising documents quickly and I will expose that scam as I did before."

"In fact Picerno, the alleged evidence is already with you in Tokyo, in the Archives of the Nunciature, no doubt. It's a chapter of the brochure published under your name for the Papal Visit in Japan, dated 22 February 1981. I remembered that you were the main organiser of the trip. That latest allegation is rather puzzling, I admit. The claimant suggested I should read one after the other some foreign words interspersed in a given chapter as an acronym."

"This is preposterous!" Turning to Mgr Altemps anxiously listening, Dorf whispered, "Marco, bring us that brochure; I saw a copy in the waiting room." Speaking into the receiver again, "Now Jacques, there was nothing political or even religious in that slim book. Fifty copies were printed, or a hundred at most. I merely put together testimonies by a dozen *hibakusha*, Hiroshima survivors. They included sportsmen, philanthropists, businessmen, scientists, fashion designer Issey Miyake, a religious superior and various artists describing how they had found the energy or inspiration to bounce back after the ordeal. The brochure was a tribute to resilience and creativeness after chaos. It was dedicated to Emperor Hirohito and Pope John Paul. The Holy Father thanked me personally after, stressing that it met his views as expressed in his Hiroshima Conference to Scientists on the 25 February following, if I recall. How on earth could it incriminate me as a Communist spy? But Marco is back with a copy of it."

"Please, calm down Picerno. I was as surprised as you are. Still, would you please read for me the title on page 21?"

"Of course. It's *Redemption Through Painting*, by Ken Kokura, the late artist. We just saw the film about him last night, by the way. There was nothing in it to embarrass me."

"I know. So I was told this morning, and I was very glad to hear it. Like you, I assumed that the safe screening of that film on Kokura would be the finishing touch to your vetting process. Now, I must make that important phone call in five minutes and I would hate to leave our conversation unfinished. So, let me read out to you what I found after combining the strange words in Kokura's text. They are disseminated between stanzas. At first, I could not make head or tail of it. Then I tried to group the words as syllables spelled in the reverse order. Brace yourself, my friend. It reads: '*Chinese master spy* Showcasing Dissent *forced me to forge this*.'"

"Totally absurd! Jacques, what connection could there ever be between this Boy Scout cipher and me!"

"I would have ignored it, Picerno, if it weren't for the second piece of evidence: your proposed coat of arms as would-be cardinal."

"What about it?"

"It's on my desk and I don't dislike it; although our expert in ecclesiastical heraldry found it rather unconventional."

"Why? It's just a bamboo tree. Many old European coats of arms include trees. This one is standing firm in the wind, bending but not breaking. I chose it because it's an Asian symbol of resilience. My Chinese contact at the Patriotic Catholic Association assured me it was a genuine Chinese ideogram."

"Precisely. In my corridor yesterday, I happened to bump into our friend Dr Shevchenko. (Further to your query last week, yes, his Chinese translation of *Centesimus Annus* will be ready, he assured me, in time for the release of the encyclical.) Out of interest I showed him your coat of arms, obviously without any mention of its intended bearer or purpose. Well, he confirmed your interpretation about the tree. From an Asian perspective, the bamboo tree means resilience."

"There. You see?"

"Indeed, but there's more. Shevchenko added that when displayed within a rectangular frame like on your draft, what looks like a stylised tree with five bent branches takes a very different meaning. Once confined, the 'tree' becomes a rather archaic ideogram meaning something like 'display opposition,' or perhaps 'showcasing dissent.' The frame turns the tree into a clenched fist: the five branches become five folded digits and the trunk figures the arm. That sign had fallen into disuse by the end of the Empire, Dr Shevchenko noted, until a dozen years ago when it resurfaced in some Government correspondence. Picerno, are you still there?"

"Yes Jacques. I can hear you very well."

"Good. Sorry to bother you with this. What I didn't tell the Professor either is that the draft of your coat of arms was accompanied, on a different sheet, by your proposed motto as future cardinal, *Dissensionem Illustrare*. As your letter explains, you chose it in reference to Acts 15:2 which you quoted, *When therefore Paul and Barnabas had no small dissension and disputation with them, they determined that Paul and Barnabas, and certain other of them, should go up to Jerusalem unto the apostles and elders about this question.* You state that the quote and motto refer to your policy of strategic concessions to the Chinese, where Beijing symbolically stands for Antioch, and Rome for Jerusalem. Now, if I didn't fear reading too deeply between the lines, I might suggest that you identify with the open-minded Saul and Barnabas, while the strict implementers of the Mosaic Law in Acts remind you of certain hard-line clergy of the Underground Church in China. They would die rather than forego the appointment of Chinese bishops by Rome rather than by Beijing, a bit like the early Mosaic Christians were adamant on retaining the rite of circumcision. Any comment?"

After a silence, Bishop Dorf answered, "If I wished Chinese bishops to be consecrated without papal mandate, Jacques, you wouldn't even be having this conversation with me. But I maintain that those who were consecrated unlawfully—or will be—should be regularised without fuss, as part of our agreed policy of strategic concessions. May I remind you of the alternative strategy claimed by Bishop Kung nearly forty years ago? *'If we renounce our faith, we will disappear and there will not be a resurrection. If we are faithful, we will still disappear, but there will be a resurrection.'* His heroic brag took us nowhere in China. We had to adapt. I called it realism. But what does this have to do with my motto, may I ask?"

Thankfully, Picerno couldn't see Mgr Jacques Pommard's short yawn and sympathetic smile. But he heard his reply, "Calm down Picerno. I've always supported you. I've no objection to your coat-of-arms and motto, but please tell me how you would translate it."

"Thank you. That's to the point. So, *Dissensionem Illustrare* means *To resolve a disagreement.*"

"It's elegant enough, if not very literal. But in the light of the unfortunate cipher found in your ten-year-old brochure, surely you see that people who don't know you as well as I do might translate *Dissensionem Illustrare* more plainly, perhaps as... *Illuminating Opposition*, or even *Showcasing Dissent*—after Kokura's code. What makes things very delicate is the nature of your 1981 Japanese brochure. If it had been a mere flyer or a circular... But no, it was the official welcoming publication for the papal visit, dedicated to His Holiness and to the Japanese Emperor. Quite embarrassing.

"Let's pray that the cipher might have been pure fantasy. I expect to hear by tomorrow whether or not our services have knowledge of this alleged Chinese master spy codenamed *Showcasing Dissent*. If they don't, then why on earth was this cipher put in your brochure a full decade ago, when you were not yet a bishop, let alone preparing for the red hat? If our services happen to know this *Showcasing Dissent* and you don't, the obvious option would be to change altogether your coat of arms and your motto.

"But it might be too late for that, I'm afraid. People in my department had to see your proposals and, as much as I trust in the dedication of my staff, I cannot exclude that some of them might know who sent me the anonymous warning about the Kokura cipher. They might inform him—or her? How could I deny the connection if it comes out? Or how can I prevent it from ever coming out? I just don't know, Picerno. It's getting a bit late and I now must call another valued collaborator. Allow me to sleep on it. Meanwhile, I recommend you comb the Archive of the Nunciature to check whether the original typescript of your brochure matches the published one. It would be a great relief to both of us if this untimely cipher were found to be a later inclusion. Let's hope for a way forward tomorrow."

Walking nearly an hour did Picerno good. On the way back though, he would take a taxi. Unable to bear his painful wait within the precincts of the Nunciature any longer, he'd

leisurely made his way north across the Kanda River towards
the old Sekiguchi Parish. Bishop Picerno Dorf had always
liked St Mary's Cathedral, the iconic monument built in 1964
by Kenzo Tange in the centre of Tokyo. Its Modernist architecture raised the visitor beyond time, he felt, up a tsunami
of reinforced concrete, towards the light well. It reminded
him of Hokusai's *Great Wave*; unlike the seamen on the iconic
woodblock print though, worshippers were quite safe under
that very solid wave of the cathedral.

Nearly thirty years later it still felt resolutely modern,
challenging and emblematic. "When would a suitable organ
be installed, though," he wondered. On three occasions,
Picerno had met famous architect Kenzo Tange. The last
time was to ask him if he could contribute a chapter to the
brochure for John Paul II's 1981 visit as he had lived in Hiroshima in the 1930s when a college student. "I would like to
have my funeral at St Mary's Cathedral," Tange had said.
Picerno felt close to the Japanese architect. Like him he had a
vision, and was trying to translate it into a yet unknown shape.
But Tange was acknowledged for his landmark monuments
all over the world, his prophetic architecture spreading all
across Japan and as far as Singapore, Paris and America. By
comparison, Picerno grumbled to himself, why was it so difficult to gain acceptance for his Chinese policy? Why so much
suspicion when results—discreet ones but verifiable—spoke in
his favour? Would his Chinese strategy remain as a monument
to his dedication and foresight, like a mausoleum?

Following the advice of Mgr Jacques Pommard, he'd spent
over an hour in the general Archive of the Nunciature with
Mgr Altemps that morning looking into the file about the 1981
Papal Visit. It contained a spare printed copy of the official
brochure, but not the original texts. The printing company
used at the time had kept no proofs of the brochure, they'd
assured Marco. There had to be more information about
Kokura. Fortunately, as First Counsellor Mgr Altemps had
clearance to access the Secret Archive. On opening the safe

in the office of the absent Pro-Nuncio, both prelates felt apprehensive, although justified by the quasi-order issued by Mgr Pommard. They glanced with excitement at the name of Ken Kokura upon a green file. It contained an account of his life written in English, and the handwritten original version—in English—of his chapter for the papal brochure. No esoteric characters showed in between paragraphs. Acronymic readings of other chapters yielded no cipher either. The compromising allegation about *Showcasing Dissent* must have been added in the typed version, either by Kokura himself, or by some other member of the Nunciature staff. No one else had been involved in the process.

Mgr Altemps was deeply apologetic to Bishop Dorf as the two men were ending their supper at the Nunciature that evening.

"I feel as if I've let you down, Picerno. I remember distinctly reading the final version in English before sending it to the printer. News of Kokura's death in hospital had just reached the Nunciature. We were running late and I didn't compare the proofs with the originals systematically. If only I had done it, surely I would have noticed the fraud."

"No, you wouldn't. No need for regret. Who would have thought of reading one after the other some cryptic syllables in one of the chapters of that book? Just get me the list of all members of staff here in 1981. The forger has to be one of them. Besides, my friend, you speak as if I were that elusive master spy. For all we know, that codename could refer to the Pro-Nuncio at the time, Archbishop Mario Pio Gaspari. Was he not once the Vatican Undersecretary of the Council for the Public Affairs of the Church? He would have known a lot about many, many people. How convenient for some, that he passed away two years after the papal visit. The spy could also have been your predecessor, the then-First Counsellor, since you were only Second Counsellor at the time."

Mgr Altemps looked inside his empty wine glass with resignation, whispering, "Or it could be *me*. That's quite plausible."

"Don't be ridiculous Marco. Why not Pommard himself or Bishop Kung! Or even Pope John Paul while you're at it? No kidding, we must find who really did it, if he's still alive."

"Picerno, I've been thinking about it since Holy Mass this morning. Time is running short and Pommard wants a solution. Seriously, why not put it on me?"

"So you're not joking? You really mean this, Marco—a sacrifice? But you couldn't tell a sheer lie, even for my sake, could you?"

"No, of course. I wouldn't lie. But it would suffice if evidence involving me were faxed to Pommard through some of our contacts. You see, I might not last as long as I'd hoped. And all I want is the success of what we've been working for all these years. I'm asking you as a friend: allow me to clear the path for you. Let *me* be *Showcasing Dissent*. I will confess to Pommard. He won't want a scandal and will let me go quietly, perhaps to retire to some monastery."

"No way, Marco! Don't even think of it. I'd rather claim that *I* am *Showcasing Dissent*. As to letting you go quietly as you suggest, that would be worse than prison! Even if you were a spy, who would be so cruel as to let you be buried alive as a typist in some flea-plagued backwater nunciature in Swaziland or Tonga, or to sweep the cloister in a Trappist penitentiary? Since on the contrary you're my friend and my teammate, we'll go to victory together, or not. However, let's hope Pommard will have found the real spy by tomorrow."

* * *

Picerno slept poorly that night. No phone call woke him up, but he got out of bed twice and walked into his office in his pyjamas to check whether a fax from Pommard had arrived. Still nothing! What were they all doing in Rome? Enjoying Easter Week in some trattoria? Did they not mind that he, at the far end of the world, was kept in dire anxiety by that infuriating cipher? His heart was beating faster than usual. How silly of him to have walked all the way to St Mary's

Cathedral that past afternoon! Exercise was recommended for his heart, but not exhaustion. It had been much too long a stretch. As if he were still in his thirties, skiing with Marco in their native Dolomite Mountains. Had the doctor not spoken sternly enough to him after his minor stroke four months earlier?

In the morning he'd attended Marco's private Mass in the chapel. Mgr Altemps was barely recognisable at the little altar. From the pews, all that met the eyes was a large embroidered cross on the back of the Roman chasuble. Marco insisted on offering Mass not only daily, but even facing East. His friend's choice of the antiquated Tridentine Mass still puzzled Bishop Dorf. And it took so much genuflecting! In his condition, the poor man should not overdo it. Contrary to custom, at the Offertory Mgr Altemps took a pause, sitting down on the sanctuary chair as if in pain. Well, it seemed that they were both old men, despite being still well under seventy. Perhaps neither of them was destined to rise much higher in the service of the Church after all. What a waste of their strategy after so much work. While reading his breviary, Picerno kept an eye on his friend standing at the altar. Altemps safely reached the Consecration. Having prayed all the hours until Vespers, Dorf rose from his pew and walked to his office again to check his fax machine—still obstinately void of any communication from Pommard.

In frustration, Bishop Dorf went to the dining room where he indulged in a more copious breakfast than needed. He managed to smile at the waitress as, with a bow, she laid before him a cheese omelette with steamed rice and pickles or *tsukemono*. She would be a beautiful woman, he admitted, if it were not for that slight limp of hers. A pity, she could have been a model, twenty years ago, instead of a servant.

"It's Hana, isn't it? Are you the new cook, or the new maid? I also saw you cleaning the offices, didn't I?"

"His Excellency is most generous to notice Hana's insignificant presence. Hana is only a temporary housekeeper covering during the Easter break. All permanent staff will be back next Monday and standards will rise again to the level His Excellency deserves."

"Temporary? Ah, that explains why I couldn't remember the names and faces of the chauffeur and of the gardener then. Like you they must have arrived yesterday, didn't they?"

"His Excellency's kind interest does us all much honour. Indeed my esteemed Uncle Byobu and Mr Han were fortunate enough as to be hired this week to serve in this glorious mansion. Would His Excellency wish more miso soup?"

Back in his office after breakfast, Bishop Dorf sat comfortably in his Chinese rosewood armchair and opened the brochure of Pope John Paul II's visit to Japan. He'd only browsed through it the day before, connecting in exasperation the awkward words of Kokura's chapter to form the fateful cipher. Since he had nothing better to do, being kept waiting by Pommard in Rome, he would now scrutinize the entire text of the poem.

CHAPTER 3
A Spy in Love

I N THOSE DAYS, ODDLY, I "FELL IN love", as most people call such a circumstance. It was the first time it had happened to me since awakening in 1945 and perhaps the only time, unless my life before the bomb ever proved otherwise. This is how it begun.

Although based in Germany, the Kravitzes, Sultan and I were still required to spend time in the USSR. We would travel there every three months or so. Once, in the winter of 1947, in between two working sessions in Moscow, our team of painting analysts had been summoned to Leningrad by Comrade Stepan Churakov. Masterpieces such as Rembrandt's *David and Uriah* needed our attention at the Hermitage Museum. The journey by train to Leningrad felt like travelling back in time to Saint Petersburg of old. Our reserved cabins for *apparatchiks*, that is, Party officials, had retained some old-fashioned flavour. Upper class travellers from the pre-Communist era might have sat on those very seats, I fancied. Only later did I learn that the father of my cherished painter James McNeill Whistler had built the railway by commission from Tsar Nicholas I. Well, Whistler junior himself then might have peered through my very window, gathering emotions and shades to inspire his future paintings.

I spent part of the journey looking with delight at the vast expanses covered with moonlit snow, swept by the shadows of pine trees and birch woods as our train glided through the night. I shared a cabin with Sultan. Did Ida, in the next-door cabin with Professor Kravitz (perhaps even with her cheek resting upon the same partition against which I was leaning) share my happiness, I wondered? The sky became overcast as we approached the coast. I contemplated the icy dawn, like a light grey curtain pulled up over a streak of rose that spread horizontally against the blue grey snow. On arrival I happened to be sitting next to Ida in the Soviet-made "ZiS" limousine, a sleek official government car. Instead of going straight to the Hermitage though, we stopped on the way at nearby Laval House, a palace on the waterfronts, where the city archives were located. Maintenance work had brought about an important discovery for the world of art, we had been told.

Comrade Stepan Churakov welcomed us in the large library with the vaulted ceiling on the first floor of the palace. Through its tall windows, one could admire the snowed Angliyskaya Embankment, along the partly frozen River Neva. Once seated in our frail-looking nineteenth-century armchairs, I felt as if transported a century earlier to Imperial Russia. Handing a glass of port to Ida, and then to us three men, Churakov explained the historical background. The discovery was a letter sent in 1844 by Count Ludwig von Lebzeltern to his father-in-law Count Jean-Charles de Laval. Lebzeltern had left Russia nineteen years earlier. At the time of writing he had just retired as the Austrian Ambassador to the Kingdom of Naples. Laval had served as a high civil servant in the Tsar's administration. A French émigré in St Petersburg, Laval had risen to prominence thanks to the special protection of Tsar Paul I, who had him marry the richest woman in Russia, heiress to copper mines in Ust-Katav and elsewhere in the Urals.

"So far, so good," Churakov commented.

But Laval's position became compromised in 1825 when his other son-in-law, Prince Sergei Troubetzkoy, was convicted of plotting the December 26 Uprising, a failed attempt to democratise the tsarist State. Prince Sergei sought refuge in the Austrian Embassy, much to the embarrassment of his brother-in-law Lebzeltern, the then-Austrian Empire's minister to St. Petersburg since 1816. Born in Lisbon only nineteen years after the 1755 Great Earthquake that had destroyed the

Portuguese capital, Lebzeltern had served as a diplomat in Madrid, Rome, Switzerland and Paris, before Prince von Metternich had promoted him to St Petersburg. Although unaware of the plot schemed by his brother-in-law, Lebzeltern was socially implicated through his close family connection with the insurgent. This led to his demotion to Naples. Over there, in addition to his diplomatic tasks, art connoisseur Lebzeltern sought important paintings to enrich the Imperial collections. Troubetzkoy was arrested, first sentenced to death, but soon "mercifully" sent to Siberia for forced labour instead. I remember how Comrade Stepan Churakov had praised the heroism and foresight of Troubetzkoy, fallen under the brutal autocratic oppression as he fought for the cause of the people.

"Men like him made possible the 1917 October Revolution," Churakov had affirmed. "No wonder that his wife Katasha was so devoted to him. Listen comrades: she obtained from the Tsar the favour of following her husband, that is, on foot across Russia all the way to eastern Siberia (indeed, a mere three hours from the Chinese border), there to share his exile. They had several children and she died over there."

I noticed Churakov's hand laid on Ida's shoulder as he concluded with a smile. "May all our loving Soviet women imitate her faithfulness."

As often, one could not really guess whether he was making a joke or uttering a threat. Churakov went on, theatrically pointing his empty glass of port at the walls of the library covered with filing boxes containing the City archives.

"Over five thousand precious volumes once sat on these shelves, while many portraits of famous poets and philosophers were displayed all around the palace, with an enormous collection of Egyptian and Greek antiquities, and paintings by European masters. The Hermitage acquired most of these treasures, thankfully. In this room before their exile, the great Alexander Pushkin and Mikhail Lermontov read revolutionary poetry. In other words, comrades, we are sitting at the epicentre of the privileged autocratic but enlightened world of yesterday. Listen to the British 'Ambassadress,' wife of Sir Edward Cromwell Disbrowe, the British Minister Plenipotentiary and Envoy Extraordinary to the Court of St. Petersburg at the time:

'Madame Lebzeltern, *née* Countess Laval, is a Russian, but married to the Austrian Minister; she speaks English like a native, is a great musician, and I mean to like her. Her father is a Frenchman, her mother an enormously rich Russian. We dined there the other day, had a splendid feast, and the ice was served in dishes of the same material; they looked like cut glass, were fluted and of a pretty shape.'

"I share your unease, comrades! While fine parties were taking place in these warm and gilded rooms, all across Russia hundreds of thousands of serfs were kept in shackles by the aristocracy, or dying of exhaustion as they built the first railway lines reserved for the country's elites. But do not judge hastily! For at the same time, under the nose of the capitalists in this very house, Prince or *Comrade* Sergei Troubetzkoy was meeting in secret with his fellow revolutionaries. A printing press was kept in his wife's bathroom. Yes, he fell—they fell, but they did not fail. Their sacrifice sowed the seed of freedom, which now all enjoy across the glorious Union of Soviet Socialist Republics."

Churakov paused for a moment, helped himself to another glass of port and, suddenly shifting roles from Soviet tribune to enlightened aesthete, added with a confidential smile, "That being said, it cannot be denied that those autocrats of old had artistic taste and intuition, as I will now illustrate. Please listen with great attention, because this letter is the likely key to a treasure. It may allow us to locate two lost masterpieces which your team will help identify and claim—for the cause of the people."

Below is Count von Lebzeltern's letter to his father-in-law, merely thirteen years older than him, which Comrade Churakov had translated for us from the French original.

"Naples, 21 September 1844. Esteemed Count and dear Father,

"Thank you for your kind letter found last week on my return from Vienna. Zénaïde and I are very well, enjoying my retirement—and the relatively cooler temperature. I am sorry to read that your gout still tortures you despite having taken red meat and sweet wines out of your diet. All the more do we mourn your physician and friend Dr von Trinius! Can it truly be nearly six months since his death? Still, you kept his concoction recipes and what joy that as a consequence this big toe of yours—or *hallux*, as Trinius would scientifically correct me—might be spared amputation. Such a reprieve is a gift from the good doctor reaching out to us mortals even from the afterlife. I can picture him as if he still walked with you across the lawns of your delightful villa on Aptekarsky Island, the doctor's and yours rightly cherished 'Isle of the Apothecary.'

"By association with the netherworld, the thought of our dear exiles is conjured up in my heart. Nineteen years since their deportation and the wound in my soul, no more than in yours, I know well, still has not healed. But I rejoice at the news of their finally settling down in more civilised conditions, especially with five young children. Seen from Naples or Petersburg, moving from Nerchinsk to Irkutsk evokes very little improvement, though. To me it sounds as distant and inhospitable as a yurt on the Moon, or an isba on Saturn. Will we be given to embrace them again, this side of Judgement?

"But we have wept enough, I believe. Here is good news to cheer you up, dear Count! First, I snatched from the greedy claws of the Marquis de Custine at least one of Bertel Thorvaldsen's reliefs. It is a delightful family scene, with blacksmith Vulcan hammering hot metal arrows for young Cupid to hand to Madame Venus, who dips them in a love philtre. The great sculptor is barely buried and already frenzied collectors are making his works nearly impossible to acquire.

"But there is more, as you will see. In Vienna the Emperor was so pleased with my two Italian armoured knights that he let me retain the Dutch paintings, as he 'has no time for mythology.' His Majesty was adamant that further acquisitions had to be Caravaggios or nothing. I feared that mere followers of the master, however gifted, would not satisfy my sovereign. I was wrong, happily. One of my depicted knights of Malta is the Grand Master Marcantonio Zondadari, I believe. The other looks very much like Adrien de Wignacourt, in a posture similar to his uncle and predecessor Olaf in Caravaggio's portrait. They will make a pleasant pair above the two doors of Archduke Franz Karl's writing-room at Schonbrunn.

"Thus, as you hoped, I took back with me the Dutch *Annunciation* and the *Mercury, Argus and Io*. Is the latter Dutch rather than Italian, though? For its broad and deep landscape is akin to Salvator Rosa's composition, more than to Abraham Bloemaert's or Jordaens' focus on the characters. But the style is strongly reminiscent of Rembrandt van Rijn, although not slavishly. I incline to identify it as the painting auctioned in Paris on 23 February 1778 according to Nogaret's *Memoirs*. If I am correct, its author is Van Rijn's talented pupil, the ill-fated Carel Fabritius of Delft, who went up in smoke with most of his workshop and pictures in the mid-seventeenth century when a gunpowder magazine exploded nearby—God rest his soul. Did I just write *Fabritius?* Yes, dear Father, and I can guess your joy when reading this attribution. It seems very probable indeed that I have got hold of one of the very few surviving masterpieces by Fabritius. I so wished that your gout might have ended, allowing you to come and see it in the flesh, so to speak—and us you, since your daughter misses you and her dear mother Countess Alexandra as much as I do.

"Talking of Zénaïde, she was little moved by our Fabritius, arguing that adultery and cruelty were no fitting topics for display in her rooms. I pleaded with her, explaining that the picture merely alludes to the myth, rather than depicts it. One does not see the pagan god Jupiter turning his mistress Io into a cow. Furthermore, nothing is shown of the beheading of Juno's spy, Argus with the hundred eyes, nor of Mercury placing the eyes of his victim on the tail of the peacock. Still, your daughter would have none of it. 'To a false god turning his mistress into a cow while ignoring mortals,' she remarked, 'I prefer the true God becoming Man for the love of the Virgin and of all of us human beings.' (I thought it tactful not to remind my dear wife that her first name means 'Life of Zeus.')

"Thankfully, she positively loved the *Annunciation*. This does credit to her piety and to the good education you gave her.

Although unfinished, the picture is strikingly beautiful. It is devoid of the Rococo niceties 'à la Boucher,' but also of any supernatural hints, strangely. No halo surrounds the head of the Madonna, graciously bent towards some letter she is holding, unless it be a necklace she examines (this area appears to be only sketched). To tell the truth, not even does the angelic ambassador show. I assume that the artist had assigned for Archangel Gabriel the space left empty to the left. A window opens there, and a curtain hangs nearby, half concealing a large darkish china jar. The standing Madonna could be any Dutch housewife in a seventeenth-century mansion. What I so wish you could see, dear Count, is the quality of the light, like milk for the eyes if those could drink. Only Joannis van der Meer has ever painted light like this man. *Indoor* light, I mean, for Claude Gellée's gilded sunsets upon seaports are still unsurpassed. How you and I love Claude, don't we, dear friend, having both grown up and later settled in coastal metropolises where we expect to end: your Marseille was my Lisbon, and my Naples your Petersburg. But I digress: back to our *Annunciation*. Van der Meer knew Fabritius, since both worked in Delft in the same period. To my knowledge Van der Meer painted but two religious scenes. What if that one, still unattributed, were his third and most important religious work?

"I must leave you now dear Father, as our darling Alexandrine is back from church with her mother. Thankfully for a nineteen-year-old lady, your granddaughter is not only pious, but also very fond of fine arts. I mean to ask her opinion about the author of the *Annunciation*. I wonder how she might react if I suggested selecting some talented painter to complete the painting.

"Yours affectionately,

"Lebzeltern

"P. S. I had the two enclosed daguerreotypes securely wrapped, trusting that they reach you unbroken after transportation across Europe. Strikingly, when reproduced on sheets of silver-plated copper, our two paintings glow with even greater freshness than on the original canvases."

There was silence. Comrade Churakov slowly walked towards a credence set in between two Egyptian sphinxes. An open box lay upon the wood. He extracted from it a precious bundle that looked as if wrapped in swaddling clothes and reverently lay it on the lap of Ida Kravitz. Taking infinite care, he then uncovered the fragile treasure. Unless my memory fails me, his voice was shaking when he announced, although confidentially, "Comrades, only one of Lebzeltern's daguerreotypes was found here. At least it is unscathed, thankfully. Lady, gentlemen, I, Stepan Churakov, co-director of the Committee of Arts of the Council of People's Commissars of the USSR, have the honour of introducing the authentic reproduction of our lost masterpiece. Only remember, as you behold the copy, to seek the original."

Through the high windows the light, made even brighter through its reflection upon the snow that covered the embankment, reached the copper plate finally exposed in Ida's lithe hands. Leaning or perhaps, I cannot tell, kneeling like a third wise man between Sultan and Professor Kravitz, I saw. That image could have been analysed as a pagan equivalent to a Nativity scene, but Fabritius had not produced any, to my knowledge. Under his natural shelter I saw the human form resting on the ground in trusting sleep, his unawareness poignantly contrasting with his forthcoming execution, watched over by a god's appointee, surrounded by an ox and further cattle and sheep. I remembered. I had seen it before, that is, the original painting. But where, and when? Time had spared this faithful reproduction displayed before my eyes, mirroring the original stranded in some closet or repository, whose finding, I then knew, would unlock my lost memory, restoring to my life meaning and direction. How mysterious, I thought, that the fortune of the Laval family had been built on copper mines, while a copper sheet, possibly produced in the Ural and sold in Italy was sent back to this very house, bearing the reproduction of such a masterpiece. I almost envied the copper plate: it had found its way home.

On Saturday morning, 3 January 1948 (four days after the death of Han van Meegeren), Heinrich knocked at my door in the students' residence. With a beaming smile, he announced, "Splendid news, Ken! I think I have found who you were. Our contacts in Hiroshima identified a Catholic college ran by so-called 'Canons of Saint Augustine,' located in the Nobori-cho section of the city. The school had been started in 1892 by the Society of Mary, the 'Marianists.' But in 1940, the Religious Bodies Law forbade Japanese from receiving salaries from foreigners. The Marianists were mostly French and thus had to withdraw. But they handed the school over to the Augustinians, who had several Japanese members. The Fine Arts teacher at the college was a single layman. He would have been about your age. On my trip to Hiroshima two months ago, I showed a priest survivor a picture of you. He identified you as the missing art teacher, 'with seventy-five percent certainty,' he reckoned."

Heinrich had long stopped smiling, as he noticed the impact of his words on my face. I kept quiet, not daring to move, not looking at him either. With gravity this time, he continued, "Nothing remained of the school after the bombing. Part of it still stood after the blast, but all went up in flames soon after. At the time, many Japanese schools were closed for want of staff, since most able men had been drafted in some military capacity or other, if you recall. Teenage children had been mustered to pull down some buildings and create firebreaks. But that school had probably retained some foreign and religious staff in addition to the Japanese, making it possible to run some classes still, for whatever children were able to attend. Whether or not the school was open that day, no staff or students survived apparently."

Heinrich looked at me hesitantly, as if deliberating whether he should tell me more about my past, and my likely identity. I had never sought information. He was the one who had kept in touch with Japan, not I, apart from a few postcards exchanged with my former roommate Yamato, whose wife was expecting a second child. Heinrich went on eventually, but the accumulation of details, like many shards of my splintered memory, felt like needles pushed into my soul.

"If you were that art teacher, you would probably have been on an errand in another part of the city when the explosion occurred. Classes would have started at 8:00am that Monday and the bomb exploded at 8:16am. Art classes generally took place in the afternoon because they required less concentration. The very patchy archives retrieved via the Augustinian order state that the art teacher was an Augustinian 'tertiary'—that means a lay associate, not a priest or a friar. His name was 'Kimio Kimura.' He must have been well acquainted with European art since he had published a study on seventeenth-century Dutch painting. Last month I wrote to the archivist at the headquarters of the Augustinians in Rome. He could find no copy of that publication but promised to enquire further. I shared this information with Professor Schulz before coming to see you. He would like you to focus on seventeenth-century Dutch painting. Although we cannot guarantee that you are Kimura, it seems worth investing your skills in that era of Western painting. Useful memories might come back, who knows?"

I had been standing all the time, listening with growing emotion. Heinrich stopped speaking as I fell heavily onto my bed, staring at the white wall. Pain spread in my neck and chest. I kept my hands flat on my thighs. Turning on the tap above the small basin, Heinrich poured water and handed me a glass which I drank without noticing it. Self-pity washed over me, overwhelmingly. I seemed to see in the distance the little Japanese art teacher, so conscientious, I assumed, so dedicated, on his last errand across Hiroshima, perhaps trying to find some paint or brushes for his painting lesson, little knowing that "Little Boy," the worst bomb ever made, was coming down on him and his young pupils, very fast. I burst into tears.

Heinrich sat next to me and put his hand on my shoulder. After some time in silence, he stood up and announced, "I expected the news to shake you a bit. I am sorry. You are likely to feel unsettled over the next few days. It can't be easy for you to contemplate adjusting to a new identity; having courageously restarted your life after what the Americans did to your city two-and-a-half years ago. Professor Schulz asks you to come and see him this afternoon to talk it all through. He allowed me to tell you of a surprise to cheer you up. You are to leave the students residence and become a lodger at the house of Professor and Ida Kravitz. Their spare room is ready for you to move in. It will almost be a family setting for the three of you. A car will await you with your suitcase at 6pm today to take you there in time for supper."

Heinrich went. I suddenly sprang up and grabbed the little basin, vomiting. Almost choking, I undid my green bow tie to loosen my throat, and lay down on my bed, eyes shut in vain. I could see the little Japanese art teacher stumbling across the fallen walls, while a child's voice wept, or sang, "*Shu Jesusu, awaremi tamai!* Our Lord Jesus, have pity on us!" But I was not a child anymore.

<hr />

When relocating from Moscow to Wittenberg, Professor and Ida Kravitz had been assigned a rather plain detached house surrounded by a small garden. On arrival with my two suitcases that evening, I was allocated a room on the first floor, adjacent to Ida's. The place was quieter than the university hall of residence. My hosts insisted that I was very welcome, but I still felt as if I was intruding on their privacy. On the first morning, when getting ready for my sword drawing practice around 5am, I realised that the desk stood too close to the bed for me to unsheathe the blade safely. Everybody seemed to be asleep. Not hearing a sound, I carefully started pushing the desk towards the door. There, I now had a wide enough empty space. I lit the candle and set it on the floor about one metre away from me. Sitting on my heels—I was by now fully accustomed to that daily posture—I spent my usual thirty minutes immobile, and managed to snuff out the flame in one swing of my sword, not as fast as previously though. I was not yet familiar with the space and sounds within my new home. Later in the morning, the three of us breakfasted together before driving to the University lab where we were working on several minor paintings from the Rembrandt studio.

In retrospect, the house of the Kravitzes, Number 12 Mauerstrasse, is where I first recall encountering a feeling close to what people with a memory call *home*, I presume. Our shared passion for our work led to fascinating discussions about the techniques of illustrious painters, but also about their religious motivations and the spiritual background of classical European art. I learnt a lot from the Professor, and also from Ida. There was kindness and discretion between us three. For instance, only then did I realise that Ida was the Professor's sister, not his wife. I don't know why, but this fact made a strong impression on me. Soon after, I was struck by Ida's resemblance to Titian's *Judith with the Head of Holofernes*, from the Galleria Doria Pamphilj in Rome (which assumes that the picture represents rather Salome holding the head of St John the Baptist.)

I felt relaxed enough to resume painting. I would give it a couple of hours, several times a week. After work, Professor Kravitz and Ida spent about twenty minutes every day playing the violin. It took place in the cellar so as not to disturb me. Since Hiroshima my right ear had healed and I could hear clearly the music ascending from downstairs, especially as I got into the habit of leaving the door of my bedroom open to the landing when they played. I liked it very much. After a couple of months, I realised that they only ever played the same short pieces of music—about a dozen, fifteen at most. Apart from that, the house was quiet. One night though, some days after my arrival, I perceived a strange noise in the other room. I had woken up much earlier than usual, for no reason, and was trying to get back to sleep. It sounded like rug-beating.

There didn't seem to be more than one person in the room. The muffled noise did not last long. After a couple of minutes, everything sounded perfectly still again. I discreetly pushed my desk away and knelt down in sword practice position.

We spent January and February 1948 analysing a dozen paintings from the Rembrandt studio, including four attributed to Fabritius. Little was known about that artist. I was sent some documentation from The Netherlands showing that there was more than one painter by that name. I had happily discovered that there were two brothers, both painters, when a *third* brother appeared. Johannes was the brother of Barent and Carel Fabritius. More siblings remained unaccounted for by art historians. Carel had died in an explosion which destroyed a large area of Delft in 1654. Of the three brothers, Carel became like a friend to me, for obvious reasons. Gunpowder had turned his city into dust instantaneously, as had occurred to mine through atom bombing. I felt as if I owed it to Carel to make his talent better known, since I had survived and not he. Many of his paintings had been destroyed in the explosion.

Experts disputed the authorship of several others. A striking *Mercury and Aglauros* appeared in a catalogue of the Dresden gallery in 1935. I was sure that it was by Carel. But no historian in Europe supported the hypothesis. It was now permanently in Boston. I would need to ask permission to visit America soon. I could not draw definitive conclusions based on reproductions: I needed to see the originals. Radiography had never been applied to these pictures. Important information awaited me under their surface, I felt. *Mercury and Aglauros* had been sold several times during the eighteenth century as a counterpart to another work by Fabritius, *Mercury, Argus and Io*, whose trace had been lost in Paris, if the hypothesis ventured by Count von Lebzeltern in his famous letter was correct. The bright reproduction of that elusive painting, displayed on Ida's lap when introduced to us in St. Petersburg, flashed in my memory. I dreamt of finding it, bringing back to light not only one but a pair of Carel's best works. I mourned him like a brother when reading about the devastation of his city. I stared for hours at some reproductions of Egbert Lievensz van der Poel's depictions of Delft after the 1654 explosion.

It gave me courage, I suppose, to look for the first time at pictures of Hiroshima, razed to the ground nearly three centuries after Delft. No one talked about it in Japan, it seemed, even though it had occurred only two years earlier. Worse, *hibakusha*, that is, atom bomb survivors, were ostracised. No one wanted to give them jobs apparently, even less so marry them. People feared long-term consequences on the health of the survivors and chose not to be associated with them. Also, the Americans in control of Japan censured information about their double crime.

Thankfully Heinrich had obtained very rare pictures of the catastrophe. He pointed at what was termed "nuclear shadows." They resulted from extreme thermal radiations. I felt as if hypnotised by the outlines of people's bodies and of objects that had blocked the heat radiation and had disintegrated within a second. There was that woman sitting on a bench by the river. All that remained of her was the shadow of where she had been sitting at the moment of the explosion. Another "nuclear shadow" was a man standing by a ladder. The ladder was perfectly projected against the brick wall behind, as if it had been a black and white trompe-l'oeil or graffiti. After seeing a little girl jumping a rope, still suspended in the air, or rather her empty silhouette burnt against the wall, I stopped looking.

Compassion for the Hiroshima victims was not the only cause for my emotion. Again, some long-forgotten memory had just been triggered. This time, it implied that I had travelled in Europe before. It was in Italy, either in Pompeii or in Herculanum, one of the two cities destroyed by the eruption of Vesuvius in 79AD. Conjured up by the nuclear shadows from Japan, Italian plaster casts of the tuff or lava hollows of what were, once fully alive, a little boy, a couple kissing, or a curled dog became vivid in my memory. I had been there before. Yes, I remembered examining the casts with other young men. I wondered if we had not prayed for the victims. We would have been pilgrims then, not scientists.

~~~~~~~~~~~~~~~~~~~~~~~~~

On Thursday, 24 June 1948, there was great excitement all across my University department and throughout Wittenberg, as the Berlin blockade by the Soviet Army was announced. Most of us approved of it, not realising that Berliners in the Soviet-controlled East Sector had voted en masse against Communist candidates. I walked home without Professor Kravitz who had been detained for an important meeting with Comrade Leonid Naumovich Rabinovich. Ida stayed at home on Wednesdays and Thursdays. Eager to ask for her views on the blockade, I expected to find her in the garden where she liked to sit in summer. I will never forget her gaze when, not having located her anywhere, I pushed open her bedroom door, which was ajar. She never told the name of her aggressor, probably because she feared retaliation on her or on her brother Professor Kravitz. I later gathered that the attacker was an influential apparatchik in the Committee of Arts of the Council of People's Commissars of the USSR. She died nine months later in difficult childbirth. Baby Anastasia was safe, thankfully. Her father was obviously Asian. I had been rather shaken by the crime and its consequences. I didn't know why Professor Kravitz would not seek compassionate support from me. Finally earning my doctorate in Art History did not even cheer me up. I had very few friends. Sultan had left Wittenberg suddenly in the early summer of 1948 in response to a long-expected promotion in Moscow. He went back to his country in December 1949 as political adviser to the newly formed United States of Indonesia.

~~~~~~~~~~~~~~~~~~~~~~~~~

In the late 1940s, I wondered whether I should move back to Japan. My old friend Yamato wrote to me regularly. He now had two children and was giving sword lessons in his spare time. Yamato had made it his mission to find out who I was before the bombing. A police officer, he was doing his best to gather plausible information matching my profile as a survivor through his professional network. He would come up with various suggestions. Once, around 1949, he told me of a missing Buddhist monk from Mitaki-dera Temple in Hiroshima. The young religious was a gifted artist and had been on an errand into town that fatal 6 August, to buy pure gold and pigments to refresh the face paint of one of the Buddha statues at his monastery. I objected that on waking under the military tent after the bombing I definitely had hair, instead of a shaven scalp as a monk would have had. But Yamato affirmed that short hair was worn by certain Buddhist religious, albeit rarely.

Another time, in 1957, Yamato was quite certain that I had been a gardener at the Hiroshima Prefectural Industrial Promotion Hall. Long before the steel shell of its ruined roof had become the familiar A-bomb Dome in the Hiroshima Peace Memorial, the edifice built in the European style by a Czech architect in 1915 had been a landmark of pre-war Hiroshima. Its yet undamaged dome reminded me of a similar one depicted by Raphael in his *Wedding of the Virgin* on display in Milan. The Hall's garden along the Motoyasu River was diligently kept and contained many trees, two separate Western-style and Japanese areas with a fountain and a gazebo. The head gardener had survived, but his assistant had gone missing. A young man of 28 at the time, he was a diligent horticulturist, spending hours on his knees bent over azalea flower beds. Yamato had shown a picture of me to a local survivor called Eizo Nomura, who had identified me with high probability as the missing assistant-gardener. In vain did Yamato have me check my right shoulder for a scar which, according to the late gardener's parents, their son had received in a fight at school.

For a couple of decades I was touched by Yamato's search for my lost identity. I daydreamed that I was, perhaps, this monk or that gardener. During the few days each new hypothesis occupied me, it felt like resuscitating young men who had been victims of the tragedy. Unlike me, these had apparently not survived. What would their lives have been like? I mourned them as brothers. But I also think that part of me slowly grew weary of the succession of candidates for the embodiment of my past life. When watching the film *Anastasia* that had just been released, I was feeling like the Dowager Empress Marie Feodorovna, when, after the Bolshevik Revolution, she was requested to identify would-be Romanov granddaughters who turned out to be imposters. I suppose that I had kept Heinrich's revelation of my past as a Catholic Augustinian lay friar and art teacher as the most plausible, perhaps because it had been suggested first. Something prevented me from seriously considering other explanations. From 1950 onwards, I realised that I did not really wish to return to Hiroshima. Besides, nowhere in Japan could I find the same opportunities for research and work as in Wittenberg.

As for Heinrich, he was never there. I missed him. On 31 January 1950 he invited me for a drink, in between two trips abroad, asking out of the blue, "Would you like to accompany me to London? We must examine a painting at the National Gallery." It was the first time a mission abroad was offered me, if one discounts my formation trips to Moscow. I could not believe it. And in London of all places, in the very gallery where the famous *View of Delft* by my cherished Carel Fabritius was displayed!

From his armchair Heinrich helped himself to another pint of beer, crossed his legs, and explained, "Ken, you have been with us four years now. You have worked very hard and have acquired valuable expertise in radiographic analysis of famous paintings. Listen carefully why we need your intervention. My friend Anthony Blunt is the Surveyor of the King's Pictures in London, a quiet position where he does a lot of good. The current director of the National Gallery, one Philip Hendy, contacted him about selling to the King's Pictures *The Entombment*, an unfinished painting attributed to Michelangelo. Hendy wants money to complete the refurbishing of his vast gallery, following the war damage. His trustees would never permit the sale of a genuine Michelangelo, but they might give in to Hendy if the authorship is doubtful. It would be in my friend Blunt's interest to accept Hendy's offer. But Anthony is convinced that Michelangelo painted *The Entombment*, and he is about to publicize his arguments.

"Why then does he not buy the painting as doubtful, hence cheaper, only to prove its authenticity once acquired? That would fit very well, if Blunt were to keep his current position as Surveyor of the King's Pictures. But for reasons that I don't need to explain now, it would be more helpful if we could find radiographic evidence to support Blunt's case and keep the genuine *Entombment* at the National Gallery. It would make Blunt's disinterestedness manifest, no less than his competence, and might obtain for him the directorship of the National Gallery, a much more prestigious appointment. There is a recent precedent, since Kenneth Clark also headed the King's Pictures, before focusing on the National Gallery exclusively. Although I am sure you will appreciate Blunt very much, when we meet him, I am only asking your expertise for the sake of science, naturally. So, that's settled. The radiographic equipment will be loaded on a plane tomorrow morning, and we can start the examination tomorrow afternoon in London."

England... The West... How thrilled I was to walk on English pavements and watch red double-deckers drive by. At every corner though, huge heaps of rubble and deep excavations reminded passers-by and tourists that London had been hit hard during the Blitz only nine years previously. Witnessing what the "capital city of free Europe" (as it was called then) had endured prompted bitter-sweet emotions in me. On the one hand I felt that it served the British right, after they had eagerly supported American nuclear research and endeavour. On the other hand, I could not exclude the thought that some innocent art teachers on their way to give their classes had been hit by German bombs and, unlike me in Hiroshima, had not survived. As Heinrich and I walked along Pall Mall, the thought occurred to me that this red-bearded policeman or that taxi driver (his hackney carriage missing a front door, awkwardly) was like me an amnesic art teacher painfully trying to rebuild his life. Everyone around me, I fancied, might well have been an amnesiac after all. Had the war made us all forget who we were, to some extent? Such a hypothesis made us all brethren, somehow. And yet, lest I forgot, were not these people our enemies, hindering the spread of socialist freedom?

We had lunch at the club of Professor Blunt, not far from Buckingham Palace. I had never entered such an elegant venue. It felt quite different from the rather trite *bierstubes* where I occasionally sat with University colleagues in Wittenberg. Although I had only been an assistant lecturer, Heinrich introduced me as "Professor Kokura." It nearly made me blush, childishly. I suddenly felt that my bow tie was much too green. Perhaps, turquoise or even blue would be more elegant. (I asked Heinrich on the way out, who replied teasingly that calling green *blue* did not apply to bow ties, only to Japanese traffic lights.) As refined as he was unassuming, Anthony Blunt reminded me of Sultan. He looked younger than forty-three. Like my Indonesian friend, he had lived in Paris before the war when, coincidentally, he had met Sultan and even Léonard Tsuguharu Foujita, the fashionable Japanese painter. As to Michelangelo, Blunt's theory was that *The Entombment* was a two-dimensional copy of *Laocoon and his Sons,* the famous sculpted group at the Vatican Museum. Pictures of the two works were displayed on our table. Blunt was skillfully swirling his red wine in a large glass, as if examining the viscosity of the liquid—but I felt as if his eyes were directed at me, through the glass. He sounded very dispassionate and yet, predatorily assertive as if describing facts rather than sharing a hypothesis.

"Remember, young Francesco da Sangallo is in the palace with his famous father, Florentine architect Giuliano. His friend Michelangelo is there, probably working on sketches for his *Moses*. Or the three might be discussing art, perhaps around a bottle of one of those Renaissance wines, Glera or La lagrima di Christo, as we are—since it was cold in Rome on that February morning in 1506—when a courtier of Pope Julius II is ushered in. He announces that, 'A spectacular discovery has just occurred in the vineyard of Felice De Fredis, on the Oppian Hill! His Holiness commands you to visit the site immediately and take note of all that is to be found.' The two friends and young Francesco (he was merely a teenager, but very bright) run to the excavation. There, a complex sculpture is carefully unearthed, a stupendous and horrifying entanglement of marble limbs and coils. Buonarroti falls on his knees. He knows. Possibly he sheds tears, being Italian. At last, the masterpiece which Pliny described so eloquently, probably brought from Rhodes some fifteen centuries earlier for the imperial collections, stands before the most brilliant sculptor of the Renaissance. Michelangelo watches the two serpents emerge from the soil as if from the sea, he sees them crawl to the high priest Laocoon and his two sons—about the age of young Francesco da Sangallo in fact and, like him, very handsome—around whom they powerfully cling, in whose flesh they spew their venom, while the muscular father tries in vain to loosen the lethal constriction. And why such a dreadful punishment inflicted by the god Poseidon? Because Laocoon had warned the Trojans against the votive horse, left outside their city walls by the Greeks, who had falsely retreated."

Professor Blunt paused, still looking at me, I felt, through his glass, which he finally brought to his lips, calmly sipping the ruby liquid. In awe, as if *The Laocoon* had been standing in our midst, we silently waited.

Heinrich then ventured, pointing at the pictures on our table, "But even though Michelangelo was struck by the unearthed statue, I see no serpents in *The Entombment*."

"The strips of cloth with which the two disciples hold the dead Body of Christ on their way to the sepulchre in the background...," Blunt quietly stated, "These are the *serpents*. The two bearers stand for Laocoon's sons. As the monstrous reptiles of the *Laocoon* form a poisonous web, forcing themselves on their unwilling victims, so the linens in *The Entombment* are the instruments of a delicate compassion for Christ, willingly carried by the disciples. The white cloths uniting the three central figures become pregnant with unsuspected meaning, it seems to me, when seen as the poetic transposition of the serpents of hate. Over several pages I have systematically described the formal resemblances in shapes, sizes, and postures between the two masterpieces. The influence of *The Laocoon* on Michelangelo's *Rebellious* and *Dying Slaves*, as well as his Sistine Chapel frescoes, is unquestionable. What I expect, with Professor Kokura's radiographic expertise, is to find evidence of such resemblances beneath the surface of *The Entombment*, which will prove the impossibility of its early dating to 1501. Michelangelo must have painted it after he had discovered *The Laocoon*, not before 1506. The formal similarities preclude otherwise."

Anthony Blunt expressed no emotion when, late that afternoon in the lab of the National Gallery, sometime after Director Philip Hendy had left the room, the small silhouette of a brazen serpent appeared on my cathode ray tube screen, in an area of *The Entombment* situated left from the head of the Apostle St John, beneath the blue background. At variance with the customary depictions of Moses' animal upon its wooden tau, after the *Book of Exodus*, the head of that snake and the coil supporting it were an exact replica of the one biting into the left hip of Laocoon. It could not have been a coincidence. Blunt was right: *The Entombment* had to be a genuine Michelangelo, even though an unfinished one. In my memory though, this victory and even my long-awaited encounters with Fabritius' paintings and with Holbein's *Ambassadors* the following day are eclipsed by the conversation Heinrich and I had, sitting on a bench in St James' Park. I suppose that was when, for the first time, I became conscious of having grown into a Soviet spy.

It was raining heavily over London that Thursday morning, 2 February 1950, I remember. That may explain why so few visitors could be seen in the National Gallery, unless my first actual encounter with Holbein's *Ambassadors* had blinded me to human interference. There I stood, a few steps away from the masterpiece. I nearly bowed to Their Excellencies John de Dinteville and George de Selve, so elegantly dressed at either end of the high table upon which lay various instruments and tools. But my business was with the mysterious skull stretched before the two men. Walking to the right of the painting, I peeped above the edge of the frame and saw the anamorphic shape condense until it floated, beautifully proportioned. Death is among the living, and little do we realise it until we change our perspective. Shifting one's vantage point takes imagination and courage. But for a *hibakusha* like me, a Hiroshima survivor, death was most effortlessly present to mind and even to stomach—as my occasional nauseas still reminded me. I had tried to forget death rather than focus upon it.

I next stepped with awe into the room where Carel Fabritius' *View of Delft* awaited me. As I looked at the city so dear to Carel, who had tragically died with it, I felt as if discovering a hypothetical *View of Hiroshima* painted before the bombing. Did I whisper these words, or did they merely flow through my mind? "I call to you, Hiroshima. Where are your busy streets and your tranquil squares, your secluded gardens and your lucrative shops? Where are your warehouses, your bridges and your piers, your schools and your hospitals, your avenues and your temples? Won't you answer me?"

The rain had stopped when Heinrich met me outside the Gallery, on Trafalgar Square. We strolled around, enjoying ourselves as mere tourists, even buying doughnuts from a street seller, before ending up on that fateful bench in St James' Park. Sitting at my side, his face towards the pond, with a smile Heinrich asked out of the blue, "Who do you work for, Ken?"

Puzzled and slightly anxious, I answered, "Well, for Wittenberg University. For the Art Department, don't I?"

He enquired further, "And who does the Wittenberg University serve, would you say?"

I ventured, "The people of the German Democratic Republic, surely."

"This is perfectly true," Heinrich replied, "and who is the strongest ally of the German Democratic Republic, more than an ally in fact, a mentor rather, even a father to the martyred German people?"

I was not sure what my friend was aiming at—unless I had known it all along. My hands tucked in the pockets of my coat, I stood up, looking in silence at the pelicans and ducks by the side of the pond.

"Well?" Heinrich insisted, nibbling a doughnut extracted from his paper bag.

"It must be Moscow," I answered.

"Indeed my friend. I meant to ask you: how does it feel for you, a Japanese survivor of Western tyranny, to collaborate in the most deserving human undertaking ever, that is, the universal liberation of the peoples?"

This time I turned towards him and plainly stated, "I am so deeply grateful that I have been given a new life, and a chance to be of use in this world, Heinrich. You know that I had lost everything. And now, I feel alive again. Wittenberg, the painting analyses and you, Sultan, and Professor Kravitz, are all I cherish most."

"Ken, this is good; but we are only manifestations of an all-powerful influence. While you cherish us and your work as you affectionately said, would you not wish to embrace more actively the dynamism that inspires us? I know that you are not political, so that the very word *Communism* does not resonate in you as deeply as it should. I'm not criticising you, please note. I respect who you are and what you've been through. But if I, your friend, asked you to commit yourself with more determination to the work of cultural liberation within the ambit of the Communist Party, would you follow me?"

I was moved, becoming aware that something very important was taking place between us, right by this bench, with the birds behind us and London all around. I sat next to him again and, letting him take my hand, whispered after a silence, "Heinrich, I feel as if, out of the rubble of Hiroshima, you and Communism have fashioned me anew, giving me shape and purpose. How could I ever not follow you?"

He then held both my hands tight, and looking me in the eyes, enquired gravely, "So, you will follow me, my friend? Even if it hurts?"

With a quickness and assurance that surprised me in retrospect, I almost protested, "If it hurts? Pain was my cradle as I awoke under a tent outside Hiroshima five years ago. Pain physical and spiritual. It is always with me. The change for me would be if pain ceased, not if it started. I will follow you then, even when it does not hurt anymore."

Heinrich put his arm around my shoulder. "Thank you Ken. Thank you on my part, and on behalf of all the oppressed, of all those peoples who hope in our help." Then he protectively announced, "Nothing needs to change about you. I mean, just carry on your valuable work as a technical expert on paintings. In fact, your mission is to alter nothing at all. You might only need to distance yourself from Wittenberg, and even from me, perhaps, if fighting the battle demands it."

While speaking he glanced inside his paper bag, distractedly crumbling the remains of his doughnut.

"Going into battle? But my work, my paintings?" I answered in dismay. "You know that I cannot fight. Surely you don't think I could ever carry a gun?"

"You can draw a sword, if I recall," he replied with a smile. "But don't you worry; no, of course you won't carry a gun. Your weapon is far more dangerous and useful to our cause. It is your paintbrush, or rather, your technical skills in painting analyses. Nobody will ever call you a Soviet spy, and in fact you will not become one, no more than you thought you were one before this conversation. For administrative purposes, purely, your name might appear in some file in Moscow under the title 'Field Agent,' but these are mere words."

"'Field Agent?' I am not sure I understand," I replied. "How would I belong then, receive directives and to whom would I report?"

Heinrich was now standing by the pond, throwing crumbs at the birds that flocked noisily around him.

"Dear, dear Ken—above anything, there must be freedom. After all, such is our goal. So, yes, some kind of link must exist, for your safety and for reporting. But yours will be light and nearly invisible. Agents in non-artistic fields may call the link a lead, for they are trained to fight as ferocious hounds, unlike you. Our scientist friends may call the link a tube or a cord. Yes, cord sounds pretty accurate, since agents are first selected like human eggs soon will be, then implanted, nurtured, activated and, only if the situation requires it—detonated."

Blowing inside the brown paper bag, now empty, he suddenly smashed it. The frightened birds flew away from him in every direction. It was my first subversion lesson. I insert here the notes I took that evening, quoting Heinrich *verbatim*.

He smiled, looking at what remained of the paper bag. "'Detonated' is a figure of speech by the way. Our agents are not physically exploded, as far as I am aware. We sometimes blow up their cover, not their body. Discovering a spy at the heart of its establishment deeply destabilises the enemy. As Sun Tzu said, 'The supreme art of war is to subdue the enemy without fighting.' Sure, we lose an agent, but we sow suspicion and unrest among all those our man or woman was in contact with, even though none of them was his accomplice. It slows the enemy down, disorganises and depresses the leaders, while undermining trust and esteem for them among the public. That is the sort of blast we like to produce."

I looked at him with a mixture of admiration and concern as he explained further. "Detonating an agent can also be used as a diversion, when we want to distract the enemy from a much more important undertaking. Let me give you an example. Have you ever heard of Professor Karl Fuchs, a Western expert on nuclear weapons? He is German, of course, but moved to the United Kingdom before the last war. Well, he is being 'detonated' as we speak. Before tomorrow, agents of Scotland Yard will have arrested him. He will be charged with having leaked secret plans of the US atom bomb to us, that is, to the USSR. After a short stay in a British gaol, we will have him transferred to Democratic Germany where he will resume his research. A charming young genius of 38, he will plead guilty—as I informed him at breakfast this morning."

Heinrich obviously didn't mention which "more important undertaking" might have been concealed behind a diversion such as the sensational arrest of Professor Karl Fuchs in England, but eleven days later a treaty of "Friendship, Alliance and Mutual Assistance" was signed by Chinese leader Mao Zedong and Soviet Premier Joseph Stalin, making the two Communist countries a force that was "impossible to defeat." On my return to Wittenberg though, I found myself thrown into such an excruciating turn of events that I was unable to pay attention to international news. Heinrich and I had just landed at Berlin Schoenfeld in the afternoon of 4 February. While I was checking that the crates containing my precious radiographic equipment were carefully loaded into our van, a couple of officials came to Heinrich. He asked me to wait for him in the vehicle as he should not be long. Returning nearly half an hour later, he frowned as he set a large envelope on my lap, commenting, "It sounds as if you will soon need to leave Wittenberg, Ken. Why on earth did you never mention this to me?"

I opened the envelope and incredulously started reading. Two official statements by Professor Chimek Kravitz and his sister, the late Ida Kravitz, claimed that I was her abuser and the father of her child, Baby Anastasia. Professor Kravitz was holding me responsible for Ida's death in childbirth, and had presented his resignation from the Painting Analyses Program if I was allowed to continue as a member of his team. This very morning, Professor Churakov had arrived from Moscow, deeply upset by this split between Professor Kravitz and myself, but determined to tolerate no hindrance to the sterling work and splendid achievements of the "Sovnarkom"—that is, the Committee of Arts of the Council of People's Commissars of the USSR. I was to be driven from the airport immediately to meet Professor Churakov at the place of my alleged crime, namely, the very house of Professor Kravitz, which I still called my home.

CHAPTER 4
Cardinal Anonymous

BISHOP DORF FLICKERED THROUGH the papal brochure. He had not paid much attention to it since Pope John Paul II's successful visit ten years earlier. Putting that booklet together had been his idea entirely. He was quite pleased with the diversity of contributors. Had not the Pope—and even Pommard—been impressed? Now what again was the title of that poem by the Japanese art expert Kokura? *Destruction? Devastation?* Ah, there it was, right after *Building Strength*, Kenzo Tange's piece on architecture. Comfortably sitting in his Chinese armchair, Picerno crossed his legs and started reading.

REDEMPTION THROUGH PAINTING

Siht

Wide Island no more, but *The Waste One* is now your name—O my city, Hiroshima!

What was, has ceased. It is daylight now elsewhere in the world, but here the darkness seems thicker than any night.

How can I still breathe while you lie dead, O my city laid waste?

Eg

Before my eyes, beyond the side of the boat carrying me towards you, nothing moves but snakes of smoke, billowing from your once comely face as horrendous hair on Medusa's head.

And how much I wish I froze to death at such a sight, when none of what lived but minutes earlier can now be found, scattered across as it all is, shrouded in ashes.

Rof

As the river carries me further along your banks, am I more than debris, floating among wood beams, dark baskets, gutted horses and sinking carts?

Dreadfully flat, your place among the living now lies open and void.

Your gates are sunk into the ground, destroyed, and your bars broken.

All they that will pass by the way will clap their hands at you: they will hiss, and wag their heads at you, saying: Is this the city of perfect beauty, the joy of all the earth?

Ot

My eyes fail with weeping, my bowels are troubled: my liver is poured out upon the earth, for the destruction of my beloved city.

I call for you, Hiroshima.

Where are your busy streets and your tranquil squares, your secluded gardens and your lucrative shops?

Where are your warehouses, your bridges and your piers, your schools and your hospitals, your avenues and your temples?

Em

Won't you answer me?

Hush!

Silence.

Silence everywhere.

Forever muted are your chatter and laughter, your shouts and songs.

Dec

I dare not weep, lest the sound of my tears falling on the wooden deck, however faintly, might disturb the sacred still-ness all around.

Death reigns.

I bow.

Rof

What organ can still be beating in my chest when before me, you my city, my very heart, lie motionless, monstrously still, having become the most striking depiction of horror?

What artist has achieved a carving on such gigantic scale, calling it *Devastation*?

If you are not Rome ablaze, yet is there a Nero nearby, admiring such a vivid depiction of the apocalypse?

Who hath kindled as it were a flaming fire devouring round about?

Tnes

Neither are you ancient Troy, O Hiroshima, since Ilion was ablaze already when a star fell from the firmament, a mere portent for old Anchises to flee his fallen city at last.

Who has poured out his indignation like fire?

Sid

And which neighbour will fly to your rescue?

Many an empire would in no time reach across the water and assist you in such dire straits, if asked.

Gnis

Why fear, O my city, why fear their ambition and their greed, as if amidst your fallen walls and under your burnt roofs, you had anything left for anyone to covet and loot?

Or are your neighbours in such need of ashes? Is dust the new gold and are firebrands more sought after than gems, that you should treasure them and fear dispossession?

Ac

Alas, I know why you should cling to these blackened remains.

But minutes ago, O Hiroshima, these calcined relics were clothed with flesh, animated by souls that felt and loved and hoped and prayed.

Wohs

My city, these smoking charcoals are what remains of your children!

The children!

Your children!

Our children!

Yps

Let walls crumble and domes explode; let bridges collapse and towers burst, if such must be our fate—but mercy for the children!

Mercy for our fellow humans!

Mercy for the little ones and for their parents!

Mercy for the adolescents and for the elderly!

Mercy for the grooms and the brides!

Ret

Mercy for the wise, such as Archimedes in Syracuse falling; and even more so, mercy for the saints such as our father Augustine within Hippo besieged!

And yet also, mercy for the sick, the prisoners, and the beggars!

Mercy for all people!

Alas, no mercy was shown.

Sam

Thousands of innocents were brushed from the face of the earth, as a butterfly from a flower, with one finger.

But the butterfly might live on, in some other garden, in some warmer climate.

Whereas you my people, were turned into smoke without even time to hug or kiss or pray.

Esen

Am I, lonely survivor, to flutter away towards another garden?

As my ship reaches your desolate bank, O Hiroshima, I want no wings, I know of no petals and I smell no fragrance.

Ihc

But if ever unclasped, my hands would paint the joy and the peace that my eyes once witnessed.

Colours might sing your beauty ere your death, and new souls would breathe the warmth of your perfumes, delighting in the sight of your splendour, O Hiroshima.

Perplexed, Bishop Dorf laid the brochure on his desk. Had Kokura really written that text? The description betrayed knowledge of European antiquity which the Japanese spy, a highly cultured man, might plausibly have acquired during his time spent in Western countries. And yet, it felt as if the narrator was not truly Japanese. Perhaps a foreign journalist had produced the original, a war correspondent posted near Hiroshima and visiting very soon after the explosion, since he was arriving by boat apparently unscathed. The bishop tried to remember his only meeting with Kokura in preparation for Pope John Paul II's visit ten years earlier. The famous Japanese, an art expert, had readily agreed to provide a chapter for the official brochure. Dorf had read with interest its English version. He'd liked the absence of Christian references. It made the appeal wider. Any sufferer, any survivor could relate to the crushing pain, to the compelling despair and to the hope eventually rising. But what of the reversed words? Were they part of the typed version he'd approved, or not? Bishop Dorf was surprised not to remember. Had these scattered syllables showed on the page, he would have caught the biblical hint, of course, even though most readers would have missed it. Kokura seemed to have imitated the *Book of Lamentations* in the Old Testament. Like the Prophet Jeremiah, Kokura had started each paragraph with a monosyllabic word, echoing the consonants of the Hebrew alphabet, or *alefbet*, rather. The *Lamentations* used to be sung during the Easter Triduum, up to the 1960s. The poem described the fate of Jerusalem besieged by her enemies.

Picerno smiled, recalling that Mgr Altemps had sought permission to retain the old breviary after the modern Liturgy of the Hours had been promulgated in 1971. Twenty years later, Dorf had become fully accustomed to the new (and shorter) readings and didn't miss at all Jeremiah's *Lamentations*. Did Kokura know about the old breviary? Had he meant the insertion of quasi Hebrew letters in his chapter on Hiroshima as an allusion to an era in history prior to 1945? What if, the bishop wondered, that rather easy cipher was only a lure? Could that enigmatic Japanese have encoded more subtle data—or worse allegations—deeper inside his text? And why only in Kokura's lines, after all? Why not through the entire papal brochure? If that chapter had been tampered with, all others could have as well. With anxious curiosity, Picerno started browsing through the brochure again, checking whether the other chapters yielded any suspicious anomalies.

Screeching interrupted him. Was Pommard sending news, at last? He jumped to his fax machine, feverishly trying to read the upper lines as they appeared on the top of the page. When the high-pitched noise stopped, Bishop Dorf stared with hatred and fear at the black printing device, now ominously silent. He finally tore off the long sheet of glossy paper and read.

Confidential:
For the attention of Bishop Picerno Dorf, Vatican Delegate
    to the U. N. Observatory of Non-Proliferation of Nuclear
    Weapons in Asia, Apostolic Nunciature in Tokyo.
Tuesday 2nd April 1991

Your Excellency,

Mgr Jacques Pommard is very sorry to have to confirm the cancellation of the announcement of your cardinalate. Recent investigations have led to this unfortunate outcome to the vetting process. Thankfully, no decisive evidence has emerged to harm your good character. The alleged connection between you and the so-called Chinese Master spy Showcasing Dissent could not be demonstrated, even though the latter's existence was corroborated. Nevertheless, persons of influence have stated their awareness of a compromising cipher found in the papal brochure published in Tokyo under your name in 1981. The same persons allegedly expressed their firm intention to divulge this fact and further compromising information about you. While not conclusive for observers familiar with the diplomacy of the Church in China, the combined evidence would undermine your trustworthiness in the eyes of a significant proportion of Chinese Catholics in China and abroad, especially in America. As you realise, this would compromise your fruitful service to the Church in China. In addition, it would jeopardize the credibility of the Holy See regarding Asian affairs, since cardinals are justly seen as the senate of the Bishop of Rome.

Mgr Pommard is acutely aware of the painful sacrifice this must represent for you, eager as you always have been to serve

Holy Church through your zeal and influence. He assures you that he has done his utmost to find a way forward, to no avail alas, and trusts in your supernatural outlook to accept this unexpected turn of events. As a token of the continued esteem in which this dicastery holds you, Mgr Pommard is glad to inform you that your appointment as cardinal next month is secured, albeit in pectore. You are no doubt cognizant of the procedure of appointment in pectore, whereby the Sovereign Pontiff honours a prelate with the cardinalatial dignity while keeping his name secret. As cardinal in pectore, you will not receive the red biretta, neither will you be able to act in public as cardinal, nor make your new distinction known to anyone. But the faithful servant of the Holy See which you always have been will no doubt draw the deepest consolation from this especial gesture of trust bestowed upon you by the Holy Father himself.

Furthermore, Mgr Pommard is anxious to consolidate your good work in China through the appointment of another cardinal supportive of your views. This other cardinal will not be in pectore but publicly proclaimed. While Mgr Pommard has several candidates in mind, some of them beyond voting age at a conclave, he is eager to secure your involvement in the designation process and invites you to suggest to him a couple of names by return of fax, should you be so inclined.

You are welcome to retain your present position as Vatican Delegate to the U. N. Observatory of Non-Proliferation of Nuclear Weapons in Asia for the foreseeable future. Mgr Pommard is confident that Mgr Marco Altemps, soon to be appointed new apostolic nuncio in Japan as previously decided, will gladly continue to lend adequate space at the Tokyo Nunciature for your administration and will appreciate your presence at his side, with the benefit of your wide experience of Asian Affairs.

Mgr Pommard assures you of his friendly esteem as ever.
Signed: Fr Hubert Lambourin,
Personal Assistant to Mgr Jacques Pommard.

Bishop Picerno Dorf was not quite ready to die. He still had a few plans to fulfil. And yet, he felt as if his hour had come as the printed sheet slowly fell out of his hands and down to the floor. The prelate clung to his rosewood throne in desperation. Pain in his chest seemed to spread to his shoulder as he collapsed on the carpet. Breathless, he tried to regain control of his emotions and thoughts. First, to find his tablets. He managed to drag himself towards the drawer in his desk and swallowed the medicine with a mouthful of Okayama Single Malt whisky, the only liquid at hand, straight from Marco's bottle. He then hid Fr Lambourin's fateful letter in his pocket and sat again while dialling the 119 emergency number. Soon transferred to a nurse, he was asked to describe his symptoms, which were deemed alarming enough to justify the dispatching of an ambulance. Suddenly though, the sick man realised that hospitalisation would definitely ruin any chances of saving his red hat. If a mildly compromised bishop could not become cardinal, even less so would a cardiac prelate, surely. Bishop Dorf gathered the remains of his strength to oppose the suggestion of the nurse. He was grateful for her advice but was already feeling "much better" and would only need to speak to his consultant later that day. He hung up with relief after hearing her reluctantly cancel the ambulance.

He wouldn't move. Please God, this had been a mere spasm. Just wait. Stay still. From his Chinese throne, Bishop Dorf surveyed his frames on the wall and his books on the shelves. Among the books, he stared at a certain cardboard box. He knew well what was concealed inside it. A red biretta and sash. When placing the order at a well-known ecclesiastical tailor in Rome on his behalf, Marco had typed the name of "Fr Hubert Lambourin" as recipient, putting any inquisitive shop staff off the scent (of Picerno). "Lambourin!" Ironically, that same miserable little secretary was the one who'd signed the fatal missive. How disappointing of Pommard to send his Quebecois henchman. The Head of the Asian Section at the Secretariat of State didn't even have the guts to break the horrible news personally to him, Picerno Dorf. Was it out of fear? Picerno smiled wryly at the suggestion. He was feeling the least fearsome prelate in the Church universal. He waited further, breathing very slowly.

What was he? Merely an old sick man in an old chair, with old ambitions now ruined, staring at a box with a brand-new biretta in it that he would never wear. Or never in public! Oh yes, he could wear it while he slept, or when brushing his teeth. He could even wear red pyjamas and, why not, use a red toothbrush! But never, ever, would he be allowed to be recognised as a prince of the Church: so dictated that absurd, petty and sadistic appointment as cardinal *in pectore*! Picerno spoke to himself ironically, "Dear *secret* Cardinal Dorf, congratulations on your never-to-be-revealed promotion! What huge influence it will bring to your Chinese policy, no doubt." Then, as his eyes met with the leather-bound volume of his own doctoral thesis on the same shelf as the biretta box, he burst into insane laughter, having realised how his nameless promotion matched the title of his book. "*The Anonymous Priest*! –by His Eminence, Cardinal *Anonymous*! Thus, my theological endeavour is now vindicated by my new status. Anonymous priests must exist, since anonymous cardinals do!"

Thanks to the tranquilisers, drowsiness overcame him at last and he fell into slumber.

~~~~~~~~~~~~~~~~~~~~~

Picerno was uncertain whether he had dozed for several minutes or much longer when he came back to his senses. His heartbeat felt normal, thankfully. His shoulder was still aching a little, but that might be merely a consequence of his fall onto the carpet, or of the prolonged resting against the back of his throne. What was he doing there, drowsing in his rosewood armchair? The dreadful news flashed in his memory again, causing fresh pain. Ah, yes, the *in pectore* cardinal... What could be done? He drew Lambourin's letter out of his pocket again. Yes, Pommard actually asked him to name the man who would wear his own red hat. How generous! How cruelly generous! Picerno was inspired to mock his superior: he would name *him*. "Dear Jacques, it must be *you*! No one knows the Asian Affairs better than you, and no one would use his cardinalatial influence more supportively of our Chinese policy than you. Why Jacques, I can't suggest Archbishop Huong, the man is senile. As to Benitez, well, last time we promoted a Filipino it didn't end well, did it? They just don't understand China. If not you, then..."

Picerno interrupted his spiteful fantasy. "Him." A name totally unexpected and fantastically providential had just crossed his mind. Closing his eyes, he paused and tried to formulate his idea with great precautions, as if in fear of seeing it vanish. How was it again? A prelate to take his place. Someone who would implement his Chinese policy. Someone he could trust absolutely. Someone who might not last long, but just long enough to do a lot of good. Someone who would keep his seat warm: who knows, by the time that docile substitute left the position vacant, the good repute of Picerno Dorf might have been cleared sufficiently for him to wear his red hat in public at last. If *that* was not inspiration... What time was it in Rome? 2:37am. It was definitely too late to ring, or too early. Even Pommard would be sleeping at that time. Picerno would wait then. Say, another five hours.

He managed to speak over the phone with his consultant, who insisted on examining his heart again that very afternoon. Very well, he would come to the hospital after speaking with Pommard. But he wouldn't ask the chauffeur of the Nunciature. For the sake of discretion, he would take a taxi. As an added precaution, he would not call Pommard via the landline. Even though the lines of the Nunciature were encrypted, he felt safer using his brand-new *Nokia Cityman* 100 mobile phone. Nobody knew that number apart from Marco, Pommard and his contact on mainland China. He checked that the device displayed a fully charged battery. Bishop Dorf was surprised that he could walk without pain to his bedroom, displaying a *Do not disturb* sign on the outside door handle. He then rested on his bed, closing his eyes with a bitter smile at the thought of his forthcoming conversation with Mgr Jacques Pommard.

"No, it's not too early, Picerno. I was expecting you to call me late last night, to be honest. Well, *Showcasing Dissent* is not an invention after all. The spy is mentioned in passing in two reports. I hadn't paid much attention. What we have about him is rather thin, but the connection with you is enough to impose utmost caution, for now. I am really disappointed. What a mess we're in, aren't we?"

"Surely that mess is not my doing, Jacques. You acknowledged that I was not compromised. The Kokura cipher itself states that it is a forgery. What bemuses me is that the ultraconservative Chinese Catholic lobby in America should hold so much clout in Rome as to make you, the Head of Asian Affairs and an enlightened man, revoke a promise made. There must have been very heavy pressures indeed."

"If the decision were mine, you would have got that red hat even sooner, Picerno. In fairness, when I mentioned it to you before the last consistory, three years ago, you said it was too soon. You expected to achieve more behind the scenes. I hope that your being still promoted to cardinal, albeit *in pectore*, eased your disappointment. In fact, that makes two of you. I must inform you of something I couldn't tell even Lambourin; hence its omission in the letter sent you. There is another 'Asian' cardinal *in pectore*. He is a Chinese, and not one you would have suggested. He was created twelve years ago, in 1979 to be precise. Unless we find a suitable Asian candidate very soon for public display as cardinal, the name of your *in pectore* colleague will be revealed next month instead."

Bishop Dorf remained silent for a while. This was worse than he had imagined. For, which Chinese prelate could have been made a cardinal in secret, if not one hated by the Chinese government, that is, one who would stand as a hindrance to the current policy? There was only one name plausible.

"Bishop Ignatius Kung Pin-mei?"

"You said so, Picerno, not I. I knew you would not like it. Anyway, listen to my plan. Since your promotion is to remain secret for now, let us choose an Asian supportive of our views, but one nearing retirement age. It will justify making your cardinalate public at the next consistory, once your alleged connection with the *Showcasing Dissent* spy has been disproved. Unlike you, I believe that Bishop Kung has nothing to do with that hoax, by the way. A man who accepts spending decades in Communist prisons cannot resort to such schemes. That would be contradictory. Regardless though, Kung's supporters in America know about the cipher and its connection with your coat of arms and motto. Even though they are mistaken, merely jumping to conclusions, they will not let you rise. Let us be realistic, however painful it is. Now, please just suggest names, as I wrote to you yesterday night through Lambourin."

Picerno remained silent for a few seconds. Closing his eyes, he gathered his strength and, bringing his lips close to the receiver, proffered two syllables as one casting a spell, confessing a sin and declaring victory.

"Altemps."

"What? You don't mean *Marco* Altemps?"

"I said Altemps. Yes, Mgr Marco Altemps is my candidate. He is dying of cancer. I know it for certain. He is my long-time friend and collaborator. Only yesterday, he offered to 'clear the path before me.' You wrote that he is confirmed as the next nuncio in Japan. Well, announce immediately his promotion in Tokyo, and few people will wonder when he is made a cardinal a couple of weeks later."

"But Altemps is not Asian, and not well-known by the Asian public either."

"Neither am I. But the persons of influence who know me also know that Altemps has been my trusted collaborator throughout my Asian career. They will deduce that I chose to remain behind the scenes with free hands, while acting through him as my red-hatted proxy. Besides, among Marco's ancestors are another cardinal and several archbishops."

"Your proposal is interesting but unexpected, Picerno. I need time to run the idea by a few people before presenting it at the top level."

"Now, listen to me carefully, Jacques Pommard. Much more unexpected and undeserved was the decision to cancel, or conceal, my cardinalate. You sacrificed me through this *in pectore* expedient. Then you asked me for a proxy. I just gave you the only name I will allow to replace me under that red hat, since I'm forbidden from wearing it. You know I have always been loyal. But let me be clear: if Marco isn't accepted, for the sake of all that I have done in China I will not be able to remain altogether silent. I have nothing to lose. Leakage will occur about matters we would both prefer kept in the archives if you fail me a second time, and that will only increase the current mess. I know you understand me. Now with all due respect, I have gone as far as I could, and I must leave you to it. Good day, Jacques."

CHAPTER 5
The Cost of Freedom

IN 1950, 4 FEBRUARY FELL ON A SATurday. Unlike London, East Germany was covered with snow. Heinrich and I had been driven straight from Berlin Schoenfeld airport to the house of the Kravitzes in Wittenberg. There were very few cars on the road that afternoon. We were now standing in my room, watching Professor Kravitz move my desk away from the wall. He pointed at a crack in the plaster.

"This is it, Comrade: just as my sister Ida said in her statement."

Professor Churakov crouched to look at an opening situated about one meter above the floor. Behind him, Heinrich and I instinctively imitated him. Through the partition, light shone from the adjacent room. Professor Kravitz went on sombrely. "All along her pregnancy, I begged Ida to tell me who had abused her. Several times she was about to reveal his name; only to stop and weep in silence, her lips tight. She wanted to protect me, she explained. She knew that I would challenge the criminal and that it might harm me and her, as the man was high up, she reckoned. At least we have her statement now. But why did she confide in me only at the end, while I was away and could not console her? When I saw the Asian features of that little creature, my newborn niece, my suspicion of Professor Kokura became a certainty."

Professor Churakov stood up again, glanced at me and read aloud a printed copy of the same statement which Heinrich had handed me earlier at the airport:

"I, Comrade Ida Kravitz, assistant to my brother, Professor Chimek Kravitz in the Painting Analyses Program of the Committee of Arts of the Council of People's Commissars of the

USSR, testify that the father of my child is Professor Ken Kokura, a member of the same Program and a lodger at our domicile. Soon after his moving into our house, Professor Kokura had expressed his sentimental attraction for me. I could not respond to it, since my work at the Painting Analyses Program needed all my attention. Professor Kokura's skilled collaboration in the same Program endeared him to me, I admit. But never did I act unprofessionally towards him. I did not suspect the faint rattling often heard early morning in his room, next to mine. When asked, Professor Kokura answered that he was moving his desk to give him space for his sword exercises. Because his room was kept dark, only too late did I notice the peephole that he had dug in the wall between our two rooms.

"On 24 June 1948, when the great Soviet Army had been deployed to protect Berlin, I was alone at home as my brother was detained at the University for a meeting with Comrade Leonid Naumovich Rabinovich. It was a very hot afternoon and I was resting in my room, my blinds shut. I awoke at about 3pm, seeing the shadowy silhouette of a man standing by me. The humming noise of the fan by my bed must have covered the sound of his footsteps. The room was dark but the sword in his hand showed him to be Professor Kokura. Though he kept silent, his blade spoke for him. I found his bow tie on the floor later on. I confess that I was afraid of dying. I told myself that if my honour were lost, at least I could carry on with my work at the Painting Analyses Program. I so much wanted to serve further the Committee of Arts of the Council of People's Commissars of the USSR.

"A few weeks later I realised that I was pregnant. I felt help-less. Thankfully Professor Kokura never came to me again. He acted all along as if he had never even thought of assaulting me. I was very afraid of confronting him, lest worse befell me. I condoned his pretence as the safer attitude for my baby, my brother and me. I am deeply sorry that my selfishness prevented me from reporting such an immoral man to the authorities. The comrade doctor has now informed me that I am likely to die in childbirth. Much as I deserve such retribution, I also wish the truth to be known for my sake, for my brother and my child. I beg the forgiveness of our Great Leader Comrade Stalin for my mistakes and weaknesses, which now cause me to cease my functions at the Painting Analyses Program. May the peoples of the USSR and of Germany be forever grateful to our Great Father of Nations for his wise and benign leadership.

"Signed: Comrade Ida Kravitz, on 20 March 1949, at Wittenberg Democratic Maternity Clinic."

Professor Churakov ended his reading. The four men—Heinrich, the two professors and the police officer—stared at me. All of a sudden, I felt very weary. I knew well that I was innocent. But I also knew that dear Ida was incapable of such a lie. And yet, her official statement left no room for doubt, while her child did look Japanese.

"What if another Japanese had attacked her in the dark as she slept that fatal afternoon, putting the blame on me?"—I protested. "Two of my fellow-citizens travelled from Tokyo with Heinrich and myself and Sultan four years ago, and one of them is still studying in Wittenberg."

Heinrich's look of pity wounded me deeply. He gently explained that the other Japanese had been questioned, whose alibi was impeccable as he was sitting for an exam session that entire afternoon.

Being suspected by Heinrich, whom I admired so much, no less than by Professor Kravitz, made me feel hopeless. Who else would vouch for me? Ida was dead (my misled accuser), and Sultan was far away… Still, I ventured, "Please, ask Sultan to stand as my witness. He was still in Wittenberg at the time and would confirm that I cannot have committed such an offence. You can telephone him in Indonesia and hear him even today." Heinrich seemed not to understand me. He motioned me towards the edge of my bed, pushing aside my sword that lay across the blanket. "Please, sit down Ken. You are under very great stress. Whom do you mean we should call in your defence? We know of no 'Sultan' in Indonesia."

I became horribly confused and insisted, "I mean our friend *Sultan*, our comrade! Prince Azmy of Serdang. He was part of the group of Asian students you coordinated. He flew with us from Vladivostok and gave Professor Kravitz and me crucial information on the Vermeer paintings forged by his relative Han van Meegeren."

In a last attempt to prove my loyalty, I leapt towards my desk and took out of the drawer a file through which I browsed feverishly until I found a group picture of our team of Asian students with Heinrich, taken outside a biergarten in Wittenberg. I pointed at Sultan. "This is him: this is Sultan, call him please."

Professor Kravitz looked the other way, as if embarrassed, while Heinrich corrected, "Ah, you mean *Zoltan*: Zoltan Maisuradze. But Comrade Maisuradze is a Caucasian, not an Indonesian. He is from Georgia like Comrade Stalin himself."

Turning towards Professor Churakov, Heinrich explained, "Comrade Zoltan Maisuradze left Wittenberg for Moscow in the early summer 1948. You may recall that he had been part of our team in painting analyses, Comrade Professor."

"I do remember him, I think," Churakov answered. Glancing at the group picture I was still holding, he remarked, "He does look Asian, as most Georgians do. But this is irrelevant. What matters to me and to the Committee of Arts of the Council of People's Commissars of the USSR is to bring this embarrassment to an end immediately. Comrade Professor Kokura, you have served with dedication in this scientific team. You could become the next Sen Katayama, earning like your fellow-countryman public recognition from the USSR and being awarded burial on Moscow's Red Square. Only time will tell. Meanwhile, we must ensure that essential work is not disrupted by a clash of cultural values between Japan and Germany. I don't know about Japan, but in Europe a woman's assent is considered necessary for a man to have his way with her. Although you bear no responsibility in the unforeseen death of Comrade Ida Kravitz, you should have asked for guidance from your mentor Comrade Heinrich before proceeding with her. You will now express your deepest apologies to Professor Kravitz for the loss of his sister, so that we may commit afresh to the important work of our department, for the liberation of all peoples."

I was stunned and remained silent. Everybody was looking at me, apart from Professor Kravitz who left the room.

As a diversion, Heinrich lifted my sword from the bed, unsheathed it and walked towards the wall. He effortlessly plunged the weapon up to the hilt into the crack, saying, "The slot fits perfectly the width and breadth of your blade." Drawing the sword out of the wall, he commented, "Look at its end, its point is badly scratched. Was it the tool you used to dig into this partition?"

I must have fainted, as I don't remember answering Professor Churakov, neither addressing Professor Kravitz, nor protesting to Heinrich, nor hearing anyone's reaction.

~~~~~~~~~~~~~~~~~~~

When I awoke, Heinrich was still sitting next to me, but alone, and the room looked different, as in a hospital.

"Here you are, my friend! I was so worried! You have remained unconscious nearly half a day. Here, Nurse, this way!"

After the nurse had checked my blood pressure, she left to ask for my meal.

I recall that Heinrich apologised. "I am so very sorry, Ken. We should not have made you a lodger at the Kravitzes. But I wish you had confided in me. Now, decisions had to be made while you slept. Professor Churakov cannot afford to lose Professor Kravitz, who wants you out of his team, whether or not you ask for his forgiveness. He dismissed my suggestion that your amnesia might have left you sincerely oblivious of your assault on his sister. 'The only plausible excuse,' he affirmed, 'would be schizophrenia. But then you must have Kokura locked up in a lunatic asylum before he attacks more members of my team, or even slashes our precious paintings with his sword.' Now Ken, I had to enquire, and the psychologist here assured me that the connection between schizophrenia and amnesia is well known. I told him about your surviving the atom bombing in Hiroshima. He said that some level of schizophrenia should be expected after such a trauma. He is to examine you as soon as possible and might recommend a trial treatment. He successfully cured patients of their mental illness within three years. By the way, your sword has been taken away. Not that *I* think you dangerous: they assured me it's a mere precaution, you know."

Heinrich paused for a while. I think I was crying, silently. My amnesia was of the past. Could it have clouded my recent memory, though, deleting any remembrance of the crime? It was true that I liked Ida. Perhaps, in fact... Perhaps I was in love with her, without having realised it. But she was no more. Then, if truly I had attacked her, was I possibly schizophrenic? Could such a man as I, armed with a Japanese sword, be let loose? The prospect of ending up in a mental institution became all of a sudden threateningly plausible. Actually, it suddenly occurred to me: was I not already in such a place? No straitjacket hindered my movements, but as I slowly tried moving my arms, I found my wrists tied to the metal railing along the mattress. Pretending not to have noticed, I felt that I had to convince Heinrich though, and quickly. If I admitted to having molested Ida, at least I would be set free. But if I denied it, I might never see my beautiful paintings again—Carel Fabritius' *View of Delft* flashed in my memory—neither my few friends. Could I face a future with white walls all around me—and iron bars?

Heinrich was looking at me attentively. I could tell that my reply to his report would be crucial. Can I say that I chose to lie? Was my friend taken in, or was he not simply relieved to see my freedom secured? My past was an enigma to me, anyway. What difference did it make if another event was added, like another shape applied to an existing painting? After all, I was a painter myself. Why not add a *"pentimento,"* a more recent layer spread upon the earlier painting of my life before the Hiroshima bombing, still inaccessible to me? *Pentimento* is the technical word for such earlier shapes and colours concealed beneath later additions to a painting. An

Italian word in picture analysis, *pentimento* literally means "to repent," that is, to repaint.

I glanced at Heinrich and managed to smile wryly, confessing, "Of course, I remember. I was just so ashamed of explaining all this in front of the professors. I am glad you are asking me now. But Ida did consent. First, we were friends. She wanted me to teach her sword spirituality. Later, I proposed to her, and we meant to get married. After a few weeks, though, she treated me as an enemy. I felt as if she had pretended to love me, merely for the sake of having a child. Once pregnant, she kept me at bay. I don't know who changed her mind. I am so sorry for what followed."

Heinrich looked deeply pleased with my answer. He held my hand (still tied to the railing) and said soothingly, "You've been through a tough time, old chap. But things are about to look bright again. Often when one door closes, another opens. Now I can break the good news to you, my dear Ken. Listen, a position is just about to be made available in England. Professor Churakov agreed to send you as associate researcher to the Fitzwilliam Museum in Cambridge, whose seventeenth-century collection needs your expertise. Professor Anthony Blunt suggested to me that you were just the person needed there. I think he very much liked making your acquaintance in London earlier this week. He has friends in Cambridge and will make you feel at home there. Assuming you recover swiftly, you could arrive there on Monday, in the middle of the Lent Term. Ida Kravitz's official report convicting you of being her molester need not be divulged, of course, as long as you serve the party well in imperialist Britain."

~~~~~~~~~~~~~~~~~~~~~~~~~

I am not sure there is much to tell about my Cambridge years. My brief was silently to "nest" inside the fabric of English social and academic life. My credentials were to be a Hiroshima survivor and a refugee from Communist Germany. Officially, I was supposed to have slipped away from my scientific delegation led by the University of Wittenberg during a seminar in London. The "delegation" was merely Heinrich, who was with me indeed at the National Gallery laboratory two days earlier, after which I had allegedly "gone into hiding." The wider public had never heard of me then, but academia hailed my defection as significant because of my achievements in radiographic analyses of famous paintings. My "skills, once hijacked by the Soviets as propaganda tools, would now be put to the service of fine arts for the benefit of all," the Fitzwilliam Museum announced. My office was there at the museum, while lodgings were arranged for me at one of the most prominent University colleges, Gonville & Caius.

There I began studying for a doctorate in addition to my Wittenberg one, this time on "Carel, Barent and Johannes: mutual stylistic influences among the Fabritius Brothers." My tutor thought that exploring the connection between the two other Dutch Golden Age brother painters Isaack and Simon Luttichuys would yield more material. But I would not be dissuaded: Fabritius it had to be. I became fond of my two rooms at the College, in a quiet corner of the main quadrangle. The bedroom was spacious enough for my sword exercises every morning: I did not need to push any desks aside before unsheathing my *katana*. The College owned classical paintings, some of which hung in the rooms of staff and privileged students. I don't know by whose influence a genuine *View of Delft after the 1654 Explosion*, by Egbert Van Der Poel, had been allocated to my little studio. I suspect that either Heinrich or Anthony Blunt had secured for me such a thoughtful welcome. I decided to dedicate several hours a week to painting. I tried watercolour for the first time and found it surprisingly rewarding. In retrospect, I think that I relished the fact that, unlike oil painting, watercolour allowed no underlayer. There was no need, no chance, no risk of hidden information surfacing ever. No *pentimenti*. All was there visible from the start.

Heinrich told me to become an Anglican. I already knew a lot about the various branches of Western Christianity.

Catholicism had inspired the very fabric of university life, even here in England, where prayers were still offered in ecclesiastical Latin, and the academic terms were named after Christian feasts: Michaelmas (autumn), Hilary (spring), and Trinity (summer). My college had three gates called "Humility," "Virtue" and "Honour." These virtues were meant to represent the moral progress of the alumni. Learning English and attending Church of England services consumed whatever free time the Museum left me. I lasted only three months in the bell ringers' guild at Great St Mary's Church. My second year at Gonville & Caius saw the preparation for the six hundredth anniversary of the founder's death in the summer of 1951. A Catholic priest, Edmund Gonville had dedicated his new college to the Annunciation of the Blessed Virgin Mary.

My position as a researcher secured enough discretion and flexibility for trips to London and abroad, mostly to the Netherlands: The Hague, Amsterdam and, blissfully, Delft. I became more familiar with Gerrit Dou, Hendrik Goltzius, Otto Marseus van Schrieck and, of course, Rembrandt. Perhaps too familiar, or indeed too passionate. The danger with sleeping agents, I suppose, is that they can become so genuinely committed to their cover activity or profession that their political allegiance nearly fades away. So it happened for me, I admit. Whereas my work on seventeenth-century Dutch paintings filled me with true intellectual satisfaction, my service to the USSR and Eastern Germany remained perfunctory. Heinrich liked it that way, however, since it made me less detectable. During the first few years, nobody in the wider public knew about me. Heinrich had made sure that my radiographic equipment followed me to Cambridge. Visiting engineers sent by Professor Churakov updated it regularly.

My radiographic expertise led to my being called upon more frequently to authenticate paintings of classical schools and styles. Since I was to embody ultra-conservative critique, part of my brief was to always reject requests about modern works of art. I ostensibly turned down an invitation to present to the British public *Gutai*, a post-war group of modern Japanese artists formed in 1954, self-defined as avant-garde. I would go as far as Impressionist depictions, stretching my interests to a respectable post-Impressionist like Lucien de Maleville—and that was the end of it. Passive allies were enrolled, such as Director Philip Hendy of the National Gallery, whom my radiography of *The Laocoon* had saved from the colossal blunder of losing a genuine Michelangelo. Professor Anthony Blunt and other art experts discreetly worked on bolstering my credibility on the academic stage.

~~~~~~~~~~~~~~~~~~~~~~~~~

When Heinrich reckoned that my standing as a member of the scholarly establishment was firm enough, he set up my first skirmish. My alleged antagonist was Jim Ede, a respected expert in modern art, and a curator of the Tate Gallery in London before World War II. After some time in Morocco, Professor Ede lived in France with his wife. But rumour had it that he was tipped to launch a new department of modern art at the Fitzwilliam Museum in Cambridge. Naïve or childish works by so-called artists such as David Jones, Jean Dubuffet, Ben and Winifred Nicholson, Alfred Wallis and even modernist sculptures by the Romanian exile Brancusi were to be exhibited within our very walls. I was asked to write in several journals and magazines against this project, contrasting true classical talent with the tedious improvisations of these alleged modern geniuses. I must admit that I quite liked some of their works, such as Brancusi's *Sleeping Muse*, which I found intriguing and refreshing. Regardless, my persona as an ultra-conservative art expert forbade any tolerance. Heinrich indicated two arguments I should use: Hiroshima, and Communism.

My status as a survivor of the Hiroshima bombing was put forward first, commanding immediate respect and interest. Emotions, not logics, were at work there against abstract art. I quote from my article in *ArtReview*:

"On 6 August 1945 in Japan, less than a decade ago, my people and I suffered the atrocious loss of the beautiful shapes contemplated in nature or designed by civilisation. Within seconds, trees and animals, houses, bridges and the very statues of our great men disintegrated. How can I not side with the world tradition of artists who imitated nature and enhanced the human figure, endowing with the permanence of marble the gracious flutter of a dove's wing, or securing eternal remembrance for the tender features of loved ones, physically dead and yet forever present to the living through carved or painted depictions of their cherished countenances? These artists keep alive before our souls the fragile shapes of our joys and sorrows. Our tears never dry, thankfully, through their talent as figurative artists. With due respect for the ingenuity of abstract sculptors and painters, I fail to enjoy their invented colours and patterns. Why?

"Because they are the luxury of spoiled children. Their homes and towns never disintegrated before their eyes. These artists are safe and comfortable in serviceable reality. Their chairs and their fridges, their gardens and their sweethearts never went up in smoke. They pose as inventors of a new perception, oblivious of the simple beauty of material things, natural or cultural. They are ungrateful. They take for granted the miracle of what is given and yet, could have been taken away. They know well how to name and to handle saucepans and apples, wine bottles and blankets, horses and cars for daily convenience—but their art obliterates those real-life companions, setting up fantasy instead, hypocritically. Allow me then to side with our scores of painters and sculptors who look at what exists, learn from it and share with us the emotion of contemplating humble reality. Wars and weathering damage the shapes and lines of the world we live in. Remedially, art should give this world permanence and even, perhaps eternity. I don't need abstract art. I have seen it all. In seconds at Hiroshima, my world turned abstract. Please, dear abstract artists, don't take me back there."

Among various reactions to my article, Heinrich alerted me to a response in the October 1955 issue of *NADIR*, the *Neo Analphabetic Dada International Review*. I immediately went to read it at the Cambridge University Library where all major periodicals could be consulted. The argument read as follows:

"Professor Kokura's Mortuary Museum.

"Professor Ken Kokura forbids modern art at the Fitzwilliam Museum. It transpires, though, that the Japanese expert has a vested interest in promoting figurative paintings against abstract ones. He built his reputation on radiographic analyses. But those would yield little or nothing at all if applied to abstract paintings. Most abstract painters indeed would shun adding a later composition over an earlier one. No need to peek below the surface of abstract works, since their inspiration forbids concealment. Their revolutionary spirit despises *pentimento*. Breaking free from conventional forms and shapes, each of their strokes hits home. They need no amending, for they are spontaneous. They hide no secret, for they lay bare the truth. They claim no lineage, for they are the beginning.

"On the contrary, painters from the past corrected their compositions to better fit conventional shapes. Subservient to the tyranny of forms, they slavishly abided by a limited visual vocabulary imposed by their bourgeois patrons. But abstract painters defy all oppressors and throw off the shackles of inherited grammar, codes and dogmas. Their paintings have the freshness and immediacy of hot blood splashed upon a white wall: no one would waste time analysing the whitewash that has nothing to tell, whereas all eyes understand the constellation of red stains spread freely on top.

"Thus, abstract paintings leave nothing to radiographers, just as living things flout autopsy. Poor Professor Kokura will soon lose his job, his clients and his relevance as abstract art eventually outshines his archaic paintings. No wonder he worries. We feel sorry for him, and we invite him to escape from the dusty morgue he calls an art gallery. Hey Ken, drop your x-ray machine and let your figurative paintings rest in peace, the poor corpses. Breathe deep and join us out here, there's life in the open air!"

I was quite upset but Heinrich was delighted. "That is just what we needed, Ken," he laughed over the phone. "You will crush their objection: it will be a triumph."

"But how on earth can I respond?" I sighed. "*NADIR* has a point, and I know very little about contemporary art."

"Nonsense! Modern artists do paint over older depictions; even if merely for want of money to buy blank canvases. I will put you in touch with Ron Hovis. He benefitted from the same technical formation as you, but we directed him towards modern art. A Picasso expert, he discovered an amazing landscape hidden under the *Crouching Beggar* (*La Miséreuse Accroupie*). The news was kept secret though, as we were waiting for the right moment. It could be made use of now. We will have you x-ray the *Crouching Beggar* and you will bring to light that landscape. It reminds one, Ron Hovis said, of the Laberint d'Horta, Barcelona's famous botanical garden. We will make a lot of noise about it. And Hovis won't claim the discovery by the way, any more than you claimed that of the brazen serpent in Michelangelo's *Entombment*. So, you can be at peace. Tackling Picasso will broaden your reputation as an open-minded conservative, and will ridicule *NADIR's* claims."

And so it happened, about a year later. With little enthusiasm, I had to fly to Canada. In a private collection in Montreal, I was given all the time I needed to examine the *Crouching Beggar*. Later in Paris I even met Pablo Picasso, whom Dora Maar had persuaded to join the Communist Party at the end of World War II. I wondered whether she might also have inspired him, years later, to enquire with the Dominican Fr Severino Alvarez about coming back to the Catholic Church in 1963, as she had done.

The project of a modern art department at the Fitzwilliam Museum was dropped, but the following year, in 1956, Jim Ede left the Loire Valley in France for Cambridge and started an informal gallery of modern art in a refurbished house at Kettle's Yard. As it happened, we became friends. Heinrich did not object, since the skirmish had achieved its purpose, namely, to make my voice heard (and listened to) on the stage of art critique.

Heinrich's second line of attack was cunning. In an article published in *Apollo* he had me, officially a refugee from Communist Germany, endorse the argument of the Communist Party in Romania who debased as "decadent" the work of Constantin Brancusi, their most famous artist. That I, little suspected of Communist sympathies, would support Soviet criticism in that particular instance, made my opposition to abstract art paradoxically less disputable. My impartiality was praised and, most ironically, I was even approached to become a Communist agent during a reception at Baroness Moura Budberg's in London. I was there with Anthony Blunt who had made his peace with Budberg (she had reported him to the British Intelligence as a Soviet agent a couple of years earlier). I declined with disdain the offer to serve Moscow, smiling interiorly at Heinrich's skilful concealing of my Soviet allegiance.

Meanwhile, Heinrich told me not to give up painting. It would do me good, he insisted, to express myself pictorially, instead of merely interpreting the productions of fellow artists. It also would enrich my "palette" as he called it, making me a more versatile agent. I would offer more angles and entries for interaction with other cultural influencers, as an artist in my own right. Anthony Blunt introduced me to Leonard Foujita in Paris, and we soon became friends. Foujita drew a parallel between us both and our two Japanese predecessors in Paris a generation earlier, Kuroda Seiki and Kume Keiichiro. I visited him in Paris nearly every year and took pleasure in learning from him. He even had two of my watercolours sold, but making a career would have required more time than I could afford. As agreed with Heinrich, painting could not become my main occupation.

In 1957, I completed my doctoral thesis on the Fabritius Brothers. That qualification now added to my radiographic expertise positioned me internationally as the leading authority on Carel Fabritius. Private collectors and museums sought me to authenticate their potential purchases, so few were the works of Fabritius known to have survived the Delft explosion. From then on and during the 1960s and 1970s, I travelled at least once a year to America and Canada, and more frequently to Europe, to give lectures and to analyse more paintings. My main motivation was to discover unknown works by Fabritius, especially his lost *Mercury, Argus and Io.*

Alas, imitations by followers of the master regularly disappointed me, when they were not outright fakes. I was not yet fully aware of the psychological drive that compelled me to seek out Fabritius. Count von Lebzeltern's letter read to us in Leningrad had spurred my interest. But only later was the deep reason for my attraction made fully clear to me. At that stage, I only knew that Carel Fabritius was an artist who had died at the age of barely thirty-two, in the same explosion which had razed to the ground most of his beautiful city, Delft, in the Netherlands. An artist like him, like him I had lost everything in a blast: I felt as if in me Fabritius had survived. I did not mean it literally, I think, as if I saw myself as a reincarnation of the Dutch painter—or did I? Finding some of his lost works somehow restored my own integrity, it seemed to me. Unconsciously using Fabritius as a proxy, I was salvaging my identity that had been scattered by the destruction of my own city, people and memory. In a corner of my study at the Fitzwilliam Museum, I had reconstructed the *camera obscura* used by Fabritius. It was a wooden box, large enough for a man to stoop inside it while looking at the small reflection of the outside view projected upon a screen through a lens. One could call this optical box the ancestor of our modern photographic cameras. The painter could then copy the projected depiction onto a piece of paper or on a canvas. It provided a three-dimensional perspective that made the composition more realistic than was previously possible.

Nearly every month, I would go on my own pilgrimage to the London National Gallery, fully reopened since 1957. There, I would spend nearly an hour in front of Fabritius' *View of Delft* and of his *Young Man in a Fur Cap.* The widow of Carel had referred to him as a "painter to His Highness, the Prince of Orange." I hoped to dig up evidence of commissions executed for the Dutch Stadholder Frederik Hendrik.

Surely, there had to be some masterpieces hidden away in some civic buildings or even in private collections, perhaps unbeknownst to their owners. I dreamed of finding the missing match of *Mercury and Aglauros*. While the latter enhanced the collection of the Boston Museum of Fine Arts since 1903, its twin painting also representing Mercury was nowhere to be found. Count von Lebzeltern was right: it was tantalisingly mentioned in the catalogues of various auctions up to the French Revolution, albeit mistakenly attributed to Rembrandt, of whom Fabritius had been the most gifted disciple. In vain, though, had I tried to trace the elusive masterpiece of *Mercury, Argus and Io*—my "Holy Grail."

There is little to say about the twenty years or so that followed. I was happily busy as an art expert, while acting as a liaison agent for Heinrich and the KGB. My role was merely to pass on messages received from active field agents. I was a very safe letterbox, that is, undetectable. I never heard from Sultan again. Something deterred me from trying to find out about him in Indonesia. I feared what he might know more than I cared to learn, perhaps, about what had happened to Ida in Wittenberg. Nor had I met Professor Kravitz again, unsurprisingly. I only knew that he had become the foster parent of his sister's daughter, young Anastasia, and was still active as an art analyst in Germany.

But from Japan, Yamato kept in touch, writing about once a year. Although working full-time as a police officer, his main interest was sword spirituality. He insisted on my duty to perform the exercise of sword unsheathing, faithfully, every morning. I admit that I seldom missed it, as it deepened my inner peace. I met with Yamato in 1962 on my first trip to Japan. I flew there from Paris with Léonard Foujita for the inauguration of an exhibition of his paintings at a major gallery in Tokyo. Foujita also took me to visit the construction site of the new Catholic cathedral. I didn't know then that he had converted to Catholicism three years earlier. Yamato had little time for Foujita or for paintings, but he was very excited by some evidence he had gathered about my alleged past, thanks to his police colleagues. Apparently, I had been a sword master before the bombing. According to him, I was of samurai ancestry. My height and age matched the profile of a missing son in an important family who owned an estate outside Hiroshima. A meeting was arranged, during which the samurai family failed to recognise me, or I them. It reminded me of the very painful episode at the hospital in August 1945, seventeen years earlier, when all of us amnesiacs were made to stand in line while relatives and friends walked by, staring at us in an attempt to identify us: taking one and leaving another as if we had been slaves up for sale. Because Yamato was disappointed, I kept my own suffering to myself. He had a wife and children, a fatherland and a profession; he could not understand my existential helplessness and my emotional vulnerability.

In 1974 Yamato retired from the police force and devoted himself to teaching Buddhist sword spirituality full time. Having invested his savings in buying and decorating a training hall or "dōjō," he deplored that his only son was pursuing a career as a civil servant for the Japanese post office rather than following him in sword practice. At least childlessness spared me that kind of disappointment: a meagre consolation for my loneliness, I thought to myself. I met again with Yamato in 1975 on his unexpected visit to England.

He had been hired by "Telluric Tours," an American travel agency specialising in geo-spirituality. Apologetically, Yamato explained that those Americans were good and enlightened people, unlike the military assassins who had destroyed our country a generation earlier. Peace activist Yoko Ono was rumoured to have granted the venture her patronage. "Telluric Tours" customers were treated as *adepts*, Yamato explained to me, not as tourists. The tours focused on locations with strong magnetic resonance. This first British trip had taken the group to Stonehenge, Glastonbury, Anglesey, Lindisfarne, ending in Scotland at the Ness of Brodgar. Such main sites were often connected to smaller ones by "ley lines," those alignments of landmarks recognised by pre-modern civilisations. As part of the staff, Yamato taught his disciples the art of "becoming sword." The weapon was to become in their hands like the rods held by dowsers for water divining. The sword became an antenna, my friend affirmed, channelling telluric currents towards the swordsman whose enlightenment was consequently accelerated.

Yamato and I met in Cambridge where he kindly visited me at the end of his British tour. That 23 May, we were sitting in a punt, serenely gliding along the River Cam. Willow boughs lush with fresh leaves created living vistas randomly concealing and revealing the back of the University colleges. Relishing the peace, we spoke sparsely. A student was standing at the rear of the boat, dexterously pushing the five-metre pole against the river bed. Our speaking Japanese enhanced the sentiment of intimate seclusion, as surely our young guide could not understand us. One hand immersed in the lukewarm water, Yamato dreamily uttered, much out of the blue, "I am turning sixty today." I smiled, knowing that this impromptu cruise, remote from fuss and noise, was just the sort of celebration he would wish.

He mentioned his stay at St Beuno's, a Christian centre supportive of Buddhism in North Wales, where ancient Japanese artefacts were on display, including two swords in pristine condition and a lacquered screen. My friend was glad to hear that I had been asked to authenticate similar exhibits connected with Catholic missionaries in seventeenth century Japan, kept in the north of England. Yamato confided that, "Some bones and teeth which they call 'martyrs' relics' are loaded with intense energy." So he had perceived during his meditation spent in St Beuno's chapel. I was vaguely expecting him to announce yet another theory to solve my identity before the Hiroshima bombing. Had Franciscan or Dominican missionaries in Japan perhaps claimed me as their lost brother?

That time though, Yamato, suggested no match. Perhaps he had come to admit, as I had, that such elucidation was best left for time or chance to provide, if ever. All in all, I found my old friend impressively composed, inwardly strong and spiritually convincing. I treasure the memory of the early morning when, in the silence of dawn, he and I meditated in my rooms during the ritual half hour. We were sitting on our heels, facing each other with our eyes shut, with a single candle lit on the floor between us. After thirty minutes during which, obviously, neither of us had even thought of checking his watch, we unsheathed simultaneously, our eyes still shut, and cut the wick of the candle twice without the slightest contact of our blades. It must have been 7am since I vaguely recall that it coincided with the Angelus bells of Our Lady of the Assumption Church in Lensfield Road.

I was in Washington for my "birthday," on 10 August 1977. Thirty-two years earlier, I had awakened under a military tent outside Hiroshima. My memory was still patchy. Cultural and professional data had resurfaced, now interwoven with the very conscious reminiscences of my life as an art expert over the past three decades. But no consistent memories had emerged about my family, childhood and youth, or religion if I had one. By then, I had become used to these blank areas on the map of my personal history. I just avoided them, as navigators of old, circumventing unchartered straits and archipelagos, sailed without further concern towards wherever their trade needed them. My "trade" was well established as a radiographer and critic of classical paintings. Although I had specialised in seventeenth century Dutch masters, I soon broadened my field of expertise and was regularly called out even for twentieth century works.

It had been decided several years ago that I would buy a flat in New York, a cosy pied-à-terre for my frequent trips to America, where I had many customers, whether private collectors or large galleries. Heinrich found me a comfortable two-bedroom flat plus study, at the corner of E 70th Street and Madison Avenue. From the balcony, I could see the roof of the Frick Collection. I had not met with Heinrich in the flesh for a dozen years. But I regularly received his directives over the phone, or through his delegates. He was pleased with the way I had blended into the establishment of international art expertise. He had me wield influence purely within the world of art, never of politics. The two areas overlap, though, which explained my presence at this very political peace event in the American capital, presided over by the new US Secretary of the Department of Health, Education, and Welfare, Joseph A. Califano Jr.

The anniversary of the Hiroshima bombing fell on a Saturday that year. The American-Japanese Foundation for Peace had selected The Peacock Room for its annual event, at the Freer Gallery of Art. Whereas the temperature in town was acceptably hot at 26°C, it was cool inside the gallery. I was familiar with the work of James McNeill Whistler, knowing well his *Little White Girl* in the Tate Gallery in London, and even better the *Lady Meux* of the Frick Collection in New York. But I had never visited his Peacock Room, created in the Japanese style for a British magnate in England, just a century earlier. The space felt grand and intimate at the same time. Blue and white porcelain on shelves alternated with panels of painted leather and gilded wood depicting splendid peacocks: some fighting, others standing peacefully. The many "eyes" on the tail feathers of the peacocks evoked fecundity, family and wealth in Japanese culture. In the early twentieth century the Peacock Room had migrated from London to Washington. The American-Japanese Foundation for Peace had seized the opportunity of the centenary of the Room to draw attention to Japanese influence upon Western art.

That morning, I had popped into the National Gallery of Art to contemplate Whistler's *Symphony in White: No. 1*, the first of his *Women in White* trilogy. I felt close to him in many respects. Not merely for the sake of his *Japonisme*, unless his style, courteous but not moralising and refined without affectation, be regarded as a genuine expression of my home country's culture. Now in the Peacock Room, oblivious to the guests swarming around the US Secretary, I looked carefully at Whistler's *Princess from the Land of Porcelain* displayed in the central panel of the room. Something about the contrast between the lady's grey kimono showing under her pink tunic puzzled me. I had seen it before, I realised. Indeed, this chromatic composition was just the reverse of the one in Whistler's *Artist in His Studio*, where a woman wearing rose stands against a grey background. Rose framed by grey, then grey showing through rose. Since both pictures had been painted in 1865, as the exhibition catalogue informed me, their inverse symmetry could not have been a coincidence. I wished to be given a chance to perform a radioscopy of both paintings and find more about such a subtle and moving embrace of rose and grey.

"Are you not Professor Kokura, the atom-bomb survivor who became an art expert?"

A Japanese woman in her fifties was smiling at me. Introducing herself as Mrs Huthwaite, she asked if I recognised her. Seeing my doubtful look, she pointed at a second Japanese woman glancing sideways at us while chatting in another group.

"My friend Tanaka, over there, wondered if it were truly you. But she was embarrassed to ask, so I did. When we briefly met thirty-two years ago my name was Motoko Fujishiro. I am not surprised that you may not remember me, for at the time I was just about to turn twenty."

I felt dizzy, as always was the case when, within the maze of my blocked memory, walls turned into doors. But this time, the reminiscence connected me with my known existence, after my "birth" on 10 August 1945. I looked with emotion, across the room, at the other woman whom I had so briefly known as "Nurse Tanaka." Was it actually her, the one who had first expressed friendship to me, whose gentle questioning had led me out of my labyrinth of amnesia, grasping a first thread in my lost identity?

We walked to her group. She was now Doctor Tanaka, a mental health consultant. I acknowledged that I was the one she thought. Possibly to conceal some slight emotion, she introduced to me a thirty-year-old-looking man, her son, also a physician. She explained that her friend, Mrs Fujishiro Huthwaite, had been working in Japan as a clerk typist for the American Army during the war, and had made most of her career in the same department, namely, the Arts and Monuments division of the Civil Information and Education Section.

"We were under the Supreme Commander for the Allied Powers," Mrs Fujishiro Huthwaite mentioned, "trying to save as many cultural objects and monuments as we could from war damage, loot or mere neglect. Former Nurse Tanaka had indicated to me your knowledge of fine arts. I met with you and her soon after to type a report. Because I took particular interest in the rare Japanese survivors connected with art preservation, when your name and story became known in the sixties, I asked Doctor Tanaka if she remembered you. Although she did recall your insight into Japanese arts—there was something to do with Hokusai's *Great Wave*, was it not?—your present name was unknown to her. The American administration provided a list of plausible matches with the anonymous patient she had examined in August 1945. But my earlier attempts at identifying you had failed, as all three Japanese I had spoken with had survived Hiroshima, not Nagasaki."

I corrected the woman. "I am sorry to disappoint you then, since I also come from Hiroshima, not Nagasaki."

Mrs Fujishiro Huthwaite and Dr Tanaka looked at each other with a hint of embarrassment. They suggested, respectfully, that my memory perhaps failed me on this point, because they had only dealt with Nagasaki survivors, not Hiroshima ones. Admittedly, the camp where I had been sent hosted patients from both bombed cities, but the two women's assignment was undoubtedly with Nagasaki victims. A second mental health team was dealing with Hiroshima amnesiacs. If I was from Hiroshima, then by mistake I must have been ascribed to the wrong group. Obviously, in the utter chaos following the double bombing that occurred within three days, such administrative oversight was to be expected. We exchanged contact details. Dr Tanaka lived in Los Angeles where she invited me to visit her if I ever travelled to the West Coast.

Mrs Fujishiro Huthwaite seemed well connected, and quite determined to make sure I was not left on my own to gaze at the subtle splendours of the Peacock Room. She now ventured, "I believe, Professor Kokura, that you have embraced the Christian religion. You might then be glad to meet with Father Pedro, standing over there, who also survived the Hiroshima bombing."

I was not particularly willing to make new acquaintances, feeling that the unexpected resurfacing of my earliest memories from 1945 called for quiet recollection, rather than further social interaction. However, my heart was touched by the sorry sight of a little priest all by himself, framed by the gilded posts of the main entrance to the Room. He seemed to have no one to talk to. I knew well how one could feel in such fashionable gatherings, if one was not deemed important. I had experienced that social loneliness in my early years in Cambridge. Since then, admittedly, people I had never seen seemed to recognise me and would approach me, rather against my wishes. The small cleric was clutching his empty hands, not even holding a glass of champagne to save face. What a contrast it was with the opposite door, near which a dozen minor guests still swarmed around the US Secretary for Education. Behind the priest, a wide cream-coloured blind hung from a canopy, bearing some emblem like a stylised beaming sun, in the middle of which the word "*shi*"—the Japanese noun for "death"—was displayed.

Dr Tanaka turned her head and gracefully glanced over her shoulder towards the priest, before resuming her conversation with her son and other guests. I followed Mrs Fujishiro Huthwaite, who eagerly introduced me to Father Pedro. His face lit up and he extended his hand with cordiality. I learned that he was posted in Hiroshima during the war as a Catholic missionary. A small hill by his house had screened him and his confreres from the blast and radiations. Because he had trained as a medical doctor before becoming a priest, he had immediately organised an emergency team, bringing first aid assistance to the thousands of victims. "Nowadays," he added with a hint of regret, "I merely sit behind a desk for admin work in Rome. Although I still travel a bit."

Father Pedro seemed aware of my field of expertise. It surprised me that a missionary priest would take much interest in classical art. By some pleasant coincidence, he even knew the religious who had asked for my services in the North of England, one year earlier. The fashionable Catholic boarding school which they ran needed more space. When about to convert an attic into a dormitory, they had come across a dusty Japanese folding screen which, they reckoned, called for proper examination. Although the pictorial style was undoubtedly classical Japanese, the figures depicted across the five articulated panels looked like Christian clerics. "Could it not be," my English clients had ventured, "a genuine seventeenth century 'byōbu' saved from destruction after our earlier colleagues had been expelled from Japan?" I was pleased to confirm their hypothesis, even suggesting that Kanō Naizen or one of his followers had painted the screen circa 1600 A. D.

Father Pedro unsettled me when he added, "I hear you once found a hidden image under a well-known Picasso. Would you ever care to take a look at his *Guernica*? The martyred city depicted on the painting is located in the Basque Country, where I come from. I was asked to help with some further celebration of *Guernica* as a follow-up to the fortieth anniversary of the tragedy last 26th April. Since you survived the bombing of your own city, Hiroshima, you might be interested in analysing such a well-known painting about a similar event, mightn't you?" At that moment, another cleric tiptoed towards us and deferentially whispered in the ear of Father Pedro, discreetly pointing at the opposite door. Over there, I noticed, the US Secretary for Education had set himself free from his ring of attentive satellites and, like a smaller planet entering the orbit of a massively more important star, now seemed to await a sign of encouragement for gliding further towards our little galaxy. With tact, Mrs Fujishiro Huthwaite gently started leading me back to Dr Tanaka. As I was leaving, Father Pedro concluded with a gentle smile his suggestion about *Guernica*, "It would be nice if you could do that for me: one Basque supporting another."

I bowed and left, feeling reassured in my earlier assumption about the superficial artistic knowledge to be expected of a missionary priest. Obviously, Picasso was born on the south coast of Spain, in Malaga, and grew up in Catalonia before making his career in Paris. He was no more "Basque" than I, then.

<hr />

I was back at my flat in New York the following day, when Heinrich rang for my debriefing. He already knew about my encounters at the Peacock Room. Little interested in Doctor Tanaka, he was puzzled by Mrs Fujishiro Huthwaite, and much intrigued by Father Pedro's invitation, which he insisted was to be accepted speedily. Only then did I realise the importance of the contact made.

"Congratulations Ken, you stood very close to the sun!"

In hesitation, I remained silent; but Heinrich effusively expounded, "Your lack of interest is a useful cover feature for a spy. But in case you truly haven't grasped it yet, you were just shown favour by one of the most influential men in the world. Such a circumstance must be made use of, Ken. Fr Pedro Arrupe is the current Superior General of the Society of Jesus, the dreaded 'Jesuits.' Under his leadership, their numbers have swollen by an extra third, totalling thirty-six thousand elite clerics, spread all over the world in every position of influence, whether in education, sciences, finances, arts or politics. As you are well aware, the Jesuits have always been the Pope's special battalion, whom he sends at whim wherever the priority interests of the Catholic Church dictate. They put special emphasis on immediate and unconditional obedience to the Roman Pontiff and they excel in all that they undertake."

I was mortified to have missed such an opportunity as that of my impromptu encounter with the Superior General of the Jesuits. Trying to make up for it, I suggested, "Perhaps, it is not too late for me to ask Father Pedro about the missing Vermeer. I know little about modern Jesuits, but I recall how, in the seventeenth century, Jesuit priests were Vermeer's patrons in Delft. They supported his conversion to Catholicism and commissioned him with his *Allegory of the Faith*. Today's Jesuits might not need long to locate and identify Vermeer's lost *Angelus*, don't you think?"

Heinrich did not sound overly optimistic.

"The lost *Angelus* again... So, you have not given up on it after thirty years? It is worth a try, I admit. A nice consolation it would be to Comrade Churakov in his retirement. But don't expect too much of 1970s Jesuits as regards classical art, Ken. They have plainly distanced themselves from it since the Counter-Reformation. Now they are social workers, not evangelists. Their new 'preferential option for the poor' has even put them at odds with their boss in Rome—so I was told. Up to then, they were obsessed with making everybody Catholic. Now, they merely want to support the proletariat. It is the sort of proselytizing we could condone. Imagine if they worked for us! I wish the Party had even ten thousand agents like these. But thirty-six thousand Jesuits make your Father Pedro more powerful than the Pope himself, and plausibly not very far below either of the new super-leaders, our First Secretary Leonid Brezhnev and US President Jimmy Carter. So, warm up your radiographic device Ken, because your next patient must be Picasso's *Guernica*. I know well that it is not your artistic style, but since the painting is still permanently displayed at New York's MoMa, I need you to visit there shortly and put in writing a few ideas until we hear from our new friend Father Pedro, the 'Black Pope.' And hear of him we will: not without a set purpose does a man like Pedro Arrupe reach out to an expert like you. How auspicious that you both survived the Hiroshima bombing!"

That conversation had revived my hope of finding Vermeer's lost *Angelus* and its likely companion, Fabritius' elusive masterpiece of *Mercury, Argus, and Io.* I looked through my window to the left end of the street, towards the roof of the Frick Collection where I had so many friends: Ruisdael, La Tour, Whistler, Vermeer, Holbein and more—but no Fabritius. I gazed further, as if across time rather than space, towards Leningrad where I had first heard about Fabritius' lost masterpiece.

I had failed to tell Heinrich, I don't know why, that the two former nurses assumed I was a *Nagasaki* survivor, not a Hiroshima one. Should I inform my old friend Yamato in Japan? No doubt this new hypothesis would prompt him to draw yet untapped information from his police network and eventually, after various unsuccessful attempts over the past thirty-two years, tell me who I really was. At my local library, I looked at pictures from pre-war Nagasaki. I did so as an amputated man would check his wooden prosthesis, that is, not in the least expecting to trigger any sensation. Black and white photographs appeared: there lay the harbour surrounded by mountains; the large Mitsubishi weapons factory; the prominent Urakami Catholic Cathedral with its octagonal dome; the historic Dutch trade warehouse, originally an Augustinian Priory; the Chinzei School by the river; the sacred Torii Gate of a Shinto shrine; etc. Many later pictures displayed the same sites and additional ones, all barely recognisable after the bombing. Yes, I felt for the sufferings undergone and for the injustice inflicted. But no particular memory connected those places with my own history. The school though—yes, the Chinzei School and children standing in line, saluting, touched me particularly. If I had been a schoolteacher, could it have been in that other city, rather than in Hiroshima? It did not seem to make a big difference to me. My life was in England, and in America.

But why on earth was Fr Arrupe interested in me if I was not even from Hiroshima? He would have had a dozen other art experts to rely upon for assistance about the *Guernica* painting. Or did he know more about my past than I cared to admit? If so, should I contact the Jesuit superior as Heinrich recommended? Did I really wish to open that door?

CHAPTER 6
Losing Face

ISFIGURED. IN UTTER DISBELIEF, Picerno Dorf kept looking at his face in the mirror held before him by Hana the housekeeper. The left side of his mouth and his left eye simply wouldn't open. However hard he tried, the muscles stubbornly ignored his command. Just as Marco wouldn't follow his order: the rascal, the traitor, the rogue! Who could have imagined that of him? But Marco was not part of his body, admittedly, whereas his eyelid and smile pertained to his integrity. The facial droop could disappear within a few days, his consultant hoped. But it could also affect him for months. In the worst-case scenario it would remain forever—that is, until death. Picerno minded disfigurement more than the loss of his left limbs. His right arm and leg moved as easily as ever, thankfully. The doctor was optimistic: on crutches, in due course, and with perseverance, he might become able to walk across his bedroom without assistance—provided there was no carpet or wire on the floor on which he might trip.

Writing was an issue of course. Why had he been born left-handed! They said the best tennis-players were left-handed: he couldn't give a hoot! Thankfully he could easily type with his right hand—too bad for Chinese calligraphy. Even holding a book was too tiring after a few minutes. Then, there was the business of getting dressed and undressed, not to mention shaving, washing and the rest. Why! Why had it come to that? Such a setback was so unfair, so atrociously frustrating when everything had gently fallen into place. Glancing again at his contorted reflection, he saw the right corner of his mouth attempt a smile reminiscent of the "happy" and "sad" paired masks, symbols of comedy and tragedy: *Sock* and *Buskin*, they were called. He looked like an improbable mix of both.

"Put it away, Hana. I've seen enough of me, sorry clown. Just leave me for now."

The housekeeper failing to understand him quickly enough, the bishop pushed the mirror aside. Speech impediment was the worst, he concluded. For all his exertions, he just couldn't manage to articulate words. He thought he heard himself correctly, but interlocutors obviously didn't. It wasn't a mere question of language: whether in Italian, German, English or Chinese, he sounded like a toddler awkwardly pronouncing his very first syllables. His nurse's explanation about "the facial nerve responsible for movement of the lips and for good muscle tone in the cheeks" had brought no comfort. He didn't need anyone to inform him that his facial nerve was badly damaged when his lips, cheeks and tongue would not work together to express the words he attempted to utter. The chalkboard they'd brought him the day before made things a bit easier, even though he felt even more humiliated to have to write as a schoolboy "more coffee" or "draw curtains" or "need loo." Pommard had also had to resort to written communication after his failed attempts to understand Dorf over the phone. To prevent confidential messages from being intercepted, Picerno had made sure the fax was moved from his office to his bedroom. Who could be trusted around him now, if not even Marco?

Left alone to rest, Picerno went over in his mind again the horrible succession of events which had led to his incapacitation. While in the office of his cardiologist, that fatal afternoon, his mobile phone had rung. On that number, it had to be very important. As he had assumed, it was Mgr Marco Altemps. Pommard had informed him of the agreed upon plan. But against every expectation, Marco objected. Worse, he was actually *begging* Picerno to dissuade Mgr Jacques Pommard from presenting his name as cardinal. Apologising to his consultant, the bishop had interrupted the examination to speak more discreetly in the empty waiting room. The voice of his friend sounded totally overcome by emotion, almost womanly, like Gao Changgong, the *Prince of Lanling*. Stammering for the first time in his life, the otherwise composed Mgr Altemps insisted that becoming nuncio in Japan was already beyond what he could comfortably take on. He was a sick man, and not one carved out for a public role. He'd supported the strategy and rise of Picerno as far as he could, but stepping in for his cardinalate was simply impossible. Bishop Dorf tried to keep calm, despite the growing tension he was feeling all across his tired body. Appealing to Marco's dedication and referring to their long collaboration in Asian Affairs, he tried his best to make his assistant see reason, but in vain.

Authority was his last resort. Sitting down and catching his breath again, his hand pressing the Nokia phone in desperation as if it were Marco's hand, while loading his voice with as much solemnity as his dizziness allowed, His Excellency Bishop Picerno Dorf ordered that Mgr Altemps had to comply in the name of obedience. There was silence over the phone, both men realising that their long friendship was being put to some unprecedented test. Such opposition had never occurred between them. There had been differences of perspective, occasional annoyances and impatience (felt by Picerno at least), but never an outright confrontation; never such a make-or-break challenge. Bishop Dorf feared that his interlocutor might collapse there and then, wherever he was calling from. If only they were speaking face to face, he would convince him.

Mgr Altemps eventually answered. Stating that he was left with no other choice, he broke the most horrifying news into the anxious ear of the *in petto* cardinal. He was set on entering a monastery! Only for the sake of Picerno had he delayed his postulancy over the past two years. But he was formally accepted at a small traditional Benedictine community in Northern Italy where he'd stayed twice of late. His cancer had made his yearning for the cloister even stronger and offering the traditional Mass again had done him good, he felt. He wished to die in peace, clothed in the black cowl, as the bell of Compline would soothingly ring over the Italian hills. If everything had gone according to plan for Picerno, he would have postponed his change of career as a last token of fidelity, and remained longer in Tokyo for six months, giving then-Cardinal Dorf enough time to have his position filled. The gravity of his illness would have won Marco easy release from the Nunciature. However, the totally unexpected occurrence of the *Showcasing Dissent* affair over the past two days had overwhelmed him. He simply could not go on. In a voice altogether shaky and assertive, Mgr Altemps announced his flat refusal. He would *not* become Cardinal Altemps.

Picerno had enough time to see himself fall for the second time that day. Providentially, the consultant soon found the prelate lying on the carpet. Emergency treatment was administered by hospital staff and after two days, the patient was stable enough for his discharge to be granted under the condition that a nurse would check on him every few hours at the Nunciature.

Had consolation come to Bishop Dorf at last, after such undeserved vexations almost sent him to his grave? Lying in his bed, his back propped up with three pillows, the hemi-plegic prelate read a note left him by Mgr Altemps:

"4 April 1991

"Beloved Friend,

"What to say but thank God for saving your precious life. I am flying to Rome this very morning as Mgr Pommard requested. He wishes to meet in the flesh and explain why I should accept being promoted to cardinal. I still find in me no strength to accept this honour, and even less merit. I know that I am unworthy. But worse is the thought of having nearly caused your death. Pray that I might do God's will, even though my own life might be the price to pay.

"Yours ever, Marco, or Brother
Enrico as Benedictine oblate

"P. S. I have instructed the staff to keep me informed of any variation in your health. The Second Counsellor Fr Domingo is in charge, awaiting the return of the Pro-Nuncio at the end of the week: Bishop William Carew wished to fly back immediately to see you, but he is detained in Rome in preparation for his transfer to Bonn and Berlin."

Bishop Dorf had felt his anger subdue slightly on discovering the better dispositions of his lieutenant. Still, there was no guarantee that Marco would accept the position. Bother, bother, and bother again! Which priest would not have danced with joy if offered the red hat on a tray! That was the problem with honest clerics: they dreaded promotion as if it imperilled their precious humility. *False* humility it often was, more subtly proud than a good plain ambition.

"Yes, I will try to rest, thank you."

Picerno doubted whether the nurse had understood his attempted reply. Leaving after yet another check on his health, she'd said very little but didn't seem alarmed. The doctor would pop in before supper. Still lying on his bed, the bishop put down on his lap the other letter he had now finished reading. It was banal correspondence from the *Observatory of Non-Proliferation of Nuclear Weapons*. Nothing of interest. Granted, the day before, another crisis had occurred at the UN about Iraq disarmament: Saddam Hussein was to surrender or destroy all his chemical and biological weapons. But that was out of his remit, since his watch was nuclear weapons. He'd checked his mail that afternoon, hoping for some news or at least for some distraction. But no: everybody seemed to be on Easter vacation. Still, he'd received cards of sympathy; assurance of prayers, etc. He glanced at a large envelope, already opened. Ah, yes, the Kokura biography. With all that had just happened, he'd forgotten about it.

Ken Kokura... That was all his fault. Why had that Japanese artist incriminated him? They'd barely met once. Or was he innocent—were they both victims of some other schemers? He had to be sure and there was no more relevant piece of information than this secret biography of Kokura's. Who knew, it could yield information never communicated to the film director of *Supero*? What if the solution to all his troubles lay within that text? By now though, his single good arm was too weak to hold the thick document. Could he not ask Fr Domingo to read it for him? Possibly, but what if any embarrassing revelation surfaced? Better not draw the attention of his young colleague to this matter. Indeed, the document was classified, having been extracted from the Secret Archive, for which a mere Second Counsellor had no clearance. Too bad, he would have to wait for Marco's return. When? When would that lowly rascal be back? He would arrive soon in Rome and would surely not meet with Pommard until the following day. Waiting, waiting, always waiting. But why not ask someone who could make no use of the confidential information? Yes, obviously! Such a brainwave led Picerno to impatiently press the "Kitchen" button on the phone by his bed, calling for emergency assistance.

The summoned domestic entered the prelate's bedroom in deferential haste, only to hear his need for immediate reading. "May His Excellency forgive Hana for her poor organisation. Hana is presently cooking the dinner and will not be able to read the book for His Excellency. But Uncle Byobu, the gardener, will readily oblige."

"Uncle Byobu" may have been a good gardener, but his spoken English was less than fluent and his reading, alas, was even poorer. Dismissed at last, the failed declaimer stepped backward with a triple bow, apologising for his incompetence and assuring that he would secure further assistance without delay. Bishop Dorf had nearly given up when "Mr Han," the chauffeur of the Nunciature, knocked at the door. He picked up the Kokura bundle fallen from the bed and, still standing in the middle of the room, started reading.

"Just sit down, man! I'm not the Dalai Lama, and you are not in the prime of life any more than I, judging from your grey beard!" Suspecting that his speech was still difficult to interpret, the bishop gestured to the elderly chauffeur that he should sit on the chair by his bed. Mr Han read English almost fluently, with as little emotion expressed, though, as if he had not understood the meaning of the words. After all, Dorf realised, the less the reader grasped, the safer. For want of a better option, he decided to give the chauffeur a chance.

~~~~~~~~~~~~~~~~~~~~~~~~

About forty-five minutes later, Picerno's improvised reader lowered the printed sheets onto his lap and paused for the third time. Was His Excellency the Bishop asleep, Mr Han wondered? It was difficult to tell whether or not the hemiplegic prelate was listening to the narration. Scratching his thin grey beard, the old Japanese didn't dare ask whether he should read any further. He had been waiting in silence for about ten minutes when he was relieved to hear a discreet knock at the door, soon opened by Hana, the housekeeper. After a deep bow to the motionless prelate, turning towards Mr Han, she brought her joined thumb and forefinger towards her open mouth, a rather unceremonial gesture suggesting that it was time for the staff meal. The hospital nurse would tell them in due course when and what His Excellency should eat. Mr Han complied, leaving the bundle of Ken Kokura's Confessions on the chair by the bed.

Picerno Dorf emerged from his slumber some time later. He had not enjoyed Mr Han's reading much. Admittedly, there was something facetious in having this confidential account read aloud by a lay employee, an interim chauffeur of the Tokyo Nunciature, thankfully unable to understand what was at stake. But the contents were disappointing. From what Picerno had heard so far, the memoirs had yielded no hint about the dreaded master spy "Showcasing Dissent." Had Ken Kokura met the Chinese fiend only later in life? Should then Picerno skip several pages or chapters to find out more quickly and eventually provide Mgr Jacques Pommard with the proofs of his innocence? Then, there might not even be a need for Mgr Marco Altemps to step in for him as cardinal. However, no clue had surfaced yet in these Confessions. What time was it? 6:23pm—Marco Altemps would not land in Rome until 10pm, Tokyo time, that is, 3pm Rome time. He might be able to meet with Pommard that same afternoon, but it would be the middle of the night here. Would Marco comply with his superiors' wishes? Should Picerno fax Pommard, asking to be informed of Marco's answer immediately, regardless of the time? Ah, if only Marco did as he was told and accepted the red hat!

Marco... Memories came back to Bishop Dorf. Their first encounter at the Asian Studies University Department in Vienna, in 1946. Picerno was back in Austria to complete his degree in Chinese after the end of WWII. He had just spent two years as a lay catechist in an Irish-run mission near Nancheng, Jiangxi Province, some six hours west from Shanghai. In Vienna one day, at the canteen, he glanced at the Japanese book opened before a boyish fresher. How incredibly shy Marco Altemps was as a student! On hearing the surname Altemps, Picerno mentioned the eponymous street and townhouse in his home city of Bolzano. Then came the striking realisation that they had grown up in the very same place in South Tyrol, although they had never met due to the difference in age (and in social backgrounds, admittedly). Marco's family still owned the historic *Altempshaus* on Via della Mostra or Mustergasse, the aristocratic street in the city centre. Marco's uncle, a fine art auctioneer, used the front room on the ground floor. By contrast, Picerno's mother had followed her parents, poor labourers relocating from Southern Italy in 1922. The Fascist Government was then eager to attract Italian-speakers in South Tyrol to counterbalance the German-speaking cultural majority. The young woman had married Klaus Dorf, a local schoolteacher and, in June 1923, their firstborn son had been named Giambattista Heinrich Picerno. His third name was that of the South Italian village where his mother had come from, a fact he was careful not to

mention, for personal reasons. Marco Altemps had left Bolzano after only a few years to live in Innsbruck and Vienna
where he had relatives. He was only 17 when Picerno first met
him. Already fluent in French and English (in addition to
Italian and German, his native tongues), the young man was
admitted into a Japanese Licentiate programme. He had a very
gentle, almost childish appearance and Picerno, his elder by six
years, had protectively taken the polyglot fledgling under his
wing. The lad suffered from asthma. Over their three years in
Vienna, Picerno's friendly nursing couldn't prevent his protégé
from being spirited away by his aristocratic family into some
posh sanatorium, sometimes for months in a row. On those
occasions Picerno found it hard not to be allowed to visit his
young friend even briefly. Marco's illness had not prevented
him from graduating with flying colours. The two friends had
met in Bolzano on summer and winter holidays. Marco had
proved a much better skier than Picerno had expected. They
had passionate discussions about the evangelisation of Asia.
Both hoped to bring the Good News to China and Japan
as missionaries. Picerno joined the Irish Columban Fathers
and Marco the Pontifical Institute for Foreign Missions. In
retrospect however, Picerno wondered at how little they had
shared about their priestly calling. They lost touch for some
years while in China and Japan, and bumped into each other
again in 1954 when a career shift brought them back to Rome
at the "Academia" to train for the diplomatic service.

The nurse interrupted Bishop Dorf's reminiscences. She
checked his pulse and reflexes, administered further medicine and called for supper. The prelate was feeling tired and
bringing the spoon to his half-paralysed mouth took him a
long time. He didn't protest when Hana the housekeeper
offered to feed him, holding the spoon to his lips. It was a
bit humiliating, but physical surrender afforded him more
energy to think. He was in two minds about reading Kokura's
memoirs any further that day. On the one hand, he wished
to stay awake until very late, in case Pommard rang him. On

the other hand, he realised that something in the behaviour of the Japanese artist displeased him. He could not put his finger on it, though. What was it? Probably his naïveté. Could he not see from the start that this German man—Heidrich; no, Heinrich—was co-opting him into the Communist party? Heinrich was obviously a Soviet recruiter, grooming potential Asian agents. Why would Kokura seem to ignore the scheme? He was literate and apparently astute. Did he not mind being manipulated, or was he so passionate an art historian that he would accept working for the Communists if it gave him better opportunities? Unless his candour was a mask concealing dubious dealings. After all, one only had his word for the veracity of his so-called Memoirs.

As Hana cleaned his chin with the napkin, Bishop Dorf managed to explain that he wished her to read the Memoirs to him. She complied hesitantly. Her reading was not as fluent as the chauffeur's, but she put more of an interpretation into it. At times though, her efforts sounded a bit annoying. Picerno would make a sign with his finger to ask her to skip what he felt was unnecessary information. Hana was determined to provide His Excellency with the highest standards of diction and intonation, never mind that it was in a foreign language. Smoothing her dress on her knees, sitting upright on the chair by the bed, she began reading the Kokura Memoirs.

Bishop Dorf was no less determined to find out and soon to produce the proof of his innocence. It had to be somewhere, hidden in the life of this dead Japanese artist, or spy, or whatever he was! Meanwhile, Pommard would see, Bishop Ignatius Kung would see, China would see that he, Picerno Dorf, was not dead yet. Disabled, he would rise again. Stunned, he would hit back. Betrayed, he would vanquish. The Church needed it. The world awaited it. To work now, to work!

PART TWO
The Figment

CHAPTER 7
Treasured Beauty

OMETHING UNEXPECTED HAP-
pened in Chicago that month. I had stayed there
many times, invited by famous art dealers for their
wealthy customers in the pharmaceutical industry. An event
that involved the presentation of my radiographic findings
in Vermeer's *Woman with a Pearl Necklace* was scheduled on
Tuesday 18 October 1977, which I was requested to attend.
At significant expense, the famous painting had been leased
for three months by its German owner, the Gemäldegalerie
in Berlin, to "Jeenaco," then only the third largest pharmaceutical company in America, specialising in women's health.
Vermeer's masterpiece was to be the emblem or mascot of
the advertising campaign for the "Uweena" oil and balm,
a revolutionary cosmetic brand designed by Jeenaco. Four
months earlier in Berlin, the Gemäldegalerie had commissioned me to examine that painting. I had discovered under
the surface a lute that used to sit on the chair now empty and
a map that used to hang on the wall now bare. I don't know
how Jeenaco had heard of my findings; perhaps through
Nestlé, another corporate client of mine three years previously. Jeenaco persuaded the Gemäldegalerie to sell them
exclusive use of my discovery for the duration of the lease.
I consented to a contract with Jeenaco to the same purpose.
Never had I been paid so much money for my expertise.
Working for sheer profit made me a bit uncomfortable. But
Heinrich had been very keen on my mercantile involvement
as it made me even less suspicious as a Soviet agent. "And
since you love this Vermeer girl," he had persuasively added
over the phone, "why would you not reveal her beauty to
the broader public? Why confine your findings to a scientific

elite when they can touch millions through this massive advertising campaign?"

Money aside, I had been very glad to work on an authentic Vermeer again. It had been my eleventh involvement in paintings by the master of Delft—or by the *other* Delft master, should I say, since Carel Fabritius was a Delft genius no less, with whom I was even more intimately acquainted. I had not totally given up hope of coming across the lost pair of masterpieces once in the possession of Count von Lebzeltern, according to his letter read to our team at Laval House in Leningrad, many years earlier. Alas Fabritius' *Mercury, Argus and Io*, no less than Vermeer's *Annunciation*, had escaped my searches in countless galleries, archives and private mansions. However, a rather troubling find in this *Woman with a Pearl Necklace* had occurred that very morning. It suggested that, unexpectedly, that latest painting might lend itself to a Christian interpretation, beyond—or beneath—the mere domestic scene. It was just thirty years, I realised, since my early success in Moscow with the *Girl Reading a Letter by an Open Window*, which had since been returned to the Gemäldegalerie in Dresden. Things had changed enormously since 1947. I was now a leading expert in seventeenth-century paintings, while my analytic tools had been improved beyond recognition through ongoing technical upgrades by my original Soviet department, discreet as ever. I smiled when recalling my early radiographies, in contrast with the laser surgery and chemical chromatic alterations which had become my usual instruments. For instance, the basket of clothes concealed by Vermeer behind the leg of his *Milkmaid*, another painting of his, had escaped my earlier investigations. But in 1974 my improved radiographies had turned the still hidden basket into a celebrated *pentimento*—at least among art experts. As a result, I had been commissioned by Nestlé, the world's largest food and beverage company, to make further checks on that painting. Their newly acquired brand Chambourcy had selected Vermeer's *Milkmaid* for a television advert and poster campaign to launch their purposely old-fashioned whole milk yoghurt in a glass jar. Vermeer's woman pouring milk conjured warmth and tradition. But they sought my reassurance that no hidden data might confuse the message if it ever came to light. It had been my first experience working for a multinational company.

That morning in Chicago, then, I had come to the Jeenaco Tower to inspect the painting arrived from Germany the day before. Nicknamed "The Needle" because of its slim silvery body and swollen head pierced with a large single eye, the tower was a sleek tubular building in the latest style of the Second Chicago School, located on West Randolph Street in The Loop. The Jeenaco board wished me to perform a routine certification of the work for which they had paid good money. Vermeer's picture was securely stored in one of the labs of the Tower where my radiographic equipment had been set up as well. It had been upgraded by my undercover Soviet engineer on arrival in America the month before. Setting to work, I easily located under the surface the lute that used to sit on the chair and the map that used to hang on the wall. These latest radiographies were of better quality. The chromatic contrasts were more refined and the contours sharper. The authentication was conclusive: unquestionably, this picture was my *Woman with a Pearl Necklace*. The improved equipment inspired me to inspect again other areas of the painting, out of curiosity. I recalled a pale underlying zone, detected in Berlin, on the figure of the young woman. To my stupefaction, this time the *pentimento* showed neatly delineated, while on my screen appeared a three-dimensional shape which anyone would immediately recognise. It changed my understanding of the painting quite sensationally. I made a mental note to write an article about it as soon as I would have the time. Meanwhile, I took high resolution pictures of the discovery, which I managed to give to the advertising team before our afternoon meeting. Despite the very short notice, they would do their best, they said, to include this additional data in the description. That would certainly interest Jeenaco deeply.

About thirty top executives and major shareholders attended this formal presentation of the Uweena campaign at the Jeenaco Tower. The conference was the finishing touch to the advertising campaign scheduled to begin a fortnight later with a grand gala launch at Chicago's Auditorium Theatre where two thousand guests were expected. Our meeting was led by Mike Drevan, a senior creative executive at the giant advertising agency BWT (Bruce W. Thompson), which Jeenaco had commissioned to launch their Uweena oil and balm. My account of that momentous event is based on the copious entry in my diary that evening and on Drevan's brochure distributed to the participants.

A medium-sized bearded man in his fifties wearing a tie with purposely clashing colours (as it seemed to me), Drevan stepped onto the platform with an engaging smile.

"Good afternoon everyone. On behalf of BWT Agency, it is my privilege to update you on the advertising strategy for Uweena Oil & Balm, Jeenaco's latest 'baby.' First, a reminder on the subliminal connotations of the name *Uweena* chosen for the new product. While auspiciously sounding like *You win a*, the name *Uweena* combines the Latin radical *juven*, for *youth*, and *veena*, the Indian noun for *lute*, about which more soon. You asked BWT to pitch the campaign high. Uweena is expensive, you told us. Uweena must be positioned as a luxury brand. But this must be done caringly, not haughtily, you insisted. You want Uweena to be launched as upmarket, but you want it to appeal to every woman, even less affluent ones. As per your brief, we have designed a two-tier campaign. First, Uweena *Oil* targets low-income and assumedly less educated women. Uweena Oil is affordable, if not cheap. The Uweena Oil advert is a variation on a recent Hollywood blockbuster. Second, Uweena *Balm* aims at wealthy women, plausibly more cultured. Uweena Balm is expensive. The Uweena Balm advert focuses on a classical painting.

"We expect the following to happen: by Christmas, ninety-two percent of American women from age 14 up will take notice of the newly launched Uweena brand. Seventy-six percent of those will purchase Uweena Oil. Sixteen percent of them will also buy Uweena Balm. Both Uweena cosmetics, Oil and Balm, are connected. So are the two adverts. As you will find shortly, both adverts are articulated around *threat* and *protection*. Every woman will want to be saved from the threat, but only those who purchased Uweena will be protected. First, Uweena Oil. To attract a very wide audience, we have secured permission from a famous director to adapt his iconic film. The Uweena Oil advert is about 'the threat.' Second, Uweena Balm. To make Uweena desirable, hence purposely little accessible, we displayed the message in a highly cultured showcase. That second part is 'the protection.' As you will see in a moment, 'the threat' is everywhere, upon every woman. But 'the protection' is available only to women educated enough to be moved by a classical painting.

"That is where Vermeer comes in. Now, gentlemen, imagine you are an average customer, man or woman. I will display before you the articulations of the campaign. Then we will watch the two proposed adverts for Uweena Oil and Uweena Balm. After that, I expect that you will have questions to ask me. Finally, I hope that we will agree on the planned campaign, so that we may finalise the advertising film and poster in the next couple of weeks, in time for the formal launch of Uweena."

~~~~~~~~~~~~~~~~~~~~~~~~

A sense of anticipation was palpable across the vast conference room. Everyone was eagerly silent. Mike Drevan paused for a little while, joined his hands almost as if in prayer, glanced upward and began.

"Our very special Uweena guest has arrived yesterday from Germany, although she is Dutch. Here in Chicago, everyone dies to see her, but you, you the happy few, will meet with her presently in this very room. She has come to help us promote Uweena, the revolutionary skincare resource for women. She has come to help us draw women's attention to our ground-breaking dermatological technology. Jeenaco chose her as our ambassadress to womankind because, despite being three hundred and thirteen years of age, that lady has the skin of an eighteen-year old maiden."

Drevan snapped his fingers and a red curtain slowly began to rise, behind which Vermeer's painting was displayed standing alone on the stage.

"Gentlemen, I introduce to you Uweena's ambassadress, the *Woman with a Pearl Necklace.*"

Awe spread across the room as all eyes converged towards the painting in the spotlight. Because it was too small to be admired from a distance, being only about 21 inches by 17, a large picture of it was projected on a wide screen behind.

Drevan went on.

"Admire how our delightful Dutch beauty has retained the freshness of her youth, with the creamy skin of her brow, cheeks and arms still unscathed by age after over three centuries. This privilege, her secret, is what Uweena now offers to every modern woman. What good news to all women then: thanks to Uweena, aging is now efficiently tackled. I don't say that aging is *overcome*, please note, because we are realistic. We don't believe in magic or superstition, but in technology. Science, pharmaceutical science, has secured victory against the enemy of womankind. And what is that enemy, I ask you? What is that relentless fiend lurking at the corner of the bathroom mirror, or detected in the contemptuous smile of a rival, or spotted on one's latest identity picture? What is that enemy? Where is it?"

The light was dimmed across the entire room, and the Vermeer painting became invisible. A talented presenter, Drevan paused for a moment alone in the spotlight. His face assumed an anxious expression while in the loudspeakers some ominous music started playing, faintly at first, then louder. The audience remained awkwardly silent as he looked around the vast conference room, slowly, now towards a curtain, then by the double door, and again under the vast table. Participants felt slightly uncomfortable, as if each one of them could be suspected of concealing that mysterious "threat to womankind." Resuming his confident smile, the advertiser went on.

"And yet gentlemen, very real is the enemy of womankind, most real indeed! Nobody dares utter the dreaded name of the ladies' doom. Very well: if you are new to Earth, or if you have never met a woman, let me enlighten you. *Wrinkling* is the enemy! *Wrinkles* are our foes. The dreaded furrows which time, worries and sorrows plough across the once smooth brows and cheeks of our beloved girlfriends, wives, daughters and nieces: such are our enemies. The war has been raging, and powerful weapons have been devised to win the battle on behalf of womankind: antioxidants, moisturizers, retinoids, glycolic acid peels and deeper peels, alpha-hydroxy acids and dermabrasion. Some successes have been achieved, yes. But victory? No alas; no victory yet. Let me illustrate this for you."

The ominous music now played louder while, on the large screen behind Drevan, a young woman appeared, swimming at the surface of a turquoise lagoon. The film was shot from below, under water, as if displaying the very angle of vision of the large shark whose powerful shape was seen at the bottom, fatally rushing towards the slender silhouette above. Simultaneously above water, a speed boat was also seen approaching, piloted by an athletic young man whose T-shirt displayed the Uweena Oil logo.

The projection was paused while, pointing at the screen, the advertiser commented, "Like myself and the whole world you've watched Steven Spielberg's *Jaws* the year before last, haven't you? What a masterpiece, that film! And now they're shooting a sequel. Well, people, before Uweena was invented, our darling women were left as if floating in the smooth waters of a lagoon protected by a coral reef through which, when least expected, sharks horribly found a way in! Like dorsal fins slitting the smooth surface of the sea, *wrinkles* slashed across the skin of middle-aged women, mercilessly. You liked *A Streetcar Named Desire*; our women dread 'A Shark Named *Wrinkle*.' For all their efforts, despite every protection, sooner or later *wrinkles* appeared! *Wrinkles* appeared and within seconds, and forever, youth was no more. *Wrinkles* appeared and bloom lay dead. I ask you then: Who would grant our sweethearts genuine and lasting skin protection? Who will preserve epidermic elasticity, volume and even restore facial contours? Who will win for them dermatological liberation?"

The audience was not sure whether to smile or not because, on the one hand the speech was light-hearted, but on the other hand millions of dollars were at stake. Unconcerned, Mike Drevan went on.

"Many centuries ago, the Roman general Julius Caesar was once asked how he'd managed to conquer so swiftly his enemy the King of Pontus. He answered in three words: '*Veni, vidi, vici*. I came, I saw, I conquered.' We, BWT, had his Latin motto printed on the packets of Marlboro cigarettes! But today, honoured representatives of Jeenaco, better than Marlboro you can say like Caesar: 'We came; we saw; we conquered.' That is, 'We tested; we invested; we produced.' More than Caesar in fact, since his victory benefitted only the Roman Empire, long defunct; whereas your achievement will change the face of womanhood for a long time, if not forever. With the Uweena skin-rejuvenation technology, you have pulled down the wall of exclusion between pharmacology and cosmetics. Up to now, many women felt guiltily vain when buying cosmetics, as if beauty was a luxury. On the contrary, Uweena demonstrates that beauty is a core part of healthcare. Modern women look after their health, as is their duty. Modern women need Uweena, to retain their beauty."

The participants started clapping, visibly taken by the rhetoric of the presenter. But Drevan soon put his index finger to his lips, hushing them. Cupping his palm near his ear, he pretended to listen to some sound yet inaudible to the audience. Renaissance music was now playing, lute music, while the *Woman with a Pearl Necklace* appeared again on the large screen.

Drevan announced, "Some will say that skincare is too important to be left to women, like war to the generals! But we say, 'Let a woman tell us now what Uweena has done for her.' Let our celebrated guest, Vermeer's beautiful Dutch maiden, show us Uweena's pledge to womankind. What you are about to hear is based on the scientific examinations of the painting by renowned expert Professor Ken Kokura, present in this room with us today. Our young beauty stands at her table, facing her mirror. She is tying around her slender neck expensive pearls probably given by her fiancé. Vermeer first painted a musical instrument, a lute, on that chair to the right; and a large map on the wall at the back to the left. They lay hidden for centuries until our expert discovered them. Why Vermeer concealed them is a mystery. But Uweena's ambassadress offers the following interpretation."

The second advert, for Uweena Balm, this time, started playing. It featured an actress dressed as a living replica of the Dutch model in the painting. She spoke as to herself with an elegant and sweet voice that sounded European.

"Will he love me? Will you love me? I stand by my mirror, young and happy. I put the final touches to my morning toilette. I tie around my throat a costly pearl necklace. How I treasure my elegant satin jacket, with its ermine-tips 'nearly as soft as your eyelashes,' so my love once declared. On the table lie my ivory comb, my powder brush and my jewel box, such powerful allies to enhance my beauty. And yet I still fear. I feared lest my love grew weary of me and looked at another. He protested, assuring me that time spent with me feels like music, while a mere smile of mine outshines the distant isles. But every music ends, and alluring are the faraway kingdoms. I wished I were his lute set on the chair, whose strings his fingers eagerly touch: I wished I were his only music. But I will age. I dreamt of spreading upon his eyes the smooth skin of my palms, so that he might forget the wide map on the wall and never should venture far away from my hands. But I shall shrink, alas; I shall whither; I shall wrinkle. And my beloved will tire of me. Who will save me from such a fate? Who will efface his lute, conceal his map—that I might be his only tune and his only compass! Who will show compassion, erasing the musical instrument from this chair, and the map from this wall? Who will spread the balm of lasting youth upon the canvas of my skin, making my beauty forever unrivalled?"

This time again, the projection paused. Drevan snapped his fingers and two aides presently brought an old-fashioned wall map and a lute, while the actress herself, dressed as on the painting, stepped onto the platform. She stood sideways, as if looking at a wall mirror and, gracefully lifting her arms, started tying the pearl necklace. One felt as if a pause button had been hit when she stopped moving, keeping her familiar posture. The resemblance with the painted original was striking. I was touched, as if watching "my" painting becoming alive. Across the wide screen behind her, my earlier radiographies of the lute and map were displayed one after the other.

Pointing at the screen, Drevan explained, "Who will rescue the lovely maiden from the threat of wrinkling? Uweena! Of course, Uweena! Always, Uweena! Gentlemen, please look carefully at these radiographies of the painting. These are the two spectacular discoveries made by Professor Ken Kokura. In-depth analyses of the *Woman with a Pearl Necklace* reveal that this very lute once rested against the leather chair in the foreground, on the bottom right corner of the painting. Vermeer painted the lute. And finally Vermeer erased the lute. Now the lute is no more. That is, it is visible now only thanks to the equipment of art expert Professor Kokura. But our bare eyes can see the lute no longer. And what of the map? On the stage is now unfolded before you the exact replica of the map originally painted by Vermeer against the back wall between the girl and the window. But that map is no more. Vermeer erased it. The painted map is now visible only with special tools, since it has been painted over. Thus, the cries for help of the lovely Dutch maiden have been answered. No lute, no map anymore. The chair is empty; the wall is bare. Nothing will ever distract her beloved from her beauty, from her love. Space and time are abolished—her smooth skin remains forever. As you can see, three hundred and thirteen years later, she radiates the same freshness and youthfulness as when Vermeer gazed at her in his workshop in Delft. Gentlemen, what the genius painter did for this young woman, Uweena does for all modern women. Uweena comes to the rescue of modern women through its revolutionary skin-rejuvenation technology. As you well know, Uweena based it on traditional Chinese science, involving no chemicals but only organic ingredients naturally sourced."

I closed my eyes and shut my ears as the participants started clapping approvingly. They had liked Drevan's presentation, with its toxic mixture of low and high levels of culture: Uweena Oil and Uweena Balm; sharks and pearls. Would it work? Oil and water don't coalesce; soon enough the former floats upon the latter. Perhaps it was just what Jeenaco and BWT intended: so to entice the broader and lower pool of consumers, that they would sacrifice much to purchase the expensive Uweena Balm, after having been hooked by the cheap Uweena Oil. I felt out of my depth. This was such a different world to mine, which focused on artistic expertise.

Now the executives and main shareholders would probably confirm their approval, and the campaign would reach its final stage of preparation before the launch. In a fortnight, my delicate *Woman with a Pearl Necklace* would be seen on every bus from New York to Los Angeles, in the subway and on television. Anyone would deem themselves intimate with her, as if they could tap on her shoulder and claim to know her secrets. At every traffic light, munching their bagels, pedestrians would dispel her mysteries. My precious radiographies of the lute and wall map, these cherished features hidden by

Vermeer for lovers of art to seek and gratefully to display, would be exposed to the indifferent gaze of commuters, of fast-food consumers and of taxi drivers. At least, Drevan had not mentioned the most important of my findings. That one would remain hidden, thankfully. But as I consoled myself with the thought, I started wondering why the advertiser had ignored that major discovery. Was not that third one even more endearing than the hidden lute and wall map?

Drevan was now exposing the machinery of his campaign, just as I had done earlier when culpably revealing the inner side of the painting for a mercantile end. But he was doing his job, and doing it well, whereas I had betrayed two friends, and more than friends—Master Vermeer and his gracious maiden. He answered a question from one of the executives, a Chinese-looking gentleman.

"Subliminally, this is correct sir. Good pictures convey more information than meets the eye at first sight. But the mind registers it: that is what matters as it will influence the decision either to buy the product if the picture is an advert, or, say, to worship the deity if the picture is religious. The unconscious message in Spielberg's *Jaws* is that every male viewer is a shark, and every female viewer is the swimming beauty. Most obviously, the shark wants the beauty. Conversely, the swimming beauty is flattered to exercise so strong an attraction. So, in our first advert, the woman is on the surface and the shark lurks below. Now gentlemen, see how Vermeer's painting works just the same in our second advert. There as well, the young beauty is on the surface and the hidden threats are beneath. She is not at sea, so the threats are not sharks. She is beautifying her skin, so her threats are wrinkles and subsequent infidelity. Our second advert will treat the lute and the wall map like Spielberg used his sharks. Combining *Jaws* and Vermeer makes the lute and the wall map ominous. The smooth skin of Vermeer's young woman will be presented as the lagoon water without ripples, protected from the threat by...Uweena Balm. But the audience will not realise all that. They will just relish the association between *Jaws* and Vermeer. That will send every viewer towards the nearest Uweena store more voraciously than the shark racing towards Spielberg's swimming beauty. Ultimately, we turn the consumer into a shark and your product into its prey. It is all about conditioning desire."

I had listened distractedly to the explanation when, hearing my name called by Drevan, I realised to my embarrassment that he wished to introduce me to the audience. I reluctantly left my chair and walked towards the platform. I felt very awkward and, spontaneously, apologised to my *Woman with a Pearl Necklace* as I came to stand near her. Like pearls to the swine indeed, I had fed her beauty to the merchants. Painful indignation rose in my heart, and I felt more anti-capitalist than I had for many, many years. After all, I was a Communist, was I not? And a Hiroshima survivor. Had not this very American people, successful and complacent, bombed my native city? Well, the *Pearl Necklace* could turn into a Pearl Harbour. Drevan's jovial smile now repelled me even more than the clashing colours of his tie. He had me confirm Vermeer's concealing of the lute and the map.

I explained that, "the very same map appeared again on a later painting whose composition was strikingly similar to the present one (of a young woman in blue reading a letter by a window). The lute was also used in other paintings. It seemed that the painter had subsequently wished to simplify the composition. He got rid of what was anecdotal. On second thoughts, he preferred displaying vacant spaces on the chair and across the wall, inviting the viewer to ponder, to pause, to seek." I refrained from adding 'rather than to spend.' "Closer to us in time and space, Edward Hopper's empty interiors offer the same questioning," I suggested. "But Hopper's spaces mostly evoke loneliness, whereas Vermeer's are full of invisible life, so it feels."

Then, Drevan crossed a line. Instead of responding to my courteous reference to a modern American painter, he ignored my spiritual opening and crudely affirmed, "In a way, both cosmetics and paint are pigments spread upon a surface to attract attention. Vermeer and his girl are in the same business as us, aren't they? With her powder brush she paints her skin, while with his paintbrush he paints his canvas. Why, they are just advertisers like us."

This casual conclusion infuriated me. It gave me the courage I lacked to ask why his presentation ignored my third finding. He would see—they would all see—that there was more to art, much more, than mercenary advertising. Art was about gratuitousness, and mystery, if such words meant anything to Drevan and his ilk.

I tightened my green bow tie, took the microphone and slowly, calmly, asked, "But what of her baby? Should it not be mentioned that she is with child?"

A long silence followed, as if something very rude had been spoken, taking aback the audience. With a smile, Drevan dismissed my query. "Well, Professor, there are many more things one could have said about the painting, I am sure. But we had to select those relevant to Uweena, as you will understand. Further, as Mr Lawry will confirm, the communication team of Jeenaco specified what should and what should not be included in the Uweena campaign. For instance, they ruled out our first draft which focused on the Chinese element, for the Uweena farms, or labs, are located in China. A pity, as we had designed great visuals with lanterns and dragons. But, following their instructions, we shifted to sharks instead."

A couple of hands went up among the audience, several voices suddenly were heard, and the Chinese-looking gentleman asked, "Still, could we learn more about the child? I can't see any depicted on the painting."

At that stage Mr Lionel Lawry, Head of Communication of Jeenaco, stood up and came on the platform. A tanned man in his late thirties, Lawry was wearing sideburns and an orange shirt with an open collar. A long red scarf, untied, dangled on his chest from either side of his neck.

Raising his arms as in an affectionate embrace, so I felt, he explained, "Thank you. Thank you so much to Mike Drevan and everyone at BWT for their sterling work! Thank you Mr Chairman, for gracing this meeting with your presence. Many of us are eager to learn more about the Vermeer painting. I assure you that there will be time for this later on, since it is staying here for the next three months (at a cost, as you know.) For now, let us conclude our business and confirm approval of the Uweena campaign. I assume that everybody is happy with the two-tier approach, and the cross-fertilisation of the two stories, Spielberg's *Jaws* and Vermeer's *Woman*? A lot of effort (and money) has been put into this already and it seems to me that the result is very promising."

The Chinese-looking gentleman who had asked the question earlier replied, "Thank you, Lionel. Personally I agree with you. But I am still concerned with what Professor Kokura has just referred to. Can he prove that the young woman on Vermeer's painting is pregnant? It does not look obvious to me that she is. Was it found out as an underlayer, like when he discovered the hidden lute and map? If it is the case, and if a child is presently hidden under the surface of the painting, so to speak, it is likely to become known sooner or later to the public, to our Uweena consumers, and then... Well..."

Lionel Lawry was supporting his elbow with one hand while scratching his right sideburn with his other hand. After a brief silence, he suggested, "You think it might muddle the message, don't you?"

The other nodded.

"You've said it. From the start, Jeenaco planned the Uweena campaign as a statement for women's independence. We were told that 1970s women were to break free from patriarchy and should crush machismo. This meant tackling the oppressive reduction of womanhood to motherhood. If Vermeer's young woman carries a child, even invisible, she is a mother, not a self-referential beauty, and the entire dynamic of emancipation is undermined."

Several participants approved, voicing their concern. Lawry came closer to the young actress impersonating Vermeer's *Woman with a Pearl Necklace*. Tired of her "necklace-tying posture," she was now standing with her arms crossed, unsure of what she was expected to do next. Addressing the audience, Lawry observed that her yellow satin jacket was what made her silhouette bulky. To prove his point, he requested her to take off the thick furred garment. She did so, revealing a thin waist and an unquestionably flat stomach.

Lawry triumphed, "You see: no baby lay hidden beneath the jacket—just hot air, if I may say." Then, staring at me, he pointedly affirmed, rather than asked, "I suppose that settles the point, Professor?"

I conceded, "Admittedly the same yellow doublet appears in other paintings by Vermeer worn by non-pregnant women such as his *Mistress and Maid* on display in New York at the Frick Collection. With so many canals, Delft would have been a rather damp place and, in winter, this thick indoor garment would keep middle-class housewives warm without compromising on elegance. Thus, I agree that it is insufficient proof of the sitter's pregnancy. But the..."

Cutting me short with a smile, Lawry concluded, "This matter is now sorted then. Thank you again. Now everyone is getting thirsty, and it is time for a break before Mike Drevan presents the Uweena posters to us. Refreshments await you in the next room, gentlemen."

The projection ended and the screen turned blank. The young woman put on her yellow jacket again and left, while everyone stood up and walked to the lobby, chatting. Only Mike Drevan, Lionel Lawry and another Jeenaco executive lagged behind.

Lawry put his hand on my shoulder and announced, "We'd better clarify this issue and move on, Professor. It is thus. Before the meeting, Mike showed me your photographs. I just had enough time to pass them by our chairman and it was immediately clear to us that we could not include them in today's presentation. However, would you care to elaborate on your finding for us, please?"

Hesitatingly, I took out of my briefcase the envelope with my latest radiographies of the *Woman with a Pearl Necklace.* The four of us kept quiet, looking through the printed sheet of cellophane held against the light. One could very clearly see the small shape of the baby curled up at the level of the woman's abdomen, his little head down. Nobody seemed to dare comment.

Finally, Lawry admitted, "Fair enough, we can see the foetus. That is, a cluster of pigments, to be precise. It reminds me of a series of sketches by Leonardo depicting the stages of pregnancy. But I wonder why Vermeer put it there in the first place. Or did he ever paint anatomy, Professor, like Leonardo did?"

Unsure how to answer, I ventured, "Not to my knowledge. Rarely enough, though, on medieval European stained glass or Bible illuminations, one does come across the unborn Child Jesus visible in his mother's womb. As in Vermeer's attempt, the contours of the foetus are superimposed on the stomach of the mother."

Mike Drevan interjected, half ironically, "But on no Christmas card did I ever see the Virgin Mary tying a pearl necklace or powdering her face. Clearly then, this painting is not a religious scene. So why on earth does the young woman carry a child! It is confusing. Really, not something we can allow at this stage of the campaign, Lionel."

Lawry agreed. "So said our chairman, an hour ago. This is why we had to skip this detail in our presentation."

In my disappointment, I was inspired to venture a last justification for including my revolutionary finding in the campaign after all. "May I offer a suggestion? As you may have noticed, the woman wears no wedding ring. Being pregnant while single was much against moral norms in seventeenth-century Delft. Protestants frowned on fornication and Catholics like the Vermeer family were strict about wedlock. Could not her pregnancy be seen as an affirmation consistent with the narrative of the Uweena campaign? A single mum, she would embody the liberated modern woman, free from traditional bonds to husband, matrimony and the like." The words sounded hollow as I spoke them though, or even treacherous. My argument had nothing to do with Vermeer's purpose, I knew well. It was artificially projected on the masterpiece treated as a mere advertising commodity. I hated myself for pushing my darling beauty into the hands of such judges as Lionel Lawry, now weighing the evidence while still wearing his hideous orange shirt and his preposterous sideburns, and Mike Drevan with his abominably clashing tie.

Lawry was scrutinising the radiography. "You are right, no ring on." He nodded. "So, the girl has been naughty... (What will her daddy say?) I hadn't thought of that." He looked pensive and finally replied, "Your suggestion is a good spin Professor, true enough. But all in all, keeping motherhood out of our campaign is safer. That is the choice we made for Uweena and we will stand by it. Now, we have deserved a drink, I reckon. By the way, this Vermeer 'baby' must not be mentioned anywhere, as per our confidentiality clause."

I nodded with embarrassment as if I had been expected to leak business secrets. The three men had nearly left the conference room when I feared lest the gag should include my own scientific publications. I anxiously enquired, "Mr Lawry, one moment please. I will respect your decision of course, but I mean to submit my latest findings about this painting, next month to *Apollo*, the leading art magazine. Although their readership is limited to experts and enthusiasts, it might benefit your advertising campaign. I hope that is acceptable."

Lionel Lawry walked back to me with the other man. I vaguely recognised him as one of the lawyers who had attended my early meeting at the Jeenaco Tower. The lawyer announced, "Professor, hopefully you recall that Jeenaco purchased from you the copyright for your radiographies. While you may write and speak about your findings on Vermeer's *Woman with a Pearl Necklace*, you are prohibited by law from communicating visual evidence for them to anyone. In other words, your radiographies are not yours anymore, but Jeenaco's. I have here the copy of the contract which you signed, with acknowledgement of payment, if you care to take a look."

I was taken aback. Obviously, I would not be able to publish without the corresponding radiographies displayed on the page. Against my natural shyness though, I felt bold enough to ask further, "But once the painting is back in Berlin, in three months, I will be permitted to take new radiographies and publish them, will I not?"

Lawry turned back and said casually, "Oh, you didn't know? Jeenaco has taken steps with the Berlin Gemäldegalerie to extend our rental period. We are confident that the Uweena campaign will be a lasting success, justifying an ongoing lease of five years as a start. Even though Vermeer's painting may return to Berlin sooner for the sake of visitors, the publication of any visual depiction of his *Woman with a Pearl Necklace* will be subject to our approval for the duration of the lease. You may apply for use of your findings regarding the lute and map, or similar details. But the girl's 'babe' remains concealed." Momentarily dropping his American accent, Lawry added with a falsely prudish smile, "That's better for the guilty mother. No gentleman would ever expose a lady to dishonour, would he? See you later, Professor."

The lawyer read aloud to me a statement in my name, confirming that I had not, in person or through a third party, taken, kept, hidden, shared or in any other way disseminated any visual evidence of my findings about the *Woman with a Pearl Necklace*, whether before my present stay in Chicago or during it; and that I committed not to do so in the future either, without prior written approval from Jeenaco for the duration of their lease of the painting. I had to sign the statement.

They left and I sat down, alone in the vast empty room. The sharks were gone. Or was I the last one of them left? On the stage in front of me, in her sober dark wooden frame, the innocent young woman I had alternatively tried to praise and prey upon was still busy tying her pearl necklace. I felt rather empty and confused as well as very, very tired.

On the plane back to New York the following morning, I relished the prospect of spending some quiet time sheltered in my flat and in my familiar neighbourhood after the three days of intense tension undergone in the alien environment of cosmetic advertising. As the aircraft landed, I decided to spend a couple of hours painting a watercolour on arrival. It had been too long since I had last held a paintbrush and I was in need of relaxation. In the taxi from the airport, what joy to see the trees of Central Park covered with yellow leaves! It was still only October. The thought of buying a dog crossed my mind. It would feel so homely to walk it around Belvedere Castle and throw sticks for him to fetch. But unless I settled in America, keeping a pet was too impractical. And how could I safely walk a dog on crowded occasions such as the concert of the so-called "Beach Boys" at the Park the previous month? To think that such rattle and bleat had taken place across the street from my dear Frick Collection. My heart leaped on sighting the familiar building—inhabited by several other Vermeer ladies—as the cab dropped me home at the corner of E 70th Street and Madison Avenue. A porter carried into the building the two heavy trunks with my radiographic equipment. All was well.

Or so I thought. As I stepped out of the lift, I found my front door slightly ajar. The flat had been broken into not long before, or the janitor would have alerted me when handing me the mail in the lobby. On any other occasion, like anyone else I would have first surveyed the damage and called for assistance. But this time, I walked into my hallway nearly without reacting as I was reading for the second time the letter opened in the lift.

"October 16, 1977, New York City

"Sir,

"For twenty-eight years you may have been expecting this. I am your daughter Anastasia. Anastasia Kravitz, not Kokura, since you never bothered to give me your surname, let alone your affection or your address. Yet, here is news from me, for your interest. I am married to Leopold, a good German man from Hamburg. Our daughter Ute will turn ten next May. I have an aunt in Cologne, my mother's sister. My uncle was Professor Chimek Kravitz, the art expert. He passed away last month after a long illness, as you may have heard. He was like a father to me, raising me as if I were his child. Uncle Chimek praised my mother Ida much. But her name can mean very little to you. You have become famous in your profession, I gather, and respected. But you abused my mother sword in hand, left her to die in anguish and fled from me your offspring, when I was most in need. Not once did you ask Uncle Chimek about me. He said that we should forgive you, though. But can I do so, unless you repent? Now that he is dead, I mean to tell the world who you really are. Not for vengeance, but for your sake, that you may take responsibility. Four leading newspapers in Europe and in America are willing to publish my story, although I have not yet disclosed your name to them. As proof of my identity, I enclose a facsimile of the official report my uncle gave me. My mother wrote it the day she died, giving birth to me. You can see her signature: 'Comrade Ida Kravitz, on 20 March 1949, at Wittenberg Democratic Maternity Clinic.' However, if you wish to meet me before I go public, I will be at the cloakroom of the Frick Collection this Thursday, October 20, at 3pm.

"Anastasia."

I walked into the sitting-room mentally aware of the chaos all over the flat but feeling emotionally numb, for now, to the shock of the burglary. Scattered books and files, twisted frames and ripped cushions were spread everywhere on the floor. It was then that something occurred that had an even greater impact on my life than Anastasia's letter and the wrecking of my home. As I pushed open the bedroom door and came near the bed I meant to sit upon, still holding Anastasia's letter open in my hand, I set foot on a frame fallen upon the floor. It was partially hidden under a shirt, but my eyes had just enough time to register the main colours of the depiction before the weight of my body would start bearing upon the fragile item and break the protective glass of the frame. What struck me in retrospect is that I knew that I was about to break the glass and, instead of deploring the accident, I was glad of it. At the very moment I heard the glass pane fracture under my shoe, I was transported some fifty years earlier and some thousands of miles away.

I was a child of six or seven. It was winter, but there was no snow. We were on a family walk along the alleyway of a park. My parents, I suppose, with my grandmother, a few uncles and aunts and perhaps some siblings and cousins were chatting light-heartedly. The alley was gravelled, not tar-macked. Frozen puddles showed here and there. Breaking their icy surface was our favourite game.

I recall no faces, I hear no voices. But I so distinctly see the tip of my small white wellington boot tread the edge of a puddle, lightly touching its solid surface, gauging its strength, testing its elasticity, until my increased pressure causes the thin transparent membrane to shatter with a tinkle. I see the crack run in two or three directions under my white foot. But the fracture is still superficial enough to leave the sheet of ice undisturbed. It still holds together and, I am clearly aware of it, it could "heal" if left to solidify again. As observed in puddles walked upon on earlier walks, shards of ice have frozen again, now aggregated to a new transparent lid, albeit uneven.

Through the ice on the surface, the inside of the puddle gapes, lined with velvety deep pink that contrasts almost organically with the dark grey gravel covering the alley. The powdery gravel is smooth enough. But the rose lining below feels appealingly softer. Its milky texture evokes some lukewarm pudding like chocolate mush, if pink chocolate exists; and feels precious and nearly alive like an oyster, one devoid of saltiness though. The protective ice lid keeps the water beneath perfectly still and yet visible. No pebble, twig or gale can disrupt the inner peace of that confined liquid, like a honeycomb cell kept mysteriously warm under the cold sky. In fact, as my foot presses through the icy surface and softly lands on the inside of the pool, no violence is felt, no cruelty, no damage, but childlike liberty or even some birth right, as if I belonged there. I do.

In my memory the puddle shines as a small, neatly delineated space, but not as if in a vacuum, not as if detached from its surroundings. Neither is one's navel, a rounded knotty depression on one's stomach, ever looked at or felt in isolation from one's entire body. It is on the contrary its geometrical centre and its chronological origin. Similarly, my little puddle sheds light on the grounds, on the people and the moods connected with this tiny event. Hazy but proximate, outer space spans as if from the puddle, like petals surrounding the calyx of a flower. There are leafless woods, not dark, not ominous. There is a vast expanse of grass combed by the brisk winter wind, sloping towards a lake that glitters under the pale sun. A few birds glide pleasantly. Rocks show here and there. And, I am sure of it, behind us stands the house. It is a mansion, several storeys high, spread out with wings. Nearby stands a little temple perched on high granite steps. The mansion is welcoming and powerful. I am no art expert there. I am a child and a son. I am no visitor there. I am home.

All this was felt in an instant as I happily anticipated the breaking of the glass protecting the fallen frame in my bedroom. I did not relish damaging the painting, of course. I just lost sight of it. The motion of my leg and foot being too far engaged, the foreseen damaged was instantaneously eclipsed by the memory released. My light stepping upon fragile glass, with precious shades of pink and grey, applied simultaneously to my artistic present and to my lost infancy. Never since my awakening under a military tent outside Hiroshima had I been able to reach behind the veil of amnesia. Sensations of *déjà-vu* had occurred many times, and I securely accessed academic and theological knowledge acquired before the bombing; but no door, no vista had ever opened into my earlier life.

The remembrance was not visually detailed. For instance, the architecture of the mansion escaped my recollection. It was built in stone, not in wood, but its style and age remained unknown. I failed to connect my notion of it with any particular building I had come across in Honshu, the main island in Japan. The small temple could be Buddhist or Shinto, or even Christian, who knows? Were the trees maples or beeches? I don't know why, oak trees came to mind. Higher up my legs than my little white wellingtons, what sort of clothes was I wearing? Western flannel trousers, or a traditional silk kimono, or a wool coat? I had no idea, neither regarding the garments of the family group that walked with me. I was still standing with Anastasia's letter in my hand. My right foot was still touching the now cracked glass of the picture. The enlightenment had occurred within a split second. I remained in that posture much longer, perhaps ten minutes or more. I did not want to let such a grace ever go away, although I knew that the memory was now mine and could be revisited at will, blissfully.

Only then did I notice that the trodden picture was Whistler's *Harmony in Pink and Grey: Portrait of Lady Meux*. I had bought that good replica a couple of years earlier. The original was up my street, literally, at the Frick Collection. Such a coincidence raised my spirits to sober ecstasy, as I realised what passage had just opened between my present affections, such as Whistler's chromatic variations, and the emotional microcosm of my early childhood. This totally unexpected access to my life before the bomb had brought me back home somehow; but it had also revealed a home amidst my later alienation. I had spent the past thirty-two years in a sort of pink and grey realm—if I can thus summarise my acquired identity as an art expert. I had lived as if in some artistic exile until the opening of the magic puddle, suddenly, had vindicated pink and grey as the very coordinates of my happy childhood instead of the later accretion, or the consolation prize, I had assumed they were.

Paradoxically, breaking the glass had mended my life, merging past and present. The gulf of amnesia was bridged, it appeared. Unbeknownst to me, continuity had guided my life. Broken down to its basic elements, a single pattern combined grey, pink, broken glass (or ice) and happiness. The identity of pattern proved that my later years had unfolded and even fulfilled the embryonic design of my prime. Like any man, my X and Y chromosomes had defined my physical and mental growth from conception. Pink and grey had done the same, I felt, as the parameters of my existential development, regardless of my lost memory. Never mind the blast, forget the amnesia: I was the very child, now grown up, who playfully trod on icy puddles. I was doomed no more, since the same shades of my innocent youth still coloured the affections of my lonely maturity.

I walked out of the flat, slammed the door and went down in the lift, nearly running to the corner of my street that housed the Frick Collection. It would have been just past noon as I recall punctual bells ringing at the nearby St Jean Baptiste Church. The gallery would not close for several hours. Even blindfolded I would have found her room. But my eyes were wide open indeed when, from a distance, I caught sight of Lady Meux's portrait. As if sun-blinded though, I lifted before my face Anastasia's letter and envelope (inadvertently kept in my hand all that time), peeping through the slot in between the two papers.

I would not come close to Whistler's *Harmony in Pink and Grey: Portrait of Lady Meux*. I considered with painful gratitude the long vertical frame that had just turned out to be the gate connecting the two halves of my life. It lay open before my eyes. The lady's beauty was not what arrested me.

It was even less her controversial fame as a Victorian socialite (a former banjo-player, she had married one of the richest men in England). No, something more intimate, truly existential, brought us together. Polite society was only too aware that Lady Meux "had a past," but my past had been taken from me. She had hoped to hide hers, whereas I had failed to find mine. Now, happily, we were even. There the lady stood, in front of a curtain concealing her dubious history or heralding her bright future. Her slightly disdainful mouth and shady gaze challenged the privileged ones, and invited the likes of me, so I felt, to step into happiness.

Like the Lady Viviane rising out of the lake in the Arthurian legend, Lady Meux seemed to have materialised out of the icy water of my childhood puddle while I, a convalescing Lancelot in Pre-Raphaelite armour, owed her my recovery. Should I, in imitation of the Round-Table Knights, devote my life to her apparitions, since I knew of not only one but three portraits of her? One in Honolulu showed Lady Meux in black, while a mysterious portrait of her wearing furs had gone missing. Thus, Whistler had painted a 'Lady Meux trilogy,' in addition to his 'Women in White trilogy.' For the present, yet, how fitting her surname sounded to me: "Meux" was pronounced "Mews," my "Muse" indeed. Recalling a picture of her driven across London in a high phaeton drawn by a pair of zebras, I wished I had been a Surrealist painter and could change the black and white stripes on the equines' backs into pink and grey coats!

CHAPTER 8
The Borny Agreement

CRATCHING THE REMAINS OF SPIRIT gum under his left nostril, Fr Hubert Lambourin nearly regretted his fake moustache. It had held surprisingly well, he admitted, now throwing into his leather briefcase, after his AC Milan football cap, the *World Youth Day* 1989 T-shirt which he had just taken off (its official Santiago de Compostela logo could have won the prize for the worst graphic design ever). A client was banging against the door, again. "*Pazienza,*" Lambourin repeated as he finished buttoning his black clerical shirt. "*Mi scusi,*" he told the tourist as he walked out of the toilets of the busy trattoria. Looking presentable again, he made his way back toward the Tiber, sorting out his impressions of the mission just completed. Stalking the pope (or a potential one) was not something he had been prepared for. Even though Mgr Marco Altemps was not even yet a cardinal, he soon might become one and, from that moment, would be granted the diplomatic status of "presumptive heir of an elective monarchy," like his other one-hundred-and-twenty or so scarlet colleagues.

Mgr Jacques Pommard had insisted on utter discretion. After a rather disappointing first meeting with Mgr Altemps the afternoon before, the Vatican Head of the Section for Asian Affairs had entrusted to his secretary an unexpected task. He was to follow Mgr Altemps that Friday morning until early afternoon. His disguise had to be very convincing. As Mgr Pommard had anticipated, Mgr Altemps had gone straight from the Anselmianum where he stayed, to the basilica of San Sisto Vecchio on the Via Appia. The monsignor had paid attention neither to the architecture nor to the paintings. Instead, he had fallen on his knees by the Madonna of the

Holy Rosary and remained there for nearly twenty minutes. His rosary beads were moving from one hand to the other while his lips muttered the prayers. He had eventually stood up. Fr Hubert Lambourin—unrecognisable thanks to his yellow moustache and *WYD* 1989 T-shirt—had folded his guidebook, ready to follow him out. Instead, the monsignor had grabbed the chair behind him and, apparently in pain, had sat heavily, catching his breath. Why, the man was sickly! It did not look promising, the secretary felt, if that would-be cardinal was ever elected pope. The white smoke might still be seen floating above the Sistine Chapel when the bells of St Peter's tolled for the sick pontiff, so soon deceased.

To conceal his identity, Dr Pavel Shevchenko had used a trick opposite to Fr Lambourin's. Leaving his lay clothes aside, he had put on a plain grey clerical shirt and trousers, hiding his bald skull under a wig, also grey. Mgr Pommard had tipped him about the sick prelate's likely destination that afternoon. As expected, Mgr Altemps had made his way to the palazzo whose name he bore, home to several collections of famous sculptures. Dr Shevchenko was not surprised when Mgr Altemps was let in without paying, having shown his identity card. After some time spent standing before the huge *Ludovisi Gaul Killing Himself and His Wife*—he sat on a chair by the colossal *Torso of Polyphemus*. He then wandered along the galleries and across the courtyard, visibly moved, as if the place conjured painful memories. On hearing Dr Shevchenko's report that evening, Mgr Pommard had wondered whether Marco Altemps was not simply trying to anticipate the party originally booked for Bishop Dorf after his first Mass as cardinal. It had been planned in that very palace the following month and, all things considered, it would do very well for Cardinal Altemps' celebration, should he eventually deign to accept the red hat. As a matter of principle Dr Shevchenko would not rule out the possibility that Altemps was "Showcasing Dissent." One had to be absolutely sure, and the red hat might be the perfect bait, he had suggested to Pommard. What Communist spy could resist the prospect of becoming a Prince of the Church, that is, potentially the next Pope. It would be like a Vatican secret serviceman promoted to party leader in Communist China!

Altemps a spy? Why not Shevchenko then? Jacques Pommard was getting a bit tired of having to suspect everybody. But it was part of his service to the Church, inescapably. By then it was nearly midnight. While brushing his teeth before going to bed, Mgr Pommard recalled that both Fr Lambourin and Dr Shevchenko had omitted a couple of meaningful facts. On meeting them separately for debriefing, he had enquired whether they had noticed any suspicious characters communicating with Mgr Altemps. Neither had mentioned the two brief exchanges which had taken place between Altemps and a *carabiniere* on the steps of the basilica of San Sisto Vecchio, and with a street cleaner by his cart near the entrance to Palazzo Altemps. Mgr Pommard was glad that, unbeknownst to his collaborators, he had witnessed these two conversations, albeit from a distance. Sitting next to him in the car, his photographer had managed to take excellent pictures of Altemps' interlocutors, whose faces were currently being checked by his department. Stalking the stalkers had proved a timely precaution, even though the two brief encounters may have been purely fortuitous. But if Mgr Altemps carried some secrets, it fell upon him, Jacques Pommard, to find out whether they were detrimental or innocuous.

The vetting process of a would-be cardinal had to be very thorough. Indeed, during a last meeting that Friday afternoon, Altemps had eventually accepted the red hat. Never too late! Poor Picerno would be so greatly relieved on reading the news. But for now the hemiplegic prelate would still be asleep in Tokyo. Wishing to secure rest for his sick colleague, Mgr Pommard programmed the fax machine to have his letter sent only a few hours later. The ability to see things from the perspective of others was a well-appreciated feature of Jacques Pommard's temperament. While others might have used that trait to secure control in a manipulative way, he seemed interested only in the comfort and happiness of his colleagues. It made him a rather popular superior.

Later that afternoon, Mgr Altemps had been sent on retreat in northern Italy according to his wish, with Fr Lambourin as chaperone. By then both men were probably sleeping in their Benedictine cells somewhere near Parma. It was time for Mgr Pommard to do the same. After a short prayer, the Vatican Head of the Section for Asian Affairs slipped thankfully into his king-size bed.

At the Tokyo Nunciature, Hana the housekeeper tiptoed into Bishop Dorf's bedroom and laid the breakfast tray on the side table. The prelate was still fast asleep. Not daring to wake him up, she tightened the bed sheet, wondering whether His sick Excellency would bestow upon her such an honour as to ask her to declaim further the Kokura Memoirs. With professional dedication, Hana opened the bundle where she'd left the narrative the night before, and silently started reading further, so as to be forewarned of more difficult words and passages.

Bishop Picerno Dorf enjoyed the blossoming cherry trees. Hana the housekeeper had wheeled him onto the patio along the main façade of the Nunciature. The weather was warm enough on this Easter Saturday, and watching the gardener, Hana's "Uncle Byobu," mow the lawn for the first time in the season, was relaxing. "Truly, we are animals," the hemiplegic prelate thought, "or how would such a trivial thing as the smell of cut grass elate us so instantly? On the other hand, when I was a boy back in South Tyrol, did the mountain cows look particularly excited by the scent of hay? Probably not. Disappointingly, cattle merely follow their instinct for food." But the bishop's mind could not escape for very long its spontaneous attraction to the business in progress, namely, Marco Altemps' cooperation in keeping the cardinal's hat "warm" for him at the next consistory. It had been several days since Monsignor Altemps' arrival in Rome and Picerno had only received a brief note from Mgr Jacques Pommard stating that, despite a couple of inconclusive initial meetings, the sick monsignor might still be persuaded to accept his appointment as cardinal.

Marco! Marco! Marco! How could he not see where his duty lay? Had he, Picerno, failed to inculcate in his junior the minimum amount of ambition necessary to achieve great things? Yes, the pair was already credited with several successes. But so much more was at hand! Why had Marco always been so shy? When at university in Vienna, he was already afraid of speaking in public. Picerno was thirty-one and Marco twenty-five when they had found each other again at the Academia, the diplomatic formation department of the Holy See. It was in 1955; no, 1954. They were together in Hong Kong four years later when the Catholic Patriotic Association appointed bishops without papal approval, splitting the Catholic Church in China. Over the following years, they had worked very hard to negotiate the evacuation of about two hundred priests and religious from mainland China—and even harder to send nearly a hundred back clandestinely.

Some were German Benedictines from the suppressed Abbey of Holy Cross in former Manchukuo, one hour north from the Korean border. Others were German Franciscans, whose superior Picerno was visiting in West Germany when, that fateful 13 August 1961, the Berlin Wall was erected. It was a Sunday, he recalled, as the news had been broken to him right after the conventual high Mass at the Franciscan friary. Cold War tensions were at their highest and Picerno's thorough knowledge of Communism in China made him a useful interlocutor with West German diplomats. That would have been when he had first heard of then-Fr Jacques Pommard, at the time a junior official at the Secretariat of State.

Pommard had conveyed his superior's wishes that Picerno should remain longer in Stuttgart, and should also travel to Rome, rather than return to Hong Kong. Important meetings had taken place, with a view to shaping the Ostpolitik of the Holy See. A small but significant victory had been the telegram of greetings sent by Soviet Premier Khrushchev for Pope John's eightieth birthday on 25 November 1961. Picerno had made useful contacts in Europe.

A year later, it was unbearably hot when, on 18 August 1962, Mgr Picerno Dorf crossed the French border and got off the train at Strasburg. He strolled around the famous cathedral, and had lunch in a restaurant on Place Broglie. A plaque on a facade informed him that the Broglie family had come from Piedmont to France and risen to prominence in the service of Church and state, with members becoming bishops and even dukes. "A Tyrolean is worth several Piedmontese," Picerno reckoned, wondering whether this first trip to France might benefit his career. A Vatican official had spoken with him in Stuttgart the week before, ordering him to attend a highly confidential meeting in Lorraine between high-level representatives of the Catholic and Orthodox Churches. The purpose was to confirm the involvement of Orthodox prelates at the long-awaited Council, scheduled to begin in Rome barely two months later, at the Vatican. Mgr Dorf walked back to the railway station and boarded his train to Metz. On alighting, he was led towards the latest Citroën DS, white with tinted windows. Behind it, another less luxurious car carried more clergy. Picerno managed to hide his emotion when sitting in the DS next to the Dean of the Sacred College, no less, the former Secretary of the Congregation for the Oriental Churches, Cardinal Eugène Tisserant.

The influential prelate, rumoured to have been nearly elected pope at the 1958 conclave, was now sent by Pope John, as he explained, to meet with Boris Georgievich Rotov, also known as Archbishop Nikodim of Yaroslavl, representing the Russian Orthodox Church—and the KGB.

"I was born near here," Cardinal Tisserant intimated in fluent German, "in Nancy. A pity you could not visit it on your way from Stuttgart. A beautiful city, truly. When His Holiness entrusted me with the preparation of this meeting, I looked for a very discreet venue. I knew the Little Sisters of the Poor, in Borny. That is where the driver is taking us now. Of course, the Sisters don't suspect who the participants are and what our purpose is."

Picerno remained quiet, guessing that His Eminence would tell him soon enough why he was included in the delegation. After a few minutes, Tisserant went on.

"Archimandrite Nikodim Rotov was the youngest Orthodox bishop ordained, at the age of 31. Two years ago, the KGB recommended appointing him to the position of chairman of the Department for External Church Relations. He was nominated as a representative of the Russian Orthodox Church, and participated in the activities of the World Peace Council and the Soviet Peace Committee. His Holiness wants a rapprochement with Moscow. It is time to improve our relationship with our Orthodox brethren, and to send the Soviets a convincing signal of Rome's readiness for dialogue. Mgr Dmitry Bogdanov, here on the front seat, is our expert on Soviet Russia. You, Mgr Dorf, will have nothing to do at all during this meeting. You were recommended to me as an expert on Communist China. Just listen and memorize. I want you to witness and inform the Government of Chairman Mao that Rome wishes to reach out to Beijing no less eagerly than to Moscow."

It had taken a quarter of an hour to reach Borny. The cars drove up Rue Jeanne Jugan along a high wall surrounding the convent of the Petites Sœurs des Pauvres, and turned right through the gates. Tall chestnut trees provided welcome shade, and a gentle breeze blew over the hill. Picerno relished the view over Metz, before following the group inside the building. The Russian prelates wore lay dress, but their long beards gave them away. Picerno smiled under his breath when realising that Cardinal Tisserant's equally profuse beard was likely to dispose the Orthodox favourably towards him. Dismissing the nuns, His Eminence insisted on pouring tea with his own hands, out of a silver samovar bearing an imperial eagle. "This appliance was found among some lost luggage of Emperor Napoleon's during his retreat from Russia," the Cardinal mentioned as he handed the cups to his guests. "An historic piece, it has remained in France for too long, I was told—one hundred and fifty years, to be precise. Would it not be a fair deed if you found it possible to return it to Russia on our behalf, Archbishop Nikodim?"

The conversations took place in German, French and Russian. Picerno had already participated in many meetings of ecclesiastical diplomacy. He liked seeing the discreet and powerful Vatican machinery at work internationally, playing a role disproportionate to its small geographical size, like the previous year, after the failed Bay of Pigs Invasion in Cuba. He warmed to Archimandrite Nikodim Rotov. The Orthodox prelate looked younger than him, beneath his abundant beard. He must have been about the same age as Marco Altemps but, unlike him, spoke with determination and authority. There was a leader, a man who could influence the course of history. Picerno smiled inwardly again, imagining the Russian as a combination of Marco and himself. He wondered whether he should not grow a beard. When leaving the room, he saw that Napoleon's samovar was left behind on the sideboard, instead of accompanying the Russians home as offered. Would it get shipped on to Moscow later by the Little Sisters of the Poor? He did not ask.

The agreement was reached. The Catholic Church would abstain from criticising Communism at the forthcoming council. In exchange, Soviet Russia would grant several Orthodox prelates permission to travel to Rome. This occurred two months later when, on 10 October 1962, the Holy Synod appointed Archpriest Vitaly Borovoy and Archimandrite Vladimir

(Kotlyarov) as Orthodox observers at Vatican II. Picerno was invited to travel back to Hong Kong where, with the assistance of Marco Altemps, unofficial meetings with Chinese representatives of the Communist Government gave hope for a release of Ignatius Kung Pin-Mei, the Bishop of Shanghai imprisoned seven years earlier. But Marco was less optimistic. In confidence, he even shared with Picerno his earnest doubts about the long-term gains of the Borny Agreement.

"We know that Communism is getting weaker in Europe. Now would be the time to expose its fallacies anew, updating its 1937 condemnation. Silence will only make oppression last longer. No less than in China, our fellow Catholics in Eastern Europe undergo violent persecution. It seems to me that we should speak up rather than keep quiet."

Picerno ascribed Marco's uncompromising stance to his youthful ideals. A lot of patience was needed to obtain any tangible results, especially there in China. Condemning oppression made one feel better. People admired protesters. But such brags yielded little fruit and often prompted retaliation, as the recent "Clear River Farm" incident had reminded them. A Christian journalist had revealed that the so-called "farm" was possibly the largest concentration camp in the world, situated in a mosquito-infested marsh some 150 kilometres outside Beijing. Thousands of "farmers" selected by the Communist Government were "eagerly" cultivating the land. They were efficiently organised as "Cadre Farm" (former civil servants from the defeated bourgeoisie undergoing re-education), the "Youth Farm" (enthusiastic young volunteers demonstrating patriotic zeal through digging miles of ditches) and even the "Garden Team" composed of female prisoners. All were expected to "have their souls cleansed by 'clear waters,'" in reference to the name of Qinghe, meaning "Clear River." Within days of the release of the article in an American Pentecostal magazine, two Catholic bishops had had their jail sentence extended, while seven priests and fifty-four Protestant missionaries had been arrested.

Undeterred, Marco had quietly suggested that, "exposing the Qinghe Farm scandal might well have been the straw breaking the camel's back, since Mao's imposed collectivist farming had halted soon after, putting an end to the largest Government-imposed famine in world history." Marco still had a lot to learn about becoming an accomplished diplomat, Mgr Dorf growled. Among other things, he should be more careful when proving his superior wrong. Thankfully, he was docile and shy by temperament, so that he would nonetheless support the official policy.

Much tact was needed indeed, since, in October 1962, the Cuban Missile Crisis unexpectedly strengthened the position of Mao Zedong. The withdrawal of Soviet missiles from Cuba made credible the assertion of the Chinese leader accusing the USSR of compromising with the West, instead of actively spreading the revolution. His *Great Leap Forward* having proved disastrous, Mao's prestige at home had waned for years: it was now growing again. Extreme caution was required of Catholic diplomats.

~~~~~~~~~~~~~~~~~~

"Would His Excellency wish Hana to apply her very mediocre skills to read some more of the Kokura Memoirs?" Now back in his bedroom, Bishop Dorf did not mind the housekeeper's suggestion. While he had nearly given up on finding clues to identify the so-called "master spy *Showcasing Dissent*," he might like some distraction, and could always choose to doze if he so wished. Hana's reading was improving, he reckoned: her elocution sounded almost fluent, as if she knew or guessed the content of every next paragraph. What a hearty breakfast it had been anyway. Digestion made him feel sleepy, but Hana's voice sounded an acceptable lullaby, a background noise.

About an hour later, the fax machine by his bed emitted a noisy screech, waking up Bishop Dorf. He must have fallen asleep once again, he realised. Hana was gone. With his non-paralysed arm, the prelate managed to reach out to the device and drowsily brought the printed sheet to his distorted face.

Confidential:

For the attention of: Bishop Picerno Dorf, Vatican Delegate to the U. N. Observatory of Non-Proliferation of Nuclear Weapons in Asia, Apostolic Nunciature in Tokyo.

From: Mgr Jacques Pommard, Head of the Asian Section, Secretariat of State, Rome

On: Friday 5 April 1991

Your Excellency, dear Picerno,

The Second Counsellor of the Nunciature, Fr Domingo, told me that you had nearly regained the use of your left hand since that disastrous stroke of yours. Congratulations! As an incentive to full recovery, I am sending you now the good news you have been hoping for.

At long last, Mgr Altemps has accepted the proposal this afternoon. Persuading him took three meetings though. In my career at the Asian Affairs, never did I encounter a cleric so afraid of wearing red. His cancer is obviously a deep concern. If he were not your express candidate in support of our Asian policy, I would not have insisted that he should become a cardinal for so short a tenure, predictably. His episcopal consecration is scheduled for Saturday, 13 April in Japan at the hands of the Archbishop of Tokyo, with you and the outgoing Pro-Nuncio as co-consecrators. Mgr Altemps will be known as Titular Bishop of Ilium, a vacant see since 1968. He chose that name out of a shortlist of three because, as he explained to me, it had been the Titular See of Michel d'Herbigny, the courageous Jesuit who set up the Catholic Hierarchy in Bolshevik Russia.

He asked permission to spend the next few days in the north of Italy, at the small Benedictine community of which he has become an oblate as Brother Enrico, before flying back to you in Tokyo. This will count as his retreat in preparation for his episcopal consecration. He had hoped to enter that monastery and soon die in peace cloistered from the world, but he is now resigned to postpone this and do his duty. Let us hope that the Gregorian chant will not make him change his mind. I sent my own assistant Fr Lambourin there with him as his driver and chaperone.

Mgr Altemps also said that he would have neither strength nor time to organise his cardinalatial Mass on Sunday, 30 June in his titular basilica and the reception following. He thus begged of you to allow him to retain all the preparation made for you before your stroke. I am sure you will permit it. I notice that your party was booked already at his family's historic townhouse in Rome, Palazzo Altemps. Well, God works in mysterious ways indeed. I hope you are pleased and that this might even help you regain the use of your left leg and facial muscles. Should your health return by then, it will enable you to facilitate Mgr Altemps' very first steps as the new Nuncio in Tokyo next week, a transitory position as per your suggestion, now that Bishop William Carew's assignment in Berlin is confirmed. Perhaps we can talk about this soon if your speech is restored.

Yours faithfully, J. Pommard

Bishop Dorf laid the fax sheet on his chest with a deep sigh of relief. At last, at last, Marco had understood where his duty lay! Picerno looked with no less satisfaction at his left hand now obeying the motion of his will unhindered. Let Marco fly back, and let them be reunited, and he would embrace him like a brother, nay, like a wayward son. Frowning though, the bishop just recalled that his assistant was actually on his way to a Benedictine monastery. Yes, Mgr Pommard was right. There was a risk that Marco might change his mind once among these Benedictine monks and might cancel his acceptance of the red hat. How wise of Jacques to have sent his Fr Lambourin along! That young Quebecois priest was down to earth. He would prevent Marco from deserting the battlefield hidden under a cowardly cowl.

Admittedly, Marco had betrayed partiality towards cloistered life decades earlier, Bishop Dorf recalled. "Yes, had he not criticised Pope Paul VI's crackdown on territorial monasteries as early as 1976—in October, wasn't it?" Marco had thought it unfair to deprive ancient abbeys from the vast territories they used to administer, and to deny abbots episcopal consecration. Picerno smiled, remembering his friend's upset about the territorial abbey of Tokwon. Founded in

Korea by the German Benedictines of Saint Ottilien, then governed by a relative of Marco's, Tokwon Abbey had been suppressed by the Communists in 1949 and might never be started again, or not on that location.

Korea was under Japanese occupation until its "liberation" by the Soviets, soon replaced by Korean Communists who shortly liquidated thirty-seven religious of either sex, mostly German. American bombs had destroyed the abbey building in July 1950. Tokwon Abbey had been a stronghold for evangelising vast territories in the Korean hinterland, all the way to the Chinese border some two hours north. The abbey had since relocated in South Korea. But Marco had contacts with underground Catholics in North Korea and was supportive of their plans to restart the Tokwon Benedictine community in North Korea, albeit clandestinely. Was he not even an "oblate" of that monastery (prior to the one in Tuscany), a distant associate while not being a monk, Picerno now seemed to recall?

Both clerics were still posted in Hong Kong at the time. Marco had an exploratory trip to Korea scheduled in the summer of 1976. He was hoping to obtain from the Communist government recognition of the former cemetery around the abbey as an "area of particular importance to the people of Korea." Because of the vast outreach of the territorial abbey during the first half of the twentieth century, thousands of Catholic converts had asked to be buried near the church and its sacramental heart, the Eucharistic tabernacle of the monks. The natives candidly hoped "to sleep better if buried close to 'Emperor Jesus,'" while awaiting the resurrection. The unusual title of "Emperor Jesus" had been invented by the Benedictine monks as an encouragement for their Korean parishioners under Japanese occupation since 1910 and, as such, forced to express submission, externally at least, to the Japanese Emperor. In 1925, Pope Pius XI's encyclical *Quas Primas* teaching the social kingship of Christ indirectly backed the monks' idea. The following year, on the accession of the new Japanese Emperor Hirohito, the Benedictines started referring to "Emperor Jesus, ruler of the world."

Bishop Dorf looked at the shelves on the walls of his bedroom. Marco had once given him a framed picture of Christ the King, had he not? The face of Jesus had Asian features. (To be very sincere, it did look rather kitsch.) The frame had been in his room in Hong Kong, at least for a while. Now, he could not remember whether he had left it behind when moving from Hong Kong to Singapore. Ah, that was it: he had let a Filipino member of staff have it. Sure, it was a gift from Marco. But not literally *all* his possessions could follow him in his relocations—now Tokyo and soon, please God, Rome—could they? His carved rosewood throne (of the Qing dynasty) had been expensive enough to ship to Japan.

Picerno resumed his reminiscences.

WWII brought Japanese occupation to an end in Korea, only to replace it by Communist persecution. Now, in 1976, a farming academy was to be built on the site of the vast Tokwon necropolis. But Marco had been tipped that Pyongyang might forego such profanation as a gesture of good will after the "Axe murder incident" of 18 August 1976, when North Korean soldiers had assassinated two US Army officers in the Korean Demilitarized Zone. Much to Marco Altemps' chagrin however, his trip to Korea was ultimately cancelled. The reason was not Pope Paul VI's proscription of future territorial abbeys, confirmed on 23 October 1976, nor even a change of heart in Communist Pyongyang, but an event of much greater significance for the two friends' Asian policy—the death of Mao Zedong on 9 September 1976. In the months immediately following the death of the "Great Helmsman," much was at stake for the Catholic Church in China. Mgr Dorf was advised to take extra caution so as not to ruin the hopes for a long-awaited improvement of the relationship with Beijing. Picerno then saw it as his duty to ask Marco to postpone his Korean trip so close to the Chinese border, and in a staunchly Communist country where his initiative

could have unpredictable repercussions. Marco was hurt by
the order but submitted to it. Bishop Dorf now realised that,
in that conflict fifteen years earlier, his assistant had already
set Benedictine life against the Asian policy of the Holy See.
Thankfully, common sense and obedience had prevailed on
both occasions.

And now his devoted assistant would prepare the way for
Bishop Dorf's elevation. Would he not?

CHAPTER 9
Death and the Princess

LADY MEUX, OR HER PORTRAIT rather, had given me life again. For the present however, no zebras but two draft horses named "Anastasia" and "burglary" were forcefully driving my life—where to? I did not know. Stepping out of the Frick Collection, I relished the rustle of the October breeze through the gilded leaves along Central Park across the street. As I walked back to my flat, elation and consternation alternated in my heart. Further bad news reached me from England that afternoon: it appeared that my flat in Cambridge had also been broken into. It could not be a coincidence. I was being targeted.

In urgent need of assistance, I had displayed the agreed signal, a half-drawn curtain on the far-left window of my sitting-room. I awaited the confirmation, which should be sent shortly, when on the building opposite the third window above the "Lanvin" sign to the left of the brown gutter pipe would also display a half-drawn curtain. However, after fifteen minutes no curtain had moved in the KGB flat. I was about to dial the secret emergency number when Heinrich himself rang me. His agents in New York had directly informed him of the signal on my window. Heinrich's previous call had been about three months earlier. We communicated a few times a year. His calls had lost their vital importance in my routine, since for decades I had stopped considering myself as a spy, really. I was what they call "a letterbox," just a friendly intermediary on behalf of the USSR which had granted me a profession and an identity thirty years before. However, hearing Heinrich sooner was a great relief, since I required his involvement urgently. As always, we spoke by allusions rather than openly and without providing context, lest the phone wire was tapped by the FBI or the CIA. It was assumed as a principle that Heinrich knew what I had been doing over the past weeks. His voice sounded geographically remote, and tired in fact, with occasional interferences, confirming my suspicion that he was not in America.

"Hello. Briefly, this is going to be tough for you, I know. But the child is in the way. It must go. I spoke with the partner today, and it is the only safe way forward. Technically, can you handle this? Too much is at stake."

"I expected it," I replied, "but how to face it? I have the letter with the official report by the mother, leaked by the uncle. Our encounter is planned for Thursday, tomorrow. I will be exposed unless you find a way. Money is not the motive, it seems. But I might well be pressured into sharing information. As if, in my capacity, I had anything sensitive to hide. Tomorrow at 3pm it is."

"No, not tomorrow. This evening you must get back whence you came this morning and solve the problem."

I became a bit agitated, and objected, "But I don't know the contact's address. Besides, I have been burgled. The flat is in an absolute mess but nothing is missing. I don't understand what they were after. And I got a phone call from England half an hour ago. My caretaker in Cambridge said my lodgings were also broken into today. What on earth is going on?"

"Calm down Ken. The address is well-known: it is the same lab where you inspected the item yesterday."

Heinrich had realised that we were talking at cross-purposes sooner than I did. Whereas I thought "the child" whom he meant was young Anastasia, my alleged daughter and likely blackmailer, he was referring to the painted child hidden under the surface of Vermeer's *Woman with a Pearl Necklace* on display at the Jeenaco Tower in Chicago. Because the situation was too complex to be dealt with safely over the phone, we resorted to the customary outdoor meeting with his anonymous representative.

I was sitting on the agreed bench inside Central Park's Dene Summerhouse, a rustic sort of spacious tree-house set on a mound. Someone came to stand on the other side of the bench. It was a woman, with a Labrador on a lead. The dog sniffed me without particular interest and went back to its mistress. I could only see her back. She was sitting casually on the banister above the rough bench. While stroking her dog and pretending to talk to it, she uttered the code meant for me. "Are all the squirrels gone?" I recited, "Your dog may have frightened them." She validated, "A pity, I had brought peanuts." Then she transmitted Heinrich's instructions.

With a shudder, I realised that my superior and long-time friend was ordering me to use my expertise not to restore or authenticate Vermeer's painting, but to damage it. For the first time in my life, I was to delete an element genuinely included by an artist in his masterpiece. The fact that it lay hidden under the *Woman*'s dress made no difference to me. Nor was I sentimentally upset by the human shape of the target. As I stressed to Heinrich—that is, to his female representative—had the shape of a flat-iron been concealed in that underlayer, I would have been equally opposed to its erasing. I would have objected just as much if the "partner," i.e. Jeenaco—how bitterly I now resented that firm!—had schemed with my boss for the deletion of the hidden lute on the chair or of the map on the wall. Anything that pertained to the integrity of Vermeer's painting, whether visible to the eye or not, had a strict right to be respected and preserved.

As I spoke, my unease grew with my insincerity since, to my dismay, I was finding myself partial to the child's shape, contrary to what I had spontaneously claimed. Count von Lebzeltern's letter read to us in Leningrad thirty years earlier came back to my memory. It described an uncompleted Vermeer. For decades I had hoped to find that painting, an alleged *Annunciation*, leading me to its historic companion, Fabritius' *Mercury, Argus and Io*. Could the *Woman with a Pearl Necklace* be Vermeer's *Annunciation*, obviously modified, enhanced, and transposed to some extra-religious setting by a talented forger such as Han van Meegeren? If such were the case, the human shape detected in the mother's stomach was essential to the composition of the work. It enormously increased the relevance of the painting, and much less than the lute or map could it be done away with.

Heinrich respected my concern, the woman assured me. He was very sorry that this painted foetus had been discovered by me so unexpectedly. But the partner was categorical. She was not at liberty to explain to me why, but a far-reaching undertaking was nearly brought to completion after years of preparation that demanded avoiding the slightest association with concepts such as motherhood and pregnancy. The *Woman with a Pearl Necklace* had long been selected as the "poster girl" for the corresponding campaign and all that was asked of me was to dissolve a cluster of pigments. Generous payments would be added to what I had already received. The woman remarked that the simultaneous searches at my two domiciles could not be a coincidence. Surely "Sammy" (the CIA) or "Georgiana" (the MI5) was behind it. "David" (the codename for Heinrich's New York contact at the Mossad) had just denied any involvement.

In addition, she intimated while still stroking her dog, the timing of Anastasia's alleged letter seemed highly suspicious. Why would she reach out to me just now, for the very first time in twenty-eight years? Clearly this only confirmed that I had recently trodden on some critical ground. Since my latest intervention was the discovery of the Vermeer's baby *pentimento*, there was good reason to assume that this was just what had triggered the two break-ins and the letter. The intruders might well have been looking for visual evidence of the painted foetus assumedly concealed in my flats. They must have guessed what major hindrance would affect our partner's plan, hence "Lioubov" (the KGB), if the visuals were made public. Thus, she enquired, was I "categorically positive" that I had not archived even a small slide of the Vermeer foetus in some discreet cache, or dropped one behind a plinth or skirting?

Of course, Heinrich's representative insisted, if my artistic scruples deterred me from flying back to Chicago that same evening, I was free to remain in New York and meet my "daughter" the following day. But if she was genuine and meant to have me repent of my crime, soon enough leading newspapers in Europe and in America—as she threatened—would reveal to the world that I was a woman molester and a Soviet agent. Since "Lioubov" could not help me prevent Anastasia's untimely disclosure, they were bound to make use of the opportunity at least and to stage it as my "detonation," causing maximum collateral damage among the scientific art establishment. "Detonation," I recalled, was the expression used by Heinrich during my early initiation in London in 1950. I would be "suicided"—a body meant to be mine would be found in my flat set afire.

Conveniently discovered intact after the arson, my handwritten confession would emphatically deny my being a Soviet agent, but would admit to Ida's rape and to my having forged most of the so-called discoveries achieved through my radiographies. Evidence would be gathered from my flat, and more would "surface" in various quarters, incriminating dozens of main gallery directors, prominent art dealers, international auctioneers, major insurance companies of cultural assets and fellow art experts now exposed as my accomplices, with "authentic" extracts of correspondence, records of our meetings in fashionable clubs and luxury hotels and detailed proofs of the bribes received—all faked or distorted. "Lioubov" had dedicated departments for such make-believe and the set-up would not take longer than a week—even down to four days if under pressure. The poisonous list of "accomplices" would soon be leaked to the media if "Sammy" (the CIA) or "Georgiana" (the MI5) tried to cover it up.

Dozens of first-rate paintings currently worth tens of millions of dollars would lose their value; the credibility of major galleries would vanish; cabinet ministers in charge of national cultural patrimony would fall. The magnitude of the impact would far, far exceed the conviction of Han van Meegeren, since he had dabbled only in Vermeers, while I had analysed masterpieces by a wide range of painters. In keeping with my "confession," the USSR and East Germany would flatly deny that I was a Soviet agent. They would reveal that I had not left East Germany of my own accord, but rather had been tried and expelled since my proven abuse of a female co-worker was a disgrace to Communist morality. Lust, with capitalistic greed and ambition, were the true motives behind what the West had praised as my "defection" in 1950. Simultaneously, "Lioubov" would instruct leftist media and politicians to make the most of the occasion. They would denounce the international collusion between art, finance and politics as further proof of capitalist manipulation, and would demand drastic cleansing of the rot in Western governance and culture.

Meanwhile, I would be exfiltrated to Moscow for debrief and formation upgrade. There, I would be invited to clarify whether or not I had committed the crime against Comrade Ida Kravitz, lest my confession twenty-eight years earlier had been obtained under duress, as my file suggested. Psychiatric assessment would be granted based on modern techniques successfully implemented under the current leadership of "Lioubov" (i.e. Yuri Andropov, head of the KGB) against imperialist agents, but equally in support of mentally defective Soviet operatives. These checks were routine procedure for agents back from the field after such a long time as myself. Beyond the twenty-year threshold, sleeping agents were prone to imbibe the enemy's mentality, regardless of their intended loyalty to the USSR. Capitalism influenced them unbeknownst to them. It was what made them undetectable, hence lethal. But of course, they needed intensive psychological care on their return home. If or when "Lioubov" were satisfied with me, I would probably practise my painting expertise in the USSR collections again, and possibly teach at a Moscow university, under a new name. My life in the West would be over of course. On the contrary, if I accepted the job in Chicago, a car would take me to a private jet this very afternoon. I would be back tomorrow and the wealthier for it. Meanwhile, "Lioubov" would solve the "Anastasia" problem and my life in the West as a sleeping agent would continue unchanged.

The lady's Labrador was now allowed to fetch a ball, giving me time to make up my mind. I tried to ignore the fear gripping my heart following the woman's thinly veiled threat of psychiatric internment in Moscow. I sought to analyse the situation with courage and honour. I would not cowardly surrender to instinctive self-preservation nor cling to bourgeois comfort. Being branded a woman's abuser should affect me less, emotionally, than any suspicion cast upon my trustworthiness as an art expert. But they wanted me to act against the most basic rule of painting conservation: "Thou shalt not tamper." If I did not, they would proclaim my alleged immorality and my usurped fame as an expert. Would I choose to become known as an assaulter according to Anastasia's claim, or as a forger according to theirs? I could be accused of lust, I felt, but not of fraud. That would cast suspicion on all my previous expert finds. Rivals would jubilantly support the claim that I had invented, not discovered, the radiographic shapes.

Where did I truly belong? Where did I wish to spend the rest of my life? England? America? Japan? Germany? Russia? Central Park spread before me in gilded autumnal sunlight with the Manhattan skyline behind it. Further away, in England, the spires of Cambridge and the Fitzwilliam Museum shone in my recent memory. In comparison, what was Moscow to me? I mean, of course I was an agent of the USSR. Having awakened in 1945 with no identity, no past, no friends, no future, no trade, I owed Heinrich, Wittenberg and Moscow more than I could ever repay. But was I ready to leave behind nearly all my life—at least the part I remembered—merely because I was a scrupulous examiner and restorer? "Thou shalt not tamper." Who would ever come to know of that baby shape under Vermeer's *Woman with a Pearl Necklace*? Vermeer was long dead; so was the woman sitter. So was her child, if she ever bore one. So were Fabritius, and Lebzeltern. So were my Hiroshima fellow-citizens. So would I soon be. Meanwhile, "Lioubov" was very much alive and its outreach was ubiquitous.

Until yesterday morning in Chicago, in the private lab at the Jeenaco Tower, no one had ever guessed the existence of that painted shape. At the same time, a very faint voice, or loud but sounding as if perceived across a very great distance, seemed to affirm otherwise. It claimed that the author's design had to be respected, regardless of who knew of it. It implied that the integrity of a work of art encompassed its genesis, its history, its various layers and anything that had affected its existence and still adhered to its substance. Whoever came across such signs, however tenuous or fragile they might seem, was honour bound to preserve them instead of tampering with them.

As to "Anastasia," the remote possibility that such a young woman might exist and considered me her father teased me more than I cared to admit. Memories of my teamwork with Ida in Moscow and Leningrad flashed back. Ida reading a book in the garden at Wittenberg, wearing that—yes, that yellow silk blouse I was fond of (chromatically speaking). What a woman: so professional, so focussed and yet, so—how to put it? Well, to meet Ida's daughter, here in New York and at my favourite New York gallery... Would she look very much like her mother, whoever her father was? Could I not persuade her of my innocence? Might we not even become friends? Was there anything I could do, even after so long, to assist her and honour the memory of her uncle, dear Professor Chimek Kravitz?

That man had been my mentor. He had guided my first steps, as that of a toddler, along the arduous but rewarding path of picture analyses. I suddenly felt ashamed of myself for having never tried to reach out to him. I had feared his reaction, since he clearly considered me his sister's aggressor. I had felt at the time that it was better left to heal with time.

In addition, Professor Churakov had expressly ordered me to keep away from Professor Chimek Kravitz until further notice. Well, his notice had never come—until this day? Professor Kravitz was a strong advocate of "non-invasive" interventions in paintings. Our modern tools, he reckoned, provided us with a vertiginous insight into any given painting without requiring any physical intrusion. What would a man like him think of erasing Vermeer's baby *pentimento*? Indeed; and how would "Lioubov" react if I did not erase the baby's shape?

As the limousine dropped me at the Jeenaco Tower that evening with my two trunks of equipment, I still did not know what I would choose to do in that lab of theirs. If I was quick enough, I might be back in Manhattan before 3pm the following day, in time to meet my alleged daughter at the Frick Collection. Meanwhile I would see Vermeer's *Woman with a Pearl Necklace* again. I might ask her what she preferred. Should not the decision be hers, after all? Surely her child was not mine, was it?

The lab had no windows. It was far below ground level, judging from the direction of the lift we took. Three Jeenaco employees escorted me down with my equipment. One was a guard, the second was the lawyer who had me sign a document the day before and the third was the Chinese-looking gentleman who, at the conference, had expressed concern about my third finding. We met no one on the way as my visit was taking place after office hours. It was about 9pm. The *Woman with a Pearl Necklace* was standing in the middle of the room. Still looking at her mirror while tying her jewel around her slender neck, she would not tell me her preference. She seemed unmoved by the forthcoming procedure.

I decided merely to inspect the painting out of scientific interest. The Chinese-looking man did not object when I slowly glided the radiographic probe across the picture. I was doing it at random, merely trying to gain time, when to my surprise I discovered yet another *pentimento* in the folds of the dark-blue tablecloth. Originally the flowing material did not conceal so much of the table leg and floor tiles. Now, its altered position made the only visible foot of the table more conspicuous. It was highlighted by the two white fragments of the tile surrounding it, as if mirroring the other twin white reflections of the window against the dark china. The two pairs of white irregular shapes were at the same distance from the horizontal edge of the table, above and below it, as if the lower pair reflected the upper pair. I commented aloud on my unexpected find, in an attempt to woo or distract the Jeenaco executives.

But the Chinese-looking one became suspicious of my intentions. He pointed out that my discovery of the altered folds of the tablecloth had nothing to do with erasing the child from the woman's stomach and commanded me to proceed without further delay. I was about to comply, when I met with a more spectacular discovery. It was not a *pentimento* this time, but a microscopic depiction of a male figure, probably a reflection of the painter himself, upon a shining part of the composition. I had encountered before such discreet signatures or "*mises en abyme,*" but never any so minute as to be unnoticeable to the naked eye. It had taken my radiographic probe to detect the tiny chromatic signal, painstakingly displayed across that meaningful area of the picture. What on earth had Vermeer meant to tell us through that code? Forgetting Jeenaco, Chicago and even the KGB, I was instantaneously consumed with a yearning to elucidate the mystery, when the guard came to stand between me and the radiographic screen, his arms crossed against his chest, forbidding further investigation. I felt like Archimedes killed by a Roman soldier in the siege of Syracuse when, captivated by a scientific problem, the Greek genius failed to heed the order yelled by the brutal invader. How could this brutish employee interfere with what might prove to be my most significant finding on Vermeer so far!

I was not Archimedes. I was weak. Still, I kept my finding to myself: Jeenaco would not have me erase that other
small shape! The Chinese-looking man pressed me to "get
to work." Glancing with shame at Vermeer's gracious lady
on her stand in the middle of the lab, I knew that a decision
had been made for me which I did not have the courage to
oppose. At my request, the *Woman* was turned back to front.
The small human shape she carried was more safely reached
from behind, since any changes would be less detectible than
through the painted surface on the side opposite. (Also, that
way I would not meet the eyes of the young Dutch mother.)
I put on my surgical protection, although I would not touch
the object with my fingers, only visiting it from a distance via
a remote-controlled probe. The canvas was laid to rest upon
a sheet of firm foam, its frame tightly caught in light presses.
Since the intervention was microscopic, avoiding the slightest
vibration was essential lest colour alteration got blurred. As
I anticipated, the lower horizontal stretcher bar of the oak
frame ran pretty close above the targeted area of the canvas.
But I managed to position the small probe in the shallow
space between the wood and the canvas: a fine, plain-weave,
linen with a thread count of 21×15 per cm^2, I reckoned.

Sitting behind the protective screen, I set to work. To
my surprise, I found that the infant shape had been applied
directly upon the whitewash canvas prime. It predated the
later composition, as if Vermeer had first painted a foetus
and only later decided to add a woman, and finally the furniture and the entire room we knew around her. Significantly
though, he had positioned the silhouette of the woman above
to coincide with the baby's shape beneath. Nothing would
have prevented him from having the concealed foetus under
the table, or behind the wall. Instead, it fitted perfectly the
natural location in the woman's superimposed womb. By contrast, I then checked, the lute and the map had been painted
after the chair and wall supporting them; even though they
had been concealed later on, making the wall look bare and

the chair empty. Thus, the foetus had been the very first item depicted on the virgin canvas.

It was a baby boy, almost the size of my thumb, his head downwards. As the tiny probe descended into the painting, my screen displayed as a mine pit the randomly selected square hole resulting from the four threads of the canvas fabric crossing perpendicularly. The probe delved further in and the whitewash against the stretched linen was quickly behind me like some evenly spread mist soon travelled across. I finally landed on the cloudy three-dimensional shape of the child. Saving minor variations, ivory was its dominant colour, with lead white as the main chemical component. Ultramarine also showed for shading the flesh tone. I identified particles of complex sodium-silicate with sulphur. Above the child or rather "behind" him, as it appeared to me since I was accessing via the rear of the painting, spread the woman's yellow jacket combining a white underpaint and lead-tin yellow, black and ochre.

I came out of the painting again and examined the best course of action to be deduced from my survey. A full range of organic pigments such as used by Vermeer was part of my equipment. I could apply a solvent on the child to dilute his contours and then paint upon him a new whitewash, blending in the original canvas primer. But recreating the white priming of the canvas out of external ingredients would take much too long and, more importantly, it might betray my intervention, since my pigments were several centuries younger than Vermeer's. Prudently, I chose instead to extract micro samples from the original whitewash on the edges of the painting. I gently sucked them out one by one with my suction device and implanted them upon the baby shape. With the microlaser, I then melted the ivory base of the child's shape and I spread the newly applied whitewash upon it with a solvent through a very thin injection needle. A further intervention with the microlaser completed the absorption of the baby shape into the primary canvas whitewash beneath it. It was a lengthy and tedious procedure. I had to take extra care to position the whitewash implants at irregular distance from each other so as to look more natural, concealing the use of my apparatus.

I took a break after midnight. The three men had understood that questioning me further only delayed the work. They were dozing in their chairs, although every time I glanced at him, the Chinese-looking man seemed to be keeping at least one eye open. Around 2am I examined my completed work. Altogether I had performed about seventy implants, covering the entire shape of the child. Thankfully, the ivory colour and the canvas whitewash blended well into one another. Some ultramarine still showed for what had been the shading of the flesh tone, but limbs, trunk, head or chest were now so blurred as to elude anatomic identification. No one could have said a baby once lay there. There were mere chromatic variations across the inconspicuous white expanse of the plain lead-white and chalk, the ingredients used in canvas priming.

I invited the two Jeenaco executives to take a look at the screen. The lawyer compared the microphotography displayed with the printed one he had kept from the day before. In his hand we could see very clearly the baby lying on his lead-white blanket, while the live picture on the screen proved the baby gone. The original matter was still there, but broken up thinly, melted and absorbed into the stronger and even white coat of the canvas beneath. No more could one guess that a human shape had once lain there than perceive a melted snowman on sea ice. The Chinese-looking man scrutinised the screen, asked for further zooming in and eventually had me print out cellophane proofs. He finally declared himself satisfied and, on behalf of Jeenaco, signed a substantial cheque which the lawyer handed to me after I had signed the receipt. I could not stand facing the painting again, and let it lie flat inside out while I packed.

Back in the lift, reaching the ground floor took much longer than on the way down. On walking out, I realised that I had been transported all the way to the top of the building, as they meant to take me back to the airport in a helicopter. That was a promotion. If I had failed in my mission, would they have had me get back to the plane on foot? As we rose from the helipad, I could not help admiring the aerial view of Chicago by night. We flew by the Sears Tower, the tallest building in the world since three years earlier. In comparison, the Jeenaco Tower, now standing on our left, looked almost modest in size. But its distinctive shape and silvery aspect made it immediately recognisable. "The Needle" was firmly planted into the urban fabric whose countless lit avenues intersected perpendicularly as warp and weft in woven material. Down "The Needle," deep into the soil, Vermeer's fair lady lay, her lovely face looking down into firm foam. She was missing something, but who knew?

On the plane, I tried to pacify my heart. I had not actually cut out or destroyed any substance in Vermeer's masterpiece, had I? All that had taken place in that basement was an alteration of form. A given form one might describe as child-like had been attenuated with no prejudice to the overall purpose of the picture. The hidden form had become even less perceptible admittedly, whereas on the surface, the visible contours of the lady, meant for display, had retained their intended harmony without losing a hint of their integrity. What is a form anyway, I questioned? A form depends on scale, on perspective, on range. If the observer changes his vantage point, the form changes with him, does it not? This is just what Holbein showed us, for instance, through his *Ambassadors'* anamorphic skull. The form of the skull is there, but barely perceptible until we step to the right. Well, I had done just that in Chicago. I had changed my vantage point and the form had changed. I had swapped ivory pigments for plain white ones, or colour for non-colour. But the pigments arranged within the dark frame of Vermeer's *Woman* were still there. And around her lovely neck, not one pearl was missing.

Back in New York before dawn, I walked into my flat, in the same state of wreckage in which I had found it the previous afternoon. There had been no time even to start tidying up. Standing in the middle of the bedroom around ʒam, my study equally laid waste as shown through the door frame, I briefly surveyed the disaster. Shattered mirrors, eviscerated cushions, torn books, heaped clothes, and slashed carpets lay everywhere. Perhaps, I bitterly thought, the succession from order to chaos was just another change of vantage point. As I had reckoned before speaking with Heinrich, I still could not think of anything missing. I stepped further towards the overturned mattress, unwittingly treading on my torn duvet that had been caught under the fallen bedside table. The duvet suddenly burst open, and the area was covered with whitish feathers. I slowly fell on the littered floor, crouched, and soon lay like a lone child amidst the white expanse, sobbing.

Anastasia did not come. I had slept like a log until past 2pm and just had time to take a shower, put on whatever fresh clothes I could grab from the floor, and hasten to the Frick Collection. I was in the cloakroom on time, furtively glancing at any Asian-looking women in their late twenties. One or two smiled back at me, but none introduced herself as my "daughter." Thus, there would be no unsavoury revelation of my alleged crime to the media. "Lioubov" had solved that issue, as agreed in our deal at Central Park the day before. Would my life resume its peaceful course then? I deeply wished so. On the other hand, I would have liked to have met Ida's daughter.

When the cloakroom attendant handed my coat back to me though, a note was included in her hand stating, "St Jean Baptiste Church, 184 E 76th St. Now." Our eyes did not meet, and I was on my way to that church four or five blocks away. It took me past the Church of the Resurrection, my local Anglo-Catholic parish. I would visit there a few times a year, when in New York. It reminded me of Cambridge. But I was in a hurry and walked further to St Jean Baptiste's, whose Italian

Renaissance Revival style I had once noticed. A music rehearsal
was taking place with three violinists. No one awaited me. I
sat down by a green marble column in a side aisle, towards the
front. I was not paying particular attention, simply relishing
the peace and admiring the brightly painted ceiling.

Soon, I realised that the tune sounded very familiar. Like
a phantom or angel from a long-faded past, the melody rose
and swirled as it used to, decades earlier, from the cellar
of the little house at 12 Mauerstrasse, Wittenberg. And I,
nearly thirty years younger, felt as if standing on the landing
outside my room in 1948, my eardrums expanding around
every note played, like the thin palms of a child cradling
soap bubbles as they soar in the warm afternoon, whose hollow spheres enshrine a living mystery and whose iridescent
surfaces, soon burst, reflect his fragile innocence. A poster
at my left announced a performance of the "Biber Rosary
Sonatas." The rehearsal lasted nearly an hour. I had heard
this music before in cherished circumstances, not knowing
then what it meant. It took me a little while to come to terms
with this revelation. Could it be that the fifteen or so pieces
of music played every day after work by Professor Kravitz
and Ida had been Roman Catholic music, and devotional at
that? If so, had it not been worship, right under my nose?
It had taken place in the cellar "so as not to disturb me," so
they had said. I felt something change in the depths of my
heart, or awaken, rather. I was not sure what it was. I surely
would not have called it *faith*, although it did feel spiritual.

I knew Christianity well. It was inevitable when living in
Europe in the 1950s and further afield, and all the more when
analysing classical paintings. On the other hand, I had failed to
explore Heinrich's discovery of my likely Catholic past. I had
been, he had suggested, an art teacher at a Catholic school run
by the Canons of St Augustine in Hiroshima. Moreover, he had
implied, I was possibly a lay member of their order. Why had
I not enquired further about this essential part of my identity?
I think I had been afraid. More deeply, it now appeared to

me, I had been angry. I had resented God for allowing the destruction of all that I held dearest: my country, my family, my trade. If religion had once been part of it, all the more was God responsible for giving my memory back to me. I would leave it to Him. I had dug long enough, and in vain. Years had gone by, turning into decades, until altering my posture had felt too late, or too upsetting. I wonder now, though, whether under the ashes of my desolate resignation, embers of faith had not kept burning all along. My zealous involvement in classical art, largely Catholic, might well have been an attempt, more or less conscious, to retain some connection with my forgotten religion, in case it revived spontaneously.

From my side pew that afternoon at St Jean-Baptiste, I could see the violinists well enough: one man and two women, one of whom looked Anastasia's age, partly Asian if not Japanese. She was wearing a long sleeveless black velvet dress with broad straps on her shoulders. The dexterity of her fingers on the instrument was remarkable, but her face impressed me more. Her long black hair was tied back, con-trasting with her pale skin and enhancing her lofty brow. She exuded neat confidence and self-effacing competence. Her eyes were shut as if she were asleep. Her graceful features alternatively displayed sadness, determination, suffering, and gentleness. It was like watching her dream at night. But the tense and brusque gestures of her head and thin arm holding the instrument tight against her neck proved that she was very much awake. I had watched Ida play her violin. She looked just like her daughter (if that Asian violinist was Anastasia): no less gracious, no less precious.

I wished she would play on, for the sheer joy it gave me, and for fear of what might happen next. Would she come to me, or leave? What was I supposed to do? Why had she not met me at the gallery, instead of sending me that message? Had "Lioubov" reached out to her and deterred her from meeting me? If so, surely the threat had not disappeared. I might have been followed to this church. I looked around, but failed to identify anyone suspicious. Worse, since this encounter was taking place perhaps by "Lioubov"'s permission, was Anastasia perhaps sent by them? Did she merely have Heinrich's approval, or was she working for him—that is, for "us?" I had taken for granted that she had no connection with my secret activities, even though she would have known of her mother and her uncle's involvement in a Soviet cultural program, as her letter showed.

The music had ceased. Having packed their instruments, the musicians walked to the side talking in a low voice before separating. Then, Anastasia knelt by the tabernacle. I waited. She rose and genuflected. Our eyes met as she came, smiling.

She said, "I am Annabel. And you are not my father." At that moment, I wished she had been my daughter.

~~~~~~~~~~~~~~~~~~~~~~~~~~~~

We sat in a quiet corner of the church cafeteria. Annabel was the author of the letter delivered to my flat the day before. Her uncle Chimek had given her my address in America and, after a few weeks, she had resolved to make contact with me. But she had altered several names to elude detection. Her uncle Professor Chimek Kravitz really had died a month before in Wittenberg as the letter had stated. He had been like a father to her, teaching her to pray, and to play the violin from the age of two. He had even made a little violin for her when she had turned seven, with the reassuring precision that catgut was a generic name referring to the bowels not of cats (she was very protective of her grey Raas), but of sheep. Later, Anastasia had changed her name to Annabel and had no further ties with Germany. Her husband was Miko, from South Korea, not Leopold from Hamburg, and their daughter was called Anita, not Ute. Her mother's sister lived in Philadelphia, not in Cologne. Annabel's family had settled in America.

The death of Professor Kravitz had prompted her to contact me at last. Wishing me no ill, she had phrased her message in a way that she hoped would force me to respond. In reality, she had known all along that I was innocent of her mother's fate. Her uncle had told her so, to my stupefaction, on behalf of her mother. Ida had identified her abuser from the start, but the man had warned her that the minute she exposed him, she and her brother would be deported to Siberia. When Ida found herself pregnant, she felt even more compelled to abide by the official version of my culpability, since how would a baby survive in exile? Greater pressures, unofficial but no less threatening, were exerted upon her by Party members to end the gestation which, unplanned, complicated the scheme of the KGB. Well informed of the reproductive legislation in the USSR, Annabel explained to me that the State police was only anticipating the reversal which took place six years later. Indeed, in 1955 Soviet Russia allowed pregnancy termination again, whereas East Germany would wait until 1972. Ida knew how advantageous "losing her child" in compliance with the KGB wishes would have been for her and her brother. But her faith precluded it, much in agreement with her love.

"Uncle Chimek" had supported her in her courageous resistance. Brother and sister would run the risk of deportation rather than harm the innocent child in any way. They were actually sent on a train as far as Irkutsk, but were called back once it appeared that they persisted in their non-cooperation. As Professor Kravitz hoped, he and Ida were found to be too valuable an asset on the team of painting analyses, so that no penalty had followed. Although he later confided to Anastasia that he doubted whether pregnancy complications and childbirth had been the true causes of her mother's death. The untimely end of the heroic mother might well have been the retaliation to be expected from the Soviet administration. As merely an assistant to Professor Kravitz, Ida could be disposed with. The KGB may have allowed the orphan child to be born as a means of pressure on her uncle. Professor Kravitz would feel personally responsible for her and would be less able to dissent now, with a baby girl in his arms. This seemed confirmed soon after, when officials warned Professor

Kravitz never to clear my name with Anastasia, "if he wanted her to live." Uncle and niece were not allowed to leave East Germany; but when Anastasia was twelve, he succeeded in smuggling her West.

As she spoke, I calculated that by then, in 1962, I was securely established as an expert in Cambridge and would have been able to help, had I known. Immediately though, I realised that it would have been akin to treason, since the USSR willed the twelve-year-old to remain on their side of the Iron Curtain. I needed to ask her, "If you know who I work for, why do you reveal all this to me?"

She gave another smile, a bit sad but confident, and responded, "I know for whom you work, but do you? My mother and Uncle Chimek were both convinced that you once were a Roman Catholic. It was Jesus Christ you worked for."

I remained silent, looking in her eyes, then at her lithe hands spread on the table behind her coffee cup. To think that fifteen minutes earlier these very fingers had played with mesmerizing dexterity, drawing such refined melodies merely by rubbing a horsehair bow against catgut strings stretched along a spruce box. Try as she might, though, she would not make me sing the tune she so much wanted to hear. I was not a violin.

She went on, "They prayed for you, Uncle Chimek told me. He confided that my mother hoped to obtain your conversion through her penances. They assumed that you had been sent as their lodger to spy on them, even unbeknownst to you. They were under suspicion of being Catholics and had to be very careful. They never admitted to their faith in your presence, but the Rosary sonatas were their daily opportunity to express their shared belief without too much risk. They could arguably justify the performance as a time of relaxation with music. They prayed for you though while playing, that you might one day awaken to your religious past. Not long before he died, Uncle Chimek was sent anonymous evidence suggesting that you had been a lay member of a religious community in Hiroshima, teaching Catholic art at the school run by the friars."

Her every word reached straight into my heart. Hearing someone I had every reason to love utter my past identity, kept secret ever since Heinrich had disclosed it to me long ago, shook my complacency. But I would not give in. Was there not even a chance, or a risk—that she might have been sent by "Lioubov" to test me? Only Heinrich could have communicated this information to Professor Kravitz. Yet, she had not enquired about their main interest, or Jeenaco's, namely, whether I had retained or hidden photographs of the Vermeer "child" in the *Woman with a Pearl Necklace*.

I challenged her. "Why do you expose yourself like this after successfully remaining hidden for so many years? Don't you fear for yourself and your family? Don't you understand that I regularly report to those whom you know? This very meeting, even the note you left for me at the cloakroom, could soon be shared with those who consider you a fugitive, and forbade your uncle and yourself ever to exonerate me."

Her back and head very upright, a grave smile on her face, she admitted, "You are right. I am taking a risk. I do it for the sake of your soul."

That word touched me deeply. When was the last time, I wondered, anyone had mentioned my "soul," and cared for it? I had a mind, that I knew well, and I applied its resources to my profession. But "soul" referred to a higher plane, a supernatural, transcendent dimension. Furthermore, "soul" implied a divine interlocutor, one eager to pursue a relation-ship, able to retribute and willing to redeem. Before I could react, she was standing with her coat on and her violin case in hand, promising as she left, "I will see you again soon, please God."

I stood and nodded, watching her walk away, gracefully.

Would I ever meet Annabel again? When I visited St Jean-Baptiste Church on the evening of the violin concert adver-tised on the poster, two violinists only, the older woman and the man, were performing Biber's Rosary Sonatas. I managed to speak to them at the end. They said that they did not know Annabel who had only offered to shadow their rehearsal on one occasion, allegedly following a recommendation from the parish. They had been deeply impressed by her talent, and asked me to let them know if I managed to find her address. And had I enjoyed the concert, they enquired, guessing that I was not a parishioner. "October is the month of the Holy Rosary in the Catholic Church, hence the selection of the Biber Sonatas."

I enquired about her at Carnegie Hall, and even at St Patrick's Cathedral. No one knew about a young Catholic violinist called Annabel. In vain did I try to forget her. I felt as if I had lost my own daughter. I admitted to some remorse after not having been more cooperative with her. What if she had been a genuine witness to the vanished faith of my youth?

Weeks went by and, for the first time in my life, I seemed to be losing interest in my work. I had left untouched, after only reading it once, the draft sent by Heinrich for a conference I was expected to deliver on Picasso's *Guernica*. I was becoming disengaged. In retrospect, I suspect that this unprecedented change was connected with the Vermeer incident in Chicago. At the same time, I was trying more than ever to bring back to actual consciousness more lost memories, further to the miraculous reminiscence I had been favoured with when stepping on the Whistler painting in my vandalised flat.

Remembrance was still not prompted at will, alas, but a dream occurred to me twice or more. It involved a bulldozer starting to pull down a house. I had seen it depicted, I reckoned, in a newspaper not long before. It surely was not a painting since the scene was displayed in black and white. A few days later I identified it as the Ipatiev House, or "House of Special Purpose," where the Russian Imperial family had been killed on 17 July 1918 after 78 days of internment. Yuri

Andropov, the then-head of the KGB (or "Lioubov") had the edifice pulled down the previous month, in September 1977, ahead of the sixtieth anniversary of the execution of the Russian Imperial family. He meant to prevent the site from becoming a shrine to autocracy since antipatriotic citizens had taken the habit of gathering in the town of Sverdlovsk to commemorate the death of the Romanovs. The Chicago Tribune had run an article about the demolition.

I don't know why the flashing picture of the Ipatiev House with its rather plain neo-classical façade falling under the bulldozer awoke me several nights in distress and horror. I felt as if something very precious wanted to live on, like a flower rooted deep in the past, which was brutally annihilated instead. That nightmare spurred me to visit my local library and search for the Romanov Family. I learnt that the four elder sisters of the young Tsarevich Alexei referred to themselves with the name "OTMA," an acronym for the initials of Olga, Tatiana, Maria and Anastasia, aged from 23 to 17. A deep emotion drew me to the ill-fated circle of the four princesses, so tragically beautiful in their white dresses, as if I had been the sickly younger brother around whom their love had unfolded the fragile protection of their persons: like the four translucent petals of a primrose sheltering a fallen bee, pride of their regal parents and late-given hope of the Empire.

Probably seventy bullets were shot, as many as the precious stones later stolen from the victims' clothes. Materially speaking, a mere swap had taken place: lead for carbon, or bullets for diamonds. All seven members of the Romanov family had been taken by night into the basement of the Ipatiev House. The killing took over twenty minutes because of the smoke and dust, also owing to the unexpected shield offered by the gems sewn into the clothes of the ladies, that made firing at them less efficacious. As moaning was still heard, the use of bayonets and pistol butts was required, then close-range shooting to finish the work. At least one of the executioners was drunk. There had been no trial, no sentence either. For the Revolution to advance, the family had to go.

Over the following couple of days, the bodies were subjected to the most violent forms of desecration in an attempt to conceal their identities. I knew I was being sentimental, but much as I tried to think rationally, invoking the liberation of the proletariat that had followed the end of Tsarist Russia as I had been taught, I failed to exonerate fully the USSR from the Ipatiev ignominy. The thought occurred to me that a regime that could show such a horrendous lack of taste and decorum was perhaps not genuinely interested in classical paintings after all. For the first time, I wondered if as an art expert I had been serving an "unaesthetic" power.

As if guessing my difficulty despite the great distance, Heinrich rang me on 28 October. Much to my surprise he invited me to terminate my involvement with him on behalf of the KGB. Why so suddenly, and after so long? What justified such a drastic change? Had I disappointed them, or become useless to them? He would not comment, even though we parted friends. I theoretically became a free man, but I was feeling more burdened and confused than ever. I thirsted for affiliation and yet, no one wanted me. I had my paintings, but they did not breathe. I was esteemed—but who would love me?

I fell into depression.

CHAPTER 10

The Terracotta Army

LYING ON HIS BED AT THE TOKYO Nunciature, Bishop Dorf attempted to smile despite the left end of his mouth still being paralysed. The future looked brighter for the hemiplegic bishop. Marco Altemps would soon be back from his Benedictine retreat in Italy and before the summer he would wear his red hat as cardinal. Less than a year later, sadly (*sadly?*) ... Ahem—less than a year later, *as diagnosed*, Cardinal Altemps would have died of cancer and Jacques Pommard would request him, Bishop Dorf, to accept the red hat meant for him in the first place. After such a successful service to the Church in China, he deserved it, didn't he?

Picerno revisited the succession of events that had led to his most daring diplomatic initiative in China. Yes, 1976 had been the real turning point in his career. And Marco Altemps had unwittingly caused it.

Various Chinese officials were greatly relieved by the demise of Chairman Mao in 1976 and hopes rose high for significant improvement for the Catholic Church, no less than for Chinese economy and culture. Mao's Cultural Revolution had proved disastrous. Over the past decade, the illustrious history of China had been savagely erased to create a new Chinese (Communist) man instead. Countless works of art and monuments of immense cultural importance had been destroyed. Providentially though, conscientious Communist officials had managed to conceal from Chairman Mao and his barbarians the most stupendous archaeological discovery in the history of modern China: the "Terracotta Army"! It had been found by chance, two and a half years before Mao's death, by a group of farmers digging a well in Lintong County, outside

Xi'an in Shaanxi. An assistant of chief archaeologist Zhao Kangmin was an underground Catholic. In December 1975, his report on the discovery reached Mgr Picerno Dorf in Hong Kong. Not much was made of it since old clay statues could obviously not help improve the fate of the Catholic Church in China. But when nine months later Mao's death revived hopes for a better relationship with China, Picerno saw in the terracotta army a golden opportunity for his Asian policy. Truly, this had been his hour of genius and yet very few people had been aware of it.

Mgr Dorf would always recall the moment when, as he was subjected for the umpteenth time to Marco's moaning about his cancelled trip to Korea, a daring plan had suddenly unfolded in his mind. Both men were chatting in their office in Hong Kong, located at the Secretariat of the Federation of Asian Bishops' Conferences. Marco was holding a satellite picture of the necropolis at Tokwon Abbey procured by a contact at the American embassy. Like sheep flocking by a barn, countless tiny rectangles showed around the darker outline of the abbey church razed to the ground. Marco repeated, "So many tombs. They trusted in the protection of the Church, and now we won't lift a finger to prevent the profanation of their graves."

"You know we meant to try if Mao had not died."

"Speak of the devil! Precisely then, how is it possible that in Communist China mere terracotta soldiers are carefully preserved, while south of the border in Communist Korea, actual remains of Catholic people, the true soldiers of Christ, will soon be bulldozed to create a farming academy!"

Yes, Picerno recalled, that was just when his brainwave had occurred. He had been gazing at Hong Kong Bay through the window, distractedly listening to Fr Altemps' recrimination as he tried to concentrate on the real issue of the day, namely, how to take advantage of the political vacuum left by Mao's death. As if the solution had been sent him by some invisible messenger, he had felt something suddenly click in his mind.

Turning towards Marco's desk, he had slowly reached for the picture of Tokwon Abbey, becoming aware of a most creative connection occurring in his brain. Could it be that the Tokwon necropolis might offer the perfect template for a much more ambitious rescue plan? What if... Bishop Dorf quickly walked to a filing cabinet, feverishly scanned the labels of various folders, selected one and, with secret exultation, opened the brief report sent to him the previous year about the Terracotta Army discovery.

He extracted a picture of the archaeological site and laid it next to Marco's picture of the Tokwon necropolis. The clay statues were probably twenty-two centuries old, the report estimated. They reproduced with startling diversity the distinctive faces and weaponry of thousands of life-size warriors with horses and carriages set as a protective guard by the Mausoleum of the First Qin Emperor. Yes, what if the Terracotta Army in Shaanxi became a symbol for China's magnanimity? Mao's Cultural Revolution had ignored (but not destroyed) this archaeological treasure. What if one persuaded his successors to display the discovery, not to boast of China's imperial past—Revolution forbid!—but to show how happily the autocratic oppression of old had been superseded by Communism. In between the lines, one might even dare to draw a parallel with Mao himself. Now that Hua Guofeng had removed the Gang of Four and secured power, the Terracotta Army could be seen as a symbol of the authoritarian policy of his predecessor, while his new tenure could herald an intelligent and magnanimous transition into the "post-Mao Communist China."

Absorbed in his scheme, Mgr Dorf had sat down as in a dream, totally oblivious of his surrounding and of Marco's inquisitive glances.

In that context, Picerno had continued, might not some sort of an agreement with the Catholic Church be envisaged? Yes, that was it! The underground Church was just like the buried army of Emperor Quin. The Party saw underground

Catholics as deplorable remains of imperialism, and yet, conceding some restrained recognition of their stubborn presence might come across as mighty benevolence on behalf of the new Communist leadership. A token of magnanimity demonstrates power much better than brutal persecution. Hordes of Communist schoolchildren might soon be shown the Terracotta Army as an impressive example of "imperial tyranny, when so many men were forced to labour and die for a monarch and his nobles." But they would also see the beauty and greatness of these stunning works of art which might impress them and, perhaps, even attract them. Similarly, brokering some sort of improved official policy, however ungenerous, with the Catholic Church might flatter the new Chinese leaders. Underground Catholics would be portrayed disparagingly, of course, but it would still improve their recognition and their hopes for better treatment.

Picerno closed his eyes. Rapt in political ecstasy he saw, unfolding in his mind, the very name of the new policy. Prophetically he murmured, "A secret meeting... With Mingdao, my hidden friend at the Chinese Patriotic Catholic Association, and senior officials from the Chinese State Administration for Religious Affairs... Some agreement, negotiated and signed... right by Emperor Qin Shi Huang's Mausoleum in... Lintong. Yes! Yes! Yes! The 'Lintong Agreement'! The 'Lintong Agreement,' which will be the historic new threshold for Catholics in China! What Cardinal Tisserant's 'Borny Agreement' was to Russia fourteen years ago, my 'Lintong Agreement' will be to China. The 'Lintong Agreement,' a masterpiece of Chinese psychology imagined and soon achieved by... By me, a modest but dedicated—and imaginative—servant of the Church in Asia."

Fr Altemps was back at his desk, typing some routine report. Mgr Dorf looked at him from behind, while his heart experienced an unexpected surge of tenderness towards his collaborator. His mention of the Tokwon necropolis had unwittingly provided Picerno with the political template he

desperately needed, and yet Marco was unaware of the importance of what had just taken place in the mind of his superior.
Altemps' fortuitous remark had occasioned in Picerno's active
brain a plan of crucial magnitude. What moved Picerno was
the gap between the incidental suggestion of his friend and
the strategic importance of the consequence still hidden from
him. It was like when St Augustine of Hippo, once tormented
by agonising intellectual uncertainty, had been prompted to
adhere to Christianity on hearing a child in the adjacent garden in Milan innocently sing a song "Tolle, lege"–"Pick up
and read!" The finest rhetorician of his time had recognised
the providential coincidence and, taking and reading at random his Bible, Augustine had received the confirmation he
had sought, turning him into the greatest Christian thinker
of the first millennium. Augustine might have looked at the
child over the garden fence a bit like Picerno had looked at
Marco: that is, as at a childlike angel unaware of the significance of his remark, as the subsequent success of the "Lintong Agreement" amply demonstrated. Yes, looking back,
this impromptu conversation in their Hong Kong office had
been Picerno's "Tolle, lege" moment.

It had taken less than a year to persuade the Chinese
authorities. Their rising leader, Deng Xiaoping, was pragmatic and understood the benefit of the proposed agreement.
Fr Altemps, Mgr Dorf and a couple of other Catholic officials
had been flown from Hong Kong directly to Xi'an airport,
whence Government cars had driven them to Lintong. The
first meeting had taken place that afternoon after a brief
presentation of the Terracotta warriors. Resting their elbows
on the metal railing, the guests had leaned in awe, contemplating the countless fierce-looking clay warriors, down below
surface-level. So many of them, and all different, as if they
were actual soldiers petrified, awaiting some resurrection.
Picerno recalled Marco's upset when finding out that he was
not included in the more important negotiations that followed.
Instead, he was driven with other lower-ranking diplomats

and less opulent American investors to further visits of the Terracotta Army. A more thorough exposition was granted them than the official presentation given to Picerno and the top brass. Marco became quite an expert in the archaeological site. The original finding had proven to be only a small part of the treasure. It was named "Pit One", after "Pit Two" and "Pit Three" were discovered, covering an area of over 20,000 square metres.

Meanwhile, the Chinese official in charge of the negotiation had affirmed that the People's Republic of China welcomed the unearthing of the Terracotta Army as a parallel for the Vatican's good will to collaborate with Beijing in exposing seditious agents of the underground Catholic Church. As the clay warriors bore culpable witness to China's imperialist history, so the Vatican was to lay bare its network of underground Catholics as a token of a new chapter in its relationship with Communist China. On reception of the list of agents, the official Chinese Catholic Church (that is, the Chinese Patriotic Catholic Association) would be pleased to commit to a protocol of collaboration with the Vatican. Mingdao, the inconspicuous friend of Picerno's at the Chinese Patriotic Catholic Association, had hailed the proposal as a success.

As Mgr Dorf walked to and fro in the garden of his residence that afternoon though, he bemoaned the dilemma he was faced with. On the one hand, his plan had worked perfectly. Chinese national pride had taken his bait. The stupendous archaeological discovery of the Terracotta Army was accepted as a symbol for a new religious policy with the Catholic Church. On the other hand, how could the Church betray her underground network? He longed to seek Marco's advice but his junior was not part of the negotiation; he would certainly have protested vehemently against giving up courageous underground Catholics anyway. The only option was to deliver names associated with the imprisoned Bishop Kung—the Communists would relish this!—only after having warned these clerics and laity to move to alternative hiding places. Did the Communists suspect anything, or was their main goal to show power? Whatever the answer, two days later, on 29 August 1977, the "Lintong Agreement" was signed. While officially kept secret from the general public, it was hailed by both the Chinese and the Vatican administrations as a great success. Mgr Jacques Pommard had praised it as "a daring amplification of the 1962 Borny Agreement," signed with the Orthodox Church and the KGB in Metz.

Such a feat had secured Mgr Dorf's diplomatic clout over the following fourteen years. He had preferred to work in the background, even turning down Mgr Pommard's earlier offer of the red hat. In hindsight, saving the red hat for later had been a mistake. But who could have expected this insufferable business of the "Showcasing Dissent" spy accusation at the beginning of the week! Thankfully he had not refused to be made a bishop ten years earlier. And there he was, recovering from his stroke in the Tokyo Nunciature, awaiting the return of Marco Altemps, his reluctant stand-in for the cardinalate.

~~~~~~~~~~~~~~~~

The sick prelate manoeuvred himself out of his bed. His left leg and foot felt alive again. With great caution, he managed to reach his antique Chinese armchair and sat with relief in the carved rosewood throne of the Qing dynasty (on permanent loan from the Chinese Patriotic Catholic Association, as secured by the ever-thoughtful Mingdao). Please God, once Marco would be made a cardinal, Picerno might even be able to fly to his luxury villa in Xi'an, nestled against a hill on the other side of Lintong Farm. It had been well over six months since his last diplomatic trip over there. In the meantime, as agreed, the staff would have planted a grown six-meter-high Chinese "chouchun" or "tree of heaven" to take the place of the one fallen in the earlier tempest. The accidental vista had opened a view of Lintong Farm in the hollow of the hill. No tractors could be heard across the vast electric-fenced area, and the several daily helicopter flights to and from Xian Xianyang International Airport sounded less intrusive than a vacuum cleaner. From Xian Xianyang, precious Jeenaco cargo was flown every day straight to Chicago. Had he lived in Michigan, he could have benefitted from such a convenient route, indulging in a monthly visit to his Lintong villa (for diplomatic purpose). But no airlines flew direct from Hong Kong, Singapore or now, Tokyo. Admittedly, the state-of-the-art aluminium architecture of the "farm" buildings made it a landmark. Nevertheless, as the Communist official had remarked when assessing the damage to the treeline after the storm, the partial sight of the nearby facility whose wide flags bore the Uweena logo ("some capitalist cosmetic brand") spoiled the enchanting landscape designed around Bishop Dorf's villa. He had therefore agreed to have it concealed immediately.

Picerno felt thirsty. Where had that Hana woman gone again? She had dropped the Kokura Memoirs while he slept and left the room. What was it about? He remembered some letters by a Dutch Jesuit in seventeenth century Japan. What was his name again? Had Hana read to the end while he rested, or perhaps skipped some chapters? Had he missed important information? He would call for her.

Hana had not offered to read further from the memoirs for two reasons, the latter of which would have led to her immediate dismissal or arrest.

First, as the official housekeeper she was quite busy cooking a batch of lamb cutlets as spiced curry with hearty vegetables, until she wondered whether His Excellency might not prefer to have the cutlets grilled and served with salad instead, in case his health condition made spice unadvisable. Should she not have enquired beforehand? She meant to do things exactly as a genuine housekeeper should.

Hana's second reason was that, while the bishop was asleep the previous night, she had "borrowed" the hundred-and-twenty-or-so pages of the Kokura Memoirs and "lent" them to her handler. Before breakfast the handler had returned the original to her and a facsimile. While the original was surreptitiously laid back on the bishop's desk, she was given only one more day to extract any relevant information from the facsimile now hidden inside a recipe book on a shelf in the kitchen of the nunciature. She would find excuses not to read aloud further the memoirs of the alleged Japanese agent, if His Excellency asked her again, as that would take her much more time than she had left to meet the deadline imposed by her department. She worked under great pressure. How long could she carry on being a spy, though?

Hana opened the cookery book as if looking at the lamb cutlets recipe, and continued to read Ken Kokura's memoirs—faster and silently.

CHAPTER 11

Delusion, Paris and Cubism

SPENT NEW YEAR'S EVE 1978 ALONE. I was seriously depressed and in growing need of medical assistance. The following letter sheds no reassuring light on my state of mind in early 1978.

Wednesday 7 March 1978, Los Angeles
Confidential
ATT Professor Ken Kokura, 841 Madison Ave, New York, NY 10021, United States

Dear Professor Kokura,

I trust this finds you well. Further to our meeting yesterday, you requested me to send you a detailed memo of our conversation at my office. You sought this report from a third party as an objective witness to help you overcome the delusion which you suspect affects you. I will do my best to put in writing exactly what we discussed. You had asked to see me for professional advice. I reminded you that although I am a mental health consultant, I do not specialise in pathologies affecting the memory. My field is Post Traumatic Stress Disorders. I focus on military personnel, lately in the aftermath of the Vietnam War. However, because I have had knowledge of you at a very early stage in your recovery process from amnesia, namely, in August 1945 near Hiroshima, I agreed to offer my expertise.

I will first recapitulate the facts you shared with me. You told me that a man named Heinrich had telephoned you last year, on 2 November 1978. You had first met him in Japan in March 1946. He had arranged for you to study art history in Wittenberg, Germany, and had guided you in the early years of your career as an art expert. He recruited you as a KGB spy while in London in 1950. You last saw Heinrich face to face on 4 March 1950 when you were accused of a crime and ordered to move to England. Since leaving Germany in 1950 you spoke with Heinrich over the phone only. He would call you every month until around 1961, when his calls became less frequent. Since 1972, you reckon, Heinrich has only called you twice a year. His representatives would meet you in public places about three times a year, following agreed signals such as half-drawn curtains. In your last-but-one conversation with him on 28 October last, you were surprised that he would not discuss any business. He preferred merely to chat about your possibly buying a dog (he insisted on a Golden Retriever, whereas you fancied a Labrador), and the more elegant shade for the new wall paint in your refurbished New York flat.

During your final conversation with him last November, Heinrich informed you that he meant to withdraw totally from your life. He asked you not to be troubled. He congratulated you on the excellent results achieved. He stated that he would not contact you further and that you were free to carry on your professional activity as if the bond with him and his administration did not exist anymore, or had never existed. Indeed, Heinrich indicated to you that it was safest if the memory of him since you left Germany was henceforth considered fanciful. To help you in this new approach, he affirmed that you had inaccurately assumed him to be politically involved, when he had always only been a university administrator and nothing else. He denied having contacted you since 1950 and claimed that the very conversation you were having with him at that moment was a figment of your imagination. He encouraged you not to worry but suggested that you might consult a mental health specialist if you felt the need. You think, but are not quite sure, that he mentioned my name further to our having met again last August at the Peacock Room event in Washington. You were deeply troubled by his staged disappearance. Later on, you started wondering if there was anything objective in what he had affirmed. You recalled that the meeting with Heinrich's representatives never took place face-to-face. You also realised that the identification protocols with these interlocutors could have been random conversations with passers-by in outdoor settings such as Hyde Park in London and Central Park in New York, or public venues such as the main art galleries in large cities. Last week you doubted whether the entire relationship with Heinrich since your relocating to England in 1950 had been real. You then contacted me for advice.

My interpretation is that such lasting delusion is plausible in your case. You confided that your mental health had never been professionally assessed since leaving the camp where we first met in 1945. Such systematic and detrimental omission on your part, for twenty-seven years, clinically surprises me. It may betray a pathological fear of confronting reality lest painful memories were identified in the process. Your physical recovery was most encouraging according to your impressions. You stated that daily sword exercises have efficiently stabilised you. Your intellectual faculties quickly returned after your ordeal and enabled you to reach academic and professional excellence. But your existential memory still has not been reactivated. You deplored the fact that biographical and emotional data connected with your family, childhood and primary education are almost non-existent. I agree that the reminiscence, last October, of the winter walk and stepping on the iced surface of a puddle was a significant breakthrough. By your own admission, this was your very first reconnection with your life before the 1945 trauma. I concur that it may lead to more such connections made.

But over the twenty-seven years that elapsed since you survived Hiroshima, the absence of personal memories might have been compensated by what we could call hypothetically the "Heinrich delusion." For want of a recalled emotional background, your mind might have built up the fictional relationship with Heinrich. His surname is unknown to you, so you said, unless "Heinrich" was his surname, not his first name. Last February, you wrote and telephoned to Wittenberg University in an attempt to identify "Heinrich." Your own identity and degree were acknowledged, but despite the many details you provided about Heinrich's role as your mentor and his selecting of students from Asia after WWII, the University has not been able to find a member of staff whose profile matches your description.

You were never charged with committing a crime, nor did the University mention this in their reply received last week. They stated that you were transferred to Cambridge University for another doctorate connected with seventeenth-century paintings at the Fitzwilliam Museum. You were appointed assistant curator there. From your arrival in England onward, your life is easily verified—but for your relationship with "Heinrich." I cannot rule out the possibility that you simply imagined the recurrent conversations with him over the phone, as well as the meetings with his representatives. "Heinrich" can have developed in your mind to satisfy the need for a friend that would connect you with Japan, Wittenberg and your subsequent assignments.

Furthermore, "Heinrich" entrusted you with an "emergency telephone number" altered every time he rang you. You told me that several times over the past twenty-seven years you were about to ring him but never did, for on each such occasion he was the one who contacted you first, within a few minutes. When speaking with you in my office yesterday, I asked you to dial before me the latest "emergency" phone number given by "Heinrich." You became extremely agitated, expressed strong reluctance, invoked compliance with the established protocol and the absence of proportionate danger. On the chair where you were sitting, you brought your folded legs against your chest and clasped your arms around them, adopting a foetal position, while you whispered like a mantra, "Unprotocolary. Unproto-colary. Unprotocolary." You finally let yourself be persuaded: you dialled the number and we both heard the speaking clock in Reykjavik, Iceland. I pointed out that "Heinrich" could not be contacted at that number. You affirmed that Heinrich had communicated this erroneous number on purpose last Novem-ber, to facilitate the severing of your relationship. I asked you if the previous "emergency" numbers could be dialled, but you answered that you successfully erased each previous number from your memory when receiving the next one, as the safety protocol dictated.

As well as meeting your need for an exclusive friendship anchored in your earliest memories, in my opinion the "Heinrich delusion" provided a satisfying explanation for your place and ties in society. Like most *hibakusha* or Hiroshima survivors, you grieved for the loss of meaning when the world you had grown in disappeared. Humans are social and political beings, and the mere confines of your profession were felt as too tight to provide you with a "Weltanschauung" or worldview. The assumption that you were a sleeping agent for the USSR, serving the cause of a global political organisation such as the KGB, satisfied your natural craving for meaning and relevance on a global scale.

You do not recall ever being involved in the Communist party. It is very likely that you never were co-opted as a Soviet agent either. Most probably you simply were, and are, a learned art expert. You looked very embarrassed on hearing my statement. I encouraged you to ask any question you may like since anything might help your assessment. You then admitted that a voice was suggesting to you, at that very moment, that I was a KGB agent simply following the instructions of "Heinrich." I told you that it would only hinder you further if I denied it, although I would not confirm the assumption either. As I type this memo though, I find it useful to affirm, for the sake of the objectiveness that you seek, that I belong neither to the KGB nor to the CIA. I am just a loyal American Catholic doctor.

You asked me to offer a diagnosis. I hesitate to do this after meeting you only for the second time in decades as a patient. With caution then, I can affirm that your profile seems to match the definition of schizophrenia, a mental disorder manifesting in frequent or permanent episodes of psychosis, entailing hallucinations, delusions and paranoia. In addition, although I am not qualified in art commentary, I would recommend that you ask yourself if you have not exhibited a tendency to perceive meaningful connections between unrelated things, such as patterns in composition and symbols. If such were the case, the diagnosis could be refined as apophenia, a type of cognitive bias which affects patients with high intellectual capacities, notably among the scientific community.

Against this hypothesis stands your interpretation of Raphael's painting, as I will now describe. Among seven images printed on paper randomly spread on my desk, you selected the only Renaissance work of art, depicting *The Wedding of the Virgin Mary* currently in Milan (Brera Gallery). I had suggested that picture test in the hope that it could reconnect you with our very first meeting in Japan, and might elicit some lost memories. I noted that you overlooked the Vermeer I had included (illustrating a luxury cosmetic brand recently advertised), as well as Hokusai's *Great Wave off Kanagawa*; an attractive Canaletto; a blue Picasso; and a couple of other paintings.

The Raphael, you said, was a good example of a composition in mirror. At first glance it looked like two paintings stacked one on the top of the other. The upper one could be called *Classical temple in a Tuscan landscape*; the lower one only seemed to refer to *The Wedding of the Virgin Mary*. You suggested that the somehow irrelevant upper half was in fact designed as an architectural equivalent of the ritual event taking place below it. You explained that the peristyle surrounds the tower like the ring does the finger of the Virgin. This, you stated, was a brilliant analogy of proportionality. You argued that Raphael had almost slavishly imitated an earlier *Marriage of the Virgin* by his master Perugino, only to differ about the outlook of the tower. Perugino's building is octagonal and merely flanked by four canopies. On the contrary, Raphael smoothed the angles and connected the canopies. He chose to make his tower cylindrical like a finger, and surrounded it with a peristyle as a ring. Thus, you concluded, the temple is a metaphor in stone of the nuptial gesture. I agreed with you that this parallel immediately unified the overall composition of Raphael's painting.

In an attempt to connect this with your need as my patient, I asked you if you did not see in it a metaphor of your life. You wondered in what sense. I said that the seemingly irrelevant upper half of the painting could figure your life since the 1945 trauma in Japan. In contrast, the meaningful bottom half would stand for the lost first half of your life. The invisible horizontal line separating the two halves could be the surface upon which you stand—the present time as you perceive it. Stooping as from a jetty, you exert yourself to lift up lost memories from beneath and set them above where meaning is sought. You would not comment upon my hypothesis, but you pointed out that I found your analysis of Raphael objective, thus ruling out apophenia, at least in that instance.

I agreed with you; but I maintained that your mind found more in the Raphael painting than you were aware. That painting attracted you among seven because it offered relevance to your entire life as an art expert. Allow me to venture the following assessment of your profession in light of the comments offered in this memo. You specialised with notable success in identifying lost elements in the composition of famous paintings. This is likely to fulfil your unconscious desire for lost personal memories. You performed with radiographies of images what you failed to achieve with your erased past so far. The surface of a painting is to you like the glass wall forbidding access to your existential history. It is my sincere hope and my prayer, dear Professor, that it might soon be granted you to step into your past prior to 1945, with even more success and personal fulfilment than what you competently accomplished as a leading art expert.

Yours faithfully,

Dr Yuko Tanaka, M. D., Psy.D.

Dr Tanaka's memo changed my life. A trusted third party, someone who had assisted me in my very first mental steps in 1945, was declaring null and void my identity as a Soviet agent. I cannot say that it convinced me, for how could I accept overnight that I had deluded myself for nearly thirty years? But it broadened my perspective and made me feel freer. I was an art expert. I was not the Tsarevitch since unlike him I had escaped the Soviet grip; but like the dead little prince, four "sisters" had watched over me from within their wooden frames: *Lady Meux*; Vermeer's *Woman* with pearls; Georges de La Tour's *St Irene* (the Louvre had asked me to confirm the authorship of this masterpiece lately surfaced in a chapel somewhere in Normandy); and Raphael's *Virgin*. In imitation of the *OTMA* acronym based on the names of the four Romanov grand-duchesses, I fancied that *LWIV* was the best combination of the four initials of my painted protectresses.

~~~~~~~~~~~~~~~~~~~~~~~

I had been back in England for five months when Yamato rang me in November 1978. He was in the middle of another "Telluric Tour," in Spain this time. The itinerary had started near the island of Ibiza, off the Mediterranean coast of Spain. There, an impressive limestone rock can be seen towering over the sea. Called "Es Vedrà," it is believed to be the tip of Atlantis, the sunken city. Yamato had experienced deep magnetic harmony when holding his sword, alone at sunrise on the top of the mountain. "The rock of Es Vedrà has had only one inhabitant, a Catholic hermit called Francisco Palau y Quer," my friend noted. His writings on Carmelite meditation had fascinated Yamato, so close they seemed to Buddhist spirituality, he confided. But I was in no fervent mood and I barely congratulated my friend on his findings.

"However," Yamato went on, "Es Vedrà is not why I am contacting you. Since then our group has travelled to various locations and we have reached the foothills of the Pyrenees in the north of Spain, at the junction of the two ancient routes of the Camino de Santiago de Compostela, the 'Camino Frances' and the 'Camino del Norte.' It is an area deeply loaded with energy, owing to the millions of pilgrims who walked these paths until the European Renaissance at least. We haven't met any pilgrims around here, but there was much interest for the sword spirituality lesson I gave at Guernica, a town in the Basque Country where we are presently.

"But listen, last night we stayed at a nearby mansion where I took part in a seminar on Buddhism. The remains of an old Roman road still show in the park and, according to local tradition, Christian Emperor Charlemagne would have travelled it on his way to Ronceval, back to France. Now Ken, you are not going to believe me I expect, but I wonder if I have not found where you come from."

I remained silent because I was still mildly depressed and unwilling to express interest in further riddles concerning my erased past.

Yamato explained, "Japanese students used to stay here before WWII. It is close to the cradle of a major Catholic religious order called the Jesuits, and during the Spanish Civil War about twenty Jesuit students from Asia were moved away from the conflict zone for shelter in that mansion. I went for sword practice upon a small hill behind the house—a ridge with an inspiring view over the estate and the country all around. There was a bench there and a stone cross bearing a Latin inscription with names and dates. I did not understand what it meant, but I noticed the word "Nagasakiensis" and suspected it referred to Nagasaki. The birth date carved by that name looked like 29 August 1920. Mr Jallier, the owner of the estate, said it was about the late Fr Xavier, a relative of his. He had never known him and asked his mother for details. She nearly cried when telling us that Xavier was a young kinsman who used to stay with them on vacation with his parents. Let me repeat to you what she said.

"The young man's father was a Japanese diplomat to the Spanish government. When the Communist forces came nearer the Jesuit noviciate in the Basque Country in 1936, the superiors feared lest their Asian features would make it impossible to conceal the identity of the twenty young students. Mrs Jallier's husband was inspired to offer them his house as a hiding place since it was secluded enough and separated from the conflict zone by a river. Wearing plain clothes rather than their black cassocks, Xavier and his fellow-students stayed there around seven months before being sent back to their home countries to complete their training. Because of WWII, Xavier was promoted to the priesthood sooner than planned and was to be ordained a priest in August 1945. The then-bishop of Nagasaki, Mgr Paul Aijirō Yamaguchi, was away, Mrs Jallier had been told, but a visiting Jesuit bishop was to have ordained the candidate. One does not know for sure because any evidence, apparently, vanished in the bombing, including Fr Xavier's body which was never found again."

I listened to Yamato's story with growing trepidation. But I was feeling irritated, rather than interested.

I finally snarled, "Thank you for your report, Yamato. But you seem to have forgotten that, if anything, I might have been a friar in a different Catholic religious order, the Canons Regular of St Augustine, not the Jesuits; based in Hiroshima, not in Nagasaki. Years ago, you thought I had been a Buddhist monk from the Mitaki-dera Temple, then a gardener at the Hiroshima Prefectural Industrial Promotion Hall. You also gathered evidence supporting my former training as a sword master in connection with samurai ancestry. In truth, I find this random digging into my alleged past rather cumbersome. What makes you think that there could be any connection between that Fr Xavier and myself? To start with, I don't speak Spanish. And by the way, how could a Japanese be a relative of a Spanish family?"

Yamato hesitated. I could hear that he was taken aback by my aggressiveness. Finally, he added, "I don't know. I am sorry to have upset you, Ken. It's when the old lady mentioned that Xavier was a talented painter. She showed me some of his works called 'crucifixions,' 'annunciations,' 'nativities'—all meant as 'illustrations for Christian catechism,' she said. Well, I just thought you might come and see for yourself. I would, if it could shed light on my past."

~~~~~~~~~~~~~~~~

I did not go to Spain. Jaded or depressed, I managed to drag myself to France later that month though, just before the closing of the Foujita exhibition which had run for the past eight weeks. That major retrospective on my late painter friend had been held at the "Centre Culturel Japonais" in Paris for the tenth anniversary of his death. In my weary condition, dreading large official gatherings, I had stalled for as long as I could. But to the formal invitation I had received as an acquaintance of Foujita another had been added, this time in my own right as a Japanese expert in paintings. The theme of this other exhibition opening at the "Chapelle de la Sorbonne" was "Japanese Illustrators in Paris." I had contributed an article to the catalogue, and finally I travelled to the French capital.

It was raining as I walked across the "Quartier Latin" towards the Sorbonne. Held in the decommissioned baroque chapel of the University, the exhibition was pleasantly eclectic. I met with Japanese artist Setsuko Ideta whose young daughter Harumi looked strikingly, I imagined, like little Anastasia if I had known her when she was five: both children were born to Eastern European and Asian parents. I was not very impressed by a series of drawings by Akira Kurosawa, which I found violent and messy, even though I still esteemed him as a powerful film director. Then I had to shake hands with the new mayor of Paris Jacques Chirac, the patron of the exhibition and a Japanese sumo enthusiast.

Just as I was hoping to be left alone, the exhibition curator asked me to settle a friendly disagreement between two Paris-based Japanese fashion designers. Both sought a fitting depiction of some woman in Edenic peace, borrowed from famous paintings, to use on a forthcoming dress. On the wall to their left, Issey Miyake was pointing at three of his sketches for a pleated fabric displaying Vermeer's *Woman with a Pearl Necklace*, which the Uweena advertising campaign had raised to unprecedented fame. But Kenzō Takada was trying to convince his colleague that Douanier Rousseau's *Le Rêve* (*The Dream*) was a much more varied source of inspiration. He had reproduced the painting as a décor for his first collection eight years earlier. I was not fond of Naïve art such as Rousseau's paintings, but I wished even more to spare my beloved *Woman with a Pearl Necklace* further irreverence as a commercial commodity. I therefore prudently suggested that Rousseau's jungle might offer a wider variety of natural shapes than would a domestic scene such as Vermeer's *Woman*. Miyake replied that for an outdoor setting he would rather use Jean-Dominique Ingres' nymph from *La Source* (*The Spring*), which was originally displayed amidst actual plants and aquatic flowers. I wish I had known at the time that Miyake was, like me, a Hiroshima survivor. I would have liked to speak with him about his life journey and mental resilience.

After a while, feeling tired, I left the main group and went to sit apart on a chair by the sanctuary of the former church, opposite a statue of Cardinal de Richelieu, a mighty patron of fine arts under King Louis XIII. What would the Cardinal have thought of the present exhibition, I wondered? I did not really think myself a believer, and yet the clash between the exhibits and the religious purpose of the sacred building made me feel awkward. Elegance and simplicity defined its architecture, whereas the heteroclite display bore no connection with religion.

As I gazed randomly, my eyes were drawn to some large illustrations, as of a children's book, on a side wall. I walked closer to examine them. Suddenly my heart ached and my stomach felt upset. It had been a long time since the side-effects of the atom-bomb had bothered me. I sat shakily on a stool, drinking my glass of water all in one go. Perspiring, I tried to analyse what was going on in my mind. Yes, the image of the children playing along a terrace looked deeply familiar. The sight of that happy band of five or six of them, dressed in somehow timeless pre-War clothes, was eerily painful. There was no denying that I had been one of them. I had stood on that very terrace as a child, a long, long time ago. If not, how could I instantaneously recall that ten steps—neither nine nor eleven—led down to the lawn, as the drawing confirmed? I also identified the statue of a maimed gladiator on its pedestal. With exultation and horror, I remembered that I had broken its wrist, one afternoon, when trying to climb on its back. I must have been less than ten years of age when the incident happened I reckoned. Then, terrified by the likely consequences of my boyish foolhardiness, I had kept quiet when inquiry had been made as to the fallen hand of the statue. And now, more than fifty years later, I was feeling so stupid for fearing to be found out and punished, there and then, in the Sorbonne Chapel.

In a way, that album picture complemented the rose-and-grey puddle reminiscence which had occurred a year earlier in my vandalised flat in New York. What frightened me was the European style of the décor. I knew that I had been a happy child, once in a family estate. But that mansion was evidently not in Japan. It was in Europe, and probably in France. No child in the group displayed Asian features. Was I to believe that I had grown up in France? How tired I was of so many preposterous suppositions. I checked the name of the author. The catalogue introduced Satomi Ichikawa as a Japanese woman who had become famous as an illustrator of children's stories. Born in Gifu, Japan, in 1941, she had moved to Paris thirty years later, and was still living here in 1978. The author of the presentation on Ishikawa's drawings was one "Brother Tristan," whose family had produced the

series *Babar the Elephant*, a seminal piece of children's literature. Then-pianist Tristan de Brunhoff had been an acclaimed
Chopin interpreter and apparently an acquaintance of Ishikawa before entering religious life as a monk four years earlier.
He commented in the exhibition catalogue:

"From my monastic retreat I readily express my gratitude for
Satomi Ichikawa's illustrated children's books. I grew up surrounded by the delightful depictions of the *Babar the Elephant*
saga. They reflected an atmosphere of family harmony and love
of nature echoed in Satomi's work. While the style of the *Babar*
illustrations was attractively plain, Satomi enriched her drawings
thanks to her feminine sensitivity and her Japanese refinement.
Children love her characters, and so do their parents buying
her books.

"Since we speak of children and of adults, may I ask, *what* is
a child? Or, *who* is a child? I lost my father when I was three
years old. Of late, having surrendered to the Heavenly Father my
entire being as a Benedictine monk, as well as my endowments
both external and internal, I thank God who calls me his child.
I am a grown man of 44 and yet, daily I learn to become a child.
Am I being childish, you may wonder? How can one become a
child, and why should one? 'Can one enter a second time into
one's mother's womb, and be born again?' (John 3:4).

"A few decades ago, a Parisian lady known as a philosopher
provocatively wrote that, 'One is not born, but rather becomes,
a woman.' I think that her statement applies better to young age
than to the female sex. To me it seems that, 'One is not born,
but rather becomes, a child.' Our poet Charles Baudelaire aptly
stated, 'Genius is only childhood recovered at will.'

"A greater Poet and deeper Philosopher than those just mentioned, indeed our Lord and Saviour Jesus Christ, announced,
'Unless you be converted, and become as little children, you shall
not enter into the kingdom of heaven' (Matthew 18:3). I thank my
friend Satomi Ishikawa for her illustrated books that rekindle in
adult hearts the innocence and playfulness of one's earlier years,
inviting one to mature into everlasting childlikeness."

Those lines by "Brother Tristan" struck some secret chord
in me. I looked with acute attention at Ishikawa's drawings

framed along the wall. Her style was classical, homely and inviting. A charming attention to detail characterised her depiction of trees and flowers, but also of the games, clothes and attitudes of the children and their pets. Above all, these children were joyful, and I then knew that I had been one of them. Deeply moved by that further revelation of my past (after Whistler's *Lady Meux* the previous year), I was unable to reflect on my childhood as suggested by Brother Tristan. My burning question was, bluntly: had Satomi Ishikawa visited that particular mansion with its terrace, lawn and statues; or had she copied them from some photograph? Even if merely replicated from a book, that house had to exist somewhere. The album had to be on her shelf and its title could be told to me. The house had to have an address and owner; one could locate it. Were I to find Mrs Ichikawa, I would probably learn where I had spent my childhood, or part of it. She was a 37-year-old Japanese. Was she standing nearby, perhaps having noticed my interest in her framed drawings? I looked around me, slyly probing the face of every Japanese woman in the vast edifice. One of them held the key to my coming home, and she did not know it. Would I dare to ask her for it?

NADIR, the *Neo Analphabetic Dada International Review*, Summer 1979

Obituary: Professor Ken Kokura

With dire concern did the shrinking world of ultra-conservative art critics learn of their discreet champion's disappearance. Professor Ken Kokura died in a train accident last 24 June, on his way back from a conference on Picasso's masterpiece *Guernica* — or rather *against* it, as will be shown. The Japanese-born British art expert was the only casualty caused by an explosion onboard the Bilbao-San Sebastian service. It occurred in the First Class carriage, over a bridge, before the train could reach the town of Azpeitia. The Basque separatist group ETA claimed the accident as a terrorist attack, but its rival organisation Iparetarrak argued that ETA was dishonestly using a railway tragedy to pose as more powerful and determined than they truly are to foster Basque independence. The few other passengers had evacuated the fateful carriage, allegedly warned by the train manager still detained by the police. Either Kokura did not understand Basque or Spanish, or he was at the bar when the warning was sent. The impact of the blast was such that the victim could not have been identified but for the documents retrieved from his luggage. Having searched the slopes and river banks in vain, the police concluded that the corpse had fallen into the water and been carried away by the powerful stream.

Chance or retribution, Kokura's demise weakens considerably the pitiable phalanx of antediluvian art critics such as Aussie turncoat Robert Hughes, arrogant snob Kenneth Clark, and antimodernist Yank John Edwin Canaday; not to mention a few other dusty ones of the same obscurantist ilk. Now those 'Three Musketeers' have lost their 'D'Artagnan.' We are not referring here to the rumoured hobby of the late Kokura, namely, *katana* or Japanese sword fighting, but to his deadly art expertise. Unlike his bereaved confreres, Kokura had based his interpretations of masterpieces upon rigorously scientific analyses. We will not deny that he had been a pioneer in art radiography from the 1950s. From time to time, his state-of-the-art x-ray apparatus would grant him chance discoveries of *pentimenti*, some less inconsequential than others. Such findings backed up by modern technology gave his obsolete views on aestheticism a seductive gloss of objectivity, all the more palatable to his bourgeois clientele, all the more deceptive for candid *ignorami* (such as you, O reader, if you think this word is Japanese for 'averagely cultured citizen').

There was something reassuring in the banal outlook of Professor Kokura. His dull green bow tie spreading its wings like a frozen butterfly above a tightly buttoned three-piece suit had become a legendary feature immediately recognisable on picture magazines and television. Coming across as shy and conciliatory, he seemed almost apologetic for having survived Hiroshima. But behind this craftily designed façade lurked an unyielding enemy of modernity. This magazine prides itself on having pierced him through from his early appearance twenty-four years ago. Since then, we followed his progress and unmasked his strategy, which could be summed up in three words: fossilisation (of art), enrichment (of the wealthy), infantilisation (of the public).

The news of our favourite enemy's death reached us as this issue of *NADIR* was about to be sent for printing, precluding a more detailed exposure of his anti-artistic influence. Watch out for our special issue this Autumn, celebrating the post-Kokura era, a welcome breath of fresh air for true lovers of modern art. As a teaser for you now, in that next issue we will expose the scandalous wealth accumulated by such a 'disinterested art lover,' comprising luxury flats in New York and London, a villa on the French Riviera and a private collection of old masters worth several million dollars. If you assumed this would all have been bequeathed to people in actual need, such as famished Cambodians or anti-nuke Hiroshima demonstrators, you are grossly mistaken. It appears that a hush-hush 'Restoration Fund Trust for Dutch Golden Age Paintings' is to pocket it all!

Should any of our readers find our condemnation unkind, would they have us wave instead the '*mortuis nihil nisi bonum*' flag of bourgeois propriety? Let them judge for themselves, then, how the late Professor Kokura treated the victims of far-right tyranny in his testament conference on *Guernica*, as witnessed by *NADIR*'s special representative at the seminar on Picasso's masterpiece, last June in northern Spain. In a world exclusive, *NADIR* is proud to give you here the full transcript of Professor Kokura's last recorded conference.

"Esteemed members of the *Guernica* Society, Reverend Fathers, ladies and gentlemen, may I thank you for your invitation to speak at this fourth '*Bring* Guernica *Home* Colloquium.' You hope and work for the return to Spain of Picasso's masterpiece, still kept across the sea in America. You oppose the prevailing opinion according to which, the relevance of *Guernica* being universal, it rightly fits in New York City, the unofficial cultural capital of the world. Instead, you argue that it belongs to the country whose sufferings it was meant to portray. You stress that the victims of the 1937 bombing of the ill-fated Basque town deserve this honour. Here in Guernica rebuilt, I stand before you in front of a replica of the original *Guernica* painting, the pride of the new Centre for Peace building. As an art expert from Asia working in America and in Europe, I am deeply honoured to contribute modestly to the compelling debate on the meaning and role of *Guernica* today. As a survivor of the Hiroshima bombing, may I express my heartfelt sympathy for the Basque victims of the 1937 tragedy. May they rest in peace.

"*Guernica* is a masterpiece, not of art, but of propaganda. Please note that, unlike George Orwell, I use this word not derogatorily. Propaganda is an essential form of communication that entails the use of fine arts, of intelligence and politics in general. Artistic propaganda reminds us that no depiction is ever neutral. Any artistic representation implies selecting a vantage point, illustrating a worldview and colouring it with one's ideological preferences. Allow me to be forthright. Visually I consider *Guernica* a pompous and unimaginative grey collage. From the angle of propaganda, I admire its efficient conflating of the injustice of war with General Franco's Government; and reciprocally its equating the innocent victims with Communists.

"Let me quote a few public figures to give us perspective. Indeed, if between 300 and 1,000 people died in Guernica's bombing, just one year earlier the Communists had assassinated between 38,000 to 72,344 Catholics priests, monks and nuns during the Spanish Red Terror. Three years after Guernica, in Katyn only, the Soviets assassinated 22,000 Polish army officers. Adolf Hitler, a failed painter, killed about 6 million Romani, Jews, Western Christians, Poles and Ukrainians in concentration camps. In Soviet Ukraine from 1932 to 1933, Joseph Stalin orchestrated the Terror-famine causing 3.5 to 5 million victims. Mao Zedong starved 35 million innocents to death in 1959-61, not counting political torture and assassinations. But let us limit ourselves to city bombing, for the sake of accuracy. During the Blitz in London, from September 1940 to May 1941, the Nazi Luftwaffe killed some 43,000 British civilians. In Dresden on 13 February 1945, American and British bombs killed 35,000 German civilians. Allow me to conclude these statistics of horror with my own country. In Japan, when bombing Hiroshima and Nagasaki on 6 and 9 August 1945 respectively, the Americans killed between 130,000 and 225,000 people, most of whom were civilians. I survived. In comparison, neither the number of victims nor the degree of injustice explains why Guernica, the smallest of modern war episodes, seems to have risen to archetypal status, outshining carnages atrociously more lethal and unwarranted. Certainly, the artistic quality of its eponymous painting fails to justify this.

"Our host at this *Guernica* seminar pointed to my expertise in finding out *pentimenti*, these hidden depictions lying under the surface of famous paintings. 'Have you found a *pentimento* in *Guernica*,' he asked me this morning, 'as you did for Picasso's other work, the *Crouching Beggar?* Are we to expect sensational revelations?' Esteemed audience, the answer is yes. I am pleased to confirm that *Guernica* is a giant *pentimento*. Beneath the alleged war scene, there truly lies...a *corrida*. Let me clarify this.

"The painting was first about bulls, not bombs. Later, the picture was given a new meaning despite no significant changes affecting its composition. Such a stupendous lack of conceptual integrity was concealed through the masterly opportunism of the painter. Pablo Picasso himself told me that this painting had nothing to do, originally, with the bombing of Guernica, for the very simple reason that the town had not yet been bombed and no major artist, not even the Catalonian painter, had ever heard of the little Basque locality. It would make news only in late April 1937. But three full months earlier, in January 1937, Picasso had received the commission from the Republican Government to paint a mural for the Universal Exhibition to be held in Paris that July. He banally selected bullfighting, a Spanish cliché recycled from *Minotauromachy*, his last significant engraving on bulls less than two years earlier. The composition of that picture resembles that of *Guernica* as if reflected in a mirror. No mystery here if one recalls that etchings are inverted in the printing process, swapping left and right.

"Inspiration was wanting though. He did not know how to make his painting strikingly original. Winter was gone, spring had arrived, and still no creative spark. How was he to present his completed work by July that summer? After three months of fruitless labour, Picasso heard of a small Basque town which had just been bombed on 26

April 1937. That was his chance, he realised. Creatively, he decided to twist and bend his *corrida* into a war scene. His close collaborator and model Miss Dóra Maar took photographs of the painting process. A member of the French Communist Party, Miss Maar inspired Picasso's shift from art to propaganda. Until then, he had not been political. He cautiously waited until the Nazis had left Paris in 1944, though, to join the Communist Party, giving in to Miss Maar. Salvador Dalí commented: 'Picasso is a Communist. Neither am I.'

"How did Picasso manage to reframe his corrida as a war scene, you may wonder? Here is the trick, or the genius, if one prefers. Picasso showed himself an adroit *torero*. He performed a dazzling pirouette. To avoid the horns of his original bulls, that is, to hide his want of inspiration about corridas, he stuck a new label all across the canvas, calling it 'war painting' instead. Picasso's friend Juan Larrea recalls how the Communist poet Paul Eluard was the one who had found the new name for Picasso's painting in progress. At that time Eluard was writing his poem *La Victoire de Guernica*. On seeing Picasso's bullfighting scene he exclaimed 'Guernica!' Picasso immediately realised the benefit of connecting his image with the Basque town recently bombed. No matter that his composition included no bombs, no planes, no swastikas, no guns or any modern weaponry, nor any crumbling roofs or walls. Their absence would enhance the evocative power of the work. *Guernica* would be its name, then. I suggest that *Guernica* should be more aptly titled *Muleta*. The 'muleta' is the matador's red cape hanging from a stick. Waved before the bull, the muleta conceals the sword about to be plunged into the neck of the exhausted beast. I say, shake off the muleta! Remove the upper layer of *Guernica*, that is, the alleged war description, and you will find the hackneyed corrida scene.

"Look, it is all before you, hidden in plain sight. Picture yourself in Las Ventas, the large bullring in Madrid. It is 9pm and still sunny and hot. You are sitting among 23,000 fellow-spectators. Suddenly they start yelling. You all rise together like a swelling wave. Why? A *picador* has just fallen from his horse as he tried to pierce the bull with his lance. All look in horror, as the beast paws the sand. The man attempts to crawl away, his leg broken. But the angry bull is now coming back, about to charge and trample upon the unfortunate horseman. To distract the beast (and win a scoop), a journalist flashes his camera. The wife and child of the fallen man scream with fear! 'Daddy!' In the middle of the painting, up here, you can see the *picador*'s horse. Right above it is the flashing camera. The bull is obviously on the far left. The wife and child are below it and the fallen *picador* lies at the bottom. He grabs the sword thrown at him by the *torero* (it is not regular, of course, but a human life is at stake). To the right, the audience is held in suspense, mesmerised by the imminent tragedy. To the far right, a helpless spectator turns his face away from the action, looking at the last sunrays shining over the edge of the vast circular arena. Unless he is praying for a miracle from heaven.

"Thus, war depiction is about as intrinsic to the initial intent of the work, a *corrida*, as would in England, where I live, a painting of a thoroughbred racehorse subsequently acclaimed as the Trojan horse outside the walls of Ilion. This could be a practical joke by the curator of the London National Gallery, swapping the signs for George Stubbs' *Whistlejacket* racehorse and Giovanni Domenico Tiepolo's *Building of the Trojan Horse*. Perhaps the most important lesson that *Guernica* teaches us, then, is the power of naming. That power can be used for good when the name expresses the essence and original purpose of the thing. But it can be misused if arbitrarily assigning a name to a thing that bears no essential relation with it. As a little diversion, you may find relevant this quote from another skilled artist, Lewis Carroll, creator of *Alice in Wonderland*:

> 'When I use a word,' Humpty Dumpty said in rather a scornful tone, 'it means just what I choose it to mean—neither more nor less.'
>
> 'The question is,' said Alice, 'whether you can make words mean so many different things.'
>
> 'The question is,' said Humpty Dumpty, 'which is to be master—that's all.'
>
> (Through the Looking-Glass, *Chapter 6*)

"Esteemed audience, I do not claim to have exhausted the semiotic riches of *Guernica*, far from it. To broaden our perspective, allow me to conclude with a couple of new interpretative suggestions.

"To start with, you may recall that five years ago in New York, artist Tony Shafrazi spread red spray paint on *Guernica*, writing the words 'Kill lies all,' as a protest statement. One could argue that he was merely doing what Picasso himself had done: adding a further layer. First, there was a *corrida*. Second, there was a war scene. Third, there were red letters sprayed, red like the *torero*'s muleta spread in front of the bull. Perhaps, I don't know, perhaps Shafrazi was only bringing the painting to its original stage—a *corrida*. I suppose it was no defacing then, but dutiful restoration.

"My second conclusive hypothesis is that Miss Dora Maar's influence might not have been solely political, but multi-layered. As a surrealist photographer, she would have been acquainted with René Magritte's *1929* seminal surrealist painting, *Ceci n'est pas une pipe*. Magritte's picture is titled *This is not a pipe* despite depicting what objectively is a pipe. Just like Salvador Dalí surrealistically said of Picasso 'This is a Communist,' *Guernica* could be interpreted as Pablo Picasso's surrealist try, if a more explicit title had been chosen, such as *This is not a corrida*.

"I thank you for your consideration."

~~~~~~~~~~~~~~~~~~~~~~~~~~

When giving that last conference in Guernica, I had read almost word for word the text of the draft sent me by Heinrich nearly two years earlier. Unlike my habitual style, his tone was provocative and ironic. No wonder it had infuriated *NADIR* and made other art reviews uneasy. Heinrich had meant it so, I guessed. Still, the emotion caused by my death was comforting. It really sounded as if I was to be regretted. On the whole, my collaborators, my clients and the wider cultured audience deplored my untimely loss. I confess that I did not altogether resist the temptation of watching my funeral on television. Standing by one's coffin and listening to one's eulogies is a phantasm of selfish and weak people. Heroes presumed dead are too busy still to care about posthumous reputation, and truly defunct ones are in heaven, receiving more rewarding palms than any earthly committee can award. But since I was neither a corpse nor a saint, I subsequently drew comfort from the display of affection and esteem following my disappearance.

Not until weeks later, though, did I have the leisure to read or watch the news. The forthcoming days were to prove a turning point in my life: indeed a further awakening.

CHAPTER 12

Grass Snake versus Cyclops

"**W**E CAN HAVE MEAT TODAY, MON-
signor: it is still Easter Week."
Fr Hubert Lambourin's chubby finger pointed
on the menu at the *braciola*, reading aloud for the interest of
Mgr Altemps. "Enjoy our dish of thinly sliced veal, pounded
and filled with *prosciutto*, fresh herbs and nuts. Our *braciola* is
served tied and seared. The robust tomato sauce in which it
is simmered makes it delightfully tender."

Red, like tomato sauce, indeed; or like a cardinal's hat.
Or... Fr Lambourin glanced at his shining red Alfa-Romeo
Spider S4 parked before them between the terrace and the
beach promenade. Under its bonnet sat a 2.0-litre twin-cam
engine producing around 124 brake horsepower. The junior
priest (he was not yet forty) smiled with contentment. Both
clerics had left Rome just before rush hour, and it had taken
them merely three and a half hours to cover the four hundred
kilometres to Carrara. He would have driven faster for the
sake of sport, but the sick monsignor on the passenger's seat
looked alarmed enough by his tamed velocity. It was Friday,
5 April 1991, five days after Easter.

The two priests had stopped at Carrara for supper, on
their way from Rome to Parma. What a delicate mission Mgr
Jacques Pommard had entrusted to his assistant! Fr Lambourin
was to act as chaperone to the exhausted Mgr Marco Altemps
during his few days of rest in a Benedictine monastery in the
north of Italy. That entailed cheering up the sickly cleric
and propping him up somehow. Now that he had accepted
to become a cardinal of the Catholic Church—at long last,
and after much insisting from both Bishop Picerno Dorf in
Tokyo and Mgr Jacques Pommard in Rome—the designated

candidate for a cardinalatial red hat was to be revived sufficiently at least to survive his formal appointment ceremony on 28 June following. Hence the meat dish. But once seated at the terrace of a trattoria by the beach, Mgr Altemps' dejected mood had manifested itself again. Ignoring the commanding view of the sea, he had shyly ruled out the meat courses, commenting that it was Friday. Fr Lambourin was quick to remind him that in Italy, as surely in Japan, the Friday abstinence of meat was lifted during Easter Week.

"Yes, of course Father. You are right. I seem to be losing my bearings a bit after this long journey from Tokyo and the busy time in Rome since landing. Well, then I will have just the same as you Father, the *braciola*. Yes, with a glass of wine, or half a glass as a start; yes, *Rosso di Montalcino* sounds just right indeed. That would do me no harm, I agree. No dessert perhaps though, if we want to arrive before Compline at San Cristoforo, don't you think?"

When the waiter brought the dishes, however, Mgr Altemps looked terrified by the quantity of food and begged Fr Lambourin to accept half of his portion (actually pushing two thirds of his *braciola* into his colleague's plate). His offer was readily accepted by the young priest who set to work with alacrity, tying a large napkin around his neck (since projections of tomato sauce were to be expected in the pressing business of feeding one's famished body) before clutching his cutlery with both fists, ready for wrestling with the veal and *prosciutto*. Mgr Altemps' sign of the cross reminded Fr Lambourin just in time that, even during Easter Week, priests should bless their food before a meal. While eating though, Lambourin observed with dismay how very slowly the monsignor ate, chewing each small mouthful for half a minute before daring to swallow it, and sipping droplets of wine from his half-filled glass more parsimoniously than if he had been a mandarin duck lost upon salted water.

Mgr Jacques Pommard had insisted on relaxation for Mgr Altemps. As the Vatican Head of Asian Affairs, the prelate's aim was double: to restore the future cardinal lest his health worsened and to continue the vetting process as was customary before promotion to the red hat. That second purpose though had not been confided to Fr Lambourin. He had only been told to report to Rome everything Mgr Altemps would do or say, however insignificant (for secretive persons, Pommard knew, are more likely to give themselves away in chitchat than in solemn speeches). Implementing the brief from his superior at the Vatican, Fr Lambourin made sure that their table conversation avoided painful or grave topics. Interested in youth evangelization, he was preparing for the forthcoming World Youth Day to be held on the following 10-15 August in Poland, at Jasna Góra in Częstochowa. Disappointingly though, Mgr Altemps expressed reservations regarding World Youth Day, wondering if it did not feel a bit like "some Catholic Woodstock."

Neither had the monsignor seemed to understand Lambourin's cheery confidence regarding his car engine "coupled with a five-speed manual transmission driving the rear wheels." Ignoring the mechanical excellence of the car, Mgr Altemps had rather irrelevantly commented on the Alfa-Romeo emblem, bearing a large cross on the left and a serpent swallowing a child on the right, "Do you know the meaning of the logo on your car, Fr Lambourin?"

Looking with perplexity at his shining roadster parked below the terrace, the young priest finally replied, "I guess there is some connection with football. The red cross looks like the emblem of the A. C. Milan."

Mgr Altemps nodded. "You are not far, really; not far at all. It is the red cross of the Municipality of Milan, worn by medieval Milanese soldiers during the Crusades. But let me tell you the full story, while you eat. When I was a student for the Vatican diplomacy at the Academia in 1954—correct, you were two years old—a colleague from Angola once staring at an Alfa-Romeo asked me if its emblem was a symbol for the battle between Christianity and Marxism. I sympathized with

him, since his country was in the grip of Communist subversion. Would you believe it: the first Angolan Communist party
was even founded by a priest, the then-Chancellor of the
Luanda Archdiocese, infamous Fr Joaquim Pinto de Andrade!
But I had to disappoint my fellow-diplomat, explaining that
the Alfa-Romeo serpent was nothing more than the '*biscione*,'
a large grass snake which the House of Visconti had on its
coat of arms 'when we ruled Milan,' if I may quote my late
grandmother (*née* Visconti)."

Reassured at seeing Mgr Altemps finally so talkative, Fr
Lambourin made sure to memorise every detail to report
to Mgr Pommard. His learned interlocutor went on, visibly
elated by the recollection from his youthful years in Italy,
"Tradition has it, Grandmamma fondly told us, that the Visconti snake refers to the bronzed serpent brought to Milan
from Constantinople around the year 1000, still displayed in
the Basilica. The sculpture is allegedly 'Nehushtan,' the very
same brazen serpent that Moses had fashioned in the desert,
and which one assumed had been later destroyed by King
Hezekiah, as you may remember."

Fr Lambourin nodded at this, which was a little lie, for he
had no recollection of the brazen serpent being destroyed,
nor of King Hezekiah. His memory of the Book of Exodus
was rather hazy. But he had no time to feel contrite, busy
as he was making mental notes of the conversation for the
interest of his superior in Rome. Those would be compared
with the Kokura Memoirs to assess possible connections
between would-be cardinal Mgr Marco Altemps and the elusive master spy *Showcasing Dissent*. Mgr Altemps brought his
glass to his lips which he sparsely moistened with wine rather
than frankly drinking, whereas Fr Lambourin eagerly swallowed two mouthfuls of *Rosso di Montalcino*. How enthralling
the sight of the sea before them, gleaming under this warm
spring sunset.

Mgr Altemps pointed with his fork at the serpent on the
right of the logo.

"The snake had survived, it would seem. Judiciously, one might interpret the Alfa-Romeo logo as an iconic summary of the Old and New Testaments: the brazen serpent on the right symbolizes the old economy of redemption prefiguring Christ, and the cross on the left refers of course to the Lord Jesus lifted up on the tau of the crucifixion. But it could also mean simply: 'Proudly made in Milan,' since at the heart of the Lombard capital, when looking towards the nave in Sant'Ambrogio Basilica, one can still admire the antique serpent on the right, opposite a bronze cross on the left, both displayed on the twin tops of ancient Roman columns."

Such an exegesis of his favourite car brand made Fr Lambourin slightly dizzy. Car wise, he was more comfortable with topics such as fuel consumption and horsepower. He would have liked to boast of his coupé's acceleration from zero to one hundred kilometres in barely 10.1 seconds. Although his companion's lack of interest in the engine disappointed Hubert Lambourin, he courteously tried to meet the other on his preferred ground, and ventured, "Oh, I see... Then Monsignor, is perhaps the word 'Romeo' a synonym for 'Omega,' since 'Alfa-Romeo' sounds a bit like 'Alpha and Omega,' doesn't it?"

Mgr Altemps smiled briefly and almost painfully before adding, "Well imagined, dear Father, but off the mark, I am afraid. Prosaically, 'Alfa' is merely an acronym for 'Anonymous Lombardian Car Factory,' while Nicola Romeo is the entrepreneur who took control of the company. However, I would support your suggestion of a Shakespearian pun connected with the name 'Romeo,' since the brand surely named their famous model 'Giulietta' in reference to the ill-fated lovers of Verona. If Friar Laurence had owned your fast car, his letter would have reached Romeo on time and the young man would have lived happily with Juliet ever after. 'In war as in love, timing is victory'—as the Japanese proverb has it."

Fr Lambourin did not like his Spider S4 to be mistaken for a Giulietta: the two models had little in common, really, beyond bearing the same Alfa-Romeo logo. But he chose not to correct his interlocutor, and the automobile topic was left at that. He dismissed the vague suspicion, briefly crossing his mind, that Mgr Altemps had been mocking him all along, or perhaps had only been playing with him. No, that would be out of character for such a self-effacing and gentle priest. Plainly, the sick cleric was finally relaxing, just as was expected. Their conversation became a bit patchy and Mgr Altemps' plate was now empty. While enjoying his extra portion of *braciola*, the young priest managed to gather in his memory some elements of artistic culture that might further entertain his valued elder.

"Here in Carrara, Monsignor, marble for the most famous sculptures in the Renaissance was quarried, I believe. Michelangelo's *David* and his *Pieta* for instance, or the Vatican's *Laocoon*."

"Yes Father, I admired the *Laocoon* some years ago. So eloquent, even with the missing arm. That is the drawback with being posted in Asia; I have had so few opportunities of seeing our ancient masterpieces from Europe. But, correct me if I am wrong: was not the *Laocoon* sculpted in Greece, like the *Torso of Polyphemus* which I was glad to see again this afternoon when I popped in at Palazzo Altemps?"

Fr Lambourin nodded again out of politeness, trusting in his colleague's memory. He also made a mental note of this allusion to the visit to the Altemps gallery where Dr Shevchenko had stalked the sick monsignor earlier that day, as Mgr Pommard had informed him. If Mgr Altemps had a shady past or a hidden agenda, he would surely not disclose so spontaneously his whereabouts on his first stay in Rome in years. Beyond his empty plate and glass, the monsignor gazed at the sea with a placid soliloquy.

"The Greeks were quite obsessed with keeping watch, it would seem, whether with one eye only, like Polyphemus the Cyclops, or with a hundred like Argos. Both were giants who ate their captives, as you may recall. For neither of them did it end well, sadly. Talking of sculptures, Chinese Emperor Qin-shihuang felt no more secure than the Greek, obviously, since he had an entire terracotta army set in array around his tomb. The site is worth a visit by the way, if you have a chance."

Feeling on safer ground this time, Fr Lambourin happily announced, "I was there already, Monsignor! Mgr Jacques Pommard, my superior at the Section for Asian Affairs, took me with him once. As you just said, I was fascinated by the number of statues of warriors, each of them with a different expression. Between us, though, perhaps what I enjoyed most was the comfort at Bishop Dorf's villa in the Shaanxi Province. What luxury! Although I wish the locals did not allow shooting parties at night! I was woken up once by barking hounds mixed with almost human screams (as of a woman), and gunshots. Dead silence followed abruptly, as if I had simply dreamt it all. But at breakfast, the villa staff explained that it was routine security drill against poachers at the local farm. Never mind, how breathtaking the view of the mountains! The Government must hold the bishop in high esteem."

"Certainly Father, they certainly do. Bishop Dorf is so dedicated and amiable. But he goes there purely for the sake of keeping good relations. Beijing would have been offended if the gift had been turned down. Well, perhaps I have just spoken too openly. Better forget this, dear Father. In our capacity, discretion is of the essence, isn't it?" Clearing his throat, Mgr Altemps added with slight hesitation, "Ahem; stuck below your left nostril Father, if you don't mind my mentioning, you seem to have a speck of cheese left from your *braciola*—surely tastier than spirit gum. Now, it is getting late: I wonder if I could not ask for a container and keep what remains of my *braciola* for tomorrow, that we might set off."

Glancing at the wall clock, Fr Lambourin rubbed his nose distractedly and finished his glass of wine, reluctantly putting away the dessert menu with its tantalizing *Torta della Nonna*, a custard tart made with sweet shortcrust pastry and pastry cream topped with pine nuts... They needed to be on their way to the abbey. On the passenger's seat, the monsignor nodded and soon fell asleep. Just as well: there would be no chitchat this time. Fr Lambourin seized the opportunity for reflecting on what he had read of the Kokura Memoirs before departing from Rome that afternoon. He had taken the file with him and hoped to complete his perusal soon for reporting to Mgr Jacques Pommard.

It took the Alfa-Romeo barely twenty minutes to reach the nearby hills of San Cristoforo, south of Parma. Although it was dark on arrival, Mgr Marco Altemps requested that Fr Lambourin might turn off his bright beams "out of discretion for the monks." Glowworms guided the car along the narrow road that led from the village, uphill, to the medieval abbey church down in the quiet vale. The mild breeze carried smells of grass and pine trees, and calls of some nocturnal bird or fox, long drawn out and quite loud squeaks. In time for Compline, Father Guest-master led the two clerics to their cells. "You will have all the quiet you need this week, since we have no other visitors booked in."

Fr Lambourin threw his bag on the small bed, put on a cassock and rushed to the abbey church where he was invited to sit in a pew. A lector started in Latin. "*Fratres: Sóbrii estóte, et vigiláte: quia adversárius vester diábolus tamquam leo rúgiens círcuit, quærens quem dévoret...* " The priest checked the English translation provided in his guests' booklet. "*Brethren, be sober and watch: because your adversary the devil, like a roaring lion, goeth about seeking whom he may devour.*" It was good to be reminded of being watchful, of course, even though this peaceful monastery nestled in a quiet Tuscan vale was possibly the safest place in the world.

The monks had just started chanting the first Latin psalm after the ritual examination of conscience when a late-coming religious hesitantly hobbled in. Recognising Mgr Altemps beneath a monastic cape (a long black hooded cloak), Fr

Lambourin recalled that the sickly cleric was a member of the Benedictine third-order under the name of "Brother Enrico." Did that entitle him to wear part of the habit though? On their way there he had boasted of being soon buried in his cape. His circumstances probably justified the privilege. Instead of joining the monks in choir, however, the exhausted monsignor slowly sat down by a pillar in the little nave, took a slow breath as if it were his last, rested his head against the column, closed his eyes and stopped moving, his cheeks and brow looking as grey and still in candlelight as if he had been carved in marble—a placid-looking gargoyle. Two or three psalms later, when Fr Lambourin gave him another glance, it seemed to him as if Mgr Altemps' hood had now fallen down his brow and nose, unless a shadow from the altar candles gave that impression. Below the hem of the black hood, the slightly open mouth of the monsignor vaguely resembled the Cyclops' eye which both men had discussed during supper. "Not a very ravenous Polyphemus, surely," Fr Hubert Lambourin smiled, praying that the future cardinal might last another two months at least. It would be such a pity to die so close to the red hat.

Compline was over and Mgr Altemps had been accompanied back to his cell by the Guest Master. Now there was quiet all around and Fr Lambourin tiptoed to the Guests' kitchenette, seeking rightful compensation for his skipped dessert at the trattoria. He carried a binder under his arm as a reminder that he was not quite on holiday (and to persuade himself that he was about to nibble while working hard, rather than merely skim the document while banqueting). There was plenty of milk, some butter and a loaf of bread for breakfast but, to his consternation, not one slice of cheese or salami, and not a molecule of chocolate. What of his dessert, then! Did these traditional Benedictine monks not celebrate Easter with choccy bunnies? And surely no convenience store would be open anywhere near, at this hour... His stomach contracted, he felt, but it might have been purely psychosomatic. The evening prospect seemed rather gloomy now; all the more since, he now recalled, no television set was visible in his cell or in the guest lounge.

Providentially though, after further searching through the kitchenette, a bag of delicious Cantuccini Toscani biscuits was found in a side cupboard, plus half an open bottle of Vin Santo di Montepulciano. What a trove! He uncorked the bottle, relishing the notes of fresh and dry fruits, almonds, and caramel. Now bringing it close to the lamp, he admired the dark yellow colour of the liquid through the glass. The sugary wine would offer a perfect combination to soften the biscuits. Mgr Altemps would surely survive the night, but the bag of Cantuccini Toscani would not, Fr Lambourin admitted without the faintest pang in his heart as he sat down at the little kitchen table, his back resting comfortably against the sink.

Smelling a second glass of Montepulciano, the priest resolved to carry on with his homework. He unfolded the binder across the small kitchen table and extracted the copy of the Kokura *Memoirs*, handed to him two days earlier in Rome by his superior, Mgr Pommard. So far, he had not found anything relevant to the vetting process of Mgr Marco Altemps. He had cursorily read about that Japanese art expert's formation in Germany and Russia, his assignment in England, the building up of his discreet influence on the stage of international art expertise including trips to Japan, America, France and Italy. Yes, the man had acted on various occasions as intermediary between Soviet agents and Western informants. But there was no sign of any clerics among those, apart from the Superior General of the Jesuits, who obviously was not a "Chinese master spy." Fr Lambourin inserted his nose into the glass, emptied and filled for the third time, as he tried to recall what other Tuscan vine had that distinctively peculiar aroma, slightly bitter or even harsh, as excess of tannins often causes. It was an attractive combination with the Cantuccini Toscani biscuits, though. Ten minutes later, one hand on the *Memoirs*, he distractedly plunged the other hand deeper inside the bag where his fingers finally met with very little edible substance left. How could it be nearly empty so soon, and the bottle as well!

Fr Hubert Lambourin probably did not hear the ambulance later that night, for he was the one carried in it unconscious on a stretcher. But the Guestmaster thanked Mgr Altemps profusely who, on entering the kitchenette to make himself a cup of warm camomile before Matins at 2:00am, had found his colleague groaning, curled up on the floor, and had immediately called for help.

In the middle of the night, several monks were standing on the esplanade outside the monastery. Fr Prior needed to put his foot down to prevent the frail monsignor, that is, "Brother Enrico," from getting into the ambulance with Fr Lambourin.

"No Monsignor! In the name of holy obedience, you will remain here and get some rest. I know he is your friend, but you have already saved his life, possibly. In your condition, you must not risk yours. By your own admission, you just spent the past hour vomiting as well, despite having consumed little of that unfortunate dish you shared for supper in Carrara. I order you back to bed, Brother Enrico. Fr Guestmaster will accompany the patient and assist him with the Last Rites if needed. After all, it is as a guest of our community and under our care that Fr Lambourin fell ill. The rest of us will now resume Matins for his welfare, and yours."

Sheepishly, "Brother Enrico" submitted to his new Benedictine superior. As he watched the ambulance drive the narrow alley up to the main road, he could not help noticing its Japanese brand, a Mitsubishi Delica Super Exceed 4WD diesel. It confirmed the article which he had browsed in the inflight magazine on his way from Tokyo to Rome, stating that three Tuscan hospitals had struck a deal with Japan, much to the fury of Fiat who deemed its 1101 Campagnola entitled to the national market for emergency vehicles. Mgr Altemps was afflicted by an exceptional photographic

memory. Over time, he forgot faces and places like everyone does, but he could read pages of texts, stored somewhere in his head, as if they were displayed in print before
him. Such an amount of data would have crammed his brain
if, by chance, his mental space had not been efficaciously
rationalised over his years of administrative service. He had
successfully applied the method of the "memory palace"
devised by Matteo Ricci, S.J. (the first Westerner to infiltrate the Chinese Empire). Being altogether submissive and
methodical made Mgr Altemps an irreplaceable collaborator,
as Bishop Dorf knew well, back in Tokyo.

～～～～～～～～～

Poor Fr Lambourin was now incapacitated, Mgr Altemps
reflected. Through the arched window of the guests' corridor, he glanced at the Alfa-Romeo of his young colleague,
stranded on the car park. It shone in the moonlight. What
was that furtive shape, over there, that leaped onto the wing
of the sports car, now jumping onto the passenger's seat as
if ready for a ride? A fox! Probably attracted by the smell of
the fatal *braciola* left in the glove compartment, the elegant
canine was trying to open it.

"Would it succeed?" Mgr Altemps asked himself as he
walked further along the corridor. The fact is, he liked foxes.
In Tyrol, they had magnificent red ones.

Closing the thick oak door of his cell, he sat at the little
desk and opened the file rescued earlier from the kitchenette.
He guessed that a couple of creased pages must have been
the ones which Fr Hubert Lambourin was reading when,
collapsing, he had fallen upon the volume. It looked like
a genuine copy of the original found in the Archive of the
Tokyo Nunciature three days earlier, on Tuesday, 2 April.
Bishop Dorf had probably faxed the text to Mgr Pommard,
who had shared it with the unfortunate Fr Lambourin. Despite
feeling rather tired by then, "Brother Enrico" thought it
timely to inspect the document.

Before leaving Tokyo he had read the Memoirs to the end, including those historic letters by a Dutch missionary Jesuit in Japan. Thus, he already knew that no objection would be found in the text against the elevation of "Mgr Marco Altemps" to the cardinalate. But he was very interested in any *handwritten* comments by Fr Lambourin or his superior. With little time left until the end of Matins (he did not wish the monks to see his light still on when he was meant to rest), he went straight to the page where he expected to find manuscript clues about the identity of *Showcasing Dissent*. After tracking innocuous scribbles with his finger down the margin, he turned the page and found a separate sheet inserted in the file. He read it conscientiously and whispered to himself with a smile of delight. "You little scoundrel!"

PART THREE
The Orient

CHAPTER 13
Calling it Home

THE CONFERENCE IN GUERNICA HAD been my farewell to art expertise. "Professor Kokura" was no more. Now hiding in northern Spain under a new identity, I was given no time to reflect on how it felt being dead. Yamato had masterminded my end. His training in the paramilitary forces and later in the police had enabled him to organise the explosion on the train. Guessing that I would disapprove of such a violent stratagem, he left me out of the preparation. A smoke cartridge which he had set up in the First-Class carriage forced the few passengers out into the Second-Class compartment. At a curve in the scenic route, over a bridge, the train was to slow down before entering a narrow tunnel for an incoming fast train to pass us by. Unrecognisable beneath his white balaclava worn under a traditional black Basque-style beret, Yamato detonated the bomb soon after, having scattered my most identifiable belongings along the rail track, even down into the river stream below us. I am pretty sure that I saw some printed sheets of my *Guernica* conference float by, and sink.

We escaped on foot along a woody path to a cache where he had left our new luggage. Older than I by a mere five years as it turned out, and looking roughly like me as far as Spaniards might distinguish between two unknown Japanese, he had me take on his identity while he would go into hiding. We were to meet two months later, on 25 August, at "Es Vedrà," the uninhabited rock near the Island of Ibiza, where he planned to spend a long eremitical retreat. Meanwhile, he shaved my head like his was, and glued on my face an artificial grey beard identical to his (thinner than Santa Claus'). I put on his Buddhist tunic, cloak and sandals, but kept in hand his *takuhatsugasa* (a mushroom-shaped straw hat worn by Japanese monks). All the while, Yamato impressed upon me to speak only in Japanese and poor English for the duration of my stay. Through woodland, he guided me to the rear of a large estate located some ten minutes from the "accident." We embraced each other with deep emotion, and he disappeared.

Following my friend's instructions, across a dense thicket I reached the walled garden. I pushed open a narrow gate of wrought iron, rusted and covered with bindweed. Surely no one had walked through there that past spring, if at all the past year. I found myself inside a disused glasshouse supported by the high wall through which I had just entered. Vegetables and flowers had grown wild, a welcome store for birds and insects. It felt hot and humid; the air was laden with pollens and with the smell of rich soil. Above me and across the glass walls, glass panes had fallen long ago. The putty that kept them in place was missing, probably eaten by slugs or birds, while through the holes, leafy stems shot into the breeze outside. High pink thornless roses screened the old glazed door through which I was to step out onto the lawn. Like many panes across the glasshouse, it seemed, those on the door were loose. The greyish rusty frame resisted my pressure at first. As the door suddenly gave in, a glass pane fell and broke against the rough tiles of the floor. I crouched behind the tall roses and waited in silence, lest anyone nearby had heard the noise and came to enquire. Hearing no sign of human life, I finally got out of the glasshouse and walked forward. It was about 6pm and still very hot and bright, that 24 June.

Earlier that afternoon Yamato had sent his luggage (henceforth mine) to the mansion where he was awaited before supper. It was the same place where he had stayed seven months earlier, in November 1978. The owner had corresponded with him since, inviting him to stay this summer to teach him and other adepts the art of sword unsheathing. About twenty men were expected the following day to begin the *kendo* seminar. Yamato was confident that I would easily be mistaken for him, since our host had only seen him once, over half a year earlier. My role was very simple. I was to stroll to the hall as if I had arrived separately and had gone out to stretch my legs or meditate in the park. I would be shown to my room and my planned adoption as "Swordmaster Yamato" would seamlessly unfold. Leaving the disused glasshouse behind, I cautiously walked towards the side of the walled garden, stopping at the end of a small orchard. The grounds looked untidy, almost abandoned indeed. But ahead of me spread some cultivated beds and at some distance across a wide lawn, surrounded by yellow gravel, stood the mansion. Hesitant to step into the open, I tightened my belt around my brown Buddhist tunic. Could I carry this pretence through? I felt oppressed and breathed noisily. To give me time, I crouched to tie up my sandal, hiding behind a trellis. I then checked my fake grey beard, lest perspiration had unglued part of it. A child's voice suddenly broke the silence, sounding clear and eerily close. "Excuse me, Sir?"

I looked around me anxiously but could only see the trunks of the fruit trees, while no one seemed to be hiding amidst the lush grass. The boyish voice asked again, respectfully confident, "Are you the Old Chinaman, Sir?"

There was still no one to be seen. I was bemused until, from the luxuriant foliage of the fruit tree under which I crouched, a dark object fell down onto the thick grass. The shape immediately bounced and stood erect, proving to be alive and talking very fast.

"I am the Chimney Sweep. Teresa is the Shepherdess. We know our roles by heart. We've been rehearsing all day. Xavier still makes mistakes. He is General-clothes-press-inspector-head-superintendent-Goat-legs, but he has very little to say, so it does not matter, does it? Grandmamma said we cannot perform until the Old Chinaman has arrived. Are you the Old Chinaman, Sir?"

He was wearing rags and his face was blackened. I would have assumed him to be just what he affirmed, a chimney sweep from the village, if we had been in Victorian England rather than twentieth-century Spain, and if his tone had not been so articulate and confident. With a clear smile, he took my hand and led me into the open, towards the mansion, explaining, "Grandmamma is on the terrace. She will be glad to meet you, Sir. You can call me Eneko." Only then did I notice that the boy was speaking Spanish and that, to my astonishment, I understood him perfectly. As far as I was aware, I had never read or spoken Spanish in my life! How could these playful words, chirped by a fluttering boy of seven or eight, reach into my mind, awake my memory and warm my heart with less explanation needed than would be expected of a robin, briskly flying across fence and brook into the neighbour's domain as if the very notion of trespassing had never existed? It felt uncanny and exhilarating. How I would have loved to reply. But I recalled Yamato's instructions warning me to speak only Japanese and little English as he did, lest my disguise was found out. With trepidation and delight, I followed my child guide across the lawn, holding my wide *takuhatsugasa* straw hat in my other hand.

Set upon a granite basement, the mansion was a vast and bulky construction in brownish bricks and white cut stone, over three floors, comprising of a central body and two higher wings, pierced all along by many high windows with faded sun blinds. Two granite staircases leading out of a protruding vestibule connected the main floor with the grounds. The building sat on the top of a small hill overlooking a mere in the distance, sheltered by copses on either side. Flanked by a Mozarabic chapel and a long orangery, it would have looked impressive in its heyday. But the grounds no less than the mansion betrayed a dire want of money. The boy introduced me to "Grandmamma" who spontaneously spoke to me in English. In her seventies, if not sixties, she looked altogether dignified and warm. She seemed to take it for granted that I was Yamato, whom she had briefly met in November past.

"Welcome back to Jallier, dear Master Yamato. I hope you had a pleasant time of meditation in the hills, earlier this afternoon. I am sorry that we were out, but Gorka, our gardener, saw you walk by earlier and confirmed your safe arrival. 'Very sensible of the foreign gentleman in robes to wear that large straw hat under such sun,' Gorka remarked. Your luggage is already in your room (the 'Samurai Room' like last year, with the shower that works best). Young Eneko will take you there, in case you don't remember the way. My son will be delighted to see you again."

The inside of the house matched my first impression. Every wall was in serious need of fresh paint, if not of replastering. The carpets were threadbare and the curtains faded. But one could tell that, some fifty years earlier, it had looked grand. Flower vases scattered here and there, as well as many gilded frames hanging from picture rails, brought colour and life into the vast rooms and staircase. Once alone, in my quarters on the first floor, I inspected my new belongings. Yamato's Japanese sword was there in its case. I would need it for my teaching session the following morning. His passport and other documents, including his return ticket to Tokyo, greatly impressed upon me the change of identity. I looked at the picture of my friend and admitted that, with my hair now shaven, my fake grey beard and my Buddhist garb, I could easily be mistaken for him. On the wall opposite my canopy bed hung an Italian-style seventeenth-century portrait of a handsome samurai, hence the name of the room. It did look familiar to me. By the bathroom door, a framed end-of-the-year class photograph made me feel melancholic. It bore the legend "San Pelayo Kindergarten, Azpeitia, 1911." I looked intently at the black-and-white silhouettes of the children, kneeling side by side on the front, sitting on the second row, standing all along behind, and probably perched on benches along the rear row. A few nuns wearing full religious habits with veils stood at either end. Some children looked shy, others confident, some others sad, or sulky. I liked to guess their temperaments, as if I were their dedicated teacher, doing my utmost to cultivate the talents, small or big, which lay hidden in their young souls. Where were they all, now, sixty-eight years later? Many of them would still be alive, perhaps even in the village or on the Jallier estate. I felt a surge of sympathy for these forty-or-so tiny figures, as if somehow I knew them, and they me. It was as if we had shared important things, they and I.

The Jallier family and I walked into the dining hall together with half a dozen people whom I soon understood to be paying guests. To make ends meet, I realised that Mr Jallier and his wife had turned the second floor of the mansion into a bed-and-breakfast for averagely wealthy tourists. The dining hall was a vast room with a high ceiling and warm blue paint peeling off above the picture rail. Various small shields with coat of arms adorned the corbels that supported the carved beams. When Mr Jallier presented me with a wide four-legged stool padded with Asian dragon material, I made my first mistake, not guessing that he expected me to dine in a yoga posture, as Yamato had done on his past visit, I later learnt. Instead, observing that my hosts and the other guests sat in the European fashion upon antique chairs, I spontaneously imitated them and set my feet upon the carpet, rather than crossing my legs in lotus position.

There were four Americans at table, plus a German and even a Japanese, the latter a priest based at the nearby Jesuit centre (he wore civilian clothes). He was elated to see a Buddhist swordsman, being himself an adept of Zen spirituality. He regretted that I had just missed our fellow-Japanese novelist Shūsaku Endō who had stayed at Jallier the week before while on a documenting visit for his next historical novel to be published within months. I knew little of Endō, a Catholic, beyond his novel *Silence* which I had read some ten years earlier. Endō had studied in France but knew little of Spain, the Japanese priest mentioned. Thus, the Jesuit had acted as mentor and translator for the Japanese novelist, travelling across Spain in the footsteps of Tsunenaga Hasekura, the seventeenth-century Japanese Ambassador to the courts of Madrid and of Rome. I nodded in appreciation and spoke little, giving me time to become accustomed to my persona as Swordmaster Yamato, instead of Professor Kokura.

~~~~~~~~~~~~~~~~~~~

I also was on my guard lest this setting, unfamiliar as it still felt, prompted any unsettling memories. Nothing struck me until after supper. The fresh fruit salad ended, the group made its way towards the vestibule, Mr Jallier and I coming last. Suddenly my eyes were attracted by a frame that I had not noticed on my way in, as it was hanging behind incomers, above a wide credence table by the dining hall door. I recognised it. It matched perfectly the daguerreotype shown us by Comrade Churakov at Laval House in St Petersburg. The small-scale replica on copper plate that I had once admired in 1947, then held in dear Ida's slender hands, now hung in its original size and colours on the wall of a decrepit Basque mansion. Finding the lost masterpiece had taken me thirty-two years, unless it was it that had found me. There it was, Carel Fabritius' lost *Mercury, Argus and Io*. I don't wish to expatiate. The shock was altogether gigantic and soft, like a child standing in a field would feel when caught in the huge shadow of a hot air balloon silently crossing the sun in a summer afternoon. It was as if I had always known that the frame was hanging there, waiting for me. The quote from Ovid's *Metamorphoses* (I.714-717), which the painting illustrated, now sounded in my ears:

When he saw that his enemy's drowsy eyes had all succumbed and were shrouded in sleep...[a]t once he stopped talking and stroked the sentry's drooping lids with his magic wand to make sure he was out.

Then he rapidly struck with his sickle-shaped sword at his nodding victim

Just where the head comes close to the neck...

All across the house, darker empty rectangles on the walls showed that various frames had been taken out in years past, perhaps sold or shared among heirs a generation earlier. Hopefully, the lost Vermeer might still hang in some other room nearby, assuming it was the other painting referred to in Count Lebzeltern's letter read to us in Russia. Strangely, in the case of the Fabritius, I felt as if the absence of it on the dining hall wall would have surprised me, rather than its unconsciously expected display. I managed not to run to the picture. But I had to find a way to come closer to it. As I walked by, I incidentally told Mr Jallier that the sword of the man on the right looked a bit like the Japanese *katana* of the samurai in my room. He answered that he had never noticed the sword. "That is strange, why would a shepherd carry such a weapon?" my host commented. "That painting is called *The Shepherds*. I have always known it on that wall. It is by some little-known Italian artist, I recall, inherited from my mother's great-great uncle who was once Ambassador in Naples. It is only worth half a year of the mortgage repayment for our crumbling estate, an expert friend of mine reckoned. You may not see *The Shepherds* on this wall at your next sword session, I am afraid. But you pointed to the man's sword. Why is he armed, after all? Well, perhaps he fears for his sheep, lest a bear attack them. Were there many bears in Italy? We still have a few, further north, in the Pyrenees."

After supper our party sat outdoors on the wide terrace overlooking the sloping field and the mere. The sun was still high in the sky on this near summer solstice evening. We watched the children perform a play written by Grandmamma after Andersen's tale, *The Shepherdess and the Chimney-Sweep*. I thanked Grandmamma who summarised the plot for me in advance, while Mr Jallier, her son, obligingly played the part of the Old Chinaman. Both Jallier parents acted or sang, supporting their four children. The group appeared to me as the embodiment of family joy, a grace I had shared in, I felt, a long time ago. The charming recreation was delivered in Spanish, so that I was careful to smile politely as if I understood little. My memories continued to unfold, and all seemed spontaneously to fall into place.

As if out of conversational interest, I asked Grandmamma if the empty pedestal, where the young *Shepherdess* girl had stood during the play, had once supported another gladiator matching the maimed one on the left. Weaponry was safe ground, I felt, for an alleged sword-master to enquire about. She looked surprised and replied, "Ah, you mean Lord Hasekura's statue? According to our family tradition, he was a samurai who visited Spain and secretly married a noble Catholic lady. His portrait is in your room. The lady was called Maria; she might have been my husband's ancestor. Hers was the statue standing opposite, but before the war it got damaged beyond repair and no replica was ever commissioned. We just got used to her empty pedestal, I suppose. But tell me, how did you like the play? Did not Eneko look a stunningly genuine chimney sweep?"

A tradition on the feast of St John the Baptist, I was told, was to light a bonfire on the empty space, ten steps below the terrace, some safe distance from the fairly dry grass in the nearby field. About fifty villagers and staff from the estate had joined the group, including a good number of children. I was given *Idiazabal* cheese and a large glass of *Txakoli Ameztoi* Basque wine. A farmer mentioned the "accident" on the train which occurred earlier that afternoon. He said that ETA might have caused it. A foreign passenger had gone missing, the man reported, but no fatalities were to be regretted. I was relieved. It was past 10pm and the sun had just set. We watched the blaze illumine the sky, outshining the nascent stars. The combined smell of smoke and grass, the popping and crackling of wood, and the slight dizziness after such a strange day exhilarated me. Several children still wore their disguise from the play, while many adults had donned traditional Basque accoutrements. It made me feel not the least out of place in my Buddhist robes and under my fake grey beard, as if we partook in the same family show. Needing no words, and unbeknownst to the people around who had never seen me in their lives, I started to feel as if, through some tender alchemy, I belonged.

Back in my room, I sat on my bed under the canopy, looking at Lord Hasekura's moonlit portrait. I recalled Yamato's mention of "Father Xavier," the young Japanese relative of Mrs Jallier, who used to stay in this mansion on vacation with his diplomat parents and had spent several months here in 1936, hiding from the Communists with his twenty fellow Jesuit students from Asia. Yamato's latest hypothesis about my lost identity had sounded the least plausible. Could it be though, that the blood once running in the veins of the seventeenth-century samurai on the portrait before me, now might flow in mine? I would not enquire. If Providence, or whichever entity claimed oversight on our lives, planned to tell me who I was, or had been, let it provide evidence. After all, I was the victim, not the detective, in what had befallen me. Let chance decide, disclose, demonstrate—or let me carry on as I had for thirty-four years since my first awakening under a military tent, somewhere near Hiroshima.

～～～～～～～～～～

In the morning, the children led by young Eneko took me for a walk across the estate. They were keen to show me their treehouse, where they kept two black-spotted white rabbits named *Pongo* and *Perdita*. After feeding the pets and playing with them, the children ran back to the mansion on hearing a bell ring: the signal for their homework session. As I watched them skip through the grove, down the slope, singing and laughing, I really felt as if the children's album by Satomi Ishikawa, once admired in the Sorbonne chapel in Paris, had come to life. I walked further up the grounds and soon found myself on the ridge where Yamato had stood. The view from there reached far across the valley to the south, while behind us, huge but distant enough to not overbear, the Pyrenees closed the perspective. I easily found the carved cross and came to the bench where, as I had known from the start, I felt, Grandmamma was sitting. On her lap lay a thick purple notebook labelled 'Cayetana J. E.,' which I suppose she had shut on hearing footsteps.

I stood a few yards to the side, between her and the cross, relishing the panoramic view. High in the sky, two buzzards were calling, one bigger than the other—unless the latter simply flew higher up. A mother, perhaps, was encouraging her young one, still unaccustomed to altitude flight. Wings extended, they glided effortlessly upon the warm breeze, like scuba divers swimming high above wide abysses, enlightened by sunbeams pouring down from on-high. Unlike the busy racket of magpies and jays, the calls of the buzzards were spaced out and majestic. They felt to my ears like some music evoking wide open spaces, eternal summers and childlike freedom. Lasting less than two seconds each time, each call felt unhurried as it travelled the vast distance between the hills across the valley and our ridge. I recognised it as the voice of happiness passed long ago.

Grandmamma and I kept silent for a while, unembarrassed. She then spoke as to herself.

"I expect you liked his *Nativity*, framed in your bedroom, and his *Exaltation of St Ignatius* on the landing? Not only did he learn from a young age about classical painters; he also loved painting. Eneko reminds me of him. Just as sensitive and artistic. Did you see at the play last night with what conviction he asked his Shepherdess, 'Are you really so brave that you'd go into the wide world with me? Have you thought about how big it is, and that we can never come back here?'"

I did not need to ask who was the "he" she was referring to, as we both knew it was Fr Xavier, her lost relative. It reminded me that I had not taken time to paint watercolours for several weeks. I should resume it.

After a while she went on.

"But the chimney sweep did come back home after his long trip up to the roof. Only, his face was sooted and his heart soothed. We will all come back home, in the end. It is a bit like you, Master Yamato, since I see you back after all, don't I? Thank God, your painful amnesia has spared the memory of your happy stay here earlier. That, you remember."

I was taken aback by her inquiry which truly sounded as if she had found me out. But she elucidated, "I am glad 'Telluric Tours' allowed you to come again as a private extra, even though I am not fond of tellurism or Buddhism, as you know. Last November, after our long conversation upon this bench, despite the cold, you said that you may probably never return. You confided that you were perceiving the divine presence upon this place, and were afraid of what you might be asked."

After a couple of minutes spent in silence, she added, "Would you mind if I revisit the past in your company? I had more to tell you last time, at your request, but I felt that it was better postponed. Since you have come back, the following should be of interest to you, I hope."

I smiled as if in acceptance of her offer, and she opened the notebook on her lap, quoting and explaining, "Thus, Xavier's father, Baron Paul Hasekura, was a distant relative of my husband, as both shared the same seventeenth-century ancestor, famous Japanese Ambassador Hasekura. The Hasekura family first made contact with us here in 1920. They were on a tour across Europe slowly recovering from the Great War. Spain had heard no gunshots but, all the same, we mourned the many victims of influenza. I was 21, three years married to 33-year-old Leoncio, Count Jallier de Etxeberria. We were childless again then; the influenza had not spared our family."

She looked sad, but composed, as if revisiting painful memories. After a short while she went on.

"My husband and I immediately took to Baron Hasekura and his beautiful wife Isabella, who was pregnant. So comfortable were they at Jallier that, accepting our suggestion, they decided to remain with us until after Isabella's delivery, rather than give birth in Paris as originally planned. Baby Xavier was born in the Samurai Room and baptised in our chapel the same day, with the names Xavier, Paul, Vincent, Cayetano, Josemaria. I was his godmother. Our affection for Baron Paul and dear Isabella was reciprocated. She would paint very fine watercolours. We kept in touch and they visited us again once in 1922. A third visit was cancelled owing to Isabella's untimely death during the Great Kanto Earthquake on 1 September 1923, claiming over 140,000 victims. God rest her dear soul. But father and son came again in 1927."

Silence followed. I was touched to have been made privy to such details. Upon her lap, Grandmamma's hands tightened around the purple notebook. I tried not to move, and avoided interpreting her confidences. But I wondered what Yamato might have told her that would justify such disclosures. Did he seriously think that he was the lost Father Xavier? He certainly showed great skill in swordsmanship, but he had been identified by his wife as early as 1945, and his family bore no connection, to my knowledge, with the House of Hasekura.

Gazing across the valley, Countess Jallier continued. "In 1934, or 1935 rather, Baron Paul was assigned to the Japanese diplomatic corps in Spain. Jallier became a true home for him, a widower, and for young Xavier. In early 1936, he permitted Xavier to enter the Jesuit noviciate a few miles away from us. You have heard, I expect, that both St Ignatius, founder of the Jesuits, and St Francis Xavier who first evangelised Japan, were Basques. The proximity of Jallier was reassuring, Baron Paul told us, since his son was barely seventeen, and in a foreign land. Six months later, the Civil War began. Soon the Communists had taken over part of our Basque Country and, as I told you last time, my husband and I were only too happy to offer our estate as a discreet shelter for the Asian Jesuit students.

"In December 1937, diplomatic relations were established between Japan and General Franco's Government who joined the 'Anti-Commintern Pact,' as I think it was called, two years later, after his victory over the Communists. In 1942, if

I am not mistaken, it was unofficially announced that Baron Paul Hasekura would become the Japanese Ambassador, a great promotion from Chargé d'Affaires. A gala dinner was offered on this occasion, here at Jallier. I still have copies of the printed menus, and some very moving black-and-white pictures of the splendid event. Some, now faded, were in colour, taken by the photographer of the Japanese embassy (at my instigation). We were delighted to see our friend honoured and to have the long-term presence in Spain of his cherished family secured. Baron Paul was a frequent guest at Jallier, whence he popped in to the nearby Jesuit noviciate to see his son. The 'Samurai Room' where you are staying was his habitual room. Xavier and his father cherished the portrait of their ancestor, understandably. My husband always insisted that ours is the original version by Claude Deruet, whereas the one in Rome is merely an authentic copy by Archita Ricci. Alas, that painting caused the demise of Baron Paul Hasekura."

She paused, lost in her memories, her hands joined on her lap, as she stared across the distant circle of hills beyond the river and the lush valley. It was getting hot, but over our bench beech branches extended the welcome protection of their luxuriant foliage. I had listened with utmost interest, because Grandmamma was now leading the conversation into my favourite territory of historical paintings; and with relief, because her double mistake made me safe. As I realised, she thought that I was Yamato, and she believed that Yamato was Xavier Hasekura, her vanished priest-samurai godson. I was grateful to her for her tact in trying to elicit lost memories in the mind of her alleged amnesic cousin, but I was sorry not to be able to respond to her painful attempts.

She sighed. "This seems so long ago, dear Master Yamato, and yet, so fresh in my mind. My husband and I went through these events so many times. He gathered all the information he could and put it all in writing. Allow me to quote from these notes, as my memory sometimes fails me—though my heart is faithful."

She had added these last words almost defiantly. Her voice and hands slightly trembling, she browsed through the thick notebook.

"Thus, it is part of official history that Adolf Hitler's Propaganda Minister Joseph Goebbels courted your country. He was on the lookout for diplomatic gifts to Japan. One of them was, so I heard, a Stradivarius violin stolen from a Jewish musician. He gave it to your virtuoso Suwa Nejiko. The chief Japanese diplomat posted to Spain was Suma Yakichiro, a man of great culture and an art collector. He was to be promoted to Berlin, while Baron Paul Hasekura was to succeed him in Madrid.

"On his visit here for our 1942 gala dinner, Suma Yakichiro was shown our portrait of Ambassador Tsunenaga Hasekura. His Japanese coat of arms was displayed on a flag in the background, opposite the vessel that had taken him to Europe. I remember how Mr Yakichiro's secretary pointed at the Buddhist swastika on our painting and commented, 'Your Excellency, look, the Empire of the Sun floating the Third Reich emblem.' Later only did Baron Paul tell us the full story. Once back in Madrid, his superior had ordered him to obtain the painting from us by any means. It was to be a key gift to cement the collaboration between Germany and its two still neutral allies, Spain and Japan. Spanish foreign minister Ramón Serrano Suñer was to present the gift to Baron Hiroshi Ōshima, the Japanese Ambassador in Berlin, in the presence of Joseph Goebbels himself, and of Suma Yakichiro whose promotion from Madrid to Berlin would then be made official.

"Baron Paul tried to dissuade his superior, suggesting he asked Count Ciano, the Italian Foreign Minister and Mussolini's son-in-law, to secure instead Archita Ricci's version of the painting kept in Rome. Suma Yakichiro made enquiries and reached the conclusion that Archita Ricci's painting was the original, while our version by Claude Deruet was a copy. His argument ran as follows: on a fresco in the Sala Regia of the Quirinal Palace in Rome, Hasekura wears the very same dress as on the two portraits. Since our painting is not known ever to have been displayed in Italy, it must have imitated the original Ricci version. Baron Paul thought it proved little, but kept quiet for our sake.

"Still, because he was posted in Spain, not in Italy, Suma Yakichiro was adamant that the gift had to come from Spain, or the project would be dropped altogether. Baron Paul refused to deprive us, his trusted friends and relatives, of such a meaningful family heirloom, and for so disputable a purpose. The following month he was recalled to Japan. It was in May 1944. He travelled with Xavier, by then a deacon, who had just been assigned to the Japan mission. We never saw them again. They went missing on 9 August 1945 in Nagasaki, where Baron Paul attended Xavier's priestly ordination. Sometimes I tell myself that if we had given away the samurai's portrait, Baron Paul might still be alive, and perhaps also Xavier.

"Now I am an old woman of nearly eighty years of age, and the portrait is all that is left to me. The expert in seventeenth-century paintings at El Prado wrote to me last year, assuring that he could raise private funds up to 45 million pesetas to buy the portrait of the Japanese Ambassador. I replied that if we had anything of value left to sell, I would know. I did not tell my son about this offer, as he would surely sell *The Ambassador*. Over my dead body. Jallier is mortgaged and we cannot repay. Next year the hall will be turned into a hotel, and we will move into the lodge. Well, I would sooner lose the estate than the portrait."

Her emotion seemed to have turned from despondency to determination. The urgent need of repair all across the hall and grounds came back to my mind, and I admired even more Grandmamma's visceral attachment to the historic portrait of Japanese Ambassador Tsunenaga Hasekura. Checking her wristwatch, she knelt down upon the grass, looking at the cross and prayed what I recognised to be the *Hail Mary*. Then she stood up again and announced that she was expected back at the mansion to prepare lunch. I immediately rose from the bench and offered her my arm. But she turned down my offer with a motherly smile, suggesting I stayed longer by myself to prepare for my sword lesson that afternoon. As she left, she pressed her notebook into my hands, inviting me to look at the photographs. She also pointed at a bottle with two glasses, on the grass by the bench. "I had brought this lemonade for us to share, but my chattering made me forget. I hope you will enjoy it. That path to the left is to the old castle, by the way, if you wish to see the ruins. The main tower still stands, though."

With surprising agility, she walked down the steep shortcut down the ridge, as she might have done daily, I assumed. I kept sight of her until she reached the bottom of the slope, concerned as I was that she might fall. I was pleased not to have given out any clue as to my true identity. It did not seem as if she had been setting traps for me. She genuinely believed that I was Yamato. I only wished he had informed me of his experience of the divine on this spot. I sat down, crossing my legs and relishing the breath-taking panorama; until with concern I suddenly remembered that all along Grandmamma had spoken in Spanish, and had rightly assumed that I understood her, whereas Yamato could have spoken only English with her, last time. Was I compromised?

I walked to the tall stone cross and read its inscription. Two trainee Jesuits had died in Nagasaki on 9 August 1945. One of them was Xavier Hasekura, S.J., born on 29 August 1920, from Aoba Castle in Mutsu Province, Japan. On the doomed day of 9 August 1945, then the feast of St John-Mary Vianney, Patron of Parish Priests, Xavier had been ordained a priest—that is, assuming the ceremony had been completed before 11:02am when the bomb exploded. If the ordination had taken place, and if I was that man, I calculated that I would presently be a 58-year-old Jesuit priest. If...

I sipped my lemonade as she had invited me to. It was refreshing and tasted surprisingly familiar. Dear Grandmamma... Dear

"Countess Cayetana." Could she truly be nearing 80? I would have thought her just past 70, if not younger. She was still a very beautiful woman. I browsed through the notebook stuffed with many old pictures, mostly of pre-war Spain. I looked with unease at a Japanese official in white tie with decorations, to whom Countess Cayetana was pointing as if making a speech. She wore a stunning red gala dress with pearls (it was true then: colour pictures existed as early as the 1930s). The distinguished gentleman had to be the father of Jesuit student Xavier. She was right: he did look very handsome, and kind.

A sudden urge to help Cayetana and her family gripped my heart. Really, this estate where they had lived for generations could not be surrendered to developers. But how to avoid it? The missing frames in various rooms bore witness to the patrimony already sold. As I walked down from the ridge, the obvious solution struck me. I stopped halfway down the slope, concentrated and smiling. Of course, the *Fabritius*! Through my American contacts, I knew that it could fetch up to twice the estimate for her dear *Samurai*. For that family portrait the Prado expert had offered 45 million pesetas, amounting to about $600,000. Even more would major galleries in Los Angeles and New York fight to secure Carel Fabritius' lost *Mercury, Argus and Io*. I gave its auction at Sotheby's in Monaco a conservative outcome of $1.5 million. This would make Jallier's future absolutely safe. But if "Grandmamma Cayetana" could not sell her *Ambassador*, how could I let go of *Fabritius*, the painting I had sought all my life? I resolved to inspect it as soon as I could discreetly do so.

~~~~~~~~~~~~~~~~~

The first sword session was a success. In addition to the twenty participants booked, members of the household had requested to attend. Even some older children had been allowed, under the condition that they would not move or speak. We were sitting on our heels in the vast orangery, wearing made-up Buddhist tunics, our hands spread on our thighs. I invited all to bow to the sword laid on a reed mat on the floor. My explanations about "becoming sword" seemed to puzzle the audience, perhaps because the translation offered by Count Jallier from English to Spanish was approximate. I could not help noticing restlessness around me after ten minutes, despite having warned everyone not to expect "action" from the start. Most of the exercise was mental preparation, regulating of breath and communing with the cosmos. It took place in strict immobility, and of course, in silence. All were looking at the flickering candle set on the floor, wondering when the blade would snuff it out. Gasp and hushed relief accompanied the final unsheathing and extinguishing. I sheathed the sword back in the scabbard and bowed to it again ritually before retiring for private meditation.

It was very hot and humid that evening, as if a storm was building up. I opened wide my window, trying in vain to cool the room. Sitting down, for some time I browsed through an old book about the embassy of Tsunenaga Hasekura in Spain and Rome. Through the window the sky had turned very dark, and thunder could be heard in the distance. I came to sit on the edge of my canopy bed, inspecting the Japanese Ambassador's portrait on the wall opposite. He looked younger than expected for a man in his position, and kinder as well. Two swords emerged from his sash. He wore an elegant silk jacket with grazing deer, over a tunic and wide trousers of light-yellow shade decorated with reeds. Was this my ancestor? Had he attended my birth on this very bed where I sat, some 58 years earlier? Had he been pleased to see his line furthered through yet one more male heir, a son of the House of Hasekura? If so, how disappointed he must have been later on. I was lost to him, or had been since 1945.

How strange his destiny, I thought, as I surveyed his martial posture and noble features. This Japanese official had left his country, one of the first of our race brave enough to do so, and had navigated all around the world on a small boat, finally reaching Spain, the epicentre of Catholic power in the early seventeenth century. How did he communicate with Catholics? What attracted him to a culture so alien to him? How did he shift from ancestral Buddhism to foreign Christianity? His change of religion was not an expedient to secure the favours of the Christian princes, king and pope, whom he was visiting. On the contrary, when back in Japan he found his newly-embraced creed forbidden, he stood firm and possibly died a martyr, followed by several among his family and servants.

I felt in my heart a tender pressure to declare myself a Catholic and his heir, not so much out of conviction as because it clearly was the only kind and meaningful thing to do. In the upper-right corner, behind him, his splendid Japanese-built galleon *San Juan Bautista* evoked his adventurous voyage. Above it appeared three figures evoking the three theological virtues of Faith, Hope and Charity. The one embodying Faith vaguely resembled the Lord Jesus sitting in heavenly glory, holding Cross, Chalice and Host; while on either side, St Francis of Assisi represented Charity, and a woman holding an anchor symbolised Hope. Further above hovered the Dove of the Holy Ghost coming down from the shining star of God the Father. A dog with a rich necklace crouched at the Ambassador's sandalled feet.

Unfurled in the upper left corner, Hasekura's coat-of-arms displayed a swastika with two crossed arrows. Thus, the Ambassador stood between the Buddhist and Christian emblems. It occurred to me that, as in Holbein's *Ambassadors*, shifting the vantage point altered the meaning of the depiction. Looking at the picture from right to left, Third Reich minister Joseph Goebbels would have hailed a healthy shift from Judeo-Christianity to Aryan paganism, from the trinity of infused virtues to the Nazi emblem. If moving from left to right though, according to the European convention, one would witness Christianisation at work, turning Eastern consciousness into divine wisdom, and man-made myths into God-revealed truths. Like my alleged ancestor, I had travelled from Orient to Occident, I had changed my creed, or rather, I had forgotten whether it was ever mine. He had kept his new faith on his return journey. What of mine?

Lightning interrupted my thoughts. I went to shut the high window, gazing at the rain that swept through the wide field. Somewhere in the vast mansion, were the children terrified, I wondered, tucked under their sheets? Was their mother by their cosy beds, calming and soothing the little ones? Perhaps, I imagined, Grandmamma was praying with them the supplication I had once come across at Cambridge in the Book of Common Prayer: *"From lightning and tempest; from earthquake, fire, Good Lord, deliver us."* Or rather, no, since Jallier was a Catholic household, it would be the Roman litany of the saints which, I was pretty sure, entailed such an invocation.

I went to bed and switched off the light. But sleep eluded me, hindered by some strange reminiscences. Many a *déjà-vu* had occurred in my mind since my arrival at Jallier. This one was particularly compelling. I saw myself in the large bed of Aunt whoever, in this very mansion, a seven-year-old-or-so on a thundering evening, with another younger child, while the adult wearing a green silky nightdress with ribbons of a slightly darker shade brought bowls of hot chocolate to quiet us. I had to wait a little to drink mine because it was still very hot. I think she then lay between us under the sheet, resting her arms on our shoulders and telling us some fairy tale, by way of diversion from the thunder and from the rain lashing against the window panes. I had grown up since. Now alone in my bed in the Samurai Room, I relished the sense of fear and comfort felt in the spectacle of natural violence unleashed, when contemplated from within a safe dwelling. It then jumped at me: the adult under whose tender hand I once lay was no other than "Aunt Cayetana." And the tale was in fact a Spanish nursery rhyme whose words now sprung out of my childhood, ringing clear and tender: "Little Prince Segismundo, dreaming in your lonely tower: awake, awake little Segismundo, for morning has broken and you are in

Mummy's garden." Cayetana would have been twenty-eight years old and, to a little boy's eyes, very beautiful. Was the younger child her own son?

I sat upright in my bed, listening to the weakening storm. It was probably moving east along the southern foothills of the Pyrenees. As I knelt down upon the sheet, I caught sight of Ambassador Hasekura's portrait facing me between the front carved posts of my canopy bed. I felt as if he was watching me. The lightning now occurred silently, thunder resounding some ten seconds later. Pale light flashed upon the samurai as if he was the one moving in and out of some bright spot, indecisively. Was he peeping at me through the frame of my canopy, as I at him amidst the fixture surrounding his painting? Who was mirroring whom? Who was awaiting the other? Was he calling me? Was I ignoring him? I looked further at the reeds and deer decorating the samurai's dress. Did it mean anything? Deer eat reeds. Brutal men would see themselves as deer, rightly feeding on any less strong creatures. But pious souls would remember the psalm I had heard sung in Cambridge at King's: *"As the hart panteth after the fountains of water; so my soul panteth after thee, O God."* Aspiring to the water of life, they would spare the reeds in imitation of the Lord Jesus of whom the Gospel affirmed, *"The bruised reed he shall not break: and smoking flax he shall not extinguish: till he send forth judgment unto victory."* With his two sharp swords, did the Ambassador slay many victims? Rather, he must have used his weapons for justice and mercy. Lying down again, I pulled the sheet over my face and managed to fall asleep.

In the morning, I was woken up by the faint sound of dripping in my bathroom. A leak from the ceiling, I realised, was probably caused by a pool in some blocked gutters after last night's downpour. The floor tiles were covered with water, now spreading towards the ornate parquet by the bedroom threshold. Immediate action was needed. Noticing a darkish lacquered china jar on the top of a wardrobe near the bathroom, I spontaneously reached for it, hoping to position it under the water ingress as a temporary solution. However, as I stood on tiptoes, my right hand grasping the neck of the jar and my left supporting its bottom, something very unexpected happened. Many small figures of children appeared on the surface of the china. They looked more or less distorted according to which area of the curved vessel reflected them. I immediately realised that the lacquered container mirrored the framed end-of-year school photograph I had examined the day before, still hanging on the wall behind me. What struck me was the very deep impression of *déjà-vu*. I truly felt as if I had made exactly the same gesture long ago, even though other children could be seen reflected in the vessel I was holding up in my hands. I stored in my memory this strange infant anamorphosis, guessing that I would need to investigate it and, hopefully, make it yield some essential information about my lost past. I positioned the lidless jar under the leak and then washed "in the best shower of the house."

I had decided to accept Cayetana's suggestion to attend Catholic worship in the house chapel. Looking in the mirror as I was again securing my fake grey beard, I recalled how Mr Jallier had promised it to be an interesting "experience of peace." Before supper last evening, he had taken me aside to apologise for the fact that Holy Communion could not be given me. "You have initiated us to Buddhist sword spirituality," he commented. "In return I wish our religion admitted you to this spiritual meal. But even though Fr Iñigo permitted it, Mother would not. We need many more *katana* sessions around here." I had assured him that I respected the rules and that I might indeed seize the opportunity to attend anyway. My beard looked convincing enough in the mirror and I left the bathroom, satisfied that the dripping water was now retained in the china jar.

Not much happened to me in the chapel, built in the Mozarabic style. I sat very close to the small sanctuary, a few steps away from the altar, right before the children. I knew the ritual already, although I had expected changes, since I had been told that Catholics now worshipped in the vernacular tongue rather than in Latin, that the priest was facing the congregation, and that the blessed bread was put on the hand, not received on the tongue. But I noticed no innovations that morning. It all took place in the manner I had witnessed when last attending a Catholic Mass in the 1960s, with my friend Léonard Foujita in Paris, at St-Roch Church, "the artists' parish." I looked at the stained-glass windows. The middle one depicted the Transfiguration of Christ on Mount Tabor, with three apostles lying on the ground and Moses and Elias on either side of the Lord. To the right of the sanctuary, a stained glass represented St Francis Xavier in surplice and purple stole, blessing with a crucifix two kneeling children, a Japanese-looking one with a thin braided ponytail, the other wearing an Indian turban. The window on the left displayed Saint Pelayo of Cordoba, a youthful martyr.

To my right, upon the whitewashed wall by the confessional, in a mahogany frame that clashed a bit with the plain decoration of the chapel, an *Annunciation* after the Dutch school attracted my gaze. A vase of fresh flowers stood in front of it. The unfinished painting looked like the lost companion of Fabritius' *Mercury, Argus and Io*. I was kneeling too far from it for a proper assessment, which also would have been irreverent during Holy Mass. Was it, at long last, the Vermeer I had hunted across several continents, in state galleries and in private collections? It bore some features characteristic of the Master of Delft. Yes, it could well be my elusive Vermeer. However, as my eyes had just set on my most desired treasure, my heart failed to engage. I had to admit, most unexpectedly, to no excitement. I felt as if the matter had lost its relevance. I cannot explain why. It was as if what I had craved to know had already been granted me. And yet, I could not spell out to myself what that gift was. I came back after the service though, to take a look, for peace of mind as a professional expert. On closer inspection, the incomplete picture proved to be an unpretentious imitation of Vermeer's style, displaying average painting skills no more impressive than mine. The image bore no signature.

Repeated bell rings drew my attention to the altar where the old priest was slowly lifting the white wafer. I remained on my knees out of decorum, not bowing my head however, unlike Cayetana and the five grandchildren, and a couple of American paying guests. I looked at the white disc in the hand of the priest and said to myself, "Could this be God?" If it was, I wondered how my mind could be so easily distracted from such a presence. How could I take any notice, for instance, of the fact that young Eneko was not wearing his chimney sweep rags anymore but had donned a red cassock and above it a white surplice with lace trimming? Why did God permit such trivial wandering of my mind, now eager to know whether the boy and his sister the "Shepherdess" had drunk hot chocolate the past night during the storm, served in bed by their mother or grandmother?

The sight of the second elevation, of the chalice, this time, suddenly ravished me. A fairly wide and smooth cup of Romanesque style was being lifted up by Fr Iñigo. The old priest was holding the knob with his right hand, while supporting the wide foot with his left. In the space between his fingers, I could see or at least I guessed what were the little figures spread side by side. It was the distorted reflection on the gilded cup of the Jallier children kneeling in the first pew. The adults were too far to the sides to show well enough but I, on the row behind the children, could see myself reflected, I reckoned. It conjured up a crucial reminiscence.

Never had a memory from my time right before the explosion surfaced. But now, that very grace had occurred. The novelty overwhelmed me. I felt as if transported in time to the 9 August 1945 at 11am, and in space to the middle-size chapel of St Aloysius Jesuit school in Nagasaki. It was the Low Mass of my ordination as a priest. A bishop was elevating the chalice just consecrated. I was right behind him, kneeling by a low lectern upon which my own altar missal was set. I recalled looking with passionate intensity at the sacred vessel which contained the Most Precious Blood of Christ under the externals of wine. I discerned, stretched across the gilded surface of the cup, the reflection of the many schoolchildren kneeling in the pews behind me. This prompted with utmost vividness the remembrance of my surprise and intuition at that moment: namely, that the children were "in" the vessel. As I watched the sacred cup ascending in the bishop's hands, I united myself with Christ's sacrifice, mentally including all the little ones under my pastoral care as art teacher and henceforth as their chaplain. I surrendered myself to God almighty, drawing to His Majesty the souls most close to me in space and in my heart: these children in the front pews, my father kneeling to the side, my mother in heaven, my fellow-Jesuits, school staff, and some parishioners.

I cannot tell if the explosion occurred during the elevation of the chalice, or later during Mass. But that elevation with our children reflected on the vessel as if "inside the cup" is the closest moment to the apocalypse I ever recalled. Later on, I meditated on the paradoxical meeting of these two gifts. The divine one was being lifted from the ground towards heaven, while the man-made one was flying down from the sky. In the sacred chalice ascending, lay the Son of Man offered as Sacrifice for the salvation of the world. From the *Bockscar* bomber, the lethal object called *Fat Man* was dropped for the annihilation of the largest Catholic community in Asia. What a sorrowful parallel, I thought. Had the opposition between God's mercy and man's folly ever been so dramatic since our first parents had fatally plucked the forbidden fruit in Eden?

I had long assumed that I had survived Hiroshima, not Nagasaki. Thirty-four years later, I seemed to have lived through both carnages. I claimed their twin impact on me. The Hiroshima bomber *Enola Gay* was ill-named after the pilot's own mother. Her first name was a palindrome, a word that allows backward reading. Rather than *Enola*, she should have been called *alone*; and all but *gay*, since she was *sorrow-striking*. She appeared to me as a modern equivalent of Eve in the Garden of Eden. Eve was also untrue to her name, since from *Mother of the Living*, she had turned out to be the *Mother of the Mortals*. Plucking the forbidden fruit, Eve had fed death to her entire posterity. Her firstborn Cain had slain his own brother Abel. Similarly, *Enola Gay* had laid her lethal egg, the bomb called *Little Boy*, drowning an entire city in atomic horror.

But, I later recalled, the Advent antiphon *Ave Maris Stella* allows of a similar backward reading of names in its second stanza: *"Receiving that 'Ave' (hail), From the mouth of Gabriel, Establish us in peace, Transforming the name of 'Eva' (Eve)."* The "Ave," Latin for "Hail," refers to the blessed Annunciation to the Virgin Mary. Her obedience and humility led her to become the Mother of the Redeemer, the New Adam Jesus Christ. She is therefore credited with transforming the name of Eve, that is, of breaking the curse of death that was cast upon men through the sin of the first mother, Eve. Mary, the New Eve, brought forth the definitive Fruit of eternal Life, her Son Jesus, the divine *Little Boy* and Saviour of all men.

That 6 August 1945, atomic radiations had instantaneously turned thousands of innocent men into mere heat and light. Through a coincidence beyond irony, this occurred on the Christian feast of the Transfiguration: that very day, America, a Christian nation, had dropped her lethal fruit. The atomic blast and cloud appeared to me as a blasphemous parody of the Gospel narrative for that feast, when Christ, *"was transfigured before [his apostles]. And his face did shine as the sun: and his garments became white as snow. And . . . a bright cloud overshadowed them."*

Would there be a redemption for Japan and America, for our modern world? Would modernity, our atomic civilisation marked by chaos and disintegration, ever be restored to order and unity? Would the contradiction in terms of a mother fatefully named "Alone"—as if the very word "mother" did not call for "children"—ever be reversed into some life-bearing "Enola," just as the death-bearing "Eva" of Eden had been changed into the grace-filled "Ave" in Nazareth? How vividly the twin atomic bombing on my country in 1945 appeared to me then as the anti-Annunciation! The Christian revelation suddenly shone in my heart as the only touchstone to assess whatever truth and bounty our nuclear age claimed. But I dreaded applying the test, sensing that it might reveal modernity as an imposture of apocalyptic scale, of which I was part.

Remembering that I was now in the chapel at Jallier, in 1979, I attempted to regain control of my emotions while ignoring the sight of the children kneeling ahead of me. Unlike those once reflected on the gilded chalice at my ordination Mass, these children were alive, thank God. I left before the end, discreetly.

As I strolled outside the mansion, now breathing freely, I relished the freshness of the early morning. No charred branches remained where the bonfire had taken place two nights earlier, on the Nativity of St John the Baptist, but only wet dark ashes floating amidst a wide pool. I noticed that the bonfire had been set in the middle of a wide shallow hole dug into the ground. It revealed, beneath the yellow gravel spread all around the mansion and down its alleys, a compact greyish layer, buried long ago, perhaps before the war. Between the edges of the wide puddle and the floating ashes, underwater, I identified a pink colour, like a milky lining covering the bottom of the shallow excavation.

The heavy rain had sifted that thin coloured mud out of the old grey gravel, I understood.

CHAPTER 14
Atomisation

"OULD THIS BE NOVOSIBIRSK? NO, we must be further north. But somewhere above Siberia, anyway." Looking through the porthole of the brand-new Japan Airlines Boeing 747-400, Mgr Marco Altemps was finding it very difficult to distract his mind. His flight from Milan would take him to Tokyo later that Saturday, although it would already be Sunday in Japan. The past night, he had been reading the copy of the Kokura Memoirs left by the unlucky Fr Hubert Lambourin. The priest was still in hospital in Tuscany, for food poisoning apparently from the restaurant in Carrara where both clerics had taken their supper, on their way to the Abbey of San Cristoforo, south of Parma. Mgr Altemps had interrupted his retreat after reading with utmost concern a document found at the back of Fr Hubert Lambourin's copy of the Kokura Memoirs.

"Strictly Confidential
ATT: Fr Hubert Lambourin, Personal Assistant to Mgr Jacques
    Pommard, Head of the Section for Asian Affairs
On Friday 5 April 1991
RE: *Showcasing Dissent* Case

Dear Father,
    Because the usual channels of communication may be compromised, I am contacting you directly. After our coordinated efforts over the past ten years, evidence has now surfaced which will lead to the identification and arrest of the so-called master spy *Showcasing Dissent*. I regret that the outcome is likely to shock you. You are still junior in this service and, although I know that you are by no means naïve, you rightly expect loyalty from your collaborators and superiors.

Undoubtedly, *Showcasing Dissent* is a Catholic cleric with some inside knowledge of the Asian Affairs. Last year, two Asian cardinals were discreetly investigated and cleared. We reached the conclusion that the traitor occupies a less prominent position, affording him a wider freedom of action. Now that the current Pro-Nuncio in Tokyo, Bishop William Carew, has also been cleared of any connection with this case, the list of suspects has been narrowed down to one. It is Mgr Jacques Pommard. But because of their administrative involvement with this issue, we must also investigate Bishop Picerno Dorf and Mgr Marco Altemps.

Our agent presently at the Tokyo Nunciature had identified evidence proving Mgr Jacques Pommard to be the master spy *Showcasing Dissent*. The proof was buried on Monday, 23 February 1981, in the tomb of the late Professor Ken Kokura. It is located at Fuji Cemetery, near the Jesuit country residence outside Tokyo. Retrieving the ten-year-old proof is a matter of vital urgency. But our agent feels under suspicion and cannot safely leave the Nunciature; Nuncio William Carew is still in Rome and unaware of the issue; and the Japanese police naturally cannot be asked to intervene. In most urgent need of a reliable outsider, we therefore ask you to fly to Tokyo at your earliest convenience and search the tomb of Professor Kokura. You must travel under strict *incognito* and go straight to the cemetery, avoiding any contact with the Nunciature.

Needless to say, you must be very much on your guard, lest *Showcasing Dissent* suspects your visit. May God protect you and Our Lady keep you safe.

Signed: Dr Pavel Shevchenko, Vice-Head
of Vatican Intelligence

In Tokyo, the recovery of Bishop Picerno Dorf seemed miraculous. If it were not for his doctor's statement just a few days earlier, one might have suspected the prelate of having faked his collapse and subsequent hemiplegia, perhaps as a drawn-out April Fool's Day joke. Admittedly, only a supremely talented actor could have motioned his facial muscles to display such a convincing distortion of the left cheek and left half of the mouth. It was now Saturday, 6 April 1991, and Picerno's face had nearly recovered full mobility. He could even walk around the room, very slowly, one hand holding the end of the bed and the other lying on the top of his imperial Chinese armchair.

He sat down again feeling a bit tired. Still no breakfast brought in. What was that Hana housekeeper doing? She normally came at 8:00am and it was already—ah? another ten minutes to go, never mind. Meanwhile, what was he to think of the Kokura Memoirs? The chapter about a long-dead Jesuit in Japan was perplexing. It did not reveal much though. Who was that "Fr Lukas Fabritius" anyway? Picerno had never heard of him when the merits of the martyrs in Japan were being discussed, prior to the beatification ceremony by Pope John Paul II on 18 February 1981. He should look him up—or ask Marco, who would surely know: he had such an exceptional memory.

But for the present, Mgr Marco Altemps was on retreat in Italy and about to become a cardinal at last, keeping the red hat "warm" for his superior when his name would be cleared of the preposterous suspicion of being "Chinese master spy *Showcasing Dissent*." Forget "Fr Fabritius," then. The real question, the only question was: who was *Showcasing Dissent*? Whoever they were, they had diverted suspicions on him, Picerno Dorf. A silly cipher had even been planted in the brochure he had put together to commemorate Pope John Paul II's visit to Japan just a decade earlier. The cryptic sentence combined syllables interspeded between the stanzas of Kokura's poem on the destruction of Hiroshima. How did it read again? *"Chinese master spy* Showcasing Dissent *forced me to forge this."*

〜〜〜〜〜〜〜〜〜〜

Reclining comfortably in his Business Class chair onboard the Boeing 747-400, Mgr Altemps read Dr Pavel Shevchenko's letter again. It was gravely disconcerting. He wished he had had a chance to visit Fr Lambourin at the Parma hospital. But there was no time and, with his colleague now incapacitated, he had taken the momentous decision to step in on his behalf. Since someone needed to look into this tomb at the Tokyo Cemetery without delay, he had purchased the first ticket available, even though at a considerable cost. Providentially, he was meant to spend the entire week in eremitical confinement, preparing for his consecration as bishop. The abbey guest master had left enough food for him in the tiny hermitage located between the monastic enclosure and the foothills of the Parco Nazionale dell'Appennino Tosco-Emiliano. He had left that night by a side gate into the countryside, wearing plain clothes. His long-range mobile telephone had allowed him to book a taxi for Milan without being noticed by the monks. By agreement, no one was to disturb the recollection of the oblate "Brother Enrico," although he was welcome to meet with the community if he so wished. Thus, Mgr Altemps knew, his absence would not be found out. He might even be back in his hermitage before the end of the retreat.

So, if the letter was accurate, Mgr Jacques Pommard was *Showcasing Dissent*. What a terrible piece of news! Never would Marco have believed that behind the courteous and attentive face of the middle-aged Head of the Vatican Section for Asian Affairs, there hid a wicked, cold-hearted and murderous Chinese agent, or "super-agent." But reading his own name with those of his trusted superiors on a shortlist of traitors to the Church had made Mgr Altemps feel all the more uncomfortable. He was somehow aware of Dr Shevchenko's involvement in intelligence, but he had never suspected that he held such a prominent position as Vice-Head of that Vatican department. Even less had Marco imagined that Fr Hubert Lambourin, this innocent young priest, who so enjoyed driving a sports car and tasting new Italian wines, was a clerical spy. After all, since appearances proved so deceptive, why would these two men not include him on the list of suspects indeed?

What were they after, anyway? What did they fear this elusive *Showcasing Dissent* was plotting? Times were difficult, assuredly. That very afternoon, he had heard on the radio about the military strikes in Iraq. In addition, an anti-Chinese Protest in Eastern Tibet had been broken up by troops. Several missionary priests had been arrested. Did Shevchenko think Mgr Pommard, or "Mr Dissent," was behind the Chinese repression? Or did he suspect him, rather, of having commissioned papal assassinations? Such things did happen indeed.

Eleven years earlier for instance, Paul VI had barely escaped stabbing in the Philippines, in an attempt to prevent his forthcoming speech in Hong Kong where, on 4 December following, he had pointedly asserted, "Christ is a teacher, a shepherd and a loving redeemer for China too." Interestingly, like Professor Kokura the attempted assassin of Paul VI was a painter, a Surrealist from Bolivia called Benjamín Mendoza y Amor Flores. Paul VI's successor, John Paul I, also had possibly been spared a violent death on 5 September 1978. KGB spy Metropolitan Nikodim was meeting him in a private audience, surely with hostile intentions despite presenting him with the gift of an historic samovar. Instead of killing the Vicar of Christ, though, he was the one who had suffered a heart attack and had died in the Pope's arms. It was rumoured that the Soviet Orthodox prelate had been received into the Church when giving up the ghost. Finally, Pope John Paul II had been truly shot by Soviet hit man Mehmet Ali Ağca on 13 May 1981, two months after his trip to Japan.

Mgr Altemps held his crystal glass to the hostess who refilled it with Mumm Champagne. Wearing lay clothes removed the risk of clerical scandal, he told himself smoothing his tie, the one with clashing colours. Besides, since he had been made to pay business fare for his flight, better not waste the privileges. Sipping his wine, he resumed his train of thought. Yes, sending tanks and stabbing pontiffs were brutal strategies, more likely to strengthen Christianity than to weaken it. One pope died, another got elected. And the blood of martyrs produced more Christians. Necessary as it may seem to the Communists, bloody violence had to be a diversion, and nothing more. Therefore, if *Showcasing Dissent* was such a master spy, would he not be involved in subtler schemes?

"Cultural Marxism" was a more efficient threat to Catholic influence. Over the second half of the twentieth century, Marxism under its cultural guise had slowly pervaded Western institutions; it had reshaped the ways of thinking, and painlessly erased religion from society, just as if God did not exist. Cultural Marxism did not deny, nor even oppose God, the Church, Christ, sin and grace, heaven and hell, the saints and the sacraments, or the Bible. It simply made them irrelevant, anecdotal, and practically forgotten. Or worse, if possible, it made Catholicism entertaining, like a drunken gladiator paraded around the arena of modernity and soon dragged back into his cell.

In other words, cultural Marxism made the Church a buffoon, not a ghost: it was safer to ridicule than to annihilate her. As long as she was visible, the Church could not be fancied to be better than perceived. But if she was flattened or pushed underground, dreamers might try to resuscitate her, glorious and attractive. As an elementary precaution, cultural Marxism should publicise its own debunking as yet another banal, right-wing, antisemitic conspiracy theory. Annoyingly, the leading philosopher of cultural Marxism, Antonio Gramsci, born just one hundred years earlier, was Albanian, not Jewish. But the mother of his lovely Bolshevik wife, Yulia Schucht, was. That should do. Ultimately, capitalists should end up thinking of Antonio Gramsci as a mythical author, like Homer or Shakespeare, not as an historic figure whose cultural intuitions were successfully implemented. However, 'By their fruit you shall know them...'

For the sake of his ministry at the Asian Affairs, Mgr Altemps had kept himself well informed of such trends. An acute observer, he had witnessed the concentric erosion of natural institutions such as fatherland, parish, worship, family and, perhaps sooner than expected, the individual itself, if one's natural sexed identity ever came to be dismissed as a mere social construct, changeable at will. "Atomisation" was the term, from the Greek *atomos* "indivisible," based on *a-* "not" plus *temnein* "to cut." Just like matter, once broken down into its core components, became plastically available for creative restructuration, so social constructs were simplified for future re-organisation.

Atomisation meant the severing or melting down of any sorts of bonds, ties, and relationships within society and within the individual. At an accelerating pace over the past hundred years, religion, patriotism, marriage, parenthood, sexuality, even individuality, were undergoing a peaceful dilution, a serene liquefaction. Everything was freed. Anyone could become anything. It fell on those with understanding of the true interests of society to inspire, to lead, and if needed to impose this unprecedented mutation of whatever existed. The definitive motto was, "You change, therefore I am."

Seen in such terms, even the word Communism became irrelevant. "Communism" was but a historical stage within a broader and accelerating process of transformation. Just a year and a half earlier, the Berlin Wall had fallen. Naïve Westerners still danced with joy on the rubble, thinking the Russian bear defunct. Their feet lying on its still warm pelt, capitalist youths watched Hollywood entertainment, not suspecting that Hollywood had become the new Leningrad, and Silicon Valley the new Moscow.

Little would these gullible bourgeois consider that if bears don't shed skin, boas do. Moscow would let them rejoice, like Mowgli in Kipling's *Jungle Book*, who thinks himself safe when bumping into huge empty organic coils, not realising that the boa, very much alive, simply outgrew its old skin, and presently lurks in deeper shadows, only greater and hungrier than before. The Polish Pontiff was hailed as the victor of Communism, whereas that ideology had merely morphed into a less detectible, hence more powerful, phase of influence.

"Yes," Mgr Altemps concluded, "this is what I would suspect a master spy of scheming if I were Dr Pavel Shevchenko.

But I am merely Marco Altemps, a sick little priest who was sent on retreat before being forced into a red cassock and hat."

In Tokyo, a knock on the bedroom door interrupted Bishop Dorf's thoughts. Hana walked in, breakfast tray in hands. With a bow she laid before him a cheese omelette with steamed rice and pickles or *tsukemono*, and miso soup. After nearly a week serving at the Nunciature, she remembered well what His Excellency liked to eat.

Picerno Dorf smiled with contentment as he savoured his soup, spoon in hand. He was done with being fed like a child: now he could eat unaided again. All was going to fall into place nicely. Marco would be back from Italy the following week. They would finalise the details for the ceremony of his installation as new cardinal and for the reception afterwards at Palazzo Altemps. Poor Marco's health would inevitably deteriorate further and, not too soon but, alas, eventually, his long-time friend and assistant would die a courageous death.

Bishop Dorf will have been cleared from every suspicion of being a spy, by then. From secret cardinal he would then be publicly acknowledged as a prince of the Church. Instead of wearing red pyjamas only, he would don the red cassock and biretta, becoming the next Asian Cardinal, *"urbi et orbi."* In anticipation, he resolved to put together a few thoughts for the eulogy at Marco's funeral, praising his friend's dedication and discretion. It could be something very moving, such as, "No Marco, cancer did not defeat you. On the contrary, you vanquished it. You are the victor because you kept hoping, serving and even smiling, against terrible odds."

Bishop Dorf would have been surprised to know that, at that very moment, his soon-to-die friend felt unquestionably alive, flying back toward Japan at very high speed.

Mgr Marco Altemps stifled a yawn. Was Siberia now left behind? According to Kokura's Memoirs, Siberia was where the Troubetzkoys and the Kravitzes had been sent into exile. The prelate looked again through his porthole towards China, wondering how far down the Shaanxi Province lay. He had fond memories of his visits to Emperor Qinshihuang's Terracotta Army, with Mgr Picerno Dorf. There, during the conferences, long-term strategies of great importance for the Church and the world had been elaborated. It was good that Western investors and philosophers had participated, in addition to Marxist and Christian delegates. On 29 August 1977, the "Lintong Agreement" had been signed. Less than fourteen years later, much had been implemented and the harvest had begun. This applied in a broad sense to the fruitful improvements in the way of thinking, but also locally to the pilot farm project run outside Lintong. There droned the *nuclear reactor*, so to speak, of the innovative policy. The Lintong farm was an interface between East and West, a nursery where valuable plants were selected, grown, grafted and enhanced for sharing with those in need. It was a world precedent of international collaboration, even blessed by the stock market, if one considered the sustained increase of the Jeenaco shares.

Mgr Altemps flicked through his inflight magazine to find again the *Uweena Balm* advert he had glanced at before lunch. There it was, in prime position. She was truly beautiful, wasn't she? Selecting Vermeer's *Woman with a Pearl Necklace* had been an inspiration, really a touch of genius. Everybody said so. Long forgotten were the pictures of historic figures once envisaged for the campaign, such as French Health Minister Simone Veil, or Fertility Regulator Margaret Sanger. Instead, Vermeer's beauty had made the Uweena campaign a phenomenal success for the past fourteen years, and counting.

How strange though, Marco suddenly recalled, to read in the Memoirs the qualms poor Professor Kokura had gone through. Yes, the cleansing of Vermeer's *Lady* in Chicago had been agonising for the Japanese expert. If he had been asked, Marco Altemps would have pointed to it as proof that Ken had been a believer, even a Christian one. Catholic training must have shaped the mind of the Hiroshima survivor so intimately that, even after years of religious amnesia he had needed the strongest possible influences exerted on him to act against what he then felt was a matter of artistic deontology. He simply could not erase that cluster of pigments from the girl's stomach. All had ended well, thankfully, and the cosmetic revolution launched via Jeenaco had received from Master Joannis Vermeer the most desirable flag, a banner held, displayed, and followed all over the world regardless of race and creed: the *Woman with a Pearl Necklace*.

Mgr Altemps declined the glass of champagne offered by the stewardess. He needed to rest for a couple of hours now if on arrival he was to explore the grave of the dead Japanese painter at Fuji Cemetery. Without assistance for the sake of discretion, he would need to shift some heavy tomb slab, and perhaps even to lift the coffin out of the cavity. All by himself? Bother! At his age and, lest one forgot, with terminal cancer?

CHAPTER 15

Motion Picture

I WAS GLAD TO BE BACK IN PARIS, strolling along the banks of the Seine. A cold winter sun gilded the Pont-Neuf, under which glided a *bateau-mouche* by the name of *Edith Piaf*. I was not wearing my Buddhist garb anymore, but trousers and a jumper; a naturally-grown grey beard had replaced the fake one. Pressing down on my shaven head my dark green cap, I stood by a *bouquiniste*, browsing through second-hand volumes, novels, outdated maps, poetry and cookbooks.

The bells of a nearby church, probably Saint-Germain-L'Auxerrois, or Saint-Roch, famous for its paintings, prompted me to hurry towards the Louvre. It was almost dark when I reached the small door to the side of the Pavillon de Flore, at the end of the south wing of the great museum, facing the Tuileries Gardens along the Seine. My last visit there had taken place in what seemed a previous life, when the director had asked me to analyse a *Sunset* attributed to Claude Gelée, two years before. Further back, in the 1960s, I had worked on Millet's *Angelus*. Lately I had also helped authenticate the celebrated *Saint Sebastian* by George de La Tour, although I missed its public installation the following year.

The appointment had been made for this Wednesday, 12 December 1979, 5pm. My Catholic contacts had asked me to provide an explanation of a few religious pictures of my choosing. It was a pleasant opportunity for me to prove my grasp of Catholic knowledge based on my professional expertise. They had insisted however on my focusing on faith, not on technicality. My belief, my spiritual conviction were what they sought to assess, not my well-established scientific ability. They were acting on behalf of the Jesuit Order, to which, allegedly, I belonged. Theirs was a delicate exercise. Resuscitating a Jesuit assumed dead in Nagasaki thirty-four years earlier, whose life since, spent in various countries, might have been scandalous or even criminal, called for extreme caution. What were they to think of my second death onboard a Spanish train as art expert Professor Ken Kokura, and of my subsequent impersonation of Buddhist swordmaster Yamato? For all they knew, I could just as well be a Soviet spy in earnest, or a freemason, sent to infiltrate the Vatican.

This test in the Louvre was a mere preliminary. If successful, I would be invited to meet Jesuit delegates. They would figure out a thorough examination of my past in the hope of a future reintegration in the Order, should no obstacle occur, and should I persist in my wish. Should I? Would I? In truth, I was not sure. It was I, as much as the cautious Jesuits, who desired a return by stages. I simply did not feel that I was a Jesuit priest. I knew their order well, based on culture and history, but it was alien to me as far as my personal memory was concerned. It would take much more than an evening in the Louvre for them to call me Father Xavier Hasekura, S.J., and for me to respond.

I walked into the narrow passage into Pavillon de Flore, and made my way to the Seventeenth Century French Department which I knew so well. I sat on a bench as the last tourists left. What quiet; what peace. Alone, with the most beautiful paintings in the world. A cleaner in a tabard was slowly sweeping the polished floor at my side, noiselessly. While she worked, I heard her speak in a low voice, not looking at me. "Master Yamato, we thank you for agreeing on this test. You asked how the Society and you could ascertain your past identity." I knew her voice! She was alive, then. More than alive, she was involved, still, in the elucidation of my life as she had been in New York on that ill-fated day in November 1977. For over two years I had hoped to see her again. Anastasia, or "Annabel"! Ida's true daughter and my would-be child. But how could such a talented violinist now turn out to be a cleaner in the Louvre? Why had she swapped her bow for a broom? Had she hurt the slender fingers which had brought back to life Biber's Rosary Sonata at St Jean-Baptiste Church?

Now she stood behind me. If only I could turn my head and see her face. But I was to pretend no one was talking to me. Did safety demand this painful stratagem? To think that they had sent her, of all handlers! They seemed to know me well, or they really wanted me: no agent would have been more likely to persuade me to defect and cross over to her side. The Jesuits had seized the opportunity of her being in Paris, performing some of Vivaldi's concertos "Per Anna Maria" – she later explained – asking her if she could introduce me to the test. She had readily accepted, rightly assuming that I would trust her intervention more than a stranger's.

She spoke further, softly and invitingly, "If you are the one we expect, you will find out the formula that explains the unity between these three paintings. It must include the following expressions: '*The deeper the...–... ...–the brighter the....*' You must discover the four missing words. In my cart you will find this text printed with the four blanks to fill; plus a Holy Bible, a blanket, a torch, a sandwich and hot coffee. You have until dawn. Pull up the blind on the middle window as a sign if you finish sooner, and you will be fetched. Security are aware of your presence here overnight 'for urgent painting analysis commissioned.' God bless you."

Could not the test have been postponed? I so much craved to see Anastasia further, to speak to her... She was the safest link to my past. Now she was gone, holding her broom I assumed, and I had not even looked in her eyes, let alone felt her hand. The dreadful thought crossed my mind that I might be hallucinating again. Dr Tanaka had warned me against holding imaginary conversations in public places, with mysterious agents whose faces I never quite saw. Had I dreamt that encounter? Was I not truly healed then from the ongoing "Heinrich" delusion? But this time I was able to check. I opened the flap to the cleaning cart and found a folded sheet of paper reading *"The deeper the...–... ...–the brighter the...."* The coffee was hot in the thermos bottle. I drank a cup, laid the flask upon the folded blanket, shut the flap again and set to work as Anastasia wished me to.

I found myself alone in Room 910. On the wall in front of me were three masterpieces by Georges de La Tour. I knew them well, in particular the last one, which I had authenticated the past year in view of its acquisition by the Louvre following its chance discovery in a chapel in Normandy. I had published several articles on La Tour, justly celebrated for the mysterious quality of his candlelit depictions. As I had observed since my visit to Jallier in Spain the previous June, Catholic terminology and theological concepts now sprang into my mind not merely as technical tools to analyse Christian paintings, but nearly as acts of faith. Whereas most of my adult life I had interpreted religious depictions as if the existence of God, and of the Christian God in particular, were irrelevant—what I now explained I also believed.

Did that make me a Catholic? I was not sure. I did not feel ready to acknowledge any corporate belonging. Neither can I affirm that a relationship had started, or been restored, between me and God. "Prayer" was too big a word for me. Praying was something I had no right or ability to perform, it seemed to me. I may be admitted to it later on, after much penance, and patience, and silence. Meanwhile, naming Catholic dogmas and articulating faith concepts was the closest I dared to come to praying. It was a way of showing God and myself that I did care and perhaps might be admitted to express my aspiration, some day, like a common suitor rehearsing his proposal in the antechamber of the princess.

The painting on the left was a Nativity scene: *The Adoration of the Shepherds*, painted circa 1645. Some humble folk from the hills of Bethlehem had come to the cave, summoned by the angels: "*This day is born to you a Saviour, who is Christ the Lord, in the city of David. And this shall be a sign unto you. You shall find the infant wrapped in swaddling clothes and laid in a manger.*" The shepherds had believed the stupendous news. Lowly and poor, they had been the early witnesses of the Incarnation: they had adored God Almighty made man.

La Tour had painted them, rustic and solicitous, a circle of artless adorers around the divine Child. His Mother St Mary sat on the left, and his foster-father St Joseph on the right.

I liked the juxtaposition of the bearded shepherd's stick and of the younger one's flute. The flute looked like a stick. Drilled through, that wood let one breathe in its holes, producing music. A third cylinder, of wax this time, showed in St Joseph's hand: his candle. That was a further improvement. The stick could be felt only by one's skin on one's back if beaten. That was the Old Testament God as feared by the disobedient Hebrew people. Better, the flute could be heard through one's ears and soon in one's very heart. That was the Messiah announced by the prophets. Finally, the candle could be seen with the eyes and its flame warmed the soul. That third cylinder evoked the Saviour incarnate, calling every contrite sinner his brother.

I watched the many elements in the composition come into play. Each of them allowed multiple connections with several others, not at random, not arbitrarily, but guided by the deposit of the Christian revelation.

These are my thoughts just as they occurred to me. I wrote them down the following day.

The postures of the five adults delineate a circular space, a kind of cell whose centre is occupied by this little face of the Child. They worship the baby God of this family temple. He is sleeping. How sweet he looks; how fragile he seems, so small in the circle of these massive silhouettes. Is it possible for a God to condescend to such reduction? He is silent, mouth and eyelids closed; nostrils wide open, however—he breathes. Is that all his teaching for now: that he lives among us?

Unless... Unless a code prohibits pedestrian, worldly, and fickle souls from accessing the temple's hidden sanctuary. It takes the time, the patience and the humility of contemplation. Everything is then illuminated... by this flame glimpsed behind the hand of Saint Joseph. It is small, fragile and clear like the Child. If the fingers folded back, suddenly the smothered flame would leave the whole scene of which it is the only light—in darkness. Now, isn't this Newborn called "Light of the Nations?" And are not the fingers of a man already stretched out to order the guards to slay him? *"Herod sending killed all the male children that were in Bethlehem, and in all the borders thereof, from two years old and under, according to the time which he had diligently inquired of the wise men."*

If therefore we look at this candle in the hand of Saint Joseph as a symbol for the Child on the straw; then let us ask ourselves in what other "hand" our Newborn lies. There, just as five shadowy fingers bend over the flame, so five figures, five faces crowning five chests lower themselves towards the Child! It is therefore a gigantic "hand" open in front of us, whose palm supports the sleeping Jesus and whose five fingers each have a human face! How to express more dramatically the core truth of the Incarnation, according to which God abandoned himself in the hands of men? He became man to nail sinful man to the Cross in his own flesh, and to resurrect in him men reconciled.

I stepped back from the painting, considering how the composition supported my interpretation. Yes, I felt that I had identified the dynamic analogy that brought together the various elements of this *Adoration*. I paced to and fro in the centre of the room, holding my hands behind my back. I was nervous, as if sitting for an examination, but also elated by my efficient mastery of Catholic concepts. I found that there was more to my theory than logic. The feast for the mind offered by my analogy between the five figures and the hand was pleasurable, not so much because it was clever as because it was true.

I sat down to drink a cup of coffee. Where was Anastasia? Should I explore the adjacent rooms and find her, perhaps waiting for my call? How much I longed to share with her my interpretation of La Tour! But on the sheet in my hand, the riddle clearly stated that the *three* paintings had to be included, not just one. Checking my watch, I found that I had already spent nearly two hours on the first panel of this triptych. I knew that tiredness might slow me down later on, so that I had to focus on the next painting while my faculties allowed it.

~~~~~~~~~~~~~~~~~~~~~

Saint Joseph the Carpenter was displayed in the middle of the wall, although La Tour had probably painted it first, in 1643: hence two years before the *Adoration* hanging on the left, and six years before *Saint Sebastian tended by Saint Irene*, on the right. The curator had rightly followed the chronology of Salvation, though, not that of artistic production: first the birth of the Saviour; then his childhood; finally, the exemplary death of his follower, St Sebastian.

In *Saint Joseph the Carpenter*, the foster-father of seven-year-old Jesus drills a piece of wood with an auger. He is bent over the wood, while the Child holds a candle. My take was that, if the activity of St Joseph was obvious, that of Jesus was subtle and invited the beholder to discover it. Our souls are before Christ like the piece of wood before Joseph. Foster-father and Son both mean to work on their chosen matter, but with different techniques, those of a carpenter and of a God respectively.

What happens in this soul that Christ, divine joiner, handles?—I wondered. What delicate tool does he use to reach men without hurting them? The painting answers us. It is again with a drill that Jesus visits us. Not the metal one, whose wooden handle Joseph grasps, but the other one, the wick protruding from the wax handle, of this candle that the Child holds in his hand. Both elongated coils are represented in the same vertical plane where the candle seems to extend the auger. But one sinks towards the ground, while the other rises towards the sky. The movement of their twists therefore unites candle and auger by its common verticality, and distinguishes them by their opposite directions. Thus, it appears to me that these two objects and their two trajectories represent one and the same spiritual dynamic: the expansion of divine grace as sought by man or as granted by God.

I crouched by the painting, trying to condense in sparse words the contrast I had identified. It was so. Yes, left to human forces alone (God forbid), the proclamation of the Gospel would be stillborn. It would progress in the world and souls only with the slowness, the arduousness of the auger in the hands of Saint Joseph, the metal penetrating the wood only in a hyperlocalized way, without the slightest impetus. Without any fruit. On the contrary, when God presides over the establishment of his peace in individual consciences and in the family of nations (peace, even with Americans, those Hiroshima bombers?), his reign spreads across shadowlands with supreme ease—or to put it better, with the instantaneity of this illumination of the flame (held here by the Child) in the pure air: God says: "Let there be light," and lo, light bursts forth!

Standing up with enthusiasm, I felt slightly ashamed, as if usurping a missionary point of view whereas I was barely awakening from my own unbelief. I leaned against the door post, wondering. Had I inertly lain like St Joseph's block of wood for the past thirty-four years, whilst boasting of my skills to capture the meaning of paintings and the truth about my past? All that time, had God offered his grace as gratuitously as the Child Jesus holding up his candle? Why had I not seen it? Were my eyes shut? Even now, were scales falling off them?

In need of physical movement, I wandered in the next-door room. It was empty and dimly lit. How many more masterpieces awaited my examination? All of a sudden, I became aware of the vast quantity of painted signs displayed around me, which so far I had seen but not *looked* at. These paintings displayed a common inspiration: whether still-lifes, landscapes or portraits, they had germinated and blossomed on the richest soil of French Catholicism. I was familiar with them from a cultural perspective, but only that night did I start connecting with them as messages truly destined for my soul. Up to now, they had been items; now they were gifts.

~~~~~~~~~~~~~~~~

Already 10pm? The faint bell, ringing from St Roch Church, made me realise that I had to hurry, as there was no need, surely, for me to spend the entire night in the Louvre. La Tour's third painting, *Saint Sebastian tended by Saint Irene,* made me feel confident. The year before, the President of *Friends of the Louvre* had requested me to authenticate it, following its discovery after WWII, in poor condition due to high humidity in the village church of Bois-Anzeray in Normandy. My radiographies showed several *pentimenti.* I was also familiar with the life of St Sebastian, the famous commander of the Emperor's Pretorian Guard, finally turned Christian and martyr. Numerous paintings and sculptures depicted him bound to a tree, his flesh pierced with countless arrows.

Saint Sebastian's biography, as it soon appeared to me, was the main axis of the composition in La Tour's masterpiece. There he lay on the ground, mourned by four Christians. Each of the four grievers evokes a decisive stage in the life of the young martyr.

I started with this young woman standing in the far right, furthest from Saint Sebastian. She refers us to the earliest event in the life of the martyr when, after having helped the Christians in secret for a long time, Sebastian decided to throw off the mask, publicly professing the faith he shared with them. The linen that half conceals the face of that young woman in the background constitutes her common attribute with the martyr. Indeed, Sebastian's only clothing seems to be the very same linen as the one across the woman's face.

The hood of the second character reproduces with exactness the dimensions, the conical structure in converging quarters and the inclination in relation to the horizontal axis of the picture—of the helmet at the feet of Sebastian, fallen officer. It reminds us that the Pretorian commandant was stripped of his armour after confessing his Christian faith.

A long and flexible cord descends from the belt of the third mourner, that woman in the centre. The cord undulates along the fabric and rests on the rock. Around the tree, one can see the rope with which St Sebastian was bound for his execution. This third relay of the cord with the rope therefore illustrates the crucial stage in Sebastian's life: the practical consummation of martyrdom.

But Saint Irene's red dress, finally, the closest to the saint among the four grievers, gives us hope thanks to the connection it suggests with the two discreet leaves "forgotten" above her torch. Does not the elegant ruffle around her waist reproduce the rounded serrations and characteristic veins of the oak leaf? Oak and martyr seemed dead, yet both are alive. In a moment, in wonder St Irene will open her mouth and eyes still closed and, thanking God she will announce: "My brother lives!"

~~~~~~~~~~~~~~~~~~~~

Midnight. Now standing between the half rolled-down blind and the large window, I looked towards the Seine flowing along the Louvre. From time to time a car drove by along the bank; a few cabs; a flashing but soundless police van. The sky had become cloudy, but it was lit from beneath by the many lampposts and other illuminations still on across the vast "City of Lights" despite the late hour. Across the river, no longer did the Pont-des-Arts graciously span the streams of the Seine towards the Institut de France, where the Académie Française meets. The bridge had collapsed after a barge rammed into it last October. I recall that my friend, art historian Kenneth Clark, had chosen that pedestrian bridge as the starting location for his epic *Civilisation* series filmed eleven years earlier, during the May 1968 student riots. Had civilisation collapsed sooner than the bridge?

To the left, the twin towers of Notre-Dame were discernible, albeit unlit. In contrast, far to the right, I could see the graceless top of the Eiffel Tower: that unfinished *derrick* whose ninetieth anniversary of completion had just been celebrated. I averted my eyes from it, giving thanks for the genuine beauty of the classical monuments surrounding me, and for genuine civilisation further displayed here in the Louvre.

Tiredness got the better of me and I sat down to eat the sandwiches before taking a nap on the padded bench, rolled into Anastasia's blanket.

~~~~~~~~~~~~~~~~~~~~

I overslept. Where was I? Awakening alone in the Louvre after midnight was not rehearsed for. Once I had found my bearings again, I set to work. It was 2.17am.

The past evening I had explained to myself, and convincingly for my examiners, I hoped, the Catholic significance of the three paintings displayed side by side on the wall of Room 910. Leaving aside radiographies and *pentimenti*, I had simply applied the dogmas of Christianity. Those had worked as efficient tools, I felt, bringing to light a wealth of meaning. For the first time I relished the orderly interaction of so many painted elements, like a discreet mechanism powered by rational faith. But this was only a first stage. I now had to elucidate the riddle for my judges to assess how much I understood, or believed, rather, about Catholicism.

The printed note unfolded in my hand, I read once more the lacunary sentence, "*The deeper the...–... ...–the brighter the....*" Providing a coordinated analysis of several paintings had not been my idea for this test. When I had mentioned La Tour as a painter whom I may like to be asked about, I merely expected my jury to test me on one or several paintings separately. Now they wanted one single formula to unlock three systems at once. That was much more challenging than I had anticipated.

My gaze scanned the three painted rectangles, searching clues as to what was "deeper" and what "brighter" according to the code. The two first paintings had identical dimensions; only, the *Adoration* was horizontal and *St Joseph* vertical, as if the original shape had rotated sideways, now resting on its narrower end. *St Sebastian* was still vertical, but of a somewhat larger size, as if the painting had grown. I noticed that not only the dimensions, but also the dates of the three works were similar, all having been painted within the same decade of 1640-1649.

That being said, they were not designed as a triptych, at least not in the way German or Spanish side-panels are hinged on a central one, whose main theme they introduce and conclude. The hazards of history often separate such panels, subsequently acquired as single pieces and displayed in different art galleries without their original counterparts. Such was evidently not the case with the three La Tours. And yet, here they were, the three of them depicting Christian themes, by the same painter, of similar sizes and times, side by side along the same wall before my eyes.

Some thread, I sensed, ensured unity between the three images. When considering them together, I felt a peaceful harmony, a rhythm, almost a tune inviting eye and mind to navigate the three rectangles as three music sheets in seamless and melodious continuity. What was their secret? What enlightening symbol would translate this colourful cipher into intelligible words? My heart felt the warmth, the depth and the life of the three-stage message displayed before my eyes, but I needed words if my mind was to account for such spiritual wealth.

It was about light and love. The three paintings depict nocturnal scenes. In each of them, a candle is held: by St Joseph, by the Child Jesus, and by St Irene. Below each candle, a body lies: the Infant, the woodbeam, and the martyr. A weapon is directed towards each body: the shepherd's stick, St Joseph's auger, and the archer's arrow. Innocuous at first (the stick does not touch the Infant), the weapon later penetrates the body (the auger drills into the wood), and finally lies immobile deep inside it (the arrow barely emerges from the martyr's torso).

I sensed that I was on to something. Yes, these various parameters seemed to be synchronised. A variation in one paradigm affected the others, as if all were coordinated. Considering the body for instance: it seems to pivot as if to remain perpendicular with the weapon to facilitate the blow. Thus, the Infant lies left-to-right under the stick coming from top-left to down-right; the woodbeam lies vertically under the auger; and the martyr lies right-to-left with the arrow piercing him from top-right to down-left.

What of the candle? Does it follow the same orchestrated pattern, I wondered? Screened behind St Joseph's opaque hand in the *Adoration*, its flame becomes visible above the Child Jesus' smaller hand (and even through its thin flesh) in the *Carpenter*, while wax, wick and flame are fully exposed in St Irene's hand in the *Martyrdom*. Therefore, in a continuous gesture across the three pictures, the candle-bearer's left hand moves away from the right hand that carries the light.

Furthermore, in the left panel of the triptych, the *Adoration*, a group of characters (Mary and three shepherds) contemplate the victim (the Infant) to the left of the candle-bearer (St Joseph); whereas in the right panel of the triptych, the *St Sebastian*, another group (three mourners) arrives from the right of the candle-bearer (St Irene), mourning the prostrate victim (St Sebastian). Only the central panel, the *Carpenter*, depicts no group of onlookers. It seems then as if, left and right, shepherds and mourners gathered around one and the same victim, enlightened by one and the same candle.

The variations between the three paintings refer then not to different scenes but to different stages in the same action. Strictly speaking, yes, there are three distinct events: Christ's Nativity, his education and his saint's martyrdom. But what La Tour suggests, skilfully in my opinion, is the continuity of a process. Christ comes into the world to save from sin fallen humanity through the free offering of his life in sacrificial death. From crib to Cross, the Nativity aims at Calvary. Even Christ's homely childhood in the tranquil household of Nazareth prepares him, his family, and his people for Golgotha, the place of the redemption. Finally, following Christ implies bearing witness to him as the truth enlightening all men, even at the cost of one's earthly life as St Sebastian's martyrdom illustrates.

~~~~~~~~~~~~~~~~~~~~~~~~~~

Those are my observations succinctly brought together. They came to my mind and heart slowly, peacefully, over the course of several hours spent long after St Roch's bells had struck twelve, in the dim light of the La Tour Room, during that mysterious night. It was not dawn yet when I heard light footsteps approaching in the main gallery. I checked my posture, only then realising that I was on my knees before the "triptych," my hands resting on the padded bench in front of me. The footsteps were coming closer and I instinctively started rising, lest a security guard found me in that implausible posture to examine a painting.

For the first time in my life, as far as I recalled, I became aware of the opportunity of a public stance as a Catholic believer. I could remain kneeling and be found in that telling position. I also could be spared the awkwardness, stand, and pretend I was merely "analysing" the pictures, as Security had been informed according to Anastasia. What would I choose?

Looking at the Infant, at the woodbeam and the martyr, I concluded that, perhaps, after all, I might do just as well if remaining on my knees. No Roman archers entered Room 910 but a friend, a daughter, a sister in faith. I did not need to turn my head when she stood behind me, nor did I jump when her hand lightly—like a dove—perched on my shoulder. I awaited no further sign, no prompting of hers, to utter what I had by then grasped of the secret: "*The deeper the wound—the brighter the light.*"

She knelt by my side, looking at the three pictures. She did not ask for the missing words. She simply commented, softly, as if we had been in church, "You have found much already, or found it again. You have found heroism. Here is Christianity: '*The deeper the wound—offered up—the brighter the light.*'"

~~~~~~~~~~~~~~~~~~~~~~~~

We walked out of the Louvre as in a dream: everything was white. It had snowed later that night, enough to coat most horizontal surfaces. We crossed the street along the riverside, following the parapet upstream. It was past 8.30am and the sun was rising. Now I could fully see Anastasia. She had changed from her borrowed cleaning staff uniform into a stylish rose coat and a beige fur hat. Despite my sleepless night I felt exhilarated by my dive into such considerations of deep faith, and by Anastasia's tender support. Do fathers feel like that when walking their bride daughters down the aisle? Her summary of Christianity, as decoded from the La Tour triptych, sounded to me like a haiku, that three-verse type of Japanese poem.

> *The deeper the wound—*
> *offered up—*
> *the brighter the light.*

My elation reached its climax when the gilded dome of the Palais Conti, across the Seine, started dazzling in the first rays of sun. We trod with great care lest we slipped, since the pavement along Quai du Louvre had not yet been cleared from the snow.

As we had first stepped out of Pavillon de Flore, Anastasia had said, "Please follow me to the Théâtre du Châtelet, over there, just four minutes upstream. That is where I performed last night; I was instructed to debrief you there. We can speak in my dressing room. If asked, since you once heard me play in New York, plainly answer that you are 'a critic from America.' After that, you will go into hiding. Please take this envelope: the address of your safe house is in it, with some money."

I quickly read on the note "Sœur Paulette, Couvent Sainte Claire, 8bis Rue des Repenties, 75009 Paris." Without much conviction, I pushed the envelope into my pocket and walked further at her side, wondering.

Anastasia's mid-heel shoes nearly made her slip in the snow by the steps onto the collapsed Pont-des-Arts on our right. I offered my arm, which she accepted. A pale winter sun was shining over the river. Pushing my cap more tightly across my shaven head, I inhaled with delight the crisp morning breeze. Anastasia's smile, though, seemed to me polite more than warm.

Unable to wait until our formal conversation in her room, and assuming that she deplored my half-failing the test, I ventured, "I am sorry that I found only two words out of four. Thank you for having disclosed the missing ones earlier. I will need time to think over it. But, will the Jesuits still want to see me, do you think?"

She waited before replying, as if distracted, and I realised that she was worried. We had passed the Louvre and proceeded towards Quai de la Mégisserie. She warned me, "Yes, they will see you. But I beg you, Master Yamato, do take extra care! You have now formally entered the process of conversion, or reversion to Catholicism. Those who trained you in the USSR will surely not allow this to become public, once they realise you did not die in Spain."

I was struck by such an abrupt shift from my all-night meditation on faith to some espionage threat. As far as I was aware, my loose involvement with the KGB had ceased long ago. I only hid further under Yamato's identity because he had secured my incognito as an incentive to visit Jallier. I would not have dared explore the alleged setting of my childhood as Professor Kokura, the art expert, in case it gave the Jallier family some obvious clues about who I really was.

Admittedly, I was worried that Yamato had not turned up at Dénia, the ferry terminal from Ibiza, at the end of his solitary retreat on the desert rock of Es Vedrà. At the hotel there, I had only found his note telling me that he had embarked on a new "Telluric Tour." My friend was experienced enough to go on without me, and I was grateful to him for having left me his authentic passport. I assumed that I would hear from him soon when contacting his wife in Japan.

In the Basque Country that past June, I had allowed Yamato to stage my death on the scenic train, as a way to force me to look into my plausibly lost identity. In a way, I had "killed" Professor Kokura to prevent any return to the comfort of my past life. I had burned my boats and was since forced to move ahead towards my plausible origin. I replied confidently to Anastasia, "My dear friend, surely I am small fry to them compared with the hostage crisis at the US embassy in Tehran, or the rumours of invasion of Afghanistan."

The only pedestrians at this crossing, we were kept waiting by the traffic light. Ahead of us, to the left, shop keepers were wheeling out cages with furred animals. It was the traditional pet market, as I learned after. Cold-sensitive species had small heaters above their cages. A few passers-by were looking at the fluffy and feathery creatures. I heard, or so it sounded, the high-pitched scream of peacocks. Intrigued by the animals, I led the way across the zebra crossing (or crosswalk), with Anastasia following at my right elbow. But she had no time for rabbits and birds. She stopped before we had reached the opposite pavement and had me turn; she looked at me in the eyes and warned, "We both know that you were part of their undercover strategy to infiltrate Western institutions. They invested a lot in you, as they once did with Uncle Chimek and Mother. Please beware. I so much wish you to come back to your..."

Her eyes suddenly widened in terror, she yelled, "Father!" – and pushed me away towards the pavement, where I fell.

An engine roared by; I vaguely heard Anastasia being hit; she collapsed near me. I got up half stunned and saw a van skidding on the snow, now veering on the pavement ahead of us, now colliding violently with cages, row after row until, avoiding a plane-tree, it managed to get back on the road and drove off.

There she lay upon the snow, both legs apparently broken. She looked unconscious, or worse. I leant over her, desperate to ascertain whether she still lived. Would she need the Last Rites? Surely, not from me! I felt no breath from her mouth, and her eyes were shut. Then I thought I heard her whisper, "Run," as her head drooped to the side.

In horror, I rose to my feet, calling for help. A couple of pedestrians arrived but my French was not up to it, and I started panicking. Everything went so fast! An ambulance was heard I think, or a police car, I was not sure, but it speedily drove by, perhaps chasing the runaway van. In front of us all sorts of animals scattered—those that had survived the hit-and-run—now let loose from their broken cages. Hamsters, squirrels, rabbits, perhaps even a snake, hens, ducks, and budgies cackling, yelping, squealing and shrieking ran or flew in every direction, even across the road where the traffic came to a halt. Soon enough, though, an ambulance arrived and medics ran to Anastasia.

Had the collision been accidental? Was Anastasia's foreboding of reprisal justified? No one there knew my connection with her. Assuming I was just one among the pedestrians, they let me walk away. Overwhelmed by fear, unable to ponder, I did as she wished me to and hurried some ten yards ahead to Place du Châtelet where, stammering, I asked a cab for "Couvent Sainte Claire, 8bis Rue des Repenties." Right behind us, Quai de la Mégisserie was in total chaos as shopkeepers and passers-by tried to catch hapless animals.

Through the cab's rear window as in a frame, my eyes were spontaneously attracted, I recall with shame, not to Anastasia's ambulance, but to the exquisite chromatic contrast offered by a peacock fully fanned out in the middle of the snow-covered road. Its tail splendidly spread in one hundred eyes, each of them of blue lapis lazuli within a green circle, as if freshly painted upon a wide white canvas. All this happened in a flash. Within the same glance, I admired another pea-cock which, having taken off, majestically ascended along the Théâtre du Châtelet. Still, as my taxi turned the corner, it was a dove, I believe, which I last saw flying by, over the snowed embankment.

~~~~~~~~~~~~~~~~~~~~~~~~~~

The feast of the Epiphany fell on a Sunday that year, as I found out in Rome that 6 January 1980. My appointment at the Jesuit Headquarters was scheduled at 2pm. It was cold and I strolled around the historic city centre. I walked into one of the famous Jesuit churches, Sant'Ignazio, where I wished to see again the breath-taking painted ceiling with trompe-l'œil architecture by Tyrolese Jesuit Andrea Pozzo. I also meant to ask St Ignatius Loyola, the founder of the Jesuit Order, to... In fact, I did not know what in particular I expected of the saint. In retrospect, expecting anything of a seemingly long dead, invisible, and personal entity was already a big step for me. Calling that entity "Ignatius" and establishing even a tenuous relationship with it, prepared me for dealing with the "elephant in the room," namely, whether or not I believed in a similar entity, that one *uncreated* though, who allegedly founded not a religious order but the Church universal, and also created the entire world out of nothing, and redeemed it through becoming man and dying on a cross.

I was kneeling at the rear of the vast Baroque church while looking at the fresco on the ceiling, trying to persuade myself that sightseeing during Sunday Mass was no lack of reverence. After all, the fresco was painted worship, was it not? The lit-urgy taking place in the sanctuary did not particularly attract me, I don't know why. It seemed to me that the woman read-ing from the ambo lacked credibility, and as musical accompa-niment in such a spectacular Baroque architecture, rather than guitars I would have suggested cellos. Suddenly, worshippers standing in the pews before me turned back and reached for my hand, shaking it, unheeding my kneeling posture.

Of course, I did not go to Holy Communion when everybody stood up in line and had the small white disc handed them. For the first time I realised that if I persisted in assuming the identity of a Jesuit priest again, I might have to receive Holy Communion daily, and even to offer Holy Mass. Admittedly, I was feeling somehow disconnected. I suppose that, all along those months of transition, I was slowly allowing myself to become accustomed to the daunting prospect of my return into the Catholic fold. I did not feel joy. Rather, I was like a mature animal, say, a bird, expected to curl up back into its eggshell—or into a crab shell, if not a chrysalis—whichever would turn out to be my true origin.

After Anastasia's accident, I had kept hidden for a fortnight at a Poor Clares Convent in Paris. It had been my best Christmas so far. I had attended their Latin liturgy with emotion and had spent many silent hours, at night in particular, in their private chapel, crouching or kneeling far at the back. I stopped my morning sword practise. Nor for want of a weapon, since I could have used a stick instead. Rather, I found myself spontaneously spending my usual half hour (and longer time in fact) in the chapel. I was still on my knees; I was still silent; my eyes were still shut. But instead of trying to dissolve into an anonymous whole, I was allowing a relationship with a personal presence. I felt as if some little flame was growing out there and, far from snuffing it with my blade as I had done for decades, I now delighted in its growth.

Sister Paulette had found out that Anastasia was still in coma. It was then, I think, that for the very first time I prayed—without naming the one I addressed, though. The memory of the La Tour "triptych" was deeply impressed on my mind. Much as I wished to visit the Louvre gallery again while being in Paris, I owed it to Anastasia to remain unseen as she had asked. Sister Paulette secured for me a discreet transit to Rome and arranged the meeting with the Jesuits. In the Eternal City, I checked in as "Mr Yamato" in another very discreet hostel ran by nuns, near the Pantheon.

The Mass was ended at Sant'Ignazio Church and everybody started chatting. Leaving the building, I ambled towards the Vatican, assured of arriving well ahead of schedule at my appointment, perhaps to pray there. On my way, before Piazza Navona, I popped into San Luigi dei Francesi, or St Louis-of-the-French. Here too Holy Mass was over, and I squeezed between tourists who stood shoulder to shoulder outside the Contarelli Chapel, to the left of the sanctuary. There, three famous paintings by Caravaggio depicted the life of the Apostle St Matthew, the infamous tax collector turned evangelist. A new coin had to be inserted every thirty seconds in a timer for electric light to flow, revealing the pictures. The images were displayed on the three walls of the middle-sized room, which looked like a large box lined with canvases.

I found a reminiscence of the La Tour triptych in the compositional thread connecting the three pictures. This time it was not the candle-versus-weapon pattern, but the *table* around which all three paintings revolved, as the life of the evangelist did: the counter of the tax collector (left painting); the writing desk of the evangelist (central painting), and the altar of the sacrificing bishop (right painting). Thus, I wondered, were these three depictions designed as another triptych? I found stimulating that invisible link between the three rectangles, as an invitation to the spectator to "connect the dots." It engaged my mind, I now realise, preparing my heart.

I attempted to explain to myself what attracted me in these images. Caravaggio's triptych reminded me of the multi-hinged solar panels on our modern satellites, such as the Russian *Soyuz* I had glanced at in *Corriere della Sera*, an Italian daily, during breakfast that morning. Like wings to the satellite floating into sideral space, its solar panels unfold to turn sunlight into energy, enabling communication between *Soyuz* and Earth. Similarly, the conjoined panels of Caravaggio's life of St Matthew hang across the gloomy expanse of the Contarelli Chapel and convert into belief the data of Christian revelation, displaying shapes and colours before the onlooker's eyes to feed his soul with food for faith.

Like satellites, the panels painted by Caravaggio are highly sophisticated communication devices. Using pigments instead of chips, they emit binary signals where true-or-false takes the place of one-or-zero. No television subscribers, but Christian souls equipped with the virtue of faith, receive and decode the signals. The core of the message is: "From the darkness of sin to the light of grace, Jesus is the Way." I was intellectually convinced, and yet, it did not seem to apply to me. Why did I linger on the outskirts of the Catholic faith? Why did I shun personal encounter with God incarnate? How could the true story of the evangelist Levi, for instance, bring clarity and peace to my own existence?

At that moment, a little bell was heard and a priest in his mid-sixties vested in white, a black biretta on his head and a veiled chalice in hand, slowly made his way into the chapel, his eyes lowered or even shut, and ascended the step below the central painting. Only then did I take notice of the marble altar standing there. The tourists near me stopped chatting or taking pictures. Out of respect, no coins were inserted into the timer for electric light anymore, so that the paintings became little noticeable, in contrast with the bright light flowing from the semi-circular window at the top. Holy Mass had begun.

It happened just as I had witnessed it at Jallier a few months earlier, and at the Poor Clares' the past fortnight. The priest was facing the altar, speaking in Latin, not once looking at those of us who stood or knelt at the rear. In the middle of the Mass, when the celebrant lifted high the consecrated host, brighter light flooded in, I seemed to notice, through the window high above the altar—in effect the only source of natural light in the entire chapel. I realised that Caravaggio's images, whose general composition was still discernible in the subdued light, included painted shadows producing the illusion that the sunlight from the window hit a three-dimensional space rather than flat canvases. A Baroque artifice, the fake shadows spread like real ones, as if sunlight had turned into pigments.

But the curved shape of the window above the altar caught my imagination. It was not a full circle, merely the upper half of a disc, made dazzling to our eyes through the contrast between the shade indoors and winter sunlight outside. Surprisingly, the priest had not moved yet, and I started wondering whether he was unwell. His hands were still lifted above his head, immobile, holding the host towards the window whose semi-circular shape it replicated. That visual analogy between bright window and white host struck me. I analysed my impression as follows.

The priest's hands, elevated partly above his head, held another white half-disc: the host drawing our gaze to itself. I knew that the lower half of the host was concealed by the priest's thumbs and screened by his head. The host was certainly a complete disc, even though I saw only its upper half. By extension I fancied that, above the altar, the window as well might be a full disc, not of bread, but of glass, its lower half *hidden behind* the painting. Two discs then, mirroring each other. The wider glass disc above looked like the smaller bread disc below. One was filled with created light, the other with the uncreated God (according to Catholic teaching).

That correspondence prompted an intuition in me. The window was to space what the host was to faith, I perceived. Just as no physical light entered the Contarelli Chapel but through that window, similarly no spiritual light entered the Church universal but through the Eucharist. Just as Caravaggio's paintings owed their composition to the central window projecting sunlight, so Catholic doctrine radiated from the Eucharistic dogma. Just as the painted shadows referred to the source of true light, so catechism, liturgy and charitable works depended on the Eucharist.

All of a sudden, it became obvious to me that the Holy Eucharist was the centre of the Catholic faith. In my mind, this realisation was still quite distinct from faith in that sacrament, or of love for Christ. But it stated with vigour and clarity that Catholicism was credible according as it showed reverence to the Holy Eucharist, at Mass and outside of it.

Holy Mass had taken well beyond the normal duration; tourists or worshippers were growing restless. After the old priest was gone, I heard a father placate his mid-twenty-year-old son, strangely wearing sunglasses indoors, "I know Fr Jean-Marie takes long to offer his Mass, Mel, but thank God for his keeping to tradition." Another tourist or attendee, seemingly in the know, confided, "He might not be permitted to use the old missal if his father had not once been the Ambassador to the Holy See."

Electric light resumed as coins were pushed into the slot again, and I took a last look at Caravaggio's three paintings. Yes, from the tax collector (left) to the evangelist (middle) and to the martyred bishop (right)—*transit* was depicted. Gold turned into ink; ink became blood. A sinner stepped into grace. Caravaggio's "triptych" well illustrated the very dynamic of Catholicism whereby, first, God became man; second, Man became food; finally, eaters became God—or no less shockingly, believers were divinised. I did not eat then, and I prayed little. But I had grasped the logic and beauty of such a process. It made sense to me.

<hr />

Generalate Borgo S. Spirito 4, 00195 Roma. I read again the address printed on the letterhead confirming my appointment. There I stood, outside the world headquarters of the Society of Jesus in Rome. From this place, as Heinrich had once told me, 36,000 highly trained priests were governed and assigned special missions, in every country, on every continent. One Jesuit was worth ten ordinary priests, he had assured. One ordinary priest could inspire at least one hundred lay people. Heinrich had reckoned further that one layman could influence about ten other people.

In contrast with such a concentration of power, the building almost disappointed me. Instead of a shining citadel flanked with high towers, protruding gargoyles, and adorned with multicoloured flags, the generalate looked rather bourgeois: a simple, inviting five-storey building, with not even a statue of the illustrious founder St Ignatius Loyola standing on the balcony. One could imagine visiting merely one's family dentist in there.

I don't know why it prompted this memory from 1947. Once in Moscow, in between two sessions of painting analyses at our laboratory, Comrade Churakov had taken our little team for a visit to the KGB headquarters. I remember standing with trepidation outside the Lubyanka building. In that same place I had feared being taken back for "debriefing" and "recycling" in 1978, when Anastasia's letter in New York had jeopardized my cover as a Soviet agent. How I had dreaded being recalled!

I walked around the little Roman square, to give me time. At the end of the narrow street on the right, the colonnade and dome of St Peter's Basilica reminded me that I was standing at the very heart of Catholicism. Did I truly want to be part of it? Why not walk away? After all, I had a trade, connections, and interests. The alleged Vermeer painting in the chapel at Jallier Hall gently gleamed in my memory. There, far away in the Spanish Basque Country, within an unsophisticated frame, the Mother of God stood on the right, looking towards a window on the left, by which a young man bowed to her, his wings almost entirely concealed behind a hanging curtain. Who would authenticate it, if I became *Fr Xavier?* Could I not pursue such a promising endeavour, after having hoped for so long to come across that painting?

Why not wait another few months before losing my independence, before taking upon me the yoke of Jesuit obedience? Admittedly, Professor Ken Kokura was assumed dead. *NADIR* was right: I had bequeathed my patrimony to the 'Restoration Fund Trust for Dutch Golden Age Paintings'—(how on earth had they found out!) But that straw charity was solely my initiative, and its chairman was no other than Yamato. He would not let me starve—especially not, I realised with tremor, since he had disappeared, *de facto* leaving me to act in his name. Since my patrimony was under my control, albeit under Yamato's identity, could I not even "resuscitate" Professor Ken Kokura, reactivating my radiography apparatus? Well, what then?

On the campanile across the square, the bell struck 2pm. I turned towards the façade of the Jesuit generalate again. To think that this was where it had all begun for me... Only then did I notice the medallion of modest size stuck against the first-floor balcony. It was a crowned Virgin with Child depicted in white against a blue background in a style reminiscent of Della Robbia's glazed terracottas. It was not much, but enough to remind me that the Jesuits had been the most prolific and successful promoters of fine arts.

Looking at the bright winter sky as if for the last time, I breathed deeply, swallowed, and walked into the building.

CHAPTER 16
Voice of the Dead

UJI CEMETERY WAS NAMED AFTER the iconic Japanese volcano nearby. As if to celebrate the octave of Easter, nature looked its best that Sunday afternoon. Indeed it was Low Sunday, 7 April 1991. At 16°C the temperature was almost warm and the "sakura" or cherry blossoms spread above the thousands of mossy graves, like a living canopy of soft pink flowers.

Walking under the trees felt like an initiation, especially when, through the roof of petals, one glimpsed the massive snow-capped silhouette of Mount Fuji. Japan's highest mountain is considered the goddess of fertility and Fuji worshippers walk through the "Funatsu Tainai Jukei," a lava tunnel symbolising the womb of the goddess. Below the mountaintop, although within the precincts of the cemetery, visitors could see the children's area. On the tomb of every child, whether miscarried, stillborn or having died in infancy, stood a statue of "Jizo," the Buddhist deity protecting dead children. According to custom, all Jizo statues were clad in red by the parents, as a token of mourning for their lost progeny and in gratitude for Jizo's care of their little ones in the afterlife.

Despite it being Sunday, a grave-digger was at work in a remote area of the cemetery. Christians were buried over there whereas Buddhists were cremated, which was cheaper and, above all, required much less space for burial. Down in the grave, the labourer in blue overalls now stood erect, catching his breath. He had managed to push aside the heavy marble slab and now, down at the bottom of the deep cavity, was busy unscrewing the lid of a coffin. A small group of about half a dozen people strolled by. They were probably a family on a "ohakamairi," a ritual visit to one's ancestor's tomb to rest his soul (*haka* is Japanese for *grave*). The mourners seemed to enjoy the idyllic weather and picturesque pink waves of the cherry trees undulating in the breeze. They stopped by a couple of cars parked at some distance under the trees, while three of them slowly walked towards the grave. On crutches and supported by his uniformed chauffeur, the older one stepped close to the tomb, enquiring of the grave-digger, "Any success, Marco? Did you find *Showcasing Dissent* lying in there?"

Unexpectedly for a *Burakumin*—a Japanese outcast—the perspiring grave-digger replied in fluent Tyrolese, "Good afternoon, Picerno. No, it seems we arrived too late. The box is empty! Kokura's bones are gone. Look, the inside is neat and clean, with not even a rib or a finger left in a corner. They must have done it yesterday or last week, since the wood shows fresh and white where the missing screws protected it until lately. The only clues are these pottery fragments and a printed picture, as if of a Vermeer painting, sealed in a plastic sheet."

Still looking up at his friend standing on the edge of the grave, Mgr Altemps swept off his brow the sweat resulting from his exertions. Coughing, he pointed out, "But your timely arrival here indicates that Dr Pavel Shevchenko has shared with you his suspicions, as I have learnt myself. Terrible business, isn't it? I would never have suspected Mgr Pommard of being a Chinese spy."

"Neither would I. It was generous of you to interrupt your retreat in Italy and fly all the way here. But why did you not simply telephone me? I would have come here straight away to investigate."

"I thought of this, naturally. But Dr Shevchenko's letter demanded utter discretion, and besides, you were still recovering from your stroke. In fact, you may not be aware that you, Picerno, and I, are also under suspicion."

"I know. As a matter of fact, I have been mandated to play the following tape to you, because it is relevant to this case. By the way, you don't mind if Fr Lambourin takes the ladder out, do you?"

Without waiting for an answer, the third man, who looked to be in his late twenties, bowed down towards the rectangular hole in the ground and swiftly pulled out of it the narrow ladder which Mgr Altemps had used to access the bottom of the grave. A bodyguard received the ladder from the priest. Like Bishop Picerno Dorf, Fr Lambourin was wearing a clerical suit.

Bishop Dorf nodded at Fr Lambourin, who next took a small device out of his pocket, commenting, "This is Sony's brand-new digital audio tape recorder. The sound is perfect, as if one heard it live. Please just listen."

A different voice, that of a ten-year-dead priest, started speaking in English. Instead of coming from the grave in which Mgr Altemps stood, though, it flowed from above ground, effortlessly bridging the decade-long gap.

"ATT: Fr Jacques Pommard, Head of the Vatican Preparatory Delegation for the February 1981 Papal Visit in Japan

"Official Statement made in the presence of Fr Jacques Pommard, of Dr Yuko Tanaka, my mental health consultant, and of Mrs Annabel Kim, née Anastasia Kravitz; at St Luke's International Hospital in Tokyo, on 20 February 1981, 3:25pm; by myself, Fr Xavier Hasekura, S.J., born on 29 August 1920 at Jallier Hall, Spain, of Baron Paul Hasekura, diplomat, and Baroness Isabella Hasekura, from Aoba Castle in Mutsu Province, Japan. This statement is recorded with my explicit consent."

The narrator's voice sounded confident, but increasingly feeble, as if under mental or physical strain.

"I, Fr Xavier Hasekura, S.J., in full possession of my mental faculties, will hereby identify the Communist spy called 'Heinrich,' referred to in the memoirs I was asked to write down as part of my process of reversion to the Roman Catholic Church and reintegration into the Society of Jesus (Jesuits). Heinrich co-opted me in Japan in early 1946, in the aftermath of the Hiroshima and Nagasaki bombings. Officially representing the

University of Wittenberg in Germany, he secured for me an academic formation as an art expert at the service of the USSR via the Soviet Committee of Arts of the Council of People. Suffering from amnesia, and left unidentified by any relatives or acquaintances, I accepted Heinrich's offer, not realising his true purpose. Only on 2 February 1950 in London did Heinrich formally enrol me as a Soviet agent. I was to live undercover in the West and pass on information as demanded, which I did. Prior to this..."

The recorded voice had slowed down considerably. It bore every sign of pain or exhaustion. After a silence though, it went on.

"Prior to this, Heinrich ordered a third party to assault a lady collaborator and had me charged with the crime. The imputed assault would not be divulged as long as I followed Heinrich's orders. Blackmail was used to keep me on a lead once I would be settled in the West. My amnesia and the lack of any known relatives or witnesses from my past made me particularly vulnerable to Heinrich's manipulation. Whereas I never saw him again, to my knowledge, after February 1950, I corresponded with him frequently thereafter. But on 28 October 1977, Heinrich informed me that I was free from my obligations towards him and the USSR. He even affirmed that the entire relationship had been a delusion of mine, implying that I had never been working for the KGB.

"Doubting my mental health, I fell into a state of depression. This providentially ended with my conversion and the reappropriation of my past. Once reintegrated as a Catholic priest and a Jesuit, I was asked to prepare for a meeting on the following 24 February with the Holy Father Pope John Paul II, with whom I was also to concelebrate Holy Mass at a large outdoor event. On arrival in Tokyo a week earlier, I was introduced to various Catholic religious and secular clerics who welcomed me most amicably. Two days ago, one of them asked me for the text of my poem *Redemption through Painting*. It is to be included in a book to welcome the Holy Father. Yesterday, I was left with the same priest to rehearse the questions I would be asked when meeting His Holiness, and the answers I was likely to give. After a few minutes of conversation, the priest smiled and said..."

The voice broke, silence followed, and the recording seemed to have stopped. Then water was asked for; one could hear ruffling and shuffling around the hospital bed; and finally, drinking. The narrative resumed slowly, interrupted by heavy breathing.

"The priest smiled and, instead of addressing me as 'Fr Hasekura,' he asked me, 'Now Ken, what's up?' His voice seemed to have changed, sounding higher pitched. Simultaneously, his face took on a different expression—with raised highbrows and a wider smile—and, despite the thirty-one years since I had last seen him, I recognised *Heinrich*. He approved of my public return into the Catholic fold, explaining that it had been part of the plan from the start. Then he congratulated me for having orchestrated my own 'detonation' on the train in Spain and my subsequent vanishing under a fake identity. 'You nearly fooled me, old boy. It took me four full months to get back onto your trail and find out your new identity.' However, he stressed that 'agents don't detonate themselves without orders.' I had acted against the rules and had incurred punishment.

"I could redeem myself though, if I followed the new instructions now communicated by him, my handler. I was to attempt to stab Pope John Paul at our forthcoming meeting. Heinrich strongly insisted on the fact that by no means was I to kill or even wound the Sovereign Pontiff. 'You must raise your dagger against him innocuously. But be sure to wait until a guard is close at hand to intervene and catch your arm *before* you might touch the Pope. Some Polish blood on the carpet, or on the *tatami* rather, would do no harm. But we are not there yet. Don't give them a martyr!' he warned. 'You will be arrested, tried, and we will make sure that the verdict exonerates you on the ground of insanity, based on the delusion diagnosis you skilfully obtained from Dr Tanaka. To sustain our claim, we will easily demonstrate your ongoing obsession with Fabritius' painting of Mercury slaying Argus, and your daily sword exercises, quite inconsistent with your meek and scholarly behaviour.'"

After a silence, the narration started again, slowly.

"Horrified, I ingenuously asked Heinrich why he wanted me to do such a thing. He smiled and agreed that, now a senior agent, I was entitled to some deeper insight than before. 'Thus,' he explained, 'this *Solidarność* trade union in Poland is causing serious disruption and we must restore order. But Japan leans towards the Western position and will probably back up the petition for negotiation with *Solidarność* and the Polish Church. An assassination attempt by you, a Japanese celebrity, on the Polish Pope during his official visit in Japan, will cause the Japanese Government major embarrassment, forcing them into diplomatic neutrality. Call it a diversion, or a gentle pressure. It worked well last time, when we sent Benjamín Mendoza to Paul VI in Manila. I should introduce you to each other since he is a painter, like you. That is what gave me the idea.

"'So,' he went on, 'that shall be your detonating, on *our* terms. After that, of course, you won't be able to function as a secret agent. But we will secure a happy retirement for you. I can already think of two American universities eager to have you as a visiting art lecturer to assert their independence of mind. As proof of your good faith as a Catholic, albeit one mentally instable, we will have you complete the conversion process of Svetlana Alliluyeva, the daughter of Comrade Stalin. She already became an Orthodox and, after due preparation by one Fr Giovanni Garbolino, she is about to move to England, settling in Cambridge where we would like you to return, befriend her and receive her into the Catholic Church. We believe that she will respond well to a converted KGB spy such as you. After that, staying in England further, you may persuade your old artistic friend Kenneth Clark, who is also ripe for conversion we are told.'

"Heinrich did not consider for a second whether my return to the Church was genuine or not. He did not even wave the usual threat of revealing my alleged crime against Ida Kravitz. His confidence in my compliance was such that blackmail felt unnecessary. Such boldness paralysed me with fear. He spoke as if assured of my assent, based on our past friendship. I knew that deep inside me lurked the faint but actual possibility of acceptance. I could see that I had been under his sway for decades and, just when I had broken free, his unexpected apparition made me lose confidence and hope.

"He then put his finger on the sorest part of my conscience. 'Ken, you and I know that from the start you remembered much more than you admitted, even to yourself. You just got used to pretending, and chose to leave your old religious self behind, like shedding skin. I never asked whether your motive was resentment against the old order of things that had failed you; or pride when helping to create a new society; or cowardice, hindering your costly return to what you still held as partially valid. Soon after awakening in 1945, you ceased to be a victim: you became a *constrictor* of your past, if I may say so, and a constructor of a better future.' I was terrified, because Heinrich was speaking the truth as if reading in my soul, although I had never expressed these thoughts with such brutal accuracy. It has been nearly a day since he found me out, and his words still burn my heart like melted lead dripping on silk."

A pause occurred. It sounded as if the bedsheet was being moved. One could hear steps in a nearby corridor, and subdued voices of staff. Fr Pommard was enquiring whether the interview should not be completed later, giving the sick priest time to recuperate. But Fr Xavier went on with exhausted determination.

"Heinrich observed that I was deliberating. He added, 'As an art expert, surely you can see that real life is not painted in black and white. Reality entails a broad spectrum of hues. Speaking as a cleric, I can tell you that our strategy is backed by powerful churchmen. Not everybody at the Vatican is satisfied with the new pontificate, and moderating the zeal of this young Polish pope would also serve the interests of Catholicism. The immediate effect will be to put a halt to the rise of the ambitious prelates organising this papal trip. Their inability to prevent the assassination attempt will make them look like fools, or amateurs to say the least, and they will be sent packing. Especially after the fiasco four days ago in Karachi. You have heard of course of the grenade that exploded right before the arrival of Pope John Paul II at Pakistan's National Stadium, haven't you? Seventy-thousand people were gathered for Mass. Not a good start for the very first stop of the pontiff's twelve-day tour across Asia.'

"'By the way,' Heinrich continued, 'I can tell you now in confidence that churchmen in high positions knew of your being planted as a KGB mole from the 1950s, and approved of a Catholic for the job. They said that amnesia was a splendid cover, and that no one needed to ask you whether it was fake or genuine. You are not our only asset. Some of our best agents don't even know that they work for us.'"

The recorded voice of Kokura had become more composed, perhaps spurred by a hint of anger.

"I was totally taken aback. I had assumed that the mixture of manipulation and delusion in which I had spent most of my life as an amnesiac had mercifully dissolved, allowing me to know myself and to relate to God and neighbour on safe ground again. But Heinrich's statement plunged me back into nightmarish uncertainty. How could the Church have condoned my being planted into an atheistic administration, and that without enlightening me? On the other hand, I was freshly returned to Catholicism. What did I really know of its ways and means? Did not the Vatican need intelligence to do good?

"After a little while, I told Heinrich that I had confessed my entire past and from now on, I aspired only to transparency in the service of God and souls. Patting me on the back, he said that he wholeheartedly supported my resolution, adding that no further mention of my past activity need occur in the future if I did as I was told. As he left the room, grinning, he turned back and, as if it went without saying, calmly stated, 'Of course, I will deny having commissioned you with this assassination attempt. On the contrary, if ever questioned I will answer that I asked you for any names of KGB Catholics, helping us to protect the Church against infiltrators, as Bella Dodd had successfully done.'"

After a brief interruption, the recorded voice concluded.

"Suddenly, I realised that Heinrich was just such a person to me. He was a Catholic cleric, and I had known him during my KGB years. It dawned on me that he was possibly *testing* me on behalf of the Church. Perhaps after all, he had been a Catholic in earnest from the start, working undercover inside the KGB. Was I meant to report him, as my definitive test to pass for full reintegration into the Catholic Church, especially when preparing to meet the Vicar of Christ himself? But how would Heinrich react if he was a Communist for real? Might he not incriminate me, suggesting I had faked amnesia and had willingly collaborated as a KGB mole? Who would trust me then? Would I even be allowed to function as a priest again? I had never yet found the courage to start offering Mass. I know that my qualms seem puerile, but please bear in mind that, up to this day, I have had very little practical experience of the Church as an institution, having just found my way back after a year of discernment.

"I went in the chapel to pray, feeling very dizzy and sick. It had been years since post-bombing nauseas had troubled me. After a while, it became clear to me that I had to report Heinrich, whatever happened. That day, yesterday, I was taken ill to this hospital where I thankfully received psychological support.

"Now uncertain of my near future, I wish to discharge my conscience before God and Church, and I solemnly declare the KGB spy 'Heinrich' to be the same person presently known as 'Fr Marco Altemps.'"

CHAPTER 17
Reborn in Japan

THE JESUIT GENERALATE IN ROME looked like any administrative centre. Walking to the front desk, I produced my letter of appointment and was speedily directed towards the "Readmission Department." A cleric ushered me into a room where other men were waiting on chairs spaced out in a wide circle. I was given the ticket number 9. Three more participants arrived. We were all sitting in uneasy silence. Were all these gentlemen in lay dress, looking so diverse in clothing, race and demeanour, former Jesuits, I wondered? Surely not the woman on the chair by the window. Unless all were examiners—the eleven of them!—called in to assess my case. Two priests in black suits walked in, chatting. They sounded rather casual, as if willing to put us all at ease. In my diary that evening, I noted down their words to this effect:

"Hello, hello everyone. Great you could all make it. We are truly sorry to have you work on a Sunday. It is just that we have been a bit swamped with readmissions over the past month and weekdays don't suffice. Well, what about introducing ourselves, as a nice start? I'm Kevin, sort of in charge of this process, but Carlos here is the one doing all the work! I am from Canada, and he is Colombian. Okay, so in your flyer, you have seen the '7 Steps' which we invited you to walk with us for this session and after. Good news, people, we have already completed Steps 1, 2, 3, and even 4! That is: Step One: You have thought of reaching out to us. Step Two: You have successfully done so. Step Three: You have passed your preliminary test based on your life situation and personal interests. Step Four: You walked into this room. Now Step Five: kindly share with everyone here who you are and what you hope for."

I was feeling dizzy, as if the room was a stage and all participants, but I, were actors. Were they all testing me?

We introduced ourselves. One had dropped a lucrative career as an investment banker, now aspiring to manage Jesuit assets instead of capitalist funds. Another apologised for his nine years spent with the Lefebvrists in Switzerland. Having finally got over his fundamentalist leaning, he was offering himself afresh for work as a Jesuit. The woman spoke on behalf of her sick husband, a Jesuit laicised fourteen years earlier. His long illness had given him qualms and he wished to explore possible readmission before he died. When my turn came, I did not mention my earlier identity, since "Professor Kokura" was officially dead. A "Hiroshima survivor turned swordmaster" provided sufficient background for my fellow-applicants, in my opinion. The only profile slightly similar to mine was a Nicaraguan Jesuit who had infiltrated the Chilean administration, had been betrayed, tortured, imprisoned for three years and assumed dead by his superiors. After his escape from jail, he had failed to inform the Jesuits, and had worked for years as a lay schoolteacher instead. He now wished to come back.

Step Five ended with a small cup of Italian coffee. I knew that in-depth scrutiny was bound to follow. Surely no religious order, and especially not the Jesuits, would take back a shadowy candidate such as me after merely a night in Le Louvre and chitchat in a coffee room. I was therefore bracing myself for some very serious investigation ahead. They would expose me or kick me out. Why had I ever set foot into that building!

We were then assigned separate interview rooms. I walked into mine, feeling rather uncomfortable. I noticed a Bible lying on the table, next to a pad and pens, and a jug of water with a glass. "Kevin" himself sat opposite me, soon joined by one I would never have expected: Dr Yuko Tanaka. She explained how, over the past two years since our chance reunion in the Peacock Room in Washington, she had accepted invitations to treat Catholic religious suffering from Post-Traumatic Stress Disorder. Most of her patients were Jesuits rescued from zones of political conflict. I was not the main purpose of her presence in Rome on this Reintegration Session, she confided. But having been tipped on my application, she wished to put her knowledge of my earlier itinerary to good use, and there she was. I was touched by her fidelity, but also anxious, guessing that a witness of my earliest awakening in 1945, and of my delusional fits in 1978, would not allow me to hide any aspect of my identity. She kept calling me "Professor Kokura" (rather than "Swordmaster Yamato") and would leave no stone unturned to assess, and hopefully to confirm, my Jesuit origin and belonging.

~~~~~~~~~~~~~~~~~~~~

Our conversation lasted about fifty minutes. I learnt from Kevin that, even as a young man, Xavier was very knowledgeable about classical paintings. He had taught himself Dutch, purely for the sake of reading first-hand correspondence from the Dutch "Golden Age." I agreed that it fitted happily with my attraction for the same era in art history, even though I still did not remember having been the young enthusiast portrayed by my interlocutor.

Having pushed to the side of the table the Bible and water, Dr Tanaka had been taking notes. She was very interested to hear that I had recently stopped my daily sword practice, using that time for mental prayer before the Holy Eucharist instead. As if speaking to herself, she announced, "For decades you would snuff out a candle with your sword, every morning. Now that you are coming to terms with your Catholic past and identity, you don't feel the need for it anymore. This change is highly significant and bodes very well. I suggest that the sword practice was a protection mechanism. It fits the psychological pattern of the 'Little Boy in the Wood,' a type of traumatic bonding. According to it, the subject (i.e., 'little boy'), finding himself alone in the wood (i.e. his helplessness) and fearing the hungry wolf (i.e. the menace), starts *howling* to identify with the predator. He attempts to convince himself that he is safe, since he cannot be predator and prey at the same time."

I objected that the attack belonged to my past—the destruction of my city—rather than threatened my future, as far as I was aware. But Dr Tanaka explained, "The person you were just before the bomb exploded, Professor Kokura, did not know of the imminent threat. You have felt for his (your) unawareness. Seeing yourself so much at risk in retrospect led you unconsciously to identify with the threat as if to cancel your past vulnerability. In that protection mechanism, the lit candle stood for Hiroshima (or Nagasaki, that is, yourself), your sword figured the bomb, and the snuffing out replicated the nuclear blast."

I was taken aback, so eerily did Dr Tanaka's diagnosis echo my interpretation of the "La Tour triptych" in the Louvre. There, a fortnight earlier, I had identified the combined movements of "victim," "weapon," and "flame" across three paintings. But I had not shared my finding with "Kevin" and Dr Tanaka yet. Nor could Anastasia have told them my elucidation, since she was still in coma according to Sister Paulette. Had I been watched all along, then? Was "Heinrich" in control even now? I made an effort to repress a bout of paranoia as Dr Tanaka went on.

"Every morning, you unwittingly impersonated the American bomber. It helped you make sense of the event, taming its horror through imitation. But the very routine of your morning sword exercise also locked you up in a traumatic posture. You were caught in an emotional loop, reiterating the sequence as would—if you allow me the blunt comparison—a demon performing an exorcism. Eventually you had to recognise that the issue lay within you."

I kept silent, shocked as I was by Dr Tanaka's analysis. I had braced myself for some painful examination, but not for being called a devil. What unsettled me most was to realise that she was probably right. Suddenly the name of the bomb dropped on Hiroshima flashed in my memory: "Little Boy." Had I *identified* with the bomb itself? Had I become "Little Boy," "in the wood" or wherever I had spent the past thirty-six years? Had I been "howling" all along, like a child prey hoping to deceive a ravenous wolf?

After a pause out of respect for my emotion Dr Tanaka concluded, now opening the Bible. "Professor Kokura, since you are now engaging with your past life as a Catholic, it might help if I reframe my diagnosis in biblical terms. Most adults harbour some nostalgia for childhood perceived as Edenic peace lost. This feature is exacerbated in your case, as an amnesic survivor of a major catastrophe. It is expected that you should long for your life before the cataclysm: a past all the more idealised since you don't remember it. I suggest that the nuclear explosion has impacted your psyche like God's avenging angel did for Adam in the Book of Genesis. Let me quote it: 'The Lord cast out Adam; and placed before the paradise of pleasure Cherubims, and a flaming sword, turning every way, to keep the way of the tree of life' (Gen 3:24). It seems to me that you have identified with the angel holding a flaming sword when, day after day, you would spring forward, sword in hand, to reach the flame of the candle, symbolically setting your steel afire. You appointed yourself fearsome keeper of your longed-for past, unawares, rather than helplessly suffer its inaccessibility."

I did not know what to answer. I recalled with embarrassment my earlier breakdown in Los Angeles when, pressed by Dr Tanaka, I had dialled the number of the speaking clock in Reykjavik, Iceland, forcing me to question the protocol allegedly set up by "Heinrich." To hide my awkwardness, I helped myself to a glass of water.

Kevin then laid on the table a metal case labelled "No 28344: Hasekura, Xavier—9 August 1945." He extracted from it two clay items and an envelope. The clay items appeared to be the darkish lid of some china jar, and a plain white-and-blue tile such as found in Delft. The large brown envelope bore the inscription, "The Dutch Painter's Papers." In it was an old stapled brochure typed in Spanish, dated 4 March 1937. Its title read: *Letters of a Dutch Jesuit missionary in Japan, summer 1663. First known translation from the Dutch original into Spanish, by Xavier Hasekura, S. J.*

Kevin announced, "Now Yamato, these papers should interest you. Xavier translated them during his formation in Spain. It seems that he had uncovered some relics or manuscripts from Japan, don't ask me how. The exhumed text lays itself open to contradictory interpretations and, unfortunately, it made Xavier's relationship with some of his formators uneasy. Jesuits in Japan were thrilled by the discovery, but in Europe, two brethren grew suspicious of it. Meanwhile, World War II was spreading from Europe to Asia, and no one had time to elucidate so secondary a matter as the authorship of three old letters. Xavier was then called from Spain to Japan, where he died in the Nagasaki bombing, as was assumed until last month when you contacted us. It seems as if these 'Dutch Letters' simply got forgotten. As you will see, they contain many clues which match very well your subsequent career as an art expert. Perhaps too well? On the other hand, the primitive ecclesiology and the crass anti-ecumenism betrayed by the letters plead for their authenticity. Their tone and scope unsavourily smack of Counter-Reformation Catholicism. I would like you to take the time to read them. Please take notes of anything which could contradict, or confirm, the identification between Xavier and yourself. We will see you again in two hours. There is a coffee station in the left corridor if you need, by the lavatory."

I was flushed, but also apprehensive, as they left the room. Loosening my green bow tie, I started reading.

"First Letter, probably written on 24 June 1663, at Nagasaki, Japan; translated from the Dutch original into Spanish by Xavier Hasekura, S.J.

"To the illustrious Joannis a Mare, Lord Master of the Guild of St Luke, Delft

"[missing words or paragraph...] with joy. It has been nearly a year since I last heard from home. But for us followers of Jesus Christ, 'home' is wherever one does the holy will of his heavenly Father, *Deo adjuvante* [i.e. by the help of God].

"Receiving Your Lordship's letter and sketches was a little miracle. Here our ships from Macau are barely permitted to anchor by a floating deck, a small artificial island called 'Dejima,' outside the mainland of Nagasaki harbour. Of all Western traders, only we, Dutch merchants, have been given access in the past twenty-two years. The Japanese granted us this favour in recognition for helping them crush the uprising by native Catholics at Shimabara between 1637 and 1638. I learnt with horror that thirty-seven thousand of those, our fellow-believers, were beheaded in retaliation. Your Lordship will understand my shame when I realised that our own fellow Delft citizen Nicolaes Coeckebacker was the one whose ship, *De Rijp*, during an entire fortnight gunned our Catholic brethren besieged in Hara Castle. The deck of Dejima burns my feet, every time my cover as a guest-painter at the local palace leads me there to procure canvases, paintbrushes and pigments. I tread on its planks in sorrowful reverence, mindful of the Catholic blood which my own country shed to enjoy trade monopoly.

"On unloading the cargo from our ships, every crate is thoroughly searched, and the faintest Christian depiction mercilessly destroyed. The same applies to export goods. Even this innocent letter will only have reached Your Lordship if its concealment in a vessel of my inspiration proves successful. Lay visitors can set foot on Japanese soil only under strict surveillance. But the last priests and friars who attempted landing were immediately arrested and executed, needless to say. May God have mercy on their souls. Those dreadful hindrances to spreading the Gospel of salvation break my heart. To think that our Father St Francis, blessed be his name, had founded such a flourishing Church in this remote kingdom. His 200,000 converts included many daimyōs [i.e., feudal lords]. Just over a century later, nearly all Christian believers are in hiding, or dead, or exiled, or worse—they have apostatised. Such...

"[missing words or paragraph...] dismay! What spiritual ruins everywhere! Parishes, priories, guilds, pious societies, so many religious paintings and statues and even the seminary went up in smoke. It reminds me of our beloved Delft after the explosion, that fateful 12 October. So vividly impressed in my memory is the sight of our hometown ablaze, that I wonder how it can already be nine years since the cataclysm. By boat along the canal, as Your Lordship heard me recall more than once, I was coming back from a business trip in The Hague on behalf of Cousin Carel. He had sent me to show a customer a mythological depiction with Mercury and Argus, for which the merchant offered less on realising that it was not by Rembrandt. Now a Jesuit and therefore a successor of those who laboured so generously here in Japan decades ago, I feel as if the consternation that writhed my heart on my return to Delft, that terrible 12 October 1654, occurred again here in Asia when, once ordained in Macao, I landed in this martyred Christendom.

"At Your Lordship's request, I readily provide below the full text of my *Lamentations on Delft* dedicated to our musical patron Master Cornelis Graswinckel. May I reiterate that the original idea comes from the poem attributed to our beloved Fr Peter Canisius, S. J., 'The Waste Vineyard,' in which he compares the spread of heresy with devastation by fire, implying that Martin Luther was the chief arsonist.

"Lamentations on Delft"

"*Ditch* no more, but *Death* is now your name—O *Delft* my city!
What was, has ceased. It is daylight now elsewhere in the world,
    but here the darkness seems thicker than any night.
How can I still breathe while you lie dead, O my city laid waste?
Before my eyes, beyond the side of the boat carrying me towards
    you, nothing moves but snakes of smoke, billowing from your
    once comely face as horrendous hair on Medusa's head..."

After whispering to myself the first stanzas a second time, I interrupted my reading of the letter. My elbows on the table, it took me a moment to remember that I was not in

seventeenth-century Japan or Delft, but in the Jesuit Generalate in Rome, on 6 January 1980. I had read the long poem
with deep emotion, wondering at the unexpected connection
it offered between my Japanese youth and my later specialising
as an expert in Dutch painting. With anxiety and anticipation,
I came back to the dead Jesuit's narrative.

"Your Lordship gladdened me with the prospect of my poem
being soon put into music under Master Graswinckel's patronage, with accompaniment by *violas da gamba*. But it should more
fittingly be played here in Nagasaki where, in truth, the damage
is much worse. In Delft, the explosion of the gunpowder magazine destroyed half our city in one minute. We mourned the
104 victims, among whom our sorely missed Carel, his wife and
children. But even though there had been a hundred thousand
of them, even though the entire city had been razed to the
ground, mere numbers would not offer an accurate assessment
of the tragedy, for natural life and possessions are not the ulti-
mate good. Nothing is truly lost, I have learnt, as long as divine
friendship is retained.

"What is so tragic here in Japan, and particularly in Nagasaki
where Christianity once prospered like a plentiful harvest, is
precisely the loss of God's revelation, of God's Church and
sacraments, of God's baptised children. Even though the entire
city of Nagasaki went up in flames in an instant, God forbid,
unjust and tragic as it would be, still, it would not compare
with spiritual damage. Apostasy is the blast to dread, because
houses and bridges can be rebuilt, whereas souls leaving this
world as fiends to their Saviour shall not change their mind in
the next. Forever, they shall hate Love. Your Lordship can now
better appreciate my torment when seeing the Evil One triumph,
uprooting the life of grace from souls. All that is left to us here
are muted prayers and covert sacrifices.

"By God's grace, though, some souls persevered until death:
our glorious martyrs. Daimyo Takayama Ukon and several of his
relatives chose to lose rank, fortune and privileges, embracing
death as exiles, rather than betray the Saviour and Holy Church.
Daimyo Hasekura, the fearless ambassador to Spain and Rome,
on his return died a Christian, and his children and servants died
as martyrs. Furthermore, secret conversions have taken place, and

I have even performed my first clandestine wedding. Praise be to the Lord Jesus who strengthens us through the witness of his saints! May our tribulations turn to the greater glory of God.

"But the woes endured by Your Lordship's family are no less my concern. Indeed, I burn to learn of Your Lordship whether Mistress Catharina has recovered from her latest childbirth so soon after her accident. I was deeply distraught by the news of her fall in the staircase a mere fortnight before her delivery. May Your Lordship be assured that I did offer the Holy Mass requested, seven of them in fact, even though the news reached me on this far side of the world long after her outcome. How I admire the patience and forgiveness of Your Lordship towards Master Willem! The mere thought of a Christian assaulting his sister, and this when she is least able to protect herself and most deserving of deference and assistance for the sake of the life she carries, in addition to her own dignity as a pious mother! O my master and friend, how this constricts my bowels and makes me want to vomit, as if I were the one whose belly had been kicked. Was it not enough for Master Willem to have called his devout mother a 'papist sow'? Worse than invectives, are blows now needed to win Catholic ladies over? Notwithstanding, your brother-in-law is more to be pitied than condemned. For his salvation as well, I offered the seven Holy Masses. Still, I would sooner excuse such a crime from the pagans among whom I have lived for nearly a year since I set foot in this 'Empire of the Sun,' as they call this realm. Few among this people have heard that God became a Child in the womb, and later appeared to shepherds and magi, raised in the Virgin's arms like the true Sun of justice. He fa... [missing words or paragraph...].

"May Your Lordship be thanked for the news from Europe, albeit it is news no more where you are, reaching me nearly a year later. Would Your Lordship send my deepest condolences to the family of our fellow-painter Adriaen Pietersz van de Venne? I loved his landscapes much. He will be missed, even though he did not share the true faith. I will pray that his soul might have been 'fished' while he had time. As to the fire in London, surely not even Protestants would accuse Catholics of such a crime! Or are we back to Nero's times? It would be like charging Catholics with having blown up Delft nine years ago, on the basis that the gunpowder magazine where the accident took place was a former Augustinian Priory. Still, I am so very sorry for the Londoners. Here in Japan, people still mourn many victims from the Great Fire of Edo, the imperial capital, some five years ago. Thankfully Nagasaki feels safe, so far. What joy to read that our convert playwright Joost van den Vondel still meets with ongoing success. How I wish I could have seen his play on the Precursor of the Lord!"

"Your Lordship was much kind to have passed on my greetings to Mistress Mathilde Megalopensis. I owe her husband my conversion, as Your Lordship remembers. Despite having abandoned his native Catholic faith and embraced the errors of Calvin, the Reverend Johannes charitably rescued my fellow-Jesuit Fr Isaac Jogues from the cruel Indians in New Amsterdam just twenty years ago. I was a boy of about nine when the spectacular story of Fr Jogues became known in Europe, including in our country. I recall how horrified I felt when learning of his capture by the natives and his one-year-long persecution, during which he managed to save a pregnant woman from drowning, and baptised one of his torturers. I was thrilled by his providential escape from savage Manhattan, sheltered by 'Dominie' Megalopensis with whom he conversed in Latin; of his landing in French Brittany half dead, unrecognisable, his fingers cut off, and of his quiet answer to his host enquiring about the missing missionary Fr Isaac Jogues, presumed captive or killed: 'He is at liberty and it is he, Reverend Father, who speaks to you.'

"I shivered on learning of the commotion of sympathy throughout Europe, of the Queen of France kissing the maimed hands of the living martyr, to whom the Pope in Rome granted dispensation to offer Holy Mass with missing fingers. Finally, I wept with joy when hearing of Fr Jogues' determination to return to the Indians where, as expected, he died a most cruel martyrdom. But what probably initiated the process of my conversion to Catholicism was to hear that Fr Jogues' torturer had later sought Holy Baptism, had taken 'Isaac-Jogues' as his Christian name, and had died at the hands of other Indians. 'If such are the Jesuits, then I too,' thought I, 'must become one!' This led to my reception into the Catholic Church, as Your Lordship also applied for when seeking another treasure—the hand of Mistress Catharina.

"Your Lordship requested traditional Japanese outfits. I am sending with this letter a light conic hat, and a precious silk robe called 'kimono.' I hope they could be included in some forthcoming paintings. Since Your Lordship is as fond of maps and globes as I am, why not indeed use the garment in the posthumous portrait of our friend from Brussels, eminent cartographer Fr Albert d'Orville, S.J.? Depicting him wearing the kimono would be a fitting tribute to his heroic journeys across China and Tibet. The hat may fit well on the head of Your Lordship's daughter playing a musical instrument, suggesting an Oriental tune.

"The three sketches sent by Your Lordship have delighted me. I took the liberty of showing them to several Japanese artists who admire our style. They are official court painters and are eager to learn our techniques. Perspective in the composition is new to them, and so is the gradation of shades. My cover as a painter myself, 'from the West,' has proved successful until now.

"But Your Lordship's petition humbles me. How would [missing words or paragraph...].

"...the scales of justice. She stands by a table, facing left, oblivious of the framed mirror on the wall opposite. The light is suffused, owing to the shut curtain. Certainly, including a discreet depiction of the *Last Judgement* on the wall behind her would be very fitting. Like Your Lordship, I favour Jacob de Backer's rendition. If it were I, though, I would leave her scales empty. It would intrigue the viewer; or simply, it may incline him to seek what the even pans are meant to weigh, if not pearls. If he is a good Christian, he will know that after his death St Michael the Archangel will set his merits in one pan and his demerits in the other, for Christ to pronounce upon his soul. On second thought, rather than Archangel St Michael, why not depict Our Lord seated in majesty, sceptre in hand, in the background?

"But no demons, no damned, since Your Lordship prefers not to display evil. I agree that nothing must frighten or repel the viewer, if the overall impression to convey is serene discernment of one's direction in life. May I suggest, though, that the blue drapery spread upon the table be pushed further to the left, revealing the lion-shape finial beneath the furniture? That carved beast could figure the Evil one, as the Fisherman warned us: *"Be sober and watch: because your adversary the devil, as a roaring lion, goeth about seeking whom he may devour."* The dramatic effect would be all the more potent as one would not, at first sight, take notice of that detail hidden in nether darkness. And yet, the wide-open mouth of the beast would remind every cautious observer of having to watch, and to pray. Perhaps, the sculpted lion could roar, below, at the same distance from the lady's wrist holding the scale as the Seated Christ above. Beast, wrist, and Christ would be on the same line. Mankind in the middle; Evil and Good at either end, depicting the choice to be made by the soul: either Moloch or Christ—Belial or Emmanuel.

"The jewels should look as ... [illegible handwriting] than dazzling pearls. Or indeed, tulip bulbs would remind Your Lordship's viewers of the precariousness of earthly investments. To think that rare bulbs once fetched ten thousand guilders, enough to purchase a townhouse on Herengracht Canal, whereas a month later in the same fatal year 1637, one could feed the same bulb to the swine. I was only a child when men lost all for flowers, but I recall the shame and bitterness that tainted many friendships long after. Unlike gold, bulbs are living things, promises of bloom, of perfume, and petals subtly variegated rejoicing a good wife's heart like Mistress Catharina's. Bulbs, though, would not glitter enough on the pans of the lady's scale or on the tablecloth. Better indeed keep to gold and pearls, then.

... [Missing paragraph or page]

"No one paints blues like Your Lordship. Your second sketch, of the housewife reading a letter, is the very embodiment of womanly grace. I long to see the painting completed. A map on the wall might be fitting. It would provide the onlooker with a bird's-eye view of country or city finely delineated, echoing the living microcosm—the dear child—being shaped within the womb of the mother standing. There is such simplicity, such gentleness in Mistress Catharina's posture. She looks as if she had just walked into the room, closer to the open window, better to read the news sent her. Your Lordship caused warm emotions to surge in my heart when stating that the letter was my very last one received from Macau. When contemplating Your Lordship's sketch, when scrutinizing the modest sheet of paper held in the lady's hands, resting on her stomach, I felt like the

Prophet Habakkuk whom *'the angel of the Lord took by the top of his head, and carried by the hair of his head, and set in Babylon, over the den, in the force of his spirit.'*

"Only, my Babylon is Japan, which the picture made me forget for a moment, while Your Lordship's household is my heart's abode, where my letter had flown. To see the sheet I held, to guess the words I wrote, spread and read with such motherly compassion and tenderness by Mistress Catharina, made me shed tears of joy. Space and time were bridged. By proxy, my letter enabled me to stand in your midst as before, to play with Your Lordship's dear children, to pray by the hearth and, O blessed memories, immobile in a corner of the studio bathed with sunshine and loaded with contemplative quiet, *'as the eyes of the servants are on the hands of their masters,'* to follow the strokes of Your Lordship's inspired paintbrush spreading across white canvases beauty without compare.

"As to the immensely generous offer of a painting for our clandestine chapel in Japan, I beg Your Lordship not to be offended by my initial hesitation. In actual fact, the 'chapel' is my studio. It provides a good pretext for visitors coming to see my paintings or enquire about our Western techniques—among them are worshippers and catechumens. Given the persecution, an overtly Catholic depiction sadly is not possible. Your Lordship understands our predicament and means the gift as a belated present for my priestly ordination in Macau, on Sts Peter and Paul last, 1662. I first thought myself unworthy of such a treasure; later I recognised that it would honour God and foster devotion even though, for safety, the Catholic identity of the image would remain implicit. With what delight I have sat then, and even knelt, before Your Lordship's third sketch of an Annunciation. To elude censure by Nagasaki custom officers, so expertly trained in Christian detection by our apostate Fr Ferreira—may God forgive him—Your Lordship has omitted Archangel Gabriel, filling with light and a gilded curtain, instead, the space on the left meant for God's angelic ambassador. This is theologically fitting, since angels are bodiless by their very nature. Furthermore, to the right, the hands of the Blessed Virgin opened in peaceful wonder and humble acceptance, Your Lordship has explained away with the ribbons of a pearl necklace, as if depicting a maiden adorning herself.

"Is respect for God and his Mother safeguarded, though, in an apparently profane depiction such as the one proposed? So did Mistress Catherina wonder, quoting to Your Lordship the opinion of our learned Fr Adriaen Poirters, S.J. In response, Your Lordship asked me how to justify his compositional choice as a Catholic artist, and my acceptance of the proposed painting as a Catholic priest. I first shared the reluctance felt by Mistress Catharina, but changed my mind since through praying and after considering the providential circumstance of persecution. In illustration thereof, I submit the following observations. Here in Japan, our 'Kakure Kirishitans' or 'hidden Christians' devised such pious stratagems, carving the Cross of Salvation on the back of a Buddha statue, or venerating the Blessed Virgin Mary disguised as statues of Kannon, the Buddhist goddess of compassion.

"My predecessors allowed them to do so, based on similar camouflages resorted to under persecution, such as were found in Roman catacombs where an innocuous anchor conceals a Holy Cross, or a fish stands for the acronym of 'Jesus Christ, Son of God, Saviour.' To delude Calvinists, did we not have recourse to the same in our country, where still-lifes displaying an empty niche surrounded with exuberant flowers, wittingly refer to the Mother of God, invisible to eyes but not to hearts?

"Lastly, when studying at Douai, I heard of the painting of a Madonna and Child purposely hidden as underlay beneath a portrait of Sir Francis Walsingham, the chief priest-hunter of Queen Elizabeth of England, and the uncle of our own Fr Francis Walsingham, S.J., of blessed memory. When searching a mansion suspected of Catholic leanings, Protestant officials were bound to assume loyalty to the Crown as they witnessed the pious nods made by members of the household walking by the image of the Queen's henchman. Finally, concealment was used even by Our Lord who, *"also went up to the feast, not openly, but, as it were, in secret."* Hiding can be legitimate and even morally necessary if chosen out of love for others, out of charity unstained by selfish cowardice. Is not the Incarnation such a concealment for love, and even the Eucharistic transubstantiation? In the former, God pure spirit becomes mere Man; while in the latter this divine Man hides under the externals of bread and wine.

"Your Lordship invited me to comment freely on the present stage of his composition. If I could be so bold, the picture being destined for our secret chapel in Nagasaki, might I request that the lute on the chair and the map on the wall be taken away? Handsome as these items are, they seem to distract from the painting's core message: namely, St Gabriel's proposal to the Blessed Virgin. Material vacancy will enhance, in my opinion, the spiritual reality of the encounter taking place.

"For the same purpose of simplification, neither would I wish a framed Cupid displayed on the wall to point at St Gabriel Archangel under the camouflage of a pagan hint. A Cupid was successfully used in Your Lordship's earlier *Girl Reading a Letter at an Open Window*. But in that case the plain context was profane love. As Your Lordship mused in his latest letter, better save such an allusion for a further depiction of courtship, or even for a merely domestic scene such as my goddaughter young Maria standing at her virginal. Does Your Lordship's precocious firstborn still play every morning as I fondly recall? Now nearing ten years of age, she must have become an accomplished musician. To think it is nearly three years since I painted an Italian landscape on the lid of her virginal, for her seventh birthday and as a farewell present from her departing godfather. I should be much obliged if Your Lordship might remind the dear child to offer one decade of her daily Rosary for my final perseverance; or would thank her for her fidelity if she has not forgotten such intercession. I keep her and her much esteemed family in my prayers ever, begging to be remembered in the Holy Sacrifice of the Mass offered on Dutch soil in the attic of dear Mr Van... [illegible: name purposely scraped].

"Your Lordship's devoted servant and friend,

Lukas Fabritius, S.J."

~~~~~~~~~~~~~~~~~~~~

I looked through the window. A few cars were driving by. I discerned with surprise the dome of St Peter's Basilica in the distance. Ah yes, Rome; 1980. That was where I was, rather than in Japan.

The thought of the coffee machine in the corridor outside my interview room crossed my mind. "Kevin" had invited me to help myself. I walked to the door but did not open it. The letters by the Dutch Jesuit exhaled a rarer aroma than Italian coffee: sacredness and identity. What would they further reveal of my past, or what future of mine would they suggest? Apprehensive and attracted, I sat again by the little table and resumed reading.

"Feast of St Ignatius Loyola, 31 July 1663, Nagasaki Palace
"To the illustrious Joannis a Mare, Lord Master of the Guild of St Luke, Delft

"Your Lordship,
"May our glorious Founder be praised for the mighty protection he has extended upon his weak son. Today, for the first time in weeks, I am able to hold a quill. This letter might be my last, and I address it to Your Lordship in thanksgiving for our friendship. Please inform our dedicated Jesuits in Delft, unable as I am to communicate with my religious superior in Edo. I mean these lines as an account of my shortened mission in this faraway realm.

"Here are the facts as much as I can understand them in my present state of confusion, isolation and exhaustion. Thus, our local ruler Daimyo Barnabas T [... name scraped] had become a Catholic in secret, together with some of his household, notably his daughter, Lady Elizabeth. To give Your Lordship a fitting idea of the young lady's virtue, beauty and wit, I would best compare her with our Amsterdam poetess and Catholic convert Maria Tesselschade. Like her, Lady Elizabeth debates on literature and philosophy, like her she can paint and sing with great talent. With my support and through my ministry, she married Lord Francis K [... name scraped], also a hidden Christian. The marriage was clandestine. The father of Lord Francis is Duke or Daimyo S [... name scraped], a powerful adviser to Shōgun Tokugawa Ietsuna who just started ruling the empire in his own right after twelve years of regency.

"Alas Lord Francis—God rest his soul—was slain by his father on 3 July past when he disclosed to him his Catholic faith—but not his marriage. Previous to this, Lady Elizabeth had been found to be with child, and her delivery is expected in about three months from now. Secretly a widow, but now lacking the protection of her spouse, she would incur dishonour for what would seem at court to be a pregnancy out of wedlock, since no husband could now claim the child as his. Her entire household would be stained by the opprobrium. The Japanese nobility have a highly developed code of honour, matching those of Spanish grandees. What they define as honour is much more precious to them than life and, once lost, it can be retrieved only through what they call an honourable death, that is, the ritual suicide or self-execution of 'seppuku.'

"Faced with the dreadful prospect of public dishonour, then, Lady Elizabeth's father Daimyo Barnabas lost courage and forsook his Catholic faith, demanding that the child should die before birth, or the mother would as well. Knowing me to be a priest (I baptised him) and her confessor, he demanded that I should persuade his daughter to save herself and the honour of her family, even at the cost of her child's life.

"As I could not assent, he denounced me as a Christian proselytiser. All my belongings were immediately confiscated. This entailed essentially my tools, my precious pigments, and my paintings. To my consternation, I was dispossessed even of the three sketches which Your Lordship had sent me, which I had so happily commented upon in my previous letter (yet to be sent with this one, please God). I had displayed the sketches on the wall opposite my bed, to meditate upon them in the evening or even when praying. The lady holding the scales was in the middle. The lady in blue reading a letter was on the right. Our secret *Annunciation* with the Virgin supposedly tying her pearl necklace was on the left.

"The memory of them helped me during the two days and two nights I spent manacled in the courtyard of the palace, hands tied high up to a post and my toes barely touching the ground. It is summer and hot here: a guard poured water in my mouth every couple of hours. Yet Daimyo Barnabas had not disclosed my priesthood, which would have meant death. Instead, he pardoned me and let me receive assistance from his household, promising that if I managed to persuade Lady Elizabeth to terminate her pregnancy, I would go free; but threatening me with death if I failed."

"Feast of St Peter in Chains, 1 August 1663, Nagasaki Palace.

"I had to interrupt my writing to Your Lordship yesterday as my swollen wrist still hurt too much. Here is the end of my account.

"Following my pardon, I have been nursed at the palace infirmary for the past fortnight. My arms and hands were in a pitiable state, and I burned with severe fever. Lady Elizabeth was granted access to my cell and assisted my nurse. She begged me not to falter, assuring that she would die like her brave husband Lord Francis, rather than intentionally harm their child.

"Something unexpected took place during those days, which I need to confide. Your Lordship is acquainted, I believe, with Japanese domestic architecture. Instead of internal walls made of stone or brick as ours in Europe, rooms are divided by light movable partitions called *shōji*, consisting of translucent paper stretched on wooden frames. This is a precaution, lest the frequent earthquakes destroyed stone walls. The doors or *fusuma* look similar, sliding sideways. Lying on my couch in my delirium, when my head was propped up for feeding, washing or merely resting, on several occasions I recall discerning silhouettes behind the partitions. Those would have been either the nurse preparing a potion, or perhaps some dignitary enquiring of her on behalf of Daimyo Barnabas how I was faring, or even Lady Elizabeth setting flowers in a vase.

"One day, the three human figures against the partition shone in my mind as some illumination. Was it morning, was it afternoon? I had lost the notion of time. But light outside must have been bright for me to see, on that occasion, three female silhouettes framed in three partitions. The peace, symmetry, and grace that flowed from this triple vista deeply impressed me. I felt suddenly very lucid, more than I had been for days. As if awakening, I listened attentively. One silhouette was the nurse, another Lady Elizabeth, and the third I assume a maid bringing a tray of food from the palace kitchen. They did not speak, but merely gestured with slow, gentle, and grace-filled care. All was taking place behind the three translucent screens, across which the lithe figures of the three young women facing to the left were smoothly displayed, in soft and living delineation. Lady Elizabeth must have been the only one with child, I suppose, although the broad sashes worn around their waists and the floating folds of the kimonos conveyed a similar impression for the other women.

"I was then reminded of Your Lordship's three sketches, which until confiscation had adorned my own room, side by side. A certain correspondence between those appeared to me. It was not merely based on their juxtaposition in space, nor was it their similar depicting of three young women. Beyond this, the identity of postures struck me. Never before had Your Lordship positioned a woman alone, standing on the right, separated by a table from the window to the left. I distinctly recall that Your Lordship's *Young Woman with a Water Pitcher* and *Girl Reading a Letter by an Open Window* both stood *between* table and window; while the busy *Milkmaid* faced the viewer, rather than the window, if I am correct.

"In contrast, the three latest projects shared the same unprecedented posture. Knowing the meticulous care Your Lordship takes in the composition of his paintings, I felt that something of particular relevance was at stake here, calling for elucidation. I did not know what it was until, from my couch, I saw the two side partitions slide behind the middle one, as the nurse meant to ventilate my cell. She had done the same every day, but only then did it prompt in my mind the thought that the three silhouettes I had admired side by side were now superimposed as if combined in one single depiction, as Your Lordship's three sketches were meant to. Such was my illumination. I realised that the lady holding the balance, the blue mother reading a letter and the young woman in yellow with pearls in the disguised *Annunciation* stood as the same person at three successive moments.

"Or better, I felt as if the three sketches sent me by Your Lordship were three moments within a single event. In my memory, I embraced them in one contemplative gaze, as if within the same frame one single image were set in motion, looking convincingly alive. What the topic of such a moving picture was, I could not identify yet. It could be an allegory of the three requirements for artistic beauty: wholeness, proportionality, and radiance; that is, 'integritas, consonantia, claritas.' Not by chance does St Thomas Aquinas refer those three to the Second Person of the Holy Trinity, Christ the Lord. In Your Lordship's painting in motion, could one not see an icon of the very process of the Incarnation, whereby the definitive beauty was given for men to see, namely the splendour of the truth in Our..."

[Missing words or paragraph...]

~~~~~~~~~~~~~~~~~~~~~~~~~

"Feast of the Invention of St Stephen, Protomartyr, 3 August 1663, Nagasaki Palace

"Blessed be Our Lord Jesus Christ, who deigned to visit his unworthy servant. With trepidation am I writing this new section of my letter to Your Lordship. This is because my entrance into the Lord's everlasting presence has become more likely; but also because my Lord's entrance into my person occurred this morning when, for the first time in weeks, I was able to celebrate the Holy Sacrifice of the Mass. Lady Elizabeth smuggled into my cell chalice, host, wine and even vestments. I had to do without missal, altar cards or crucifix, but I believe in conscience that the Lord approved my action under the circumstances. In addition, lest I were prevented from offering Mass soon again, I have hidden in this room the tiny chalice containing a few consecrated hosts. As Your Lordship can see, we are very much united in Eucharistic secrecy, and while I lie in my Japanese cell turned chapel, I can fancy myself present in Holland, in the Delft attic where my fellow-Jesuit performs the sacred rite clandestinely for such a pious household.

"Moreover, at my request, Daimyo Barnabas has restored to me Your Lordship's three sketches, now pinned on the partition opposite my couch. I don't know whether this favour is a good or bad omen: it may indicate a change of heart in Lady Elizabeth's father, but it could equally foretell my end, if meant as a last wish granted before execution.

"The nurse took away my paper and quill yesterday, stressing that it strained me too much whereas rest was still very much needed. She is right and I still do feel very weak in body, not in soul though. On the contrary, the illumination brought about two days ago has not faded away. I assumed that offering Holy Mass today might outshine the memory of the combined silhouettes on my paper partitions and of Your Lordship's sketches. But it only refined my understanding of this concurrence. I can see now, and humbly submit to Your Lordship, that all *three* sketches, not merely the last one, depict the wondrous event of the Annunciation. At least, this is what I would modestly suggest the three paintings should evince, once completed. They could be seen as a triptych figuring the three parts of the Angelus when, throughout the world, at dawn, noon, and dusk, we Christians commemorate the wondrous event of God becoming man in the womb of the Blessed Virgin Mary.

"Thus, the lady with the yellow jacket tying her pearl necklace would illustrate the first lines of the Angelus: '*The Angel of the Lord declared unto Mary, And she conceived of the Holy Spirit.*' Second, the lady with the dark jacket, holding the balance, would refer to the middle verses: '*Behold the handmaid of the Lord. Be it done unto me according to thy word.*' Third and finally, the lady with the light blue jacket, reading a letter, would conclude the prayer: '*And the Word was made flesh. And dwelt among us.*'

"Might Your Lordship allow me to explain why following that order seems meaningful to me? The yellow lady's posture expresses happiness about and attention to an apparition just occurring. Whose? We know this is God's Archangel, invisible to sinful eyes; but our Japanese and Calvinist custom officers may think nothing of it, assuming her merely to be watching her own face in the mirror as she ties her necklace. She is more youthful than the two other ladies, and her thick furred jacket, rather than her pregnancy, may explain her swollen waist. While the Blessed Virgin Mary only conceived by the Holy Ghost, any mother can consider for herself the great wonder of welcoming human life.

"The next painting of the woman holding the balance is, I suggest, the middle stage. It illustrates the core of the Angelus prayer, when we hear the Immaculate speak directly. At that moment, God becomes man in her virginal womb. This most intimate moment explains the light subdued through the curtain now shut, and the veiling of her head for deeper recollection. Most relevant then would be the representation of Christ as Judge behind the woman just become his mother. She knows already that her '*child is set for the fall, and for the resurrection of many in Israel, and for a sign which shall be contradicted.*' The scales of judgment in her hand show that she meditates in awe on the salvation of souls to be wrought by Christ, with her motherly cooperation. Her jacket has lost its external radiance of the previous stage, having turned dark from yellow, but it is now partly open, revealing a bodice of coral shade. This signals the humility of the Virgin Mother henceforth carrying a hidden treasure, '*All the glory of the king's daughter is within.*' In strong contrast with the dark hues all across the painting, this bright coral opening spectacularly points to the marvel of human conception.

"In the third image, the woman's stomach has swollen, making her pregnancy more noticeable. It is the third part of the Angelus prayer, presenting the *fait accompli* of the Incarnation. The curtain has been opened again, but the window does not show anymore. Why? Because outside stars need mentioning no longer, the woman now carrying within her a brighter light than any created ones, her very Son, true Sun of Justice, about to be cast upon the world. The letter she reads symbolises Scripture: both the Old Testament heralding the rising of her Son, Star of Jacob, and the New Testament fulfilling his coming. Thus, the letter should not be seen as distracting the young mother from the wonder of her pregnancy. Rather, it is meant for us. Since it involves a third party, the letter shows that the relationship between Mother and Son invites others to join in, instead of excluding them.

"I fear, lest my bold interpretation displease Your Lordship. Does it not, though, conform to what we discussed at length in those blessed days of my apprenticeship in Delft, when Your Lordship deigned to share with me his wish for a depiction of God's Incarnation less conventional and more intimate than classical representations? Trusting in Your Lordship's benignity, I dare summarise my musings as follows.

"Overall, if we consider the three sketches as one single image in motion, we realise how fittingly they describe the 'obumbrating' or 'overshadowing' of the Virgin by the Holy Ghost announced by Archangel Gabriel: '*the power of the most High shall overshadow thee.*' Your Lordship described that very alternating of light and shade upon the woman. Light flows bright first, then it is subdued, then it becomes bright again. Another feature of continuity is the disappearance of the pearls. They figure prominently as the focus of the action occupying the woman in yellow tying them around her neck, or more logically, untying them. In the middle image, their absence from the pans of the balance is what makes the pearls noticeable. Instead of being weighed, they lie on the table and over the box, in discarded abundance. In the third picture, the pearls are barely discernible on the table, behind the box. They seem to have been forgotten. Does it not contradict Scripture, which states that, '*the kingdom of heaven is like to a merchant seeking good pearls. Who when he had found one pearl of great price, went his way, and sold all that he had, and bought it*'? I suggest that the natural and created pearls lie discarded because the Virgin has found, and now treasures within her, a supernatural and divine pearl, the Saviour Child now growing in her womb.

"The nurse demands that I should cease writing at once. One should always obey one's doctor, I was taught, when he acts as he should for the preservation of life. Your Lordship, when shall I see your face again? When again shall we walk to and fro in your studio, the cherished sanctuary of so much beauty conceived? When, pacing with hands behind our backs, shall we further discuss the betterment of the composition of a painting in progress? Joannis, O Joannis, when shall we kneel with your household before the hidden Madonna, and entrust to the Mother of God our country, our family and our souls? When shall I det... [missing words, sentence interrupted].

~~~~~~~~~~~~~~~~~~~~~~~~~~

There was a knock at the door of my interview room at the Jesuit Generalate. "Kevin" popped in to see how I was doing with my reading of the Dutch Letters. Well, he had his answer without my uttering a word, on seeing me on my knees, silently weeping.

I smiled at him. He nodded and left me in peace.

After some time, sitting down, I summoned up in my memory the artistic argument of the Jesuit missionary. So, according to "Fr Lukas Fabritius," because these three small paintings, and only these, have similar dimensions, depict a woman standing alone indoors, facing left toward a window across a table, and were painted within the same period of time, they would constitute a triptych? The priest had described them as an Annunciation in motion—an obumbration. Light, shade, light. Proposal, acceptance, gestation. The Angelus. The lady and the cloud. It was an interesting hypothesis. Had Johannes

Vermeer received his friend's letters and vestimentary gifts, though? Possibly, since several of his later paintings included kimonos and at least one conical hat, I recalled. But if Vermeer had read the Jesuit's letters, could they have influenced the composition of his three pictures in progress?

I knew Vermeer's work well. Out of the thirty-four paintings by the master of Delft, the *Woman with a Pearl Necklace*; the *Woman Holding a Balance*; and the *Woman in Blue Reading a Letter* appeared side by side before the eyes of my mind. I smiled bitterly when realising that the patient network of correspondences identified by the dead priest, the threads connecting so many details within each frame, but also the filaments uniting all three paintings within one organic system of signification were the opposite of the *atomisation* which Heinrich had explained to me on several occasions. Every detail, whether a table, a dress, a cheek, a pearl, a finger or a leonine finial was called into a convergence of meaning that left its singularity unscathed while marrying it with other items; each of those, then, glowing with brighter significance. One could express this approach to Vermeer's paintings as vital and universal.

~~~~~~~~~~~~~~~~~~~~

I did not need to read the last letter of the dead Jesuit. I knew his end. I saw the weapon and from experience I assessed the dexterity of the blow as if my own arm had struck it. It had all come back to me. Yes, I *had* typed those sentences a long time ago, over there at Jallier Hall, in the Basque Country. I had known them almost by heart. Now I recognised who I was. It felt as if I had known it all along, but was prevented from acknowledging it. I recalled the Seventeenth Century Dutch Painting student, not daring to tell his tutor the discovery he had made. I could see the youthful Jesuit, a teacher of fine arts on his errand across Nagasaki some days before the bomb exploded. I watched the young deacon prostrate in the school chapel, about to be ordained a priest. A cross-section of my life before the bomb was displayed before the eyes of my mind. The various layers of my history, of my personality, and of my relationships superimposed, producing a figure that felt alive: me.

"Me." How deep a word. I had assumed that self of mine destroyed, atomised, scattered in 1945. Why had I condoned the delusion that I bore life in me no longer, when all I needed was to listen with all my love to the faint heartbeat persisting in my soul? It assured me that I was not lost, that it was up to me to overcome the horror, to reconnect, grow forth and bear fruit.

Had I trusted a fraud? Had I befriended a fiend? Had I espoused a lie? If so, from so unnatural a union, what monstrous offspring had come out of me since my awakening under that military tent in August 1945! Waste. Embers. Death.

O my city laid bare, O my soul in ashes. And yet, survival, rebirth, redemption, is but one call away. Ah, that I may utter it!

Lord.

Saviour.

Christe, eleison.

Please have mercy on me. Show me your comely face again, that I may live forever, O *Vision of Peace.*

~~~~~~~~~~~~~~~~~~~~~

[Translated from the Dutch original into Spanish. Handwriting and paper differ from the previous letters.]

"To the illustrious Joannis a Mare, Lord Master of the Guild of St Luke, Delft

"Feast of Our Lady of the Snows, 5 August 1663, Nagasaki

"Jesus!

"Friend, you who were to me like another Jonathan, allow me with David to sing, '*This is the day which the Lord hath made: let us be glad and rejoice therein!*' Today, O Joannis, I will see God. How the riddles of our earthly pilgrimage suddenly become clear and readable to me! How plainly lies and errors fall like scales all around! '*God is light and in him there is no darkness. If we say that we have fellowship with him and walk in darkness, we lie and do not the truth. But if we walk in the light, as he also is in the light, we have fellowship one with another: And the blood of Jesus Christ his Son cleanseth us from all sin.'*

"Two days ago, Daimyo Barnabas denounced me as a Catholic priest, since I had failed to persuade Lady Elizabeth to harm her unborn child. As a last chance, I was ordered to trample upon a picture of Our Lady with Child, a "fumi" as they call it, as proof of my repudiating the Christian faith. If I complied, I would live. I refused. Did I change my mind about concealment and cunning for Christ, as justified in my earlier letter? No. But when the legitimate authority most solemnly demands of us Catholics to confess our belief, we owe the State, and Christ, and Church, to use signs according to their objective meaning. Because our soul is the shape of our body, according to the natural unity granted our person by the Creator Himself, we cannot, then, keep a belief contrary to the signs we display. In other words, divine love concealed in our souls dies when contradicted by our bodily signs. Trampling upon a depiction of Our Lady with Child is the sign authoritatively set by Daimyo Barnabas and his officers as my abandonment of the Catholic faith. In that solemn and unambiguous context, trampling would be apostatizing. God forbid!

"Daimyo Barnabas wishes Lady Elizabeth married soon to another mighty lord, who would never wed her if pregnant, even less so if he knew her to be a Christian widow. She must appear a respectable Buddhist maiden. My Lady is the one writing down for me the words you are reading. Courageously, she obtained permission from the guard to stand by my cage with ink and quill. I have an angel for my scribe! That guard, and others among the palace staff and townsfolk, are 'Kakure Kirishitans' or 'Hidden Christians.' This gives me courage to remain faithful until the end, thus strengthening them, while also relying on their prayer for me now, and for my soul after. As Your Lordship found if this sheet of paper now rests in your hands, it was hidden as underlay within the Japanese conic hat I sent as gift. For safety, a copy lies hidden, together with my two previous epistles, sealed inside the lid of the large dark China jar also sent to Your Lordship. In the silk kimono though, no surprise is to be sought. (For Your Lordship's pious attention, Lady

Elizabeth insists on mentioning that these few items of mine may, by God's grace, one day be treated as relics.)

"Like many good but weak men, Daimyo Barnabas was afraid and chose ambition against dread. So did I. I chose elevation to heaven, rather than fear of men. My trial was short and I will die today. I am held on the city's main square within a small cage of 'bamboo'—an indigenous timber, flexible but strong. My abode was draped with white material lest the burning sun killed me before the time of my execution this afternoon. But through a little hole before my eyes, I can see outside. The Lord has shrunk my habitat by stages, preparing me for this last one. I first enjoyed the comfort of my quarters at the palace, entailing workshop, sitting-room and bedroom. Later, I lay on a couch in my infirmary cell. Now I crouch in the narrow confines of this cage. Here I can neither stand nor sit. It reminds me of Your Lordship's 'camera obscura,' the small wooden cabin we assembled in Your Lordship's studio long ago, as instructed by our late Carel—God rest the soul of my poor cousin. How thrilled we were when, with precision unrivalled, through a peephole, the outside view was projected upon the inside screen, ready for us to paint! Now I feel like a child in the womb, but one endowed with the use of reason and free will.

"Today is my 'Visitation,' after the feast last month. Then, the six-month-old Precursor leaped with joy in the womb on hearing Our Lady's salutation to her cousin Elizabeth, his mother. The voice of the Immaculate caused the Baptist to be filled with the Holy Ghost, revealing to him the presence of the Messiah, like him yet unborn. As I lay concealed within the thin walls of my tent, I hear Lady Elizabeth's encouragements as she sits next to me, and I pray that the child she carries be soon grafted into the Lord our Saviour through Holy Baptism, and conformed to Him through every virtue and, please God, one day be granted even the priestly character. How I long to be born and, at long last unhindered, to sing the praises of the Lord and serve Him in eternity! I know that my time on earth has been a mere preparation to real life in heaven. Holy Mother Church has told me about eternity. To us Catholics, Earth is a womb with a view into everlasting bliss. Holy Church is our Mother, carrying us in the water of Holy Baptism and feeding us the Substance of life in the Most Holy Eucharist, while pointing at the evergreen pastures of Eden regained. To us death is birth. May St Nicodemus intercede for me, he who enquired of the Lord, *'How can a man be born when he is old? Can he enter a second time into his mother's womb and be born again? Jesus answered: Amen, amen, I say to thee, unless a man be born again of water and the Holy Ghost, he cannot enter into the kingdom of God.'*

"I shall be pierced to death with swords. Will the blade first reach my chest, or my back, or my head? God knows. The steel will tear the cloth draped over my cage like a membrane and disjoin the bamboo canes like ribs, before it does the same for my skin and bones. And yet, to God I sing, *'thou hast possessed my reins: thou hast protected me from my mother's womb... My bone is not hidden from thee, which thou hast made in secret: and my substance in the lower parts of the earth.'* Hidden in my tunic, I carry with me the Eucharistic Lord, a fragment of a Host consecrated earlier. I will consume it fifteen minutes before the time appointed for my passing. Thus, I will not leave the Lord. My embrace of Him in faith will simply turn into the Vision of his Face. I will no longer run the risk of losing his friendship: forever secured, grace will have turned into glory.

"O Joannis, how I long to be born to life eternal! For twenty-seven years I have enjoyed my sojourn, perhaps too much, in this shady dwelling called Earth. Handling paintbrushes with you has prepared me, thank God, to be handled by God as his priest, no longer spreading pigments on canvases, but anointing souls with grace instead. If our paintings on earth have helped souls catch a glance of beauty supernal—and my friend, we know they have—how could we not trust in God's ability, so much greater than ours, to draw splendour irresistible out of our trials embraced in faith and hope, and offered up with burning charity?

"Isaac carrying the wood for his own sacrifice asked his father, *'Behold, fire and wood: where is the victim for the holocaust? And Abraham said: God will provide himself a victim for an holocaust, my son.'* I wish for an image to be painted, to the greater glory of God and I ask Him, my Father, 'Behold, canvas and frame: where are pigments and paintbrush for the picture?' And I hear in my heart God's awesome promise, 'Those will be provided, my son.' Yes, a paintbrush of sharp steel will be dipped into the reddest of pigments, to spread on the canvas of my tent.

"I long for St Paul's promise to be fulfilled in me: '*You are the epistle of Christ, ministered by us, and written: not with ink but with the Spirit of the living God.*' I have always wished to know what exactly the Lord was writing on the ground, with his finger, while proud men accused the adulteress. It had to be something which, in God's merciful economy, would counterbalance the sins of the woman and of her accusers. Perhaps was it his own name that Our Lord wrote in the dust, then: 'God Saves,' in anticipation of his redeeming Passion and Death. This afternoon, if my life can atone for the sins of Japanese souls and mine, and foster their conversion, Christ may write my name in the dust of this market place.

"Lady Elizabeth begs me to tell why I am dying. If I must now disclose the secret of my King, then hark: I am dying to be with Christ. I am dying because He died for me first. I am dying because He wills to save souls through this small sign. I am dying for the love of the innocents such as Lady Elizabeth and her little child. I am dying for the love of those fallen and misled by Satan, that they might be touched and might surrender to Love incarnate, Jesus Christ. I wish them no harm, but every blessing.

"When Samaria rejected the messengers of the Lord, '*his disciples, James and John, ... said: Lord, wilt thou that we command fire to come down from heaven and consume them? And turning, he rebuked them, saying: you know not of what spirit you are. The Son of man came not to destroy souls, but to save.*' I wish no fire from on high cast upon Nagasaki, but the fire of heavenly charity. Oh, that divine fire, how ardently I pray that it may pour upon every soul in this great empire like at Pentecost! '*And suddenly there came a sound from heaven, as of a mighty wind coming: and it filled the whole house where they were sitting. And there appeared to them parted tongues, as it were of fire: and it sat upon every one of them. And they were all filled with the Holy Ghost.*'

"The following words of mine are to the generous, courageous life-bearing mother, Lady Elizabeth. This afternoon my friend, my sister and daughter, pray that the Lord may write my new name in the dust of the market square: not Lukas then, but 'Boanerges'–'Son of Thunder'; when the scorching sun will shine high through the cool foliage of the tabunoki trees, in the cloudless sky graciously travelled by some red-crowned crane."

CHAPTER 18
Bones and Skin

TANDING BY KOKURA'S EMPTY grave at Fuji Cemetery, Bishop Dorf felt the need to sit down on a nearby bench. It felt weird to listen to the voice of the late Japanese played on the recorder ten years after his death. Worse though, was to hear him accuse so pointedly his friend Mgr Altemps of being a murderous spy. Presently Marco was sitting at the bottom of the tomb, silent as dead. Was he perhaps stunned by the charge just made against him, or heroically relying on divine intervention to clear his good name? Whom to believe?

Had not Kokura proved to be a liar in the past, when contributing to the papal brochure? The artist had claimed authorship of his poem *Redemption through Painting* in 1981. But the past night, when browsing through the Kokura Memoirs, Picerno had realised the imposture. According to the Dutch letters, Fr Lukas Fabritius was the true author of the poem, not Kokura. Picerno was mortified to have missed that detail when Hana had read it aloud for him. He had been dozing like an old man just while an important clue was coming to light! Making up for his blunder, he had read *Redemption through Painting* several times again with acute attention.

"*Wide Island* no more, but *The Waste One* is now your name – O my city, *Hiroshima!*"

The text slavishly imitated the seventeenth-century *Lamentations on Delft*:

"*Ditch* no more, but *Death* is now your name – O *Delft* my city! What was, has ceased. It is daylight now elsewhere in the world, but here the darkness seems thicker than any night…"

The two poems were identical, except for a few minor differences. Thus, Kokura had shamelessly copied Fabritius.

Cheater! How unworthy of an artist like him, and of a priest since, by then, art expert Ken Kokura had admitted to being Fr Xavier Hasekura, S. J. The Jesuits had given him a year to settle down in his recovered identity. Then, after further psychological examination, he had officially been recognised by the Holy See as a Catholic priest and invited to resume his ministry as a consecrated man. It had all played out very well in fact. Pope John Paul was coming to Japan and the "resurrection" of Fr Xavier Hasekura, S. J. was presented as a living symbol of Japan's Catholic past revived through the warm attention of the Vicar of Christ. Hasekura was to con-celebrate the main papal Mass with one hundred and twenty priests. Most frustratingly though, he had fainted a few days before the Mass, had been taken ill soon after, and had died in hospital the following day. What a waste! Clearly, the emotion had been too much for the old Hiroshima survivor. Finding himself home as a priest again and about to be paraded as a trophy and the centre of attention next to the Holy Father had all proved too much mental stress after thirty-six years spent in amnesia and delusion.

Standing on the opposite side of the tomb, Fr Lambourin kept quiet, as if awaiting Bishop Dorf's reaction about the tape just played. But Picerno needed more time to process the information. From his bench he looked at the cherry flowers fluttering in the afternoon breeze. It was pacifying. This time he did not ignore the uncomfortable suggestion that he might bear some responsibility for Fr Xavier Hasekura's untimely death. Had he not pushed the sick man too much? After all, Hasekura was an atom-bomb survivor. Was he still affected by the radiations? His infuriating insistence to be left out of the limelight may not have been motivated by false modesty, but by a genuine lack of physical and mental strength (a bit like Mgr Altemps). But Dorf had been ada-mant that Hasekura had to play his part, and all of it. The opportunity of producing on the stage of the papal visit a resurrected Jesuit, son of a samurai and descendant of the seventeenth-century convert ambassador to Spain and Rome, was simply too good to be missed. He had only met him once, in fact. His detailed instructions had been expressly conveyed to the reluctant priest by Marco Altemps. Picerno remembered how then-Fr Altemps, a bit too soft as usual, had pleaded on behalf of Fr Hasekura.

"He has never felt capable of offering Mass since his return to the priesthood. He says that the prospect overwhelms him and that, as an added hindrance, using another rite than the one in which he had been trained before the bomb would be beyond his strength."

Then-Mgr Dorf had dismissed such concern with impatience. "I know he has never said the New Mass, neither the Old in fact, since in 1945 the bomb fell in the middle of his Ordination ceremony. But he is not expected to perform any difficult task. All he has to do is put on the Papal Visit vestments, stand by the altar when asked, raise his arm with the other concelebrants and read the words of Consecration from the order of service. And also, yes, he should clasp his arms around the Pope at the exchange of peace. Surely, there is nothing daunting about that! I am sorry Marco, but Fr Hasekura must comply. He took a year to decide whether he wanted to function as a Catholic priest again. Well, now that he's been accepted as one, he must do as he is told. A gentle pressure might be just what he needs to find his feet again amongst us all."

~~~~~~~~~~~~~~~~~~~~~~~

Fr Lambourin pointed at the tomb, reminding Bishop Dorf that urgent action was needed.

Sitting upon the fractured coffin at the bottom of Fr Hasekura's grave, Mgr Altemps was looking at the rectangle of blue sky above him lined with pink petals from the overhanging branches of the lush cherry trees. On either side he could see, first, the tips of four shoe soles, and further up, the heads of the two clerics leaning towards him. His reaction was awaited after such a blunt accusation by the dead Japanese artist.

Finding the situation almost comical, Marco Altemps eventually broke the heavy silence and commented, "This setting is more fitting for a Spaghetti Western film, I think. You, Picerno, would now ask where the bags of dollars are hidden, since they are not in the coffin. Soon enough though, Red Indians will attack.

"However, since we all have more important things to do, let me thank you for playing this tape. First, are you absolutely sure of its authenticity? Anyone could read such a statement. One would need at least Mgr Pommard's confirmation, since allegedly he was present. But of course, Mgr Pommard is in Rome and is the chief suspect in Dr Shevchenko's letter to—to *you*, Fr Lambourin: glad to see that your food poisoning did not prevent you from arriving here as fast as I did."

At that moment, Marco noticed the tips of two more shoes becoming visible on the edge of the grave, while a third voice spoke, coming straight out of Mgr Pommard's placid face. "Dear Mgr Altemps, I am here and I readily confirm that I witnessed the statement you just heard, spoken by Fr Xavier Hasekura, S.J. as he lay dying in hospital ten years ago. Over the past decade, its contents have contributed to our more cautious policy regarding infiltration. Hiding this interview from you made you less guarded, serving our purpose better. But earlier this week, the surfacing of the *Showcasing Dissent* cipher leading to your acceptance of the cardinalate prompted us to confront you with Fr Hasekura's accusations. Thus, can you tell us whether he told the truth about you, or not?" Mgr Pommard recalled Dr Shevchenko's earlier suggestion of using the red hat as a bait. Had it served its purpose? Had a master spy been caught at last, thanks to their long patience and risky gamble?

His back leaning against the cavity wall, Marco Altemps sighed and replied, "With respect, since Fr Lambourin sees no objection to your presence Mgr Pommard, despite your being the prime suspect in Dr Shevchenko's incriminating letter, then I see it my duty to confirm that I have been serving for years as member of 'Pro Deo,' the Holy See's intelligence section under the authority of the late Fr Felix Morlion, OP, a unit recently absorbed into Dr Shevchenko's department. Compartmenting protocols may have led to Dr Shevchenko being unaware of my membership, just as I did not know his. I must emphatically demand that you keep what I am about to say strictly confidential.

"What I do affirm, now, is that Fr Hasekura invented this conversation as well as any other connection between me and a so-called 'Heinrich.' On the contrary, I was astonished when hearing that the elusive Soviet spy Ken Kokura had boldly decided to enter the Church in plain sight, through the front door, having exhausted the benefits of his faked amnesia. To see him involved in the papal visit to Japan meant high risk, and scheduling a meeting for him with the Holy Father was folly. As soon as I had a chance to meet with him in private, I eventually confronted him. But he ignored my threats, boasting of having all the backing he needed to carry on his mission now overtly as a Catholic priest. This meant that he had fellow-spies here in Tokyo, at the Nunciature, at Archbishop's House, or even in the Vatican. I had indeed been following Ken Kokura for decades. He was remarkably cunning and blended faultlessly in the establishment of international art expertise. His 'resurrection' conveniently coincided with the preparation of the papal visit.

"Can I please get the ladder down again as I am getting a stiff neck talking to you all from below, and would appreciate clarifying matters aboveground?"

As if unaware of Mgr Altemps' request, Bishop Dorf asked, "Marco, what you said is very useful. Thank you. But we have another query, if you don't mind. Mgr Pommard, standing next to me here, told me that over the past ten years you have been under special surveillance, albeit discreet, from his department. They checked the whereabouts of 'Heinrich' based on the Kokura Memoirs. Notably, every time 'Heinrich' appeared in Japan, in Germany, in Russia, in England or even when he was presumed to be in America, like at the Uweena conference in Chicago, guess what? You also were away from your desk, travelling. In fact, as I look back, I see that these coincidences started from our young days at university when I thought you were resting at a sanatorium for your asthma; it ended with... well, it ended today, when we all assumed you to be on retreat in Italy, only to find you in a grave in Japan. How do you account for this, please?"

Mgr Marco Altemps stood up on the coffin, still at the bottom of the grave. His tone expressed weariness. He replied, "Don't tell me that you still assume the so-called Kokura Memoirs to be genuine? Whatever truth they contain was skilfully twisted and craftily interspeded with pure fiction. Yes, Kokura was born in Jallier Hall as Xavier Hasekura, he became a Jesuit, and lost his memory in 1945. But his amnesia ended much earlier than he claimed, and it was invoked as an ideal pretext to explain his 'return' home to the Church, after decades spent working against her as a KGB agent. Imagine: the poor victim 'had forgotten' who he was! How convenient. Is that credible, though?"

All remained silent, until Fr Lambourin respectfully submitted that one Joseph Stalin had also been a seminarian aiming for ordination as an Orthodox priest, before becoming the USSR ruler.

Mgr Altemps patiently observed, "Indeed, dear Father, but Comrade Stalin never claimed to have 'forgotten' that earlier part of his existence. Neither did Stalin express a change of heart, begging for readmission into the Orthodox Church which he had so spectacularly persecuted. Kokura is small fry in comparison with Stalin, but unlike the Russian tyrant, our Japanese spy did mean to 'come back' to the Church, hoping to harm her further from within."

"But how exactly does that account for your absences," Bishop Dorf insisted, "all coinciding with the appearances of 'Heinrich'?"

"Your Excellency truly wants to go to the bottom of this mystery, it would seem. Very well: Kokura's basic preparation for plain-sight infiltration was to create an account of his life that would exonerate him while implicating a trusted cleric. It is clear that someone with intimate knowledge of my comings and goings has informed him. Shifting the blame on me in that way is as convincing, seriously, as would be a suspicion raised against you, my old friend, merely because of your aunt Bella Dodd, the same KGB agent who boasted of having planted hundreds of crypto-Communists inside Catholic seminaries, as we all just heard Kokura mention."

On hearing this, Bishop Dorf shook from head to toe on his crutches and Fr Lambourin had to catch him, lest he fell into the gaping grave. The prelate became as red as the cardinal's hat which he feared he might now have missed for ever.

Seeing Mgr Pommard look at him with surprise and expectation, he finally stammered, "This is totally ludicrous! I only met the woman when visiting my mother's relatives on holiday, down in Southern Italy. All my mother and her ever had in common is the surname of Visono."

But Mgr Altemps pushed his pawn forward.

"Of course. Nobody suggests otherwise. And how again is the town called, where your mother and her sister the KGB spy grew up?"

As Bishop Dorf would not answer, Mgr Pommard had to intervene. "Come on, Picerno, surely that piece of information cannot compromise you!"

As one confessing the most shameful deed, the bishop whispered, "'Picerno.' My mother's family, the Visonos, is from Picerno, a small town in the province of Potenza. I cannot fathom why my parents chose 'Picerno' as my first name, when my baptismal register states 'Giambattista Heinrich Picerno.'"

From the bottom of his tomb, Mgr Marco Altemps apologised.

"I am very sorry. I meant to cause no embarrassment. Nobody would believe for one second that KGB spy Aunt Bella Dodd, from Picerno, might have encouraged her young nephew, Picerno, to begin a successful career in Church diplomacy... Nor that Auntie Bella had any hidden or shared agenda when, travelling back several years in a row from America via Naples to Picerno (Town) for the traditional feast of S. Rocco on 16 August, she would chat with Nephew Picerno after lunch (and four glasses of fruity Nero D'Avola), at one end of the terrace of the family house (I saw the pictures), asking about his ministry and contacts. Finally, no one would be so rash as to draw any problematic conclusion, on hearing that in 1952, having become a Catholic at the hands of TV star Bishop Fulton Sheen, Bella Dodd lost every interest in her successful nephew, much to his disappointment as he hoped to parade his famous convert Auntie in Rome (and why not in New York?), whereas she would have none of him. To be sure, being named after the hometown of a KGB spy does not mean that one is a KGB spy. Bearing the same name can be purely coincidental. For instance, the daughter of the American ambassador in Berlin in the 1930s was called Martha Dodd and yet, she was not related to Bella Dodd."

Fr Lambourin interrupted inquisitively, as one eager to show how well informed he was. "Excuse me Monsignor, I seem to remember that, like Bella Dodd, Martha Dodd herself *was* a KGB spy, or rather, an NKVD spy, as it was called in 1936 when Soviet agent Boris Vinogradov recruited her. So I recall from her obituary last August in *The New York Times*. Or am I mistaken?"

Bishop Dorf looked at young Fr Lambourin with a mixture of incredulous exasperation and murderous contempt. Mgr Altemps said nothing, but his face displayed deep satisfaction, as if he was glad to be proven wrong about the young priest whom he had underestimated. A rather uncomfortable silence followed, mercifully ended by the monsignor in the tomb.

"Gentlemen, I was merely putting a case, to invite all of us to caution, if not to benevolence, when hearing so-called pieces of evidence merely uttered by an absent and now defunct witness, himself a confessed KGB spy for decades, the notoriously elusive and opaque personality 'Professor Ken Kokura,' also known as 'Swordmaster Yamato,' and lately 'Fr Xavier Hasekura.' But *I* am the one under suspicion here, if I remember correctly, not Mgr Picerno Dorf, nor Professor Ken Kokura. Then, to answer your query, dear *Picerno*—sorry, dear *Heinrich* from Picerno; sorry again, dear *Giambattista*, from Bolzano—I readily admit that my intelligence missions as assigned by 'Pro Deo' regularly led me to travel around the world, obviously under some plausible pretexts. Certain pieces of information cannot be gathered sitting behind a desk, you know. But I see that Kokura's skills dazzle you still, even ten years after his death. Very well. I read again his alleged memoirs on the plane last night, and I will now list the *missing* chapters for your interest. Do not expect pleasant gossip, though, gentlemen.

"Death in hospital of Vermeer forger Han van Meegeren on 30 December 1947 in Amsterdam, aged barely 58. Four days earlier, on 26 December 1947, the last day to appeal the ruling condemning him for forgery, Van Meegeren suffered a highly suspicious heart attack. I have the written testimony of Kokura's intimate friend, *Sultan*, also known as Prince Azmy of Serdang, stating that Kokura had accompanied him on his first visit to Van Meegeren in early October 1947. Kokura was most eager to acquire from the forger as much secret information as possible about Vermeer's paintings. This was to give him future credibility as a sagacious art expert and to invent the so-called 'Dutch Letters,' just as much a forgery as his entire Memoirs, of course. He purposely selected a Hispano-Olivetti M40 typewriter used in Spain in the 1930s, and later planted his 'Dutch Letters' as a piece of 'evidence' in the Jesuit archive in Rome, probably in the 1950s. The original handwritten letters in seventeenth-century Dutch never surfaced, for the obvious reason that they never existed.

"Kokura's trick was exposed, though, by his shameless recycling of the fake 1663 *Lamentations on Delft* into the 1981 *Redemption Through Painting* chapter of the Papal Visit brochure. He simply copied his forged poem about a Dutch Jesuit describing Delft after the 1654 explosion, and pasted it as if it were written by a Hiroshima survivor weeping on the Japanese city bombed in 1945. You may wonder, then, how soon Kokura first used the precious information extracted from Van Meegeren in October 1947? Well, the answer is simple: immediately! He staged with it the 'discovery' of the Cupid, during his first analysis of a Vermeer in Moscow. This occurred merely a week after his first meeting with Van Meegeren. Professor Kravitz and his sister Ida were suspicious of Kokura from the start, hence his intention of doing away with them as soon as it was safe enough, as he attempted in Wittenberg.

"Seeing how well his claimed discovery of a Vermeer *pentimento* had worked, he went secretly back to Amsterdam and persuaded Van Meegeren to put together as many facts as he could about the so-called 'Vermeer triptych,' enticing him with the practical joke of a forged correspondence by an imaginary Dutch Jesuit. Van Meegeren could not resist the prospect. Having been convicted as a painter forger, he would have his revenge through literary forgery. Sadly, the sick man did not know that Kokura was up to no joke. As soon as the invaluable data on Vermeer was in his hands, he made sure that Van Meegeren would share it with no one else ever after.

"Assault on Ida Kravitz on 24 June 1948 in her house at Wittenberg. I have a further testimony of Prince Azmy of Serdang, to whom Kokura boasted of having had his way with his lady-colleague. Serdang accepted to be the official culprit while Kokura was planning to let himself be 'wrongly' accused. He meant to pose as a victim of blackmail by the KGB later on. He had planned his return to the Church from the start, as you heard in his version of our meeting. Kokura was killing two birds with one stone as he was simultaneously showing the Kravitzes his power, and securing their silence about the dubious origin of his Vermeer findings.

"Death of Leonard Foujita on 29 January 1968 near Reims in France. Foujita had converted to Catholicism and the remorse for his earlier complicity with Kokura weighed on him increasingly. Foujita probably did not know that Kokura was a spy, but both had haunted places of ill repute in Paris. He warned Kokura to amend his life and repent, or he would disavow him as a friend and possibly expose him. So did his widow testify, adding that Kokura forced his way into her sick husband's bedroom. A few hours later, Foujita was found dead."

The three clerics, standing above Mgr Altemps, had listened with stupefaction. They had never considered such possibilities, which the man in the grave, below their feet, presented as proven facts. They felt as if they had known him only superficially until then. Watching him was like attending a chess game by some Russian grandmaster playing ten or fifty adversaries simultaneously. One could see his powerful brain following five, ten or twenty different threads at a time. As he spoke, without any notes or written support, one could almost hear him assess other proofs referring to earlier circumstances, weighing them and ordering them in the most convincing way, all the while he spoke of something totally different. His mind seemed to function better than modern computers, Fr Lambourin mused. Those operate on two levels of memory: volatile for data presently processed; archived for data permanently stored. But Mgr Altemps' brain knew no such difference, as all data were processed simultaneously, or so it seemed to his speechless audience as he carried on.

"Next. Disappearance of swordmaster Yamato on 24 June 1979, never seen again since. Yamato had been working for us since 1953; or perhaps since 1954 when Picerno and I started at the Academia in Rome. (I apologise for the uncertainty and I promise to check our records shortly.) Kokura treated him as a friend and this position allowed Yamato to keep us informed. He managed to attract Kokura to Spain. We had finally discovered Kokura's birthplace at Jallier and we hoped that if he visited there, family members might recognise him, leading him to make some mistake and betray himself. Apparently Kokura had genuinely forgotten that part of his life. The painting by Fabritius, *Mercury, Argus and Io*, was used as bait.

"Unfortunately, Kokura found Yamato out and eliminated him before any feedback on the visit reached us. I have the report of the Azpeitia forensic surgeon who identified the remains of a man of Asian ethnic type found hanging on the cliff below the railway bridge where the First-class carriage exploded. The man was the same size and build as Yamato, like him with a large scar on the torso, left by a sword fight during their meeting in Cambridge in May 1974. The Japanese-speaking student who steered the punt down the River Cam was our informant. He confirmed that, while on the punt, both men had violently clashed over Yamato's 'Telluric Tours,' because Kokura demanded an introduction to peace activist Yoko Ono, whereas Yamato maintained that he did not know her enough to justify it. Four years later, then, Kokura did not only take Yamato's passport. He also took his life, making sure his new identity would not be unmasked while his friend's corpse would be found late enough to pass as Kokura's own body, making his staged death irrefutable.

"Next victim in Kokura's busy summer vacation. Fall of Countess Cayetana Jallier de Etxeberria on 16 August 1979. The old lady soon realised that Kokura truly was Fr Xavier and that, an amnesiac no more, he was now fully recovered and knew Jallier to be his birthplace. To her dismay though, instead of embracing his past identity, bringing much joy to her and her family, Kokura pretended to be swordmaster Yamato.

"When the valuable *Mercury, Argus and Io* painting by Carel Fabritius got stolen from Jallier Hall merely a week after the departure of 'Master Yamato,' Countess Cayetana grew deeply suspicious. I have a written statement from Gorka, the gardener at Jallier Hall. Gorka has a very keen eye. He had first spotted 'Yamato' in the park, even before his official arrival, as Countess Cayetana had once observed. He told me that his late mistress had enquired of him several times, with utmost insistence, whether he had seen Master Yamato sneaking around during his stay, and whether anyone by Master Yamato's description had been identified in the area since. Gorka confirmed to her, and later to me, that the very day of the theft he had noticed Yamato, from a distance, entering from the rear of the disused glasshouse into the walled garden where the gardener was inconspicuously cutting flowers for the church. It was the feast of the Assumption of Our Lady and the entire family was gathered in the chapel rehearsing hymns for the forthcoming Mass.

"The following day, Countess Cayetana 'fell' on her way down from the ridge where she liked to sit, despite knowing so well the path down to the hall. She remained unconscious for a couple of hours, before dying."

At that stage, Mgr Pommard nodded to Fr Lambourin, and pointed towards the ladder lying on the grass. As the young priest stabilised the ladder down against the bottom of the grave, Mgr Pommard commented, "Mgr Altemps, please come up to us. You have provided us with crucial insight into this very complex case. If you please, let us sit together on the bench over there to conclude this matter."

As Marco stepped out of the tomb and onto the grass, not even a hint of relief showed on his face. He really looked like a conscientious administrator, doing his best to submit every relevant piece of information for his superiors to assess a situation. No one would have believed that his reputation, his red hat and his freedom were at stake. Once seated on the bench under the cherry tree in-between Bishop Dorf and Mgr Pommard, he went on as if he found it his duty to omit nothing of the truth, even at the risk of making his audience weary.

"Thank you Monsignor. Explaining the situation while sitting is easier, I confess.

"Next. Doing away with Anastasia Kravitz. As her October 1977 letter to Kokura in New York clearly stated, Kravitz had eventually found him out. She challenged him about the assault on her mother. Kokura knew her to be a heavy liability. She would soon expose his pretence of spy delusion, proving that he had been, and still was, a ruthless Soviet agent. She had slipped through his claws after the violin performance in New York, but he would not miss a second chance, never mind that she was his daughter.

"Thus, we come to the 'accident' of Anastasia Kravitz on 13 December 1979, on Quai de La Mégisserie in Paris. Kokura stalked her on her way to Théâtre du Châtelet where she was to perform that day. She obviously never met her homicidal father in Le Louvre the night before. Kokura pushed her under the van. It took me a while to obtain evidence. One of the pet shop assistants was passing by on his way to work that winter morning. He remembered seeing those two pedestrians talking in the middle of the snowed road, apparently unaware of the risk of cars skidding to avoid them. He was about to warn them when he saw the grey van come near, and merely had time to glance at Kokura pushing the woman before the vehicle. The shop assistant reported this to the police but the Asian-looking assassin had run away, prudently lying low at some convent under the pretence of being a Catholic convert hunted by the KGB.

"I could go on with countless instances, petty crimes in comparison, such as the fake burglary of Kokura's flat in New York in 1977, after the one in Cambridge which he staged two days before he would have the caretaker alerted, giving himself time to get back to New York and fly to Chicago for the Jeenaco presentation of the Uweena Campaign. I have found the Cambridge taxi driver who took him back to Heathrow airport on 16 October."

There was a pause, soon ended by Bishop Dorf. Sitting on the bench next to Altemps, the sick prelate pensively inquired, "This is astounding, Marco. But what of the entire Jeenaco business then, since you mention it? The Jeenaco company exists for certain. They are a very successful cosmetic brand, based in Chicago, as Kokura wrote. I know for a fact that they receive freight daily from China where manpower is cheaper: but that is not espionage, surely. So, at least Kokura did not invent Jeenaco, did he?"

"Thank you, Your Excellency. You put your finger on it. In truth I lack evidence at this stage. Jeenaco is a real firm, you are right. But I do suspect that Kokura falsified his account of the meetings at the Jeenaco Tower. The 'Chinese-looking shareholder' he described is likely to have been none other than himself. Unless the 'advertising executive Mike Drevan,' conveniently concealing his features behind a beard, was yet another of his impersonations. (Please note that I am only conjecturing about that particular point. I am sorry that I don't have the proof at hand, but the advertising agency BWT told me that 'Drevan' had left their firm in 1978 and they did not have his current contact details, understandably, thirteen years later. I hope to obtain formal identification of 'Drevan' by next week.)

"Thus, I am pretty sure that Kokura was not present at the advertising committee meeting on 18 October 1977, at least not as 'Professor Ken Kokura.' Nor was he ever asked to 'erase a baby shape' from Vermeer's *Woman with a Pearl Necklace* on 20 October. For no 'baby' was ever painted there in the first place, as any conscientious Vermeer expert would confirm. Alleging that *pentimento* was a very convincing trick to throw us off the scent of 'Showcasing Dissent.' Indeed, if the readers of his Memoirs believed that Professor Kokura was once pressured into tampering with a Vermeer painting in Chicago, leading to his nervous breakdown and depression, they would never suspect him of being, instead, the one setting up Jeenaco as the commercial outlet implementing his Chinese scheme.

"Even more skilful was Kokura's simulation of hysteria when examined by Dr Yuko Tanaka on 6 March 1978 in Los Angeles.

Her clinical testimony is perhaps the only genuine piece of evidence in Kokura's Memoirs. Even that one, however, was faked by Kokura, since it was based on his false pretences. It was of great importance for Kokura to be diagnosed as delusional. Making 'Heinrich' appear as a figment of his neurotic imagination would make the same 'Heinrich' impossible to debunk as a premeditated invention of his. Common forgers hide reality behind fiction but, always three steps ahead, Kokura concealed the fiction behind the delusion. Highly regarded by State and Church as a consultant, and endowed with the strongest credibility as the first mental health nurse to have examined Kokura after his 'awakening' in 1945, Dr Yuko Tanaka unwittingly cemented Kokura's pretence. His meeting with her in the Peacock Room in Washington was obviously not impromptu, as far as he was concerned. An eerily shrewd psychologist, Kokura guessed, I suspect, that her womanly compassion would blind Dr Yuko Tanaka. It inclined her to trust one posing as a deserving man, a fellow-Catholic and a Hiroshima survivor. All the more since she felt morally indebted to him. Indeed, unlike her family now American, *he* had not deserted Japan at the hour of need.

"But the gravest omission in the so-called Memoirs of master-spy Ken Kokura is, as we all realise, his masterminding of the 1977 Lintong Agreement. Working under the usurped identity of one Mingdao, a Communist official at the Chinese Patriotic Catholic Association, Kokura let loyal churchmen assume that the Agreement was their diplomatic triumph. In reality, they were unwittingly lending him a screen to conceal the real deal, namely, a bio-industrial template for spreading cultural Marxism across the Western world. To secure such an achievement, Kokura would take zero chances. He left 'Heinrich' out of it, fooling us through 'Mingdao,' a puppet whose fantastic shadow he enigmatically named 'Showcasing Dissent,' the most elusive and dreaded spy of the Cold War in Asia. Kokura's Lintong Agreement bore fruit beyond expectations. Contrary to the selected Eastern and Western investors and policy-makers in the know, to this day the general public will swear that in Lintong, the primary or even the *only* matter of interest is the Terracotta Army, a world-famous tourist destination. Such successful make-believe bears Kokura's dazzling signature and remains to this day his most enduring feat, one which historians and strategists will delight in analysing twelve years from now, once the relevant documentation will be declassified."

On the bench and behind it, the four men remained silent for a while, looking at the sun declining on the horizon through the cherry trees. Marco Altemps neither smiled nor frowned: his weary face merely manifested his painful duty done. One of his three listeners looked perplexed, another embarrassed, and the third lost in thought.

Mgr Jacques Pommard was the first one to speak. Standing up, he announced, "Well, thank you Mgr Altemps. I am glad that we took this opportunity to hear all that you had to share. I suppose that it alters our perspective quite a lot, and I will need to get back to the Nunciature to speak with Dr Shevchenko in Rome. Still, I am afraid that the plans for your cardinalate will have to be put on hold indefinitely. I am sure you understand that we have heard too many preoccupying statements here this afternoon. Such a decision as creating a new cardinal requires better visibility than is granted us at the moment. Furthermore, I will commission a new assessment of your liver cancer by a consultant of my choice who will also report to me on Bishop Dorf's heart condition. Finally, I ask you to remain at the Tokyo Nunciature until further notice. The same applies to Bishop Picerno Dorf until this matter is fully clarified. Neither of you is to travel anywhere without my explicit permission. Are we agreed?"

Bishop Dorf nodded absently. But Marco Altemps now seemed truly relieved at last. After coughing several times, he replied, "Yes Monsignor. But I am so sorry to disappoint

Bishop Dorf. I know how much he desired me to prepare the way for him in the Sacred College. The truth is, as you both know, I never wished this responsibility lain on my shoulders. Perhaps, with this crisis now burst open and no further obligations to fulfil, I might even be permitted to retire in my monastery as I had planned. I only left it yesterday because I thought it my duty to advise my superiors. I have long obtained leave from my Provincial at the Pontifical Institute for Foreign Missions, and I am quite content to be buried in a Benedictine black cowl, perhaps sooner than we think. Meanwhile I will eagerly pray for those called to wear scarlet robes and hats."

Mgr Pommard concluded in a cheerful mode, perhaps to soften the atmosphere after the stressful episode of the interrogation in the tomb.

"All is well then, or nearly. We have a spare seat in the car for you if you need, Marco, by the way. Fr Lambourin and I must depart at once, though, but if you wish to stay longer, I recall that Hana the housekeeper made sandwiches and tea for us. She is over there, waiting by the service car."

"Thank you, Monsignor. I will definitely avail myself of food, having eaten nothing since before landing in Tokyo. But the airline provided me with a rental car which awaits me down there. I will drive myself home and see you back at the Nunciature, then."

~~~~~~~~~~~~~~~~

Now a free man again, Marco Altemps relished his first strides across the lawn under the pink ecstasy of blooming cherry trees. The second limousine was already sailing through the gates, driven by the bodyguard, while Mgr Pommard was speaking with Fr Lambourin at the back. Marco could now breathe in peace. What a terrible ordeal had just ended! He had nearly been buried alive in his grave, so to speak—that is, in Kokura's grave.

Leaving Bishop Dorf to rest on the bench by his chauffeur, Mgr Altemps reached the service car and thanked the middle-aged housekeeper for the plate of ham and cucumber sandwiches, nicely wrapped in a freshly ironed napkin. She bowed deferentially and said, "Would Your Reverence permit Hana to share a memory for a happy future, if such a request is not too bold?"

Puzzled, Mgr Altemps nodded rather than spoke, his mouth being full of food.

"It is this. From where she was asked to wait over the past hour, Hana could not fail hearing Your Reverence speak once of a *grey* van. Well, the Kokura Memoirs did not mention the colour. But the van was red."

Mgr Altemps choked on his second cucumber sandwich, looked the housekeeper in the eyes and sternly asked, "And how would *you* know that, woman?"

"Because Hana saw Your Reverence at the wheel that winter morning in Paris, aiming for Fr Xavier on the crosswalk. I, Hana, that is, *Anastasia*, only had time to push him towards the pavement."

It was the first time Mgr Altemps was taken off guard, perhaps since his teenage years. But his very quick brains riposted, "Well done! I expected Kokura to have schemed ways of getting at me even beyond the tomb. I must praise his imagination and his determination. But enough fiction. Now the proven facts: Anastasia Kravitz died in the accident, as you seem to forget; and she was a violinist, not a cleaning-lady. Any Asian-looking woman can fake a limp as an attempt to impersonate her, as if she had survived. The van was a grey 'Renault Estafette' model R2136/37, its number plate 7286 WU 75 stained with blood: I saw the picture. Next time, check your facts better. Whoever you are, I see that you are not a genuine housekeeper. For such scandalous insinuation I shall report you immediately to Bishop Dorf as a spy put in here by... probably by Bishop Ignatius Kung, am I not right?—to undermine the work of this Nunciature."

By then, "Uncle Byobu," the gardener of the Nunciature, was walking back to the cars, a hoe on his shoulder. He had been tasked with pulling the slab back in place over the empty tomb. As Hana instinctively stepped towards him, as if for protection, Altemps ordered, "You, gardener, lock up this woman in the car right now! She came here under false pretences."

But "Uncle Byobu" merely stood before the cleric, immobile, hoe in hand.

Marco Altemps recovered his self-control and uttered, "I see... Nor are you a gardener, then?"

Uncle Byobu assented, "I am a gardener, Your Reverence, but I am not Hana's uncle."

"Fine. Another trick from Kokura, I assume. Let me guess: will you claim to be 'Swordmaster Yamato' risen from the dead? If not, where is your garden anyway?"

"My garden is at the relocated Tokwon Abbey in South Korea. I am Brother Gerard, a Benedictine oblate. Before that, though, I was called Prince Azmy of Serdang, later known as 'Sultan'—not 'Zoltan Maisuradze.' By your order long ago, through my grievous sin and for my redemption, Hana is my daughter. And for Your Reverence's amendment, I say that Ken Kokura was with me in Moscow when Van Meegeren died in Amsterdam. My uncle Han, the Vermeer forger, died a natural death. Kokura did not kill him."

Now surprisingly composed again, Mgr Marco Altemps gently objected, "My good man, if you were 'Azmy' and I the so-called 'Heinrich,' surely you would have reported me half an hour ago when I was at the bottom of the grave, surrounded by clerics and a bodyguard who could have easily arrested me. Why such a far-fetched pretence now? Is it cash you are after? Perhaps I can help. If your agency employer does not pay you properly, I can advise you on Part-time workers' rights. This is part of what we churchmen call the 'Social Teaching of the Church,' a complicated name, I know, but meant for your protection."

There was, perhaps, a hint of spite in the voice of "Uncle Byobu," as he declared, "Your Reverence need not trouble himself about us. Fr Xavier asked us to spare you, as he also was once given a chance. Besides, he told us, Your Reverence's is not the soul he is most anxious to assist."

As if slightly losing patience, but still in a quiet voice, Mgr Altemps retorted, "I see. For all your preaching, you are but a blackmailer, and not a convincing one at that."

In vain would they try, Marco well knew, if backed by such poor allegations.

No charges were ever pressed, however. His accusers had probably realised that they had failed the test.

Meanwhile, "Uncle Byobu" had presented the sealed plastic envelope found in the empty coffin. Altemps had left it there but now, snatching it out of the gardener's hands, he quickly tore the seal open. It contained three items.

The main one was the lid of a china jar. The lid was darkish and unadorned, its inside cracked as if a cavity lay concealed further in.

The second item, next to it, was a square white tile displaying a small blue figure standing sword in hand. It was similar to those many small characters sketched on blue-and-white Delft tiles, protecting the bottom of walls from mops in many Vermeer depictions of domestic interiors. No wings showed on the back of the little man, Mgr Altemps observed, unlike the "fishing Cupid" Delft tile displayed in other Vermeer paintings. Both clay objects were wrapped within a single sheet of paper: the third clue.

One side of the sheet was a colour copy of *The Woman with a Pearl Necklace* with a close-up of the lid of the china jar. On the reverse of the sheet was displayed what again looked like a man, sword in hand, unless it were a painter holding his *maulstick*, the baton used transversally to support the hand holding the paintbrush. It looked a painted replica of the white-and-blue tile. But upon the sheet, the man's face was of ivory shade, and he stood looking up towards a large rectangle above him, like a free-standing screen whose actual symmetry was distorted through being reflected upon a spheric surface. The depiction looked like a close-up on an enormously bigger painting. But it could also be a detail, fantastically enlarged, of a normal-size image. Then, the actual scale on canvas of the swordsman or painter would have been microscopic. However, that would have required tools of such small size, and a technique of such unprecedented precision, as to preclude the inclusion of this miniature in paintings produced before the twentieth century.

Mgr Altemps challenged the gardener.

"Is that all your ammunition, my good man? Kokura's symbolic 'bones' and 'skin'? So what? A hidden reflection of the painter upon a shiny surface is a cliché of Dutch painting, as in Van Eyck's *Arnolfini Spouses*. But fine, I will play fair. So, if I am the spy 'Heinrich,' as you obsessively claim, rather than a Vatican secret serviceman, then you must prove that you are 'Sultan.' Surely Kokura would have told Sultan, his intimate friend in the painting analyses team, whether this tiny swordsman-painter reflected on the lid of the china jar in *The Woman with a Pearl Necklace* was genuinely by Vermeer, or added by the forger Van Meegeren, or even by Kokura himself. What do you say?"

Uncle Byobu had looked with emotion at the picture in the hands of Mgr Altemps. He had closed his eyes and, after a short silence, replied, "My uncle Han van Meegeren never worked on this painting. In Chicago, Kokura did, once in the Jeenaco laboratory, according to his Memoirs. In my opinion he would have needed several hours to paint this microscopic figure, one coloured spot at a time. But he was being watched closely by a guard and therefore would not have been allowed to proceed. For this area of the painting was too distant from the *Woman*, whose dress he was to alter through the back of the canvas, if I recall."

Mgr Altemps interrupted him. "Pretty well deduced so far, really. But I will need more than that. At least you have convinced me that you are not a gardener."

Uncle Byobu paused briefly, looked at Hana the housekeeper, and concluded as if unaware of Marco's sarcasm.

"This leaves only Vermeer. His style normally does not involve hidden codes or riddles. For him to make such an exception, spending a vast amount of time to add such an invisible detail on the tip of the lid of a rather nondescript piece of china, Vermeer would have needed a very strong personal motivation. The Dutch Letters provide it, but Your Reverence thinks them not genuine."

Mgr Marco Altemps gave a sympathetic smile and concluded with a cough.

"Just as I expected. Your allegations remain unsupported. All you can produce are vague hypotheses. You just gave me the proof that it was not Kokura who sent you against me. An expert like him would have furnished you with compelling arguments. Now, I understand that this is the end of your week of interim service at the Nunciature. A chance for you. Make yourself scarce immediately, and report to your master, Bishop Ignatius Kung, that his stratagems have utterly failed. And if it is of any consolation to His Excellency, tell him that he can have my red hat! I am retiring to a monastery. I have had more than my share of cloak-and-dagger, double-dealings, and smoke-and-mirrors. Keep these toys, by the way, since you probably planted them yourself in the coffin after you gathered up Kokura's bones, now bagged up in the boot of your car, I presume."

A sad smile on his weary face, Marco left the printed sheet and the clay items in the hands of astonished "Uncle Byobu." He walked back, coughing, to his rental Nissan *President Sovereign* and drove away. The sick monsignor still needed to offer his private Mass, having been travelling for nearly two days. Feeling too tired to bring the car back to the rental agent that evening, he decided to go straight to the Nunciature and fulfil his priestly duty in the little house chapel. As he anxiously checked his watch, he was relieved to see that his Mass would begin just one hour from having swallowed his cucumber sandwich, in conscientious observance of the Eucharistic fast. He might need to mention this latest fasting concern to his confessor at the cathedral, however, to help him tackle his enduring scrupulosity.

It had been a day of toil, if not of tears, an exhausting hurly-burly. But he had fought the good fight. Ultimately, he knew well, the battle was about *souls*—so Holy Church taught.

Mgr Marco Altemps could not agree more.

The Invisible Messenger

ROM HIS BENCH, BISHOP DORF HAD watched the second limousine of the Nunciature drive down the slope between two lines of cherry trees, soon followed by Marco Altemps' vehicle. Mgr Pommard was eager to speak with Dr Shevchenko as soon as possible, back in Tokyo, and had taken Fr Lambourin with him. After loading the picnic case and gardening tools in the boot of their modest service car, Uncle Byobu and Hana had finally gone as well. He was alone, at last.

In a meditative mood, the bishop looked successively at Fr Xavier Hasekura's grave in the distance, at the countless Buddhist tombs across the hilly grounds, and finally at the scattered groups of late visitors. It was getting cool as the afternoon was drawing to a close, and he tightened his purple cashmere scarf around his chest. By his watch it was past 5pm and he relished following the imperceptible descent of the sun upon the horizon. He stood up, resting on his right leg, as the left one had not yet regained full motricity since his hemiplegia. A couple of birds could still be heard from time to time. He felt like walking a bit under the flowery branches, without help though—and he withdrew his arm from that of the chauffeur placidly standing at his side, a hand on the wheelchair that had been extracted from the car.

Contrasting sentiments alternated in Picerno's soul. Relief had followed the painful episode of Mgr Altemps' examination. Was he innocent? Was he guilty? Or did his responsibility lie halfway between both? Bishop Dorf perceived that Mgr Pommard knew more than he had expressed today. As Kokura's recorded interview showed, Pommard had been watching Altemps for the past decade. "And watching *me* as well!" Bishop Dorf realised with surprise, protesting to himself, "But I am not a Soviet spy." Was Marco a spy? One who was about to be made a cardinal: had a Communist spy, then, got that close to being possibly elected pope? That sounded preposterous.

And yet, could Altemps have told lies all along, ever since they had first met as students in Vienna forty-five years earlier? He recalled Marco's shy introduction at the cafeteria of the Asian Studies University Department, in 1946. Memories of their skiing excursions sprung back to his mind. Then, Marco's first absence for treating his asthma in a sanatorium had occurred. Was it plausible that the brainy and sickly young Tyrolese with whom he had shared so much might have flown to Japan instead, as a Soviet recruiter?

What of the postcards Picerno had conscientiously addressed to "Waldsanatorium, Davos, Switzerland", where Marco's uncle, a fashionable patient after the Great War, had inspired Thomas Mann with one of the characters of his *Magic Mountain* (Picerno had immediately borrowed the novel from the University library, lest Marco found out his plebeian ignorance of Mann). And if Marco was in Japan or Germany, rather than in Switzerland, what of the replies received from him, treasured letters elegantly written on expensive paper with *Waldsanatorium* letterhead? How could the brilliant young student have fooled his family, his teachers and his best friend all at once? No, deception was not plausible.

But later on, was it on behalf of 'Pro Deo,' the Holy See's intelligence section, that he had secretly spent time in Wittenberg, London and other places? "And all this behind my back, I, his official superior!" Bishop Dorf tried to dismiss surges of resentment and of wounded pride, likely to cloud his judgement. He could see better, now, that he had always enjoyed his seniority over Marco Altemps despite, or rather because the young man was his better intellectually and socially. Picerno, the son of a working-class father and an immigrant mother from poor Southern Italy, found security and gratification in the faithful submission of the younger aristocratic but unassuming boy. There was more to his relationship with Marco than vanity, for sure. They had worked in brilliant complementarity, understanding each other at once, and agreeing without need for words on the allocation of tasks—under Picerno's avuncular leadership.

The culmination of their teamwork had been the decisive "Lintong Agreement," signed on 29 August 1977 near the recently unearthed Terracotta Army of a dead emperor. "Just like me now," Bishop Dorf thought with a bitter smile, on seeing himself surrounded with so many tombs, while his prospect of ever wearing red, to rule over Asia—or even white, to reign over the world—was now as good as dead. But Marco had just made the strangest insinuation about the Lintong Agreement. As if its object had been other than what he, the chief negotiator, had assumed.

Furthermore, Marco had positively affirmed that Kokura and Mingdao were the same person. Perhaps were they even one with the elusive "Showcasing Dissent," then. That would clear Marco. But, he suddenly realised, Mingdao was the one who had suggested the design of his coat of arms as future cardinal barely a fortnight earlier, whereas Kokura had been dead ten years. Thus, they could *not* be the same man. Why had Pommard not pointed out such an inconsistency in Marco's justification?

Unless... Was not Kokura's body actually missing from the grave? Could it be that the dreaded spy had not died in earnest during Pope John Paul II's visit in 1981? Was he still at large then, scheming treacheries more lethal than ever? But Marco held Kokura to be dead. Having displayed such a detailed knowledge of the alleged crimes of the missing Japanese, could Marco plausibly be mistaken about the latest survival of the Communist art expert a decade earlier? Or was Mgr Altemps implicated as well after all? Had Picerno's masterpiece, the Lintong Agreement, been Marco's secret achievement—against the interests of the Holy See?

How bewildering!

Bishop Dorf felt like sitting down for a while but, for want of benches close at hand, he waved at the chauffeur who diligently pushed the wheelchair for the prelate to rest. The possibility of Altemps' secret identity was opening before Picerno a ghastly vista. He recoiled from looking at it. And yet, he had to consider the hypothesis that Marco's involvement in China had not been what he had understood. He smiled, remembering his friend's grimace when excluded from the important meetings with the Communist representatives. Instead he had been sent "to take a better look at the Terracotta Army," like a child given twopence to buy an ice-cream while grown-ups discuss grave matters.

A fantastic thought dawned on Bishop Dorf, captivating his imagination like an evil revelation. He was not sure how to define it. He had no proof. The suggestion was visual, more than intellectual. It was an image reflected on the surface of water. Triumphing with his "Lintong Agreement," Picerno had naturally assumed that he was the chief actor, and Marco his valued manservant. But all of a sudden, the image felt as if reversed, and the bishop was seeing himself floating like a two-dimensional puppet, a flat projection of the actual mastermind standing on the bank, namely Fr Altemps, radiating power, penetration and mastery.

What if Mgr Dorf's so-called "important meetings" with the Communist officials had been a bag of lollipops thrown at him to keep him busy with background actors, while in some designated venue Marco had been shaping the future in earnest with the true delegates from East and West? Who had been the child, and who the grown-up?

The most tortuous and fantastic hypotheses spun in Picerno's suspicious imagination, as had once plagued jealous Othello. Thinking of it, then, could not Marco have orchestrated the Terracotta Army analogy from the start, astutely planting the idea into his superior's mind, when... Yes! when mentioning the Tokwon Abbey necropolis spread around "Emperor

Jesus"? If verified, would Marco then be found to be much more than the so-called Soviet spy "Heinrich"? Was he not, in truth, the dreaded Chinese master spy *Showcasing Dissent?*

Was he not, to Picerno, like the murderous god-spy Hermes in Fabritius' painting—why was Kokura enamoured with that rather uninspiring picture?—lulling the hundred-eyed giant Argus with tales, the better to get rid of him? Picerno had thought himself supremely informed, detecting everything and scheming successfully. And yet, by his side, the one he trusted as his companion was empowered by *Zeus,* or so it seemed, to cut off his head and claim control of more than a sacred cow like the nymph "Io": instead, to subvert and highjack his cherished Asian policy.

∿∿∿∿∿∿∿∿∿

No, Bishop Dorf decided, this was falling into paranoia just like Kokura had! Was Picerno, a rational man, now contaminated with such pathological suspicion, perhaps because of having stayed too long here in Fuji Cemetery by the tomb of the dead Japanese? Was he cursed like the Egyptologist Lord Carnarvon and his team along the Nile, dying strange deaths after violating the sepulchre of Tutankhamun in the Valley of the Kings? Nonsense! Bishop Dorf pushed his hands further into the pockets of his black suit and flexed the muscles of his arms. Again, he protested to himself: Mgr Altemps was *not* a god in disguise, nor a warlock. By all accounts he was a dutiful assistant and that was the end of it.

On the contrary, ten years earlier Kokura must have relapsed into his customary fits of delusion. The shock of finding himself a churchman again after decades would have unsettled him. He would have felt as if Marco Altemps looked slightly like his imaginary "Heinrich," and would have persuaded himself of this preposterous new KGB assignment—stabbing Pope John Paul, no less! Unsurprisingly, the unfortunate Japanese Jesuit had succumbed to the emotional toll. But let the dead bury the dead. He, Picerno, was alive, even without a red hat; and so were Marco and the others.

If Kokura had merely imagined "Heinrich," though, as clinically confirmed by Dr Tanaka, it left unresolved the question of the "Chinese master spy." Who was *Showcasing Dissent* then, if not Marco? It had to be one within Picerno's close circle, since the name had been inserted as a warning in the very brochure printed for the papal visit ten years earlier. After all, why not Pommard himself! But Pommard had agreed to secure the red hat for Marco. Since Marco was loyal, and if Pommard was a Chinese spy, the latter would rather have manoeuvred to be made a cardinal himself. No, Pommard had to be left out of this; and Lambourin was too junior: just a kid with a Roman collar. If not Marco, if not Pommard, only Dr Pavel Shevchenko remained. What, the Vice-Head of Vatican Intelligence? That sounded a bit far-fetched. Or else, of course...

Bishop Dorf wheeled his chair further among the tombs, determined to ignore his sudden perspiration and accelerating heartbeat. Feeling a tension in the muscles of his face, he attempted to smile in vain, dreading another fit of hemiplegia. He wheeled himself faster and purposely broadened the scope of his deliberations to evade the dreadful thought that had just occurred to him.

Over the fourteen years following the 1977 "Lintong Agreement," like every distanced observer Picerno had witnessed unprecedented changes in Church and society. He had accepted the optimistic narrative because it was everybody's interpretation. The Church was adapting to modern times, and that predictably required painful surrenders and updates. Among many aspects, the loss of Latin as a common idiom, of a sacral liturgy, of a sacrificial priesthood, of the Catholic claim to exclusive possession of the truth, all practically abandoned—had not bothered him much.

Instead, he had welcomed renewal like a breath of fresh air, such as the license given to married couples to regulate their procreation as they saw fit. Paul VI's encyclical *Humanæ*

Vitæ heralded a new type of magisterium, exhortative, not authoritative—at least, that was how most prelates, all over the world, had implemented it. Unlike him, Marco had bemoaned the dissolution of mores, the melting away of the time-proven norms of conjugal morality, of clerical discipline and dogmatic affirmation.

Now in the early 1990s, looking back at two or three decades of experimentation, Picerno found himself admitting that things were not as good as promised. As for his allocated area, China, well, to be brutally honest, his policy had not yielded significant fruit. Against his will, the underground Church was stronger and proactive, whereas his own study commissions, his ambitious circulars and his diplomatic meetings with the Communists had not improved religious freedom by an inch.

Worse even, Marco had sometimes implied that Bishop Dorf was turning a blind eye to the widespread mistreatment of vulnerable human beings. He was too busy with schemes and policies, and looked as if numbed when hearing of the fate of those whose rights were trampled on and whose blood was unjustly shed. What was the remedy: more time spent kneeling? Mgr Altemps had teased his friend and superior, asking if he remembered the old Mass of his youth and early priesthood, and whether he would consider celebrating it again on occasions. He had even offered to serve it for him as a traditional "Low Mass of a Bishop."

⁓⁓⁓⁓⁓⁓⁓⁓⁓⁓⁓⁓⁓

Bells rang at some distance. It was just 6pm: perhaps the signal for the last visitors to exit the cemetery before the closing of the gates? Or, from the nearby Jesuit residence, the Angelus bell? No, Bishop Dorf remembered, it could not be the Angelus, for in Eastertide the *Regina Cæli* is prayed instead. That incidental mistake brought back a memory to his mind. Long ago in the Louvre, in the late 1960s, he and Marco Altemps were accompanying a delegation of Chinese Communists.

Walking by Jean-François Millet's famous painting *The Angelus* (1859), one of the Chinese referred to it as a proletarian depiction, calling it *The Poor Potato Harvest*. Mgr Dorf (he was not yet a bishop) could not resist showing his better grasp of the painting. He politely corrected the Communist, pointing at the tiny steeple on the horizon, to the right of the woman.

"The peasant and his wife are not concerned with the potatoes in the basket at their feet. They bow their heads in recollection, rather, because they hear the bells being rung at the village church for the Angelus, a Christian prayer marking the end of the day's work. Thus, they are not lamenting a meagre crop, but entrusting their lives to God who became man to save them. Noticing the small steeple to the right of the woman changes the meaning of the picture."

Bishop Dorf recalled how the Chinese officials had looked impressed, if not converted.

Making him look like a fool, though, Fr Altemps had candidly commented, "If I may add a precision, the painting was originally called *Prayer for the Potato Crop*. But when the rich American who had commissioned it failed to pay, Millet added the church steeple and renamed the picture *The Angelus*, the better to appeal to Catholic buyers. Millet neglected to alter the postures of the peasants, who should have been kneeling for a weekday Angelus; not standing."

Picerno remembered having been pleased by Marco's intervention: although it contradicted him, it diplomatically supported the first remark by their valued Communist guest. The latter beamed with contentment, feeling that he had been proved right from the start.

Fr Altemps had suggested further, "However, it may be of interest to recall Salvador Dalí's intuition. The Spanish Surrealist painter was convinced that the couple were mourning a dead child. In 1963 he had expert radiographer Ken Kokura x-ray *The Angelus* on behalf of the Louvre. To everybody's surprise, the test revealed a child's coffin at the feet of the woman, instead of the potato basket."

"It cannot be the Angelus." Now alone at dusk in the nearly deserted cemetery, a sick sixty-seven-year-old prelate, Picerno Dorf contemplated the breath-taking layered panorama of lawns, trees, mountains and gilded clouds; and suddenly felt overwhelmed. He seemed to be connecting at last with a hidden part of his mind, one that had tried to draw his attention to essential issues for years, without success. He could now take heed of that secret voice, or tune, in his soul. It was not reproachful, not condemning—that would have been bearable. Instead, the voice was encouraging, forgiving, soothing. But its very tenderness and compassion implied that he, a loyal servant of the Church and a distinguished diplomat, was wanting. More than wanting, he was worthy of pity, in need of healing.

But why? How? What was it that he should have done, or seen, or opposed? Was he God Almighty? Could he stop at will the spread of evil? Still, an intimate admission of guilt pervaded his faculties. When standing in Kokura's tomb half an hour earlier, Marco had made mortifying allegations against him, based on his chats with Auntie Bella Dodd, then a KGB spy. Such nasty insinuations, and in front of Pommard! Never had Marco behaved viciously to him until then.

"I deserved it though," Bishop Dorf admitted, even though it had occurred some forty years earlier. Yes, he recognised that he had been a useful idiot to Auntie Bella, leaking information without suspecting who she worked for. When she had converted, he had thought it only fair that he should benefit from her fame. But she had kept her young and ambitious nephew at bay. However, his main guilt was something else and much, much deeper, he now knew. From beyond the grave, Kokura's words quoting 'Heinrich' in the recording heard earlier that afternoon, seemed to include him.

"You are not the only one. Some of our best agents don't even know that they work for us."

He then understood, with excruciating stupefaction and unexpected relief, that *he* must have been *Showcasing Dissent* all along. The realisation conjured the memory of King David being told his crimes by the prophet Nathan. "Thou art the man." Everything became clear to Bishop Dorf, his spiritual enlightenment increasing as the twilight dimmed his eyesight.

Yes, sunset was imminent. The light was nearly gone. Picerno caught a last glimpse of Kokura's tomb further down the lawn, only then realising the strangeness of its having been found empty after ten years. Something moved in his heart, not physically felt, but still concretely perceived. He was tired, and thought how silly it would be if he were to weep now before his domestic. What would the chauffeur think of "His Excellency" shedding tears in the sunset like a Romantic poet? Well, Mr Han surely had no knowledge of Romantic poets anyway. What could he know of Schiller or Hölderlin, Marco's favourites?

Yet, why this awkward impulse, leading Bishop Dorf, a man of considerable learning and influence, to ask for the opinion of a mere employee? How could a temporary driver, probably passed retirement age judging by his grey beard, decide whether he, Picerno, "was more to blame" than Marco? What would Mr Han advise a man to do, a prelate of Picerno's stature, who "felt that he had perpetrated a terrible crime by omission?"

No reply came, no judgement was heard. The chauffeur smiled deferentially. As was to be expected, either he did not understand, or he thought himself unqualified. And yet, why was it that, as if prompted by the very silence of the humble driver, an admission flashed in Picerno's soul like a firebird flying across a winter sky?

"What they grow at Lintong Farm by the Terracotta Army, *the horror*—I ignored for gain."

Picerno felt his wheelchair pivot very slowly towards the rear of the cemetery. The sun was now setting over the tombs where the red-cladded Jizo statues seemed to have shared their scarlet with the entire scenery, even with the great volcano behind. For a while the two men, one sitting, the other standing behind with hands upon the handles of the chair, looked silently at Mount Fuji swelling in the distance like a formidable crimson wave.

At first, Picerno assumed that the voice he had heard then had to be his, speaking fluent German. But he later recalled a hint of English accent when the voice had suggested, like a confessor speaking to his penitent, "And for your salutary penance, my child, will you please name this colour that you see?"

THE END

ABOUT THE AUTHOR

French-born British author FR ARMAND DE MALLERAY, FSSP, grew up in the Loire Valley and Paris. He left France in 1994 after completing a Master's Degree in Modern Literature at the Sorbonne in Paris. He taught French at the Military Academy in Budapest before joining the Priestly Fraternity of St Peter in 1995 in Bavaria, where he was ordained in 2001. His first priestly assignment was in London, Southwark Archdiocese. He served in England since, apart from five years in Switzerland, then in an administrative position at his Fraternity's headquarters. Since 2008, he has been the editor of *Dowry*, the quarterly magazine of his Fraternity in the UK & Ireland. Fr de Malleray has been chaplain to the international *Juventutem* youth movement since its inception in 2004 (cf. www.juventutem.org), and to the Confraternity of St Peter, his Fraternity's international prayer-network for priestly vocations until 2021. Since 2015, he is the rector of St Mary's Shrine in Warrington, Liverpool Archdiocese, where he also oversees the apostolate of his Fraternity in England and promotes vocations to the priesthood and to the religious life.

Printed in the USA
CPSIA information can be obtained
at www.ICGtesting.com
LVHW051410100823
754634LV00001B/35